Fishi
Eastern New York

D0916376

Help Us Keep This Guide Up to Date

Every effort has been made by the author and editors to make this guide as accurate and useful as possible. However, many things can change after a guide is published—trails are rerouted, regulations change, techniques evolve, facilities come under new management, etc.

We would love to hear from you concerning your experiences with this guide and how you feel it could be improved and kept up to date. While we may not be able to respond to all comments and suggestions, we'll take them to heart and we'll also make certain to share them with the author. Please send your comments and suggestions to the following address:

The Globe Pequot Press
Reader Response/Editorial Department
P.O. Box 480
Guilford, CT 06437

Or you may e-mail us at:

editorial@GlobePequot.com

Thanks for your input.

Fishing
Eastern New York

SPIDER RYBAAK

FALCON®

GUILFORD, CONNECTICUT
HELENA, MONTANA

AN IMPRINT OF THE GLOBE PEQUOT PRESS

A FALCON GUIDE ®

Copyright © 2004 by The Globe Pequot Press

All photos by Ray Hrynyk unless otherwise noted.
Text design by Casey Shain
Maps created by Trailhead Graphics © The Globe Pequot Press

ISSN 1544-8428
ISBN 0-7627-1100-0

Manufactured in the United States of America
First Edition/First Printing

To Susan, for enriching my life beyond words.

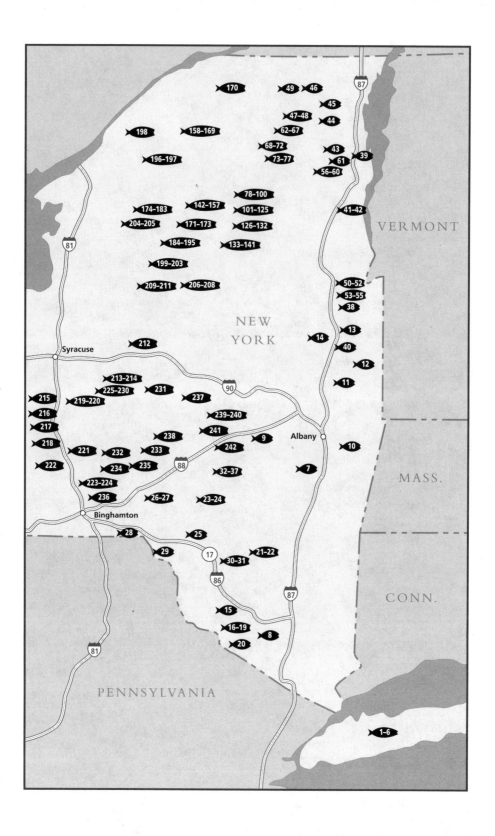

Contents

Acknowledgments

Completing a work this ambitious all by myself would have taken more years than I have left—not to mention gas money and time away from Susan, the cats, and my favorite fishing spots. An army of people helped me with everything from locating obscure sites and popular hot spots to setting me up with lodging, guides, local experts, regional fishing techniques, site dimensions, stocking statistics, maps . . . You get the picture. Mentioning everyone would add twenty or more pages to the book. So here's a list of those I bugged most of all (at least twenty times) at all hours: Rich Preall, Frank Flack, Gary Marchuk, John Rucando, Mike Flaherty, Stephen Litwhiler, Mike Seymour, Fred G. Henson, Charles Guthrie, Robert Angyal, Norman McBride, George DeChant, Tracy Montoni, Ron Kolodziej, and Scott Shane.

Introduction

A lot of folks think New York is one big metropolis, the ideal setting for martial-arts and cop flicks. But there's more to the place than just concrete jungle with a strip park running down its deepest canyon. Indeed, the Empire State has a great big backyard, more than 45,000 square miles' worth, and it's all watered by the finest fishing habitat you'll find anywhere.

There's so much water here, in fact, that no matter where you stand, you're never far from shore. For instance, 90 percent of New York's northern and western boundaries end in water. Lake Champlain, its canal, and the Hudson River run the length of the state's east side, a distance of more than 300 miles. Even the relatively dry south end spawns, and is largely bordered by, the mighty Allegheny, Susquehanna, and Delaware Rivers.

Huge largemouth bass for the taking at Fort Pond. ERIC FIELDSTADT, PHOTOGRAPHER. USED WITH PERMISSION.

And then there's the interior: glacial lakes, impoundments on state forests and wildlife management areas, countless reservoirs, tributaries, and outlets, abandoned and working canals, Catskill Mountain streams (cradles of American fly fishing), numerous Adirondack Mountain lakes and ponds, and wild rivers that run down these ancient rocks like crooked seams in a geologic baseball cap.

The New York State Department of Environmental Conservation is charged with maintaining these fisheries. Unlike the rest of the bureaucracy, this agency does its job efficiently and productively. A recent Cornell University study estimates that freshwater fishing in New York generates a positive economic impact of $3.6 billion annually.

Just about anything that swims in the temperate waters of the Western Hemisphere can be found here. You can troll for trophy salmon or muskies; fly fish for monster steelhead, brown trout, largemouth bass, and northern pike; jig for 10-pound walleyes and world-class lake trout; fish with live bait for ancient and bizarre-looking critters like bowfins, eels, burbot, and gars; ply tidal rivers for shad and stripers; or simply sit on a dock and dunk worms for bullheads, sunfish, perch, carp, sheepshead, suckers, you name it.

You name the setting, too. From lakes so vast you can go out beyond sight of land, to mountain brooks you can step over and city creeks where trout chase moths under streetlights, New York's got it all. And while no one can guarantee you'll land the trophy swimming around in your dreams, you can count on catching memories that will last a lifetime.

New York's Wildlife

While puma sightings have been reported all over upstate New York in the past decade, their numbers are so small, you have a better chance of catching a wide-eyed fish called Wanda than seeing a mountain lion.

About the most dangerous critter you are likely to encounter is a black bear. These can show up just about anywhere in rural New York: I've run into two of them in forty-five years of fishing, and both snuck away. Still, if you see one clumsily lumbering down the trail or splashing upcreek toward you, make enough noise to be noticed, then make yourself as big as you can.

The Adirondack Mountains have moose. While not particularly violent, their sheer size makes them dangerous. It's probably a good idea to avoid approaching females with calves, especially by canoe.

And then there are coyotes, 11,000 by some estimates. Corrupted by timber wolf genes, they are fully 30 percent larger than the western variety. And though their howls have probably cut some camping trips short, there is no record of one hurting a human. Several have crossed my path over the years but when they winded me, they split so fast I was left wondering if I'd ever seen one in the first place.

Besides dump ducks (gulls), the friendly skies over the state's waterways are loaded with kingfishers, blue herons, cormorants, wild ducks, and Canada geese. Loons thrive in remote waters and large bodies with swampy areas. Bald eagles are making a comeback; you can expect to see them on popular streams like the Salmon River and Beaver Kill, as well as deep in the Adirondack wilderness.

Insects are plentiful, ubiquitous, and can really bug you. Yellow jackets and bald-faced hornets have sent more than one angler diving for cover. In late spring, blackflies rule the air over backcountry creeks. Some are so aggressive, an old-timer once told me he's seen them chase trout. While that's stretching things a bit, they can swarm in such numbers from mid-May through June, especially in the northern half of the state, they'll drive an unprotected fly fisher off a stream in the middle of a mayfly hatch. What's more, not all insect repellents discourage them—indeed, some actually seem to sound the dinner bell. Those containing DEET work well. Most roadside streams and lakes are sprayed to keep blackflies in check, but waters in wild forests and wilderness areas are not.

Finally, we have a lot of mosquitoes, establishment attempts at eradication notwithstanding. They've become particularly troublesome lately because some carry West Nile virus, a pathogen known to be fatal to crows and humans. Mosquitoes are especially active at dusk and dawn, near shore around ponds, lakes, canals, and slow-moving rivers. They don't cotton to most insect repellents. Folks wishing to avoid harsh chemicals are encouraged to wear Bug-Out or similar mesh garments over their regular clothes.

New York's Weather

New York has a temperate climate with an average annual temperature of about 48 degrees Fahrenheit. But that doesn't mean we don't get wild swings. Most winters, temperatures drop below zero. Indeed, several winters in the 1990s saw record-breaking snowfall and temperatures so low, some self-proclaimed environmentalists burned their copies of Al Gore's *Earth in the Balance* for kindling. The Adirondack village of Old Forge regularly makes it onto the national news by registering temperatures lower than 30 degrees below zero. While most lakes in the northern tier (roughly north of I–90) develop ice caps thick enough to support large RVs, southern-tier waters generally only get about six weeks of ice thick enough to walk on.

Summer is hot and humid. Temperatures vary with elevation. The Mohawk and Hudson Valleys get a lot of days in the high 70s and 80s. The Catskills are normally 5 degrees cooler and the Adirondacks are as much as 10 degrees cooler.

Spring and fall are the reason many New Yorkers put up with winter and summer. Temperatures range from 55 to 65. And while many complain it is always cloudy or raining, the truth is, the sun shines about half the time.

Finding Your Way

The maps in this book were drawn from a variety of sources. In most cases, actual mileage was recorded by visiting the site. Odometers aren't all created equal, however, and when combined with factors such as weather, rest stops, and garage sales, readings can vary. While I've made every attempt to present accurate distances, please accept them as approximations at best.

Catch-and-Release

One thing all competent anglers with average luck can expect to do in New York is catch fish. So many, in fact, that some will have to be released eventually, for reasons ranging from the fish being out of season or too small, to catching more than you feel like cleaning, to a sense that you simply don't feel like killing anymore. And then there are those who practice catch-and-release religiously. Whatever the reason, it is in the best interest of all concerned for the critter to be released unharmed. Here are some simple pointers to ensure you release a fish with a future instead of a dead fish swimming.

- Avoid going after big fish with ultralight tackle. The cruel, frustrating struggle for freedom can exhaust them beyond recovery.

- Use a net only when absolutely necessary. Nets tear mouths, rip gills, break fins and teeth, scratch eyes, and remove slime—an important barrier against harmful bacteria.

- Keep the fish submerged in water, even when unhooking it.

- If you must remove a fish from the water, always wet your hands before touching it and place it on something wet.

Releasing a 16-inch brown trout caught in the Ausable River. This fish was hooked deeply and had to be removed from the water so that the angler could cut the line as close to its mouth as possible.

- If the fish is hooked deep in the tongue, guts, or gills, cut the line. Fish are bleeders, and an internal wound as small as a pinhole can be fatal. By leaving the hook in place, healing will occur around it as it rusts away. No hook is worth a life.

- Never lift a pike by squeezing its eyes with your fingers.

- Keep fingers out of a fish's gills.

Fish Consumption Advisory

While the doctor may tell you that fish is healthy, the state advises that you eat no more than 0.5 pound of fish per week caught from any of the state's waters, including municipal reservoirs. What's more, the *New York State Department of Environmental Conservation Fishing Regulations Guide* lists three pages of streams and lakes from which you should only eat 0.5 pound per month, or none at all.

Best Times to Fish

All fish feed most actively around dusk and dawn. Some biologists and successful anglers claim that the moon influences feeding; commercial calendars such as Rick Taylor's "Prime Times" list the best days and most productive hours. Still, some fish like catfish, eels, and walleyes feed best at night, especially when there's no moon, while yellow perch and northern pike feed best during daylight. The rest—from trout and bass to salmon, muskies, crappies, and sunfish—feed whenever they feel like it.

Security Notice

The terrorist incidents of September 11, 2001, commonly referred to as 9/11, have taken a big bite out of fishing opportunities. In the name of national security, the government has slapped a security zone around all dangerous waterfront structures. For instance, anglers are forbidden to fish within 1,000 yards of nuclear power plants and must stay at least 25 yards away from all bridge abutments. For further information, contact the Coast Guard number in the appendix.

Regulations

New York has so many fishing regulations, it takes the *Department of Environmental Conservation Fishing Regulations Guide* about forty pages just to list them all. Pick up the pamphlet when you buy a license, memorize the general regulations in the front of the book, then check the special regulations by county to see if additional rules apply to the spot you're going to fish.

Public Fishing Rights

The state has purchased easements along hundreds of miles of streams. These sites are normally posted with square yellow signs announcing PUBLIC FISHING STREAM. Access is limited to the stream and the band of land 33 feet from the bank. Activities other than fishing are prohibited.

Fly fishing on the Connetquot River. ERIC FIELDSTADT, PHOTOGRAPHER. USED WITH PERMISSION.

Camping

Generally, primitive camping is allowed on state land in the Adirondack and Catskill Parks, and in all state forests.

- Groups numbering up to nine can spend up to three nights at any given site. Larger groups and longer stays require a permit from the local forest ranger.

- As a rule, camp must be set up at least 150 feet away from any road, trail, or source of water. Exceptions exist, however, in sites designated by a CAMP HERE disk.

- Primitive sites that are not in campgrounds are on a first-come, first-served basis and cannot be reserved.

- Lean-tos are not for exclusive use and must be shared.

- Camping is prohibited above 4,000 feet in the Adirondacks and above 3,500 feet in the Catskills.

Many state parks have campgrounds, and some even rent rustic cabins. Contact the park directly (see State Parks in the appendix for addresses and phone numbers) for informational brochures.

The Adirondack and Catskill Parks also have public campgrounds, but these are operated by the New York State Department of Environmental Conservation. Contact the regional office (addresses and phone numbers listed in the appendix) for informational brochures, or check online at www.dec.state.ny.us (click on "DEC Camping Information"). Reservations for all campgrounds can be made by contacting the New York State Camping/Cabin Reservation System at (800) 456–2267 or online at www.ReserveAmerica.com.

How to Use This Guide

Numerous books have been written about fishing in New York. None, however, has covered every spot—there are so many that the task would be of encyclopedic proportions. This book is also limited in scope. It only includes waters that are open to the public and are relatively easy to access.

The book is broken down into six regions: Long Island, Hudson Valley, Catskill Mountains Region, Adirondack Mountain Region, Mohawk Valley, and Susquehanna Drainage: East. Every region's major sites will be named, numbered, and described in the following way:

Key species: This section will include all the fish commonly sought in the spot.
Description: Each spot will be described. Lakes will have their acreage or square miles given, as well as average and maximum depths. Streams will contain information on their sources, lengths, and mouths.
Tips: Site-specific tips will be mentioned here.
The fishing: This section will give details on the fishery, including stuff like typical sizes, bait and habitat preference, state stocking statistics (fish stocked by local clubs or county and federal hatcheries will not be included), and special regulations.
Directions: How to get here from the nearest major town. Since one of the main focuses of this book is to introduce traveling anglers to the state's fishing, the directions will be the easiest way to go—not the shortest. In the case of streams, the major routes paralleling them will be given.
Additional information: This section will contain on-site camping information, boat launches, campgrounds, shore-fishing access, and other site-specific information.
Contact: State and local agencies to contact for information on the site. Phone numbers and addresses will be listed in the appendix.

Lettered sites below numbered ones include access points, campgrounds, and directions.

Web sites, addresses, and phone numbers of contacts are listed in the appendix.

Map Legend

Featured Fishing Site	🐟 20
Interstate Highway	90
U.S. Highway	89
State Highway	83
County, Local, or Forest Road	280
Trail	- - - - -
Railroad	⊢⊢⊢⊢⊢
State Line	— - — - —
Boat Ramp	🛥
Campground	▲
Parking	🅿
College	▪
Gate	⊢•
Ski Area	⛷
Lock	⌄
Waterfall	⫽
Bridge	≍
River, Creek, or Drainage	———
Reservoir, Lake, or Pond	⬭

Fish Species of New York

Brook Trout *(Salvelinus fontinalis)*

General description: This beautiful fish normally has a deep olive back decorated with a labyrinth of wormlike markings. Spots on its sides are red and blue; a white line traces its reddish lower fins. A member of the char family, its mouth and appetite are greater than your average trout's.

Distribution: The state's official fish, brookies are also called natives or speckled trout and can be found in clear, cold brooks, streams, ponds, and lakes throughout the state. They are the fish of choice for anglers hiking into remote Adirondack Mountain ponds and streams.

Additional information: Brookies assume their most striking colors in autumn when they're ready to spawn. Males often have bright red bellies and large hooked jaws. Their propensity for eagerly taking worms, salted minnows, flies, small spoons, spinners—you name it—has earned them the distinction of being the easiest trout to catch. The state's smallest trout, most range from 4 to 10 inches long. Fish around 18 inches long are possible, and the state record, caught in Boy Scout Clear Pond (site 68) on April 27, 2001, is 5 pounds, 14 ounces.

Lake Trout *(Salvelinus namaycush)*

General description: Like brookies, this delicious member of the char family isn't exactly the brightest fish in the tank. It has a relatively big mouth and an appetite to match. Its back is generally gray or green; the sides are silvery or gray and speckled with light spots. The belly is white, and its tail is forked.

Distribution: Another native New Yorker, this species prefers cold, deep water and is often sought in depths exceeding 100 feet. They are present in Lake Champlain and deep ponds and lakes in the Adirondack Mountains.

Additional information: One of the larger trout, lakers easily reach 20 inches, and 30-something-inch fish are common in Lake Champlain. They spawn in autumn in shallow water over gravel. The state record, caught in Lake Ontario on May 5, 1994, is 39 pounds, 8 ounces.

Brown Trout *(Salmo trutta)*

General description: Sporting deep brown backs, this species' color lightens into golden sides splashed with red and brown spots surrounded by light halos. Sometimes the red spots are so bright that they look like burning embers. Mature males sport kypes (curved lower jaws) that are often hooked so extremely, they seem deformed.

Distribution: Imported back in the 1830s from Germany, browns found America to their liking and have prospered. Far more tolerant of warm water than brookies or lakers, they do well in every kind of clean, oxygenated water, from deep lakes to shallow streams.

Additional information: Purist fly fishers consider the brown the savviest of trout. Its propensity for hitting a well-presented dry fly has endeared the species with some of the world's most famous authors—Dame Juliana Berners, Izaak Walton, William Butler Yeats, and Ernest Hemingway, to name a few. Especially colorful when they spawn in autumn, browns assume a brilliance that perfectly complements this colorful season. The state record, caught in Lake Ontario on June 10, 1997, weighs 33 pounds, 2 ounces.

Rainbow Trout or Steelhead *(Oncorhynchus mykiss)*

General description: This species has a deep green back that melts into silvery sides. A pink stripe stretching from the corner of the fish's jaw to the base of its tail is what gives it its name. The upper half of its body, its upper fins, and the entire tail are splattered with black spots.

Distribution: Native to the West Coast, rainbows were first introduced to New York in the nineteenth century and have been here ever since. They can be found in deep, cool lakes and cold streams throughout the state. Relatively easy to catch, they are often stocked in inhospitable urban creeks because biologists know the vast majority will likely be caught way before summer heats the creek to unbearable temperatures. Those that survive the early season's line-dancing anglers seek out spring holes or migrate downstream to cold lakes or the ocean.

Additional information: Anadromous rainbows are called steelhead. They run up streams in autumn to feast on the eggs of brown trout and salmon, often staying the entire winter. Come spring, steelies and domestic rainbows run up streams to spawn, providing trout enthusiasts with some of the year's most exciting action. The state record, caught in Lake Ontario on May 22, 1985, tipped the scale at 26 pounds, 15 ounces.

Splake *(brook trout–lake trout hybrid)*

General description: A cross between lake trout and brook trout, these hybrids can look like either one. The only way to identify them exactly is to examine their innards.

Distribution: The state stocks them in the Adirondacks in ponds like Green (site 84) and Boy Scout Clear (site 68) and lakes such as Meacham (site 69) and Limekiln (site 185).

Additional information: Splake are larger than brookies but generally don't reach the size lakers do. Unlike other hybrids, splake can reproduce; they spawn in autumn. The state record, caught in Little Green Pond on June 29, 1983, is 12 pounds, 15 ounces.

Atlantic Salmon or Landlocked Salmon (Salmo salar)

General description: The only salmon native to the state, Atlantic salmon generally have deep brown backs that quickly dissolve to silvery sides splattered with irregularly shaped spots, which are often crossed.

Distribution: Currently, this species is maintained almost exclusively through human intervention. They are most heavily stocked in Adirondack Mountain waters ranging from large ones, such as Lake George (site 38) and Lake Champlain (site 39), to tiny places, such as Moose Pond (site 62). They are also stocked in other regions, including suitable habitats such as Neversink Reservoir (site 15) and Otsego Lake (site 240).

Additional information: This species is the only salmon that survives the spawning ordeal, often returning to procreate a second, sometimes even a third time. Considered the classiest salmon, catching one, especially on a fly, is many a fly-fishing purist's greatest dream. Atlantic salmon spawn in autumn. The state record, caught in Lake Ontario on April 5, 1997, weighs 24 pounds, 15 ounces.

Kokanee Salmon (Oncorhynchus nerka)

General description: The landlocked version of sockeye salmon, this fish is silvery but turns red when spawning.

Distribution: The state stocks them into Taylor, Connery, and Lower Mitchell Ponds and Kushaqua and Limekiln Lakes, all in the Adirondacks.

Additional information: One of the smaller salmon, they average about 10 inches. Their mouths are very delicate; some anglers actually tie a rubber band onto their line to act as a shock absorber when setting the hook. Two techniques are used to catch them: First, you can chum with oatmeal and then still-fish with a red worm on a tiny (14 to 20) hook; second, try trolling slowly with a red worm about 18 inches behind a Lake Clear Wobbler. They spawn once, in autumn, and die. The state record, caught in Twin Lakes on September 24, 1995, is 2 pounds, 10 ounces.

Cisco or Lake Herring (Coregonus artedi)

General description: This silvery fish has a rounded, cigarlike body and is often described as resembling an oversized smelt.

Distribution: They are present in deep, cold lakes such as Hatch (site 227).

Additional information: Primarily plankton eaters, ciscoes will take dry flies, tiny garden worms, small minnows, and spoons. They spawn in autumn. The state record, caught in Lake Lauderdale on January 25, 1990, weighs 5 pounds, 7 ounces.

Lake Whitefish (Coregonus clupeaformis)

General description: These fish generally have brown or blue backs that fade into silvery sides and white bellies.

Distribution: Formerly distributed widely throughout the state, pollution has run them out of most of their range. They are, however, still found in cool, deep places such as West Caroga Lake (site 141), Indian Lake (site 127), and Otsego Lake (site 240).

Additional information: Zebra mussels feed on the same phytoplankton that lake whitefish eat, prompting some experts to warn they will wipe out the whitefish in waters occupied by both. Others counter that zebra mussels simply redistribute the biomass by laying their waste on the floor, which will result in explosions of bottom-feeding invertebrates—which whitefish also eat. While the jury is still out on the zebra mussel question, most scientists agree that alewives, which feed heavily on whitefish fry, can send the population into a nosedive. The state record, caught in Lake Pleasant on August 29, 1995, is 10 pounds, 8 ounces.

Largemouth Bass or Bucketmouth *(Micropterus salmoides)*

General description: The largest member of the sunfish family, this species is dark green on the back, with the color lightening as it approaches the white belly. A horizontal row of large, black splotches runs along the middle of the side, from the gill plate to the base of the tail. Its trademark is its huge head and mouth. The ends of the mouth reach past the eyes. This is one of the two species that the New York State Department of Environmental Conservation includes under the heading of black bass in the state *Fishing Regulations Guide.*

Distribution: Found in lakes, ponds, and sluggish streams throughout the state, except in the highest Adirondack ponds.

Additional information: Occurring in the entire lower forty-eight states, inclined to hit artificial lures of every description, the largemouth bass is America's favorite game fish. It'll hit just about anything that moves and is notorious for its explosive, heart-stopping strikes on surface lures. This species spawns in spring when water temperature ranges from 62 to 65 degrees Fahrenheit. The state record, caught in Buckhorn Lake on September 11, 1987, is 11 pounds, 4 ounces.

Smallmouth Bass or Bronzeback *(Micropterus dolomieu)*

General description: Brownish in color, the smallmouth is easily differentiated from the largemouth because the ends of the mouth occur below the eyes. One of America's most popular fish, it is granted equal status with bucketmouths in most bass tournaments. This is one of the two species the New York State Department of Environmental Conservation includes under the heading of black bass in the state *Fishing Regulations Guide.*

Distribution: Found in lakes and streams throughout the state.

Additional information: Spawns in late spring and early summer when water temperatures range from 61 to 65 degrees Fahrenheit. The state record, caught in Lake Erie on June 4, 1995, weighs 8 pounds, 4 ounces.

Muskellunge *(Esox masquinongy)*

General description: The largest member of the pike family, this long, sleek species commonly reaches 35 pounds. The back is a light green to brownish yellow, and the sides can have dark bars or blotches. Its most prominent feature is its duck-billed mouth filled with razor-sharp teeth. Only the upper halves of the gill covers and cheeks have scales—a fact normally used to differentiate muskies from northern pike and pickerel.

Distribution: Muskellunge occur in Lake Champlain (site 39), the Delaware River (site 29), and the Susquehanna River drainage.

Additional information: The Ohio and Great Lakes strains occur in the state. Muskies spawn in late April through early May when water temperatures range from 49 to 59 degrees Fahrenheit. The state record, caught in the St. Lawrence River in 1957, is 69 pounds, 15 ounces.

Caution: Keep your fingers out of the gill rakers; they are sharp enough to shred human flesh.

Tiger Muskie or Norlunge

General description: This species is a cross between a male northern pike and a muskie. Its body is shaped the same as a true muskie, but its colors are more vivid; its sides have wavy, tigerlike stripes. Its teeth are razor sharp.

Distribution: They are bred in hatcheries and released into rivers and lakes such as Durant (site 184) and Canadarago (site 239) to provide trophy fishing and to control runaway populations of hardy panfish such as white perch.

Additional information: These strikingly beautiful hybrids are sterile. The state record, caught in the Tioughnioga River on May 25, 1990, is 35 pounds, 8 ounces.

Caution: Keep your fingers out of the gill rakers; they are sharp enough to shred human flesh.

Northern Pike or Pikasaurus *(Esox lucius)*

General description: The medium-sized member of the pike family, this long, slender fish is named for a spear used in combat during the Middle Ages. Its body is the same as a muskie's, but its color is almost invariably green; it has large, oblong white spots on its sides. Its cheeks are fully scaled, as are the top halves (only) of its gill plates. Its teeth are razor sharp.

Distribution: In large and midsized rivers and lakes throughout the state.

Additional information: Spawns in April through early May, in water temperature ranging from 40 to 52 degrees Fahrenheit. The state record, caught in Great Sacandaga Lake on September 15, 1940, is 46 pounds, 2 ounces.

Caution: Keep your fingers out of the gill rakers; they are sharp enough to shred human flesh.

Chain Pickerel (Esox niger)

General description: The smallest member of the pike family, its body is shaped exactly like its larger cousins, but its green sides are overlaid in a yellow, chain mail-like pattern. Its teeth are razor sharp.

Distribution: In ponds and lakes throughout the state.

Additional information: Spawns in early spring, in water temperature ranging from 47 to 52 degrees Fahrenheit. The state record, caught in Toronto Reservoir in 1965, is 8 pounds, 1 ounce.

Caution: Keep your fingers out of the gill rakers; they are sharp enough to shred human flesh.

Walleye (Stizostedion vitreum)

General description: The largest member of the perch family, it gets its name from its large, opaque eyes. A walleye's back is dark gray to black and fades as it slips down to the sides, which are often streaked in gold. It has two dorsal fins; the front one's last few spines have a black blotch at their base. Its teeth are pointed and can puncture but won't slice. Nocturnal critters, walleye often enter shallow areas to feed. If the moon is out, their eyes catch and hold the beams, spawning stories of ghosts and extraterrestrial sightings by folks who see the eerie lights moving around in the water.

Distribution: In cool lakes and rivers throughout the state.

Additional information: Walleyes spawn in early spring when water temperatures range from 44 to 48 degrees Fahrenheit. The state record, caught in Kinzua Reservoir on May 22, 1994, weighs 16 pounds, 7 ounces.

Sauger (Stizostedion canadense)

General description: The second largest member of the perch family, sauger look like walleyes. They can be differentiated from their larger cousins by the two rows of black, crescent markings running the length of their front dorsal fin. In addition, they lack a white spot at the bottom tips of their tail and anal fins.

Distribution: Although historically sauger have been found in the Great Lakes and their tributaries, Lake Champlain boasts the state's largest population.

Additional information: Sauger spawn in spring. The state record, caught in the Lower Niagara River on September 30, 1990, weighs 4 pounds, 8 ounces.

Yellow Perch (Perca flavescens)

General description: This popular panfish has a dark back that fades to golden-yellow sides overlaid with five to eight dark, vertical bands. Sometimes its lower fins are traced in bright orange.

Distribution: Found in every type of water throughout the state.

Additional information: Spawns from mid-April through May when water temperatures range from 44 to 54 degrees Fahrenheit. The state record, caught in Lake Erie in April, 1982, is 3 pounds, 8 ounces.

Black Crappie *(Pomoxis nigromaculatus)*

General description: Arguably the most delicious of the state's panfish, this member of the sunfish family has a dark olive or black back and silver sides streaked with gold and overlaid with black spots and blotches. The front of its dorsal fin has seven or eight sharp spines followed by a soft fan.

Distribution: The state's most common crappie, it is found in still to slowly moving water throughout the state.

Additional information: Spawns in late spring when water temperatures range from 57 to 73 degrees Fahrenheit. The state record, caught in Duck Lake on April 17, 1998, weighs 3 pounds, 12 ounces.

White Crappie *(Pomoxis annularis)*

General description: This species looks pretty much the same as its black cousin but is generally lighter and only has six spines on its dorsal fin.

Distribution: Found in lakes, ponds, and slow rivers throughout the state.

Additional information: Spawns late spring and early summer when water temperatures range from 57 to 73 degrees Fahrenheit. The state record, caught in Kinderhook Lake on December 18, 1988, is 3 pounds, 9 ounces.

Bluegill *(Lepomis macrochirus)*

General description: One of the most popular sunfish, its color varies. It has anywhere from five to eight vertical bars running down the sides, a deep orange breast, and a dark blue, rounded gill flap.

Distribution: Lakes, ponds, and slow-moving rivers throughout the state.

Additional information: Ounce for ounce, bluegills are the sportiest fish. Fly fishing for them with wet flies and poppers is very popular. The species spawns in shallow, muddy areas near vegetation in summer. The state record, caught in Kohlbach Pond on August 3, 1992, is 2 pounds, 8 ounces.

Pumpkinseed *(Lepomis gibbosus)*

General description: This popular sunfish is the most widespread in the state. Its color ranges from bronze to dark green, and its gill flap has an orange-red spot on its end.

Distribution: Ponds, lakes, and slow-moving streams throughout the state.

Additional information: Spawns in shallow, muddy areas near vegetation in early summer. The state record, caught in Indian Lake on July 19, 1994, is 1 pound, 9 ounces.

Redbreast Sunfish *(Lepomis auritus)*

General description: This small sunfish rarely grows beyond 6 inches; an 8-incher is considered a trophy. It has a long, narrow flap at the end of the gill plate that is black for its entire length. The upper side has rows of red and orange spots, while the bottom side has rows of orange spots. The cheek and gill plate usually have blue, wavy

lines. Mature males have a deep orange breast, belly, tail, and second dorsal fin.
Distribution: Lakes and deep, slow rivers.
Additional information: Spawns in shallow, muddy areas near vegetation in early summer. As of press time, there was no state record.

Rock Bass, Redeye, or Googleye *(Ambloplites rupestris)*

General description: Another member of the sunfish family, it is dark brown to deep bronze in color, heavily spotted in black, and has big, red eyes.
Distribution: Found in rocky, shallow areas of streams and lakes throughout the state.
Additional information: Spawns over rocky areas in late spring and early summer. The state record, caught in the Ramapo River on May 26, 1984, is 1 pound, 15 ounces.

Channel Catfish *(Ictalurus punctatus)*

General description: The largest indigenous member of the catfish family, it has a dark brown back, white belly, forked tail, and barbels around its mouth. Juveniles up to 24 inches have black spots on their sides. Spines on the dorsal and pectoral fins can inflict a nasty wound.
Distribution: Found in deep channels of lakes and large rivers throughout the state, often in heavy current.
Additional information: Spawning takes place in summer, when water temperature reaches between 75 and 85 degrees Fahrenheit. The state record, caught in Lake Lauderdale on July 15, 2001, is 30 pounds.

Brown Bullhead *(Ameiurus nebulosus)*

General description: Having a dark brown back and white belly, this member of the catfish family has barbels around its mouth. A relatively square tail distinguishes it from the channel catfish.
Distribution: Great variety of habitats. It's tolerance of high temperatures and low oxygen levels allows it to live in places other fish can't. It is found in virtually every type of water, from Adirondack ponds to the Old Erie Canal.
Additional information: Spawns in muddy areas from late June through July. Both parents guard the schooling fry for the first few weeks of life. The state's record, caught in Sugarloaf Pond on April 26, 1998, is 6 pounds, 9 ounces.

White Perch *(Morone americana)*

General description: A member of the temperate bass family Percichthyidae, this species' back can range in color from olive to silvery gray. Its sides are pale olive or silver.
Distribution: New Erie Canal (site 212) and the Mohawk and Hudson River drainages.
Additional information: They spawn from mid-May through mid-June, when the

water temperature reaches 52 to 59 degrees Fahrenheit. The state record, caught in Lake Oscaletta on September 21, 1991, weighs 3 pounds, 1 ounce.

White Bass *(Morone chrysops)*

General description: Same as white perch but with bold, lateral stripes.
Distribution: Primarily found in the Mohawk River drainage.
Additional information: This species' populations undergo boom and bust cycles. One year, huge rafts dimple the surface in summer; the next year they're as rare as hen's teeth. They spawn in late spring. The state record, caught in Furnace Brook on May 2, 1992, is 3 pounds, 6 ounces.

Striped Bass *(Morone saxatilis)*

General description: Dark back with silvery sides and black, horizontal stripes.
Distribution: Hudson River and tributaries.
Additional information: This anadromous species runs coastal rivers and spawns in mid-May through June in water ranging from 58 to 68 degrees Fahrenheit. The state record, caught in the Hudson River on May 9, 2000, is 54 pounds, 3 ounces.

Burbot, Ling, or Lawyer *(Lota lota)*

General description: Looking like a cross between a bullhead and an eel, this species' color is yellow-brown overlaid with a dark mottled pattern. It has a single barbel on its chin and deeply embedded scales that are so tiny, they are almost invisible.
Distribution: Lake Champlain and the Susquehanna River drainage.
Additional information: Found in water up to 700 feet deep, individuals range from 12 to 20 inches. They are the only freshwater fish in the state that spawns in winter. Females lay up to one million eggs at a time. The state record, caught in Black River Bay on February 14, 1991, weighs 16 pounds, 12 ounces.

Freshwater Drum or Sheepshead *(Aplodinotus grunniens)*

General description: Overall color is silvery with a blue to olive-brown back and a white belly.
Distribution: The Mohawk, Hudson, and Susquehanna River drainages.
Additional information: Sheepshead have small, round teeth for crushing snails and have a taste for zebra mussels. They use muscles around their swimming bladders to produce drumming sounds. Spawning takes place in summer, from July through September. The state record, caught in Ganargua Creek on May 26, 1995, is 24 pounds, 7 ounces.

Common Carp *(Cyprinus carpio)*

General description: A brown-colored, large-scaled fish with orange fins, it has two barbels on each side of its upper jaw. Some are leatherlike with no scales or spotted with disproportionately large scales.

Distribution: Native to Eurasia, the species was introduced into American waters around 1830 and found the habitat good. Carp thrive in warm waters, and can be found everywhere from the Great Lakes to abandoned canals, farm ponds, and in lower reaches of creeks and brooks.

Additional information: Like many introduced species, carp suffer an image problem. Recently, however, European anglers have discovered the state's tremendous carp fishery, and the species is gaining in popularity. A good way to catch them is find a spot that looks fishy and still-fish with a piece of baked potato about the size of a bouillon cube, a marble-sized piece of white bread, or several kernels of canned corn. They will also hit worms. One of the most exciting ways to catch them is to sight-fish in a sluggish creek, slowly working the bait to the fish. They spawn in late spring when water temperature reaches 62 degrees Fahrenheit. The state record, caught in Tomhannock Reservoir on May 12, 1995, is 50 pounds, 4 ounces.

American Eel *(Anguilla rostrata)*

General description: A snakelike fish with a pointed head, its dorsal fin starts midway down its back, wraps around the end, and become continuous with the caudal and anal fins, reaching halfway up the belly.

Distribution: These fish are found in the Hudson River drainage and in the New Erie Canal.

Additional information: Nocturnal by nature, these fish are often caught at night on worms by bullhead anglers fishing in swamps and marshes, and by walleye anglers fishing large minnows on the bottom in canals or in holes below dams. After hatching in the Atlantic Ocean, the larvae migrate to fresh water, where individuals live for varying lengths of time before maturing and returning to the Sargasso Sea to spawn and die—a life cycle known as catadromous. Mature adults migrate back to sea in autumn. The eel's life span is unknown, but one was kept in captivity for eighty-eight years (Vladykov, 1955). Females migrate for great distances inland, while males stay close to the sea. The state record, caught in Cayuga Lake on July 25, 1984, is 7 pounds, 14 ounces.

Bowfin *(Amia calva)*

General description: Easily recognized by its primitive appearance. It has a long, flat head, a large mouth full of sharp teeth, a dorsal fin running along most of its back, and a rounded tail; males have a large spot at the upper corner of the tail's base.

Distribution: Mostly found in the Great Lakes drainage—but some inland waters such as Bashakill Marsh (site 8) are loaded with them.

Additional information: The sole surviving member of the Amiiformes family, a species that was around when dinosaurs roamed the countryside, bowfins spawn in shallow water in spring. The state record, caught in Bashakill on June 5, 2000, is 12 pounds, 8 ounces.

American Shad *(Alosa sapidissima)*

General description: A silvery, large-scaled fish with a single dorsal fin in the middle of the back.

Distribution: The Hudson and Delaware Rivers.

Additional information: An anadromous species, it runs up coastal rivers in late spring and early summer to spawn. The state record, caught in the Hudson River on April 30, 1989, is 8 pounds, 14 ounces.

White Sucker *(Catostomus commersoni)*

General description: A large-scaled, cylindrically shaped fish, its back and sides are olive-brown and it has a white belly. They normally range from 10 to 20 inches.

Distribution: Throughout the state, in just about every kind of water, from small streams to the Great Lakes.

Additional information: Although their flesh is sweet in early spring, it gets funky as the water warms up. About the only use most anglers have for white suckers is as bait. Their young are among the hardiest minnows, capable of living for hours while hooked through the back. Many anglers kill them needlessly; this is a waste, because suckers are valuable forage for everything from pike and bass to muskies, walleyes, and trout. By killing them, especially when they're spawning in spring, you deprive prized game fish of a valuable food source. The state record, caught in the Hudson River on May 13, 1994, is 5 pounds, 3 ounces.

Rainbow Smelt *(Osmerus mordax)*

General description: A cylindrically shaped silver fish with an olive back, it generally sports a noticeable silver stripe and a pink or blue iridescence along it sides. It has a large mouth for a small fish, with two large canine teeth on the roof of the mouth. Smelt normally range from 6 to 9 inches but can reach 13 inches.

Distribution: Found in Lake Champlain; they have also been introduced into numerous inland lakes throughout the state, including some in the Adirondack Park.

Additional information: Smelt are considered a delicacy wherever they are found. They ascend small streams in spring to spawn, and are often taken in large quantities with dip nets. There is no state record.

Connetquot River · Nissequogue River · Lake Ronkonkoma · Carmans River

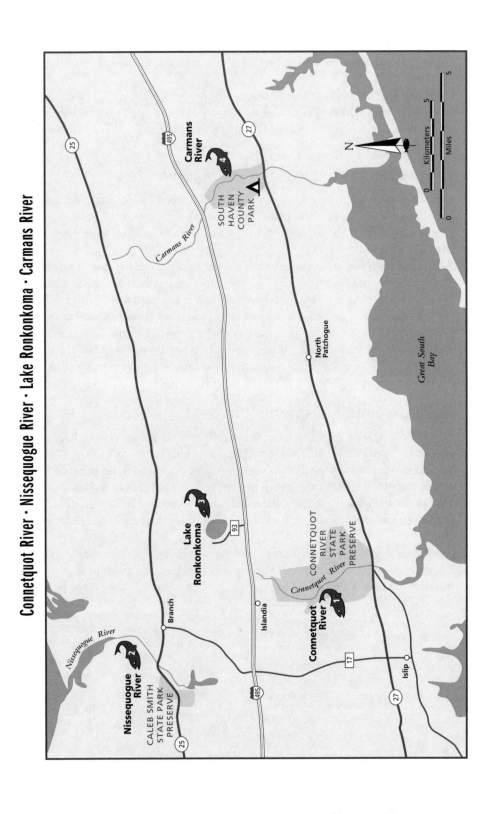

LONG ISLAND

Comprised of 1,723 square miles, Long Island's creeks and rivers have a history as hot spots for sea-run trout. Heavy development, dense populations, pollution, you name it, have eliminated most of the year-round trout habitat, greatly diminishing stocks of returning sea-run trout. Still, this huge suburb of New York City offers top-notch fast-water trout fishing, as well as lakes containing bass, walleyes, perch, and black crappies.

1. Connetquot River

Key species: Brook trout, brown trout, and rainbow trout.

Description: Bubbling up from the heart of the island, this 6-mile-long, spring-fed river's route is a refreshing strip of wildness in a seemingly endless suburb.

Tips: If you plan to fish in the preserve on a weekend, reserve your spot two weeks in advance.

The fishing: The state stocks 300 9-inch browns yearly in the stream outside Connetquot River State Park Preserve. In addition, the tidal section gets a few sea-run trout that can run as heavy as 5 pounds. They respond to worms and spinners.

In the tidal section, the minimum length for trout is 12 inches, the daily limit is three, and the season is year-round.

Directions: Head east out of Islip Terrace on NY 27 for about 3 miles.

Additional information: Most of this river flows through Connetquot River State Park Preserve. This fee area is managed as a fantasy fishery for fly fishing only. Annually, the hatchery on site releases up to 45,000 trout ranging from 8-inch yearlings to 26-inch brood stock, offering fly anglers a better-than-average chance at catching a big trout. Each angler must register in advance and is assigned a session (7:00 to 11:00 A.M., noon to 4:00 P.M., 5:00 P.M. to sunset) on a fishing platform stretching over a 500-foot-long beat (there are thirty). Barbed hooks are prohibited, and the session limit is two trout. Fishing is allowed by permit only, from February through October 15. Catch-and-release fishing only in February and March. Reservations for permits can be made up to two weeks in advance.

There is no public camping on the river. There are, however, several motels in the area.

Contact: New York State Department of Environmental Conservation Region 1, Long Island Convention and Visitors Bureau, and Connetquot River State Park Preserve.

2. Nissequogue River *(see map on page 20)*

Key species: Brown trout, rainbow trout, and brook trout.

Description: This river springs up from the heart of the island and flows north to feed Long Island Sound.

Tips: Almost any cream-colored fly pattern catches fish.

The fishing: The state stocks 700 brown trout averaging 8 inches and 400 two-year-olds averaging 14 inches in the section stretching from the mouth upstream to the Caleb Smith State Park Preserve. In addition, the tidal section gets a few sea-run trout that can reach 5 pounds. They take worms and streamers.

In the tidal section, the minimum size for trout is 12 inches, the daily limit is three, and the season is year-round.

Directions: Take NY 25 west from the village of Branch for about 1.5 miles.

Additional information: About a mile of this stream winds through Caleb Smith State Park Preserve, a fee area dedicated to providing a fantasy fishery for fly anglers. Each week during the season, anywhere from 100 to 250 trout ranging from yearlings to surplus brood stock are stocked, giving fly fishers a better-than-average shot at a big trout. Fly fishing only, by permit only. Reservations for permits can be made up to two weeks in advance. Anglers are assigned a four-hour session (7:00 to 11:00 A.M., 11:30 A.M. to 3:30 P.M., and 4:00 to 8:00 P.M.—or sunset, whichever comes first). The minimum size for trout is 9 inches, and the session limit is two. Only fly fishing with conventional fly-fishing tackle is allowed. This park also offers pond fishing for trout, largemouth bass, and panfish. Bucketmouth season runs from July 1 to October 15, their minimum length is 15 inches, and the daily limit is one. The daily limit for panfish is fifteen.

There are no public campgrounds on the river, but several motels are located nearby.

Contact: New York State Department of Environmental Conservation Region 1, Long Island Convention and Visitors Bureau, and Caleb Smith State Park Preserve.

3. Lake Ronkonkoma *(see map on page 20)*

Key species: Largemouth bass and walleye.

Description: This 229-acre lake averages 15 feet deep and drops to a maximum depth of 70 feet. The largest lake on Long Island, its entire shoreline is surrounded by suburbia, a large county park, and two municipal bathing beaches.

Tips: Jig scented, curly-tailed grubs along the drop-offs of deep holes.

The fishing: Largemouth bass range from too small to more than 20 inches. They are primarily targeted with topwater lures and soft plastic baits cast in and around shallow structures. This used to be the best bass spot on the island but, according to state aquatic biologist Fred G. Henson, an explosion in the populations of white and yellow perch has led to stunting in both species and heavy predation on largemouth fry—which isn't good for future generations of bass. The state is tackling the problem in two ways: by increasing the minimum length for black bass and by stocking walleyes, a species with an appetite for perch. Roughly 5,000 1.5-inch fingerlings (raised in ponds) and 5,000 5-inch advanced fingerlings (raised in the hatchery) have been stocked annually since 1994. By 2000 a few lucky anglers caught keeper walleyes, and "eyes" that size—and bigger—are being reported with increasing regularity. They take jigs and deep-diving crankbaits fished deep during daylight, and floating-diving crankbaits fished in anywhere from 5 to 15 feet of water at night.

The minimum length for largemouths is 15 inches. The regular season is from the first Saturday in June through November 30. Catch-and-release fishing for bass is allowed from December 1 through March 15. The minimum length for walleyes is 18 inches, and the daily limit is three. Gas motors are prohibited.

Directions: Head east on I–495 out of Islandia for about 1.5 miles to exit 59, then go north for about 0.75 mile on NY 93, which parallels the lake's west bank.

Additional information: The state launch for cartop craft on Victory Drive, on the west bank, has parking for fifteen cars. There is no public camping on the lake. There are several motels in the area.

Contact: New York State Department of Environmental Conservation Region 1, and Long Island Convention and Visitors Bureau.

4. Carmans River *(see map on page 20)*

Key species: Brook trout, brown trout, and rainbow trout.

Description: This river seeps out of the sand and gravel on Long Island's rural east end and weaves south for about 9 miles to feed Great South Bay.

Tips: The longest stretch of water open to public fishing is in Southaven County Park.

The fishing: According to regional fisheries manager Charles Guthrie, natural groundwater streams such as this are ideal trout habitat because they don't feature wild swings in water temperatures. This river supports one of the island's greatest populations of wild brook trout. Ranging from 4 to 8 inches, they hit just about any fly. The state stocks roughly 130 15.5-inch, 930 14-inch, and 710 9-inch brown trout, along with 1,700 9-inch rainbow trout annually. They hit nymphs, dry flies, streamers, in-line spinners, and worms.

Trout season is from April 1 to September 30.

Directions: Take NY 27 exit 58 north in the village of Shirley, turn west onto Victory Avenue, travel about 0.25 mile, and follow the signs to the county park.

Peconic River

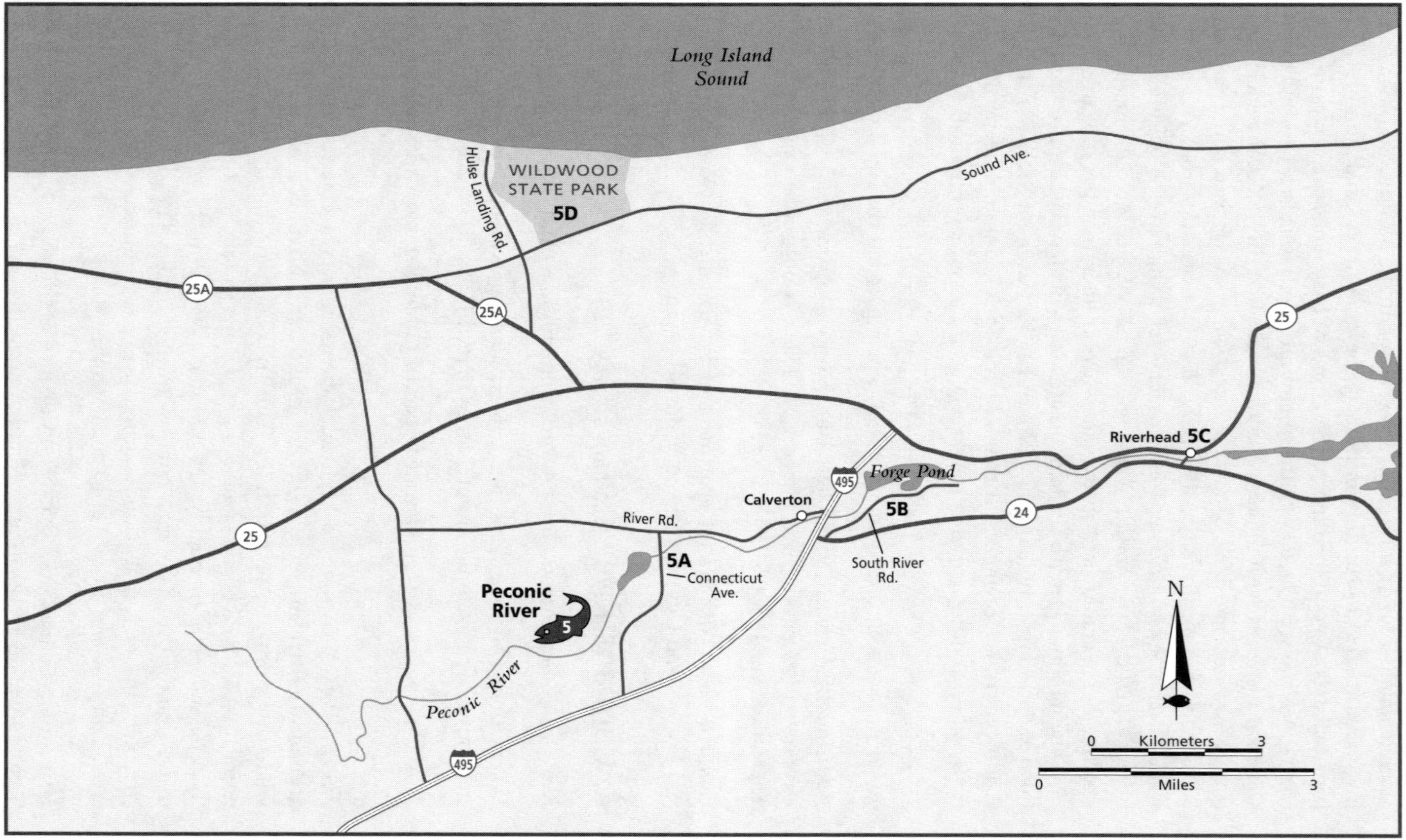

Long Island Sound

WILDWOOD STATE PARK **5D**

Hulse Landing Rd.

Sound Ave.

Riverhead **5C**

Forge Pond

5B

South River Rd.

Calverton

Connecticut Ave.

5A

River Rd.

Peconic River **5**

Peconic River

N

Kilometers

Miles

25

24

495

25A

25A

25

Additional information: South Haven County Park, a 1,356-acre fee area set in unspoiled native forest and wetland, offers a 3-mile stretch of Carmans River managed for trout, as well as 132 campsites and hot showers. The campground is open mid-April through mid-October. A permit, available from the county parks, is required to fish the river. There are three special trout-fishing-regulation areas: no-kill fly fishing, fly fishing only, and freestyle angling. In the latter two, the minimum length is 9 inches and the daily limit is three.

Contact: New York State Department of Environmental Conservation Region 1, and Long Island Convention and Visitors Bureau, and Suffolk County Parks.

5. Peconic River

Key species: Brown trout, largemouth bass, chain pickerel, black crappie, and yellow perch.

Description: Running from west to east for roughly 15 miles to feed Flanders Bay, this stream is dammed in several places, creating warm-water impoundments.

Tips: Jig or drag scented, soft plastic lures along weed edges.

The fishing: The state stocks about 300 brown trout ranging from 9 to 14 inches into the headwaters annually. They hit worms and nymphs. The river's bread-and-butter fish is the largemouth bass. Ranging anywhere from 12 to 22 inches, they take anything from Jitterbugs and Hula Poppers worked on still summer evenings to buzzbaits, spinnerbaits, and lipless crankbaits such as Cotton Cordell's C-29 Super Spot Minnows. Chain pickerel range from 15 to 25 inches and voraciously attack jerkbaits and worms on spinner harnesses. Yellow perch running from 6 to 12 inches and black crappies of 8 to 10 inches are plentiful; try jigging Beetle Spins and 2-inch curly-tailed grubs on bottom or swimming them through the water column.

The daily limit for black crappie and yellow perch is fifteen of each species.

Directions: NY 25 parallels the river in—and west of—the hamlet of Riverhead.

Additional information: Indian Island County Park in Riverhead, on the river's mouth, offers 150 campsites, picnic sites, and hot showers. The campground is open year-round, but restricted to self-contained units like RVs between November and March because the utilities are shut off.

Contact: New York State Department of Environmental Conservation Region 1, Suffolk County Parks, and Long Island Convention and Visitors Bureau.

5A. Public Access

Description: This site has a beach launch for cartop craft and parking for five cars.

Directions: Take River Road west out of Calverton for about 1 mile and turn south onto Connecticut Avenue.

Additional information: A state Department of Environmental Conservation permit is required to launch here.

5B. Public Access *(see map on page 24)*

Description: This site has a beach launch for cartop craft and parking for ten cars.

Directions: In the hamlet of Calverton, on South River Road, 0.5 mile east of Edwards Avenue (NY 24). (South River Road comes off NY 24 less than 0.5 mile east of I–495 Bridge.)

Additional information: This site is on Forge Pond, a 120-acre impoundment averaging 6 feet deep.

5C. Public Access *(see map on page 24)*

Description: This site has a beach launch for cartop craft and parking for five cars.

Directions: On NY 25, in the village of Riverhead.

5D. Wildwood State Park *(see map on page 24)*

Description: This 760-acre park offers 322 campsites (including 80 with full hookups), hot showers, picnic areas, and surf fishing in Long Island Sound.

Directions: Head west out of Riverhead on NY 25 for about 5.5 miles and turn north onto NY 25A. Travel for about 1.5 miles, turn east onto Sound Avenue, then head left at the traffic light onto Hulse Landing Road.

6. Fort Pond *(see map on page 28)*

Key species: Largemouth bass, smallmouth bass, and walleye.

Description: This 192-acre pond averages 8 feet deep and has a maximum depth of 27 feet. It is surrounded by vegetated bluffs bearing hillside cottages.

Tips: Cast jig-rigged 4-inch finesse worms for suspended walleyes and smallmouth bass.

The fishing: This lake's largemouth bass range from 12 to 22 inches, but the vast majority are undersized. They hit spinnerbaits and walking baits such as Zara Spooks. Smallmouths average about 14 inches, and a full 20 percent of the fish caught by anglers are legal sized. More plentiful than bucketmouths, they are usually targeted with crayfish and plastic worms. This pond is overpopulated with yellow and white perch, a situation that has led to stunting of both, and to decreasing populations of black bass because the perch prey on their fry. The state is combating the situation with walleyes, a species known for preying on perch. Roughly 4,000 1.5-inch fingerlings (raised in ponds) and 4,000 advanced fingerlings (hatchery raised) have been stocked annually since 1997. They seem to be doing their task, and walleyes ranging from 18 to 24 inches are available. They respond to worms

Netting a pickerel on the Peconic River. ERIC FIELDSTADT, PHOTOGRAPHER. USED WITH PERMISSION.

drifted plain, trolled on spinner harnesses, or tipped on bucktail jigs. The minimum length for black bass is 15 inches, and the season extends from the first Saturday in June until November 30. In addition, catch-and-release bass fishing is allowed from December 1 through March 15. The minimum length for walleyes is 18 inches and the daily limit is three. Gas motors are prohibited.

Directions: Head east out of East Hampton for 12 miles on NY 27.

Additional information: The state-operated beach launch for cartop craft in the village of Montauk, off Edgemere Road, has parking for about twenty cars. Theodore Roosevelt County Park, 2.5 miles east of the village of Montauk on East Lake Drive (off NY 27A), offers camping for self-contained units such as RVs on its outer beach. The campground is open May through October.

Contact: New York State Department of Environmental Conservation Region 1, and Long Island Convention and Visitors Bureau.

Fort Pond

A good catch at Fort Pond. ERIC FIELDSTADT, PHOTOGRAPHER. USED WITH PERMISSION

6A. Hither Hills State Park

Description: This 1,755-acre fee area offers 160 no-frills campsites, hot showers, picnic areas, fishing in a freshwater pond, and surf fishing in the Atlantic Ocean. The campground is open from early April through mid-November.

Directions: On NY 27, about 9 miles east of East Hampton.

The fishing: Fresh Pond, completely surrounded by the park, covers 35 acres and contains one of the island's best warm-water freshwater fisheries. Largemouth bass range from 1 to 3 pounds, and 5-pounders are present. They respond to buzzbaits and scented plastic worms. Yellow perch running from 8 to 12 inches are plentiful, and black crappies of about the same size are available. Both like small minnows, 2-inch scented curly-tailed grubs, and tubes. Pumpkinseeds and bluegills range from 8 to a whopping 10 inches and love tiny poppers, wet flies, and worms. Brown bullheads (locally called catfish) average 10 inches and hit worms fished on bottom.

The regular season for black bass runs from the first Saturday in June through November 30. No-kill bass fishing is allowed from December through March 15. The daily limit for yellow perch, black crappies, and sunfish is fifteen of each species.

Additional information: The park's eastern boundary contains "walking dunes," which constantly shift with the wind.

HUDSON VALLEY

For the purposes of this book, the Hudson River will be divided into two sections: upper and middle. The fast-flowing upper river, from its source down to Hudson Falls, is covered in the Adirondack Mountain Region section (site 130). The slow-moving, freshwater, tidal river from Troy to Newburgh is listed as the Mid Hudson River.

7. Mid Hudson River

Key species: Striped bass, American shad, largemouth bass, smallmouth bass, and walleye.

Description: New York's largest river, the 315-mile-long Hudson falls from Lake Tear of the Clouds, high on Mount Marcy in the Adirondacks. Gathering strength from the numerous tributaries it picks up while storming through the mountains, it earns its title as New York's greatest river at Cohoes where it is joined by the Mohawk River. The section below deals with the big water described by New York's senior aquatic biologist Mike Flaherty as the "perennially freshwater portion of the tidal river." Stretching for roughly 95 miles, from the Troy Dam to Newburgh, the tidal swing in this section averages 4 feet per day.

Tips: The biggest stripers are available in mid-May.

The fishing: This massive stream contains everything from monster sturgeon and tiger muskies down to yellow and white perch. It is most famous for its incredible bass and shad fisheries. Striped bass range from 0.5 to 40 pounds but average 6 pounds. While some are caught year-round, this anadromous species' greatest numbers and largest specimens run upriver in spring when water temperatures hit the upper 40s, igniting their urge to spawn. Primarily targeted with blood worms, eels, live and cut herring, and bunker, they are also taken on Bomber Long "A"s and Rebels. Millions of American shad averaging 5 pounds run upstream each spring to spawn, as well. They hit red-and-yellow and red-and-white shad darts. Generous populations of largemouth bass ranging from 2 to 7 pounds, and smallmouths running 1 to 5 pounds, have been drawing national bass tournaments here since the 1970s. Schools of both species hang out in tributaries and their mouths for a couple of weeks after spawning. Afterward, the bucketmouths find cover in water chestnut colonies, weed beds, bands of vegetation clinging to the edges of channels, and shallow structures such as pilings and docks. Smallmouths seek out deep structures, including pilings, wrecks, bridge abutments, and the human-made rock piles surrounding the river's numerous beacons. Both species take minnows, crayfish, crankbaits, soft plastic jerkbaits, Texas- and Carolina-rigged worms and craws,

Mid Hudson River

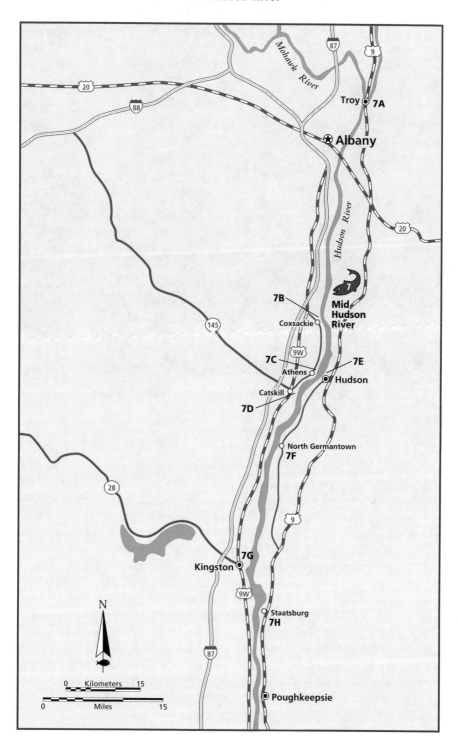

Drop-off where weed flat dives into deep water, a classic Hudson River largemouth bass habitat.

jig-rigged soft plastics ranging from tubes to curly-tailed grubs—you name it. Walleyes up to 7 pounds have been showing up with increasing frequency lately, especially near the mouths of tributaries. Most experts attribute this emerging fishery to stockies escaping from reservoirs and lakes in which the state is trying to establish the species. They hit bucktail jigs fished plain or tipped with a worm or minnow, worms drifted and trolled on harnesses, and minnowbaits.

The key to catching all these species is understanding how they respond to the tide. For instance, American shad feed most actively during the period of slow current just before the tide direction changes, while stripers seem most active during a running tide. Largemouths dive into weed beds during ebb tide and spread out to feed at high tide. At night, a rising tide often lures herring—and stripers—onto shallow flats and into tributaries. Tide tables and charts are sold at local sport shops, published in regional newspapers, and covered during weather reports.

Catch-and-release fishing only is permitted from the Troy Dam upstream to Fort Edward. Striper season runs from March 16 through November 30; their minimum length is 18 inches, and the daily limit is one.

Directions: US 9 parallels the Hudson's east bank, and US 9W parallels the west bank.

Additional information: Numerous motels and a few public campgrounds are available in the communities along the river.

Contact: New York State Department of Environmental Conservation, Columbia County Tourism, Albany County Convention and Visitors Bureau, Greene County Promotion and Tourism Department, Rensselaer County Tourism, Ulster County Tourism, and Dutchess County Tourism.

7A. Troy Public Access *(see map on page 31)*

Description: This site has a paved ramp, loading docks, and parking for about fifteen rigs.

The fishing: Wide, canal-like, flowing through a highly populated area loaded with structures ranging from dams and locks to bridge abutments and docks, what this stretch lacks in terms of quality moments steeped in solitude, it more than makes up for with good bass fishing. Drift crayfish and 3-inch minnows for smallmouth bass and work surface plugs, jerkbaits, and jig-'n'-pigs along the edges of flotsam, decaying timber, and weed beds for largemouths.

Directions: At the west end of 123 Street, city of Troy.

7B. Coxsackie Public Access *(see map on page 31)*

Description: This site features a concrete ramp and parking for thirty-five rigs.

The fishing: Extensive weed beds north of the village and a variety of structure along the village waterfront make this area "bucketmouth heaven."

Directions: In Riverside Park, at the end of Reed Street, hamlet of Coxsackie.

7C. Athens Public Access *(see map on page 31)*

Description: This site features a paved ramp and parking for thirty-five rigs.

The fishing: The riprap around area beacons and the broken shoreline north of the village hold largemouths all season long. Work deep water with curly-tailed grubs or tubes on jigheads and rip jerkbaits and buzzbaits over the shallows. The flats south of the small lower island are a striper hot spot, at high tide, all summer long. Try Red Fins and ThunderSticks.

Directions: Off NY 385, in the village of Athens.

7D. Dutchman's Landing Public Access *(see map on page 31)*

Description: Around the bend from the mouth of Catskill Creek, this site has a paved launch, parking for seventy-five rigs and fifty cars, a concession stand, picnic facilities, and toilets.

Largemouth bass caught in the Hudson at Catskill Creek.

The fishing: The drop-off south of the mouth of Catskill Creek is a shad hot spot in May. The mouth of the creek for a way upstream is a hot spot for postspawn largemouth and smallmouth bass. Additionally, this launch is a popular staging area for tournaments, and bass released after the events usually hang around for a while in the fertile waters. They will hit everything from jerkbaits to crankbaits, crayfish to minnows. Lately, walleyes in the 2- to 6-pound range have been showing up in the creek to spawn. They are primarily taken with Rapalas and Red Fins. Huge stripers come into the creek at high tide in May to pig out on herring running upstream to spawn. They hit Rebel Minnows, Bomber Long "A"s, and live herring.

Directions: Take a left just before the end of Main Street, village of Catskill.

7E. Hudson Public Access *(see map on page 31)*

Description: This site has a hard-surface ramp and parking for forty-five rigs.

The fishing: The drop-off stretching the length of riprap north of the village of Hudson holds smallmouths and stripers all summer long. Both respond to minnow-imitating crankbaits and surface poppers.

Directions: Water Street, city of Hudson.

7F. North Germantown Public Access *(see map on page 31)*

Description: This site has a hard-surface ramp and parking for twenty rigs.

The fishing: Area beacons are surrounded with riprap—prime largemouth bass habitat. Jig curly-tailed grubs and tubes along the rocks, or drift 3-inch minnows over them.

Directions: At the end of Anchorage Road, hamlet of North Germantown.

7G. Charles Ryder Park Public Access *(see map on page 31)*

Description: This site features a two-lane concrete ramp and parking for fifty rigs.

The fishing: A long, shallow flat stretches down the center of the river from about 0.5 mile above the Kingston-Rhinecliff Bridge for almost 2 miles downstream. During the spawning run, mid-April through mid-June, stripers are forced into the channels running along both shores but prefer the narrower west channel. Locals anchor in about 20 feet of water and fish for them with blood worms and herring.

Directions: Head north out of Kingston on NY 32 for about 1.5 miles, turn east onto Ulster Landing Road (CR 37), and travel about 1 mile to Charles Ryder Park.

7H. Mills Norrie State Park *(see map on page 31)*

Description: This fee area features fifty-one no-frills campsites, ten cabins, hot showers, a marina, a paved launch ramp, parking for forty rigs, miles of shore-fishing access, playgrounds, hiking trails, and two nine-hole golf courses. The park is

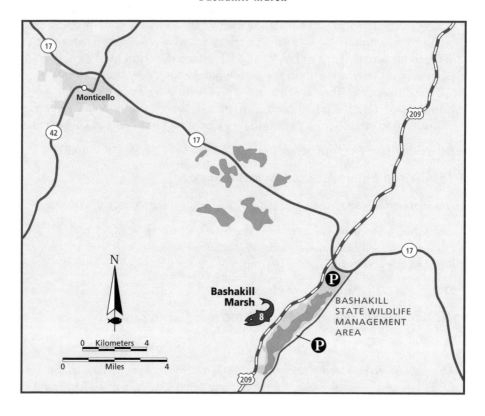

open year-round; the campground is open mid-May through the last weekend in October. Free day use off-season.

The fishing: The weed beds in and around the marina hold hawg largemouth bass that respond to spinnerbaits and jerkbaits. Across the river, forage spawning in Black Creek draws stripers from mid-April through June. Target them with crankbaits and free-lined minnows.

Directions: Head north on US 9 out of the village of Poughkeepsie for 9 miles to the village of Staatsburg.

8. Bashakill Marsh

Key species: Largemouth bass, chain pickerel, sunfish, and bowfin.

Description: The crown jewel of the Bashakill Wildlife Management Area, this swamplike 800-acre impoundment averages about 4 feet deep and is loaded with weed lines, lily pads, and bog and cattail mats.

Tips: Tip Road Runner Jigheads with scented 1- or 2-inch curly-tailed grubs.

The fishing: This fabulous wetland complex boasts a good population of bucket-mouths in the 2- to 5-pound range. Go for them with jig-'n'-pigs, Zara Spooks, and floating worms. Chain pickerel typically range from 15 to 25 inches and take the same baits as the largemouths. This is sunfish heaven. Bluegills get up to a pound and hit worms and wet flies. There is a large population of bowfins. These primitive-looking critters respond best to live bait, especially minnows.

Bass and pickerel can be taken year-round.

Directions: Take NY 17 (soon to become I–86) east out of Monticello for about 9 miles to exit 113 just south of Wurtsboro, then head south on US 209.

Additional information: The state has several launch ramps and parking areas off US 209 and off South Road, which parallels the east bank. Camping is prohibited in wildlife management areas. Several private campgrounds are available nearby.

Contact: New York State Department of Environmental Conservation Region 3, and Sullivan County Visitors Association.

9. Thompsons Lake *(see map on page 38)*

Key species: Rainbow trout, brown trout, smallmouth bass, largemouth bass, chain pickerel, pumpkinseed, and yellow perch.

Description: This spring-fed lake covers 128 acres, averages 41 feet deep, and drops to a maximum depth of 60 feet. Its shoreline is heavily developed in private residences, and there's a state park and campground on the northwest shore.

Tips: Night fish with Christmas tree rigs.

The fishing: The state stocks roughly 1,700 rainbow trout and 600 brown trout averaging 9 inches annually. Growth is decent—most end up ranging between 12 and 16 inches. From fall through spring, they can be taken near shore on live bait. Come summer, they suspend in deep water by day and can be taken on minnows fished below slip bobbers and lures trolled deep. On some summer evenings, they will rise to feed on hatching insects. Smallmouth bass in the 12- to 15-inch range are plentiful. They hang out along deep shelves and respond to diving crankbaits and 3-inch grubs fished on drop-shot rigs. Largemouth bass go anywhere from 12 to 20 inches and take buzzbaits and surface baits cast around their haunts, primarily the weed beds on the south end. Pickerel normally ranging from 15 to 20 inches share this range with the bucketmouths and have a taste for jerkbaits. Pumpkinseeds reaching up to 8 inches and yellow perch stretching the tape to 12 inches can be found all along the shoreline and respond to worms and wet flies.

Directions: Head west out of Albany for about 8 miles on NY 85 to its intersection with NY 157. Turn north onto NY 157 and travel for about 5.5 miles.

Thompsons Lake

Additional information: Thompsons Lake State Park is a fee area offering 135 no-frills campsites, hot showers, a swimming beach, and a hard-surface launch. The campground is open from mid-May through mid-October. A day-use fee is charged to noncampers when the campground is open; free day use is allowed off-season. A municipal launch on the south end of the lake, off NY 157, has a paved ramp and parking for about five cars.

Contact: New York State Department of Environmental Conservation Region 4.

10. Kinderhook Creek *(see map on page 40)*

Key species: Brown trout.

Description: Running for 45 miles before feeding the east side of the Hudson River south of Albany, only the upper half of Kinderhook Creek remains cool enough year-round to support trout.

Tips: Caddis imitations and Blue-Winged Olives, fished early in the morning and at dusk, match just about anything hatching in June and July.

The fishing: The state annually stocks about 15,000 8-inch brown trout and 1,650 averaging 14 inches into the stream upstream of Corsey Road, in Columbia County. Survival is decent in the creek's insect-rich environs—11-inch trout are typical. They take worms, minnows, streamers, and flies.

Downstream of Adams Crossing, the trout season remains open until November 30.

Directions: US 20 and NY 66 parallel the best trout water.

Additional information: The state owns public fishing rights on about 90 percent of the creek stretching from NY 43 in Stephentown downstream to Malden Bridge. Access is plentiful off the shoulder of US 20 and at bridge crossings. No public camping is available on the stream, but there are private campgrounds and motels in the area.

Contact: New York State Department of Environmental Conservation Region 4, Columbia County Tourism, and Rensselaer County Tourism.

10A. Public Access

Description: This site has parking for about five cars.

Directions: Head east on US 20 out of the village of Nassau for about 6 miles to NY 66 and turn north. Travel for about 1 mile, then turn east onto Tayer Road.

11. Saratoga Lake *(see map on page 41)*

Key species: Largemouth bass, smallmouth bass, chain pickerel, northern pike, walleye, yellow perch, sunfish, and black crappie.

Kinderhook Creek

Saratoga Lake

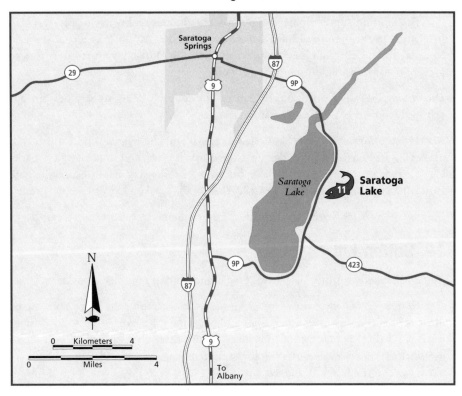

Description: This 3,764-acre lake averages 25 feet deep and has a maximum depth of 96 feet.

Tips: In summer, troll Rattlin' Red Fins and ThunderSticks 20 feet deep over 35 feet of water.

The fishing: This lake is most popular for bucketmouths ranging from 1 to 4 pounds. They'll take spinnerbaits, buzzbaits, Texas-rigged worms, and crankbaits run along weed edges and breaks. Smallmouths ranging from 0.75 to 3 pounds are common on rocky bottom and respond well to Carolina-rigged Exude finesse worms and curly-tailed grubs. Pickerel in the 1- to 2.5-pound class hang out in weeds, where they attack Exude RT Slugs and nightcrawlers on spinner harnesses worked quickly through openings in the weeds and along their edges. Recently the state has been stocking more than eight million walleye fry annually. They've grown to range from 2 to 5 pounds and respond well to rattling crankbaits ranging from C. C. Rattlin' Shads and MirrOlure's 92LSR series to Bomber "A"s, Rat-L-Traps, and Mann's Loudmouth Jerkbaits. Sunfish from 0.5 to 0.75 pound are plentiful and respond to worms and small poppers. Yellow perch ranging from 7 to 10 inches and black crappies from 9 to 12 inches are abundant and will take small minnows and scented 2-inch curly-tailed grubs.

The limit on sunfish (bluegills, pumpkinseeds, and redbreasts) is fifty per day from June 16 through the Friday before the first Saturday in May. From the first Saturday in May through June 15, the daily limit for sunfish is reduced to fifteen to prevent overharvesting during their spawning period.

Directions: Take I–87 north out of Albany for about 20 miles to Saratoga Springs exit 14, then take NY 9P east for about 3 miles.

Additional information: The Saratoga Lake boat launch, located on the north end, off NY 9P, has a hard-surface ramp, parking for forty rigs, and some overflow parking. There is no camping on the lake, but a lot of folks stay at Moreau Lake State Park, 10 miles north (take I–87 to exit 17, then head south on US 9 for about 1 mile).

Contact: New York State Department of Environmental Conservation Region 5.

12. Batten Kill

Key species: Brown trout, brook trout, smallmouth bass, and tiger muskie.

Description: Spawned in the Green Mountains of Vermont, the New York leg of this world-famous trout stream is about 30 miles long. Ranging from 80 to 100 feet wide, crossed in spots by wooden bridges, it runs through Rich Preall's beat, carving what the state senior aquatic biologist describes as "a beautiful valley that looks like a piece of the Catskills moved north."

Tips: Work streamers through the deep pools below covered bridges.

The fishing: The stretch from the Vermont border to the village of Shushan, a distance of roughly 8 miles, is prime wild trout water. Browns outnumber brookies nine to one. Both typically range from 8 to 12 inches but 15-inch brookies and 20-inch browns are present. From Shushan to Battenville, the state annually stocks roughly 12,500 browns averaging 8 inches and almost 1,000 averaging 14 inches. Lately the fish haven't been doing too well in this 10-mile stretch, and the size of those caught coincides with the size of the stockies. Some blame the trout's inability to thrive in this section on the disrepair of its stream-improvement structures (roughly 350 structures ranging from cribs and V-notches to riprap and pool diggers).

Battenville is about as far downstream as trout can survive. From here, smallmouth bass up to 16 inches are plentiful and respond well to minnows and crankbaits. Recently, the state has been stocking several hundred tiger muskies annually. If they take, there should be some keepers in the river between Middle Falls and the mouth by the time this book is published.

Trout season is year-round in the stretch from the Vermont border to the covered bridge at Eagleville. Only artificial lures may be used. The minimum size is 10 inches, and the daily limit is three.

Batten Kill

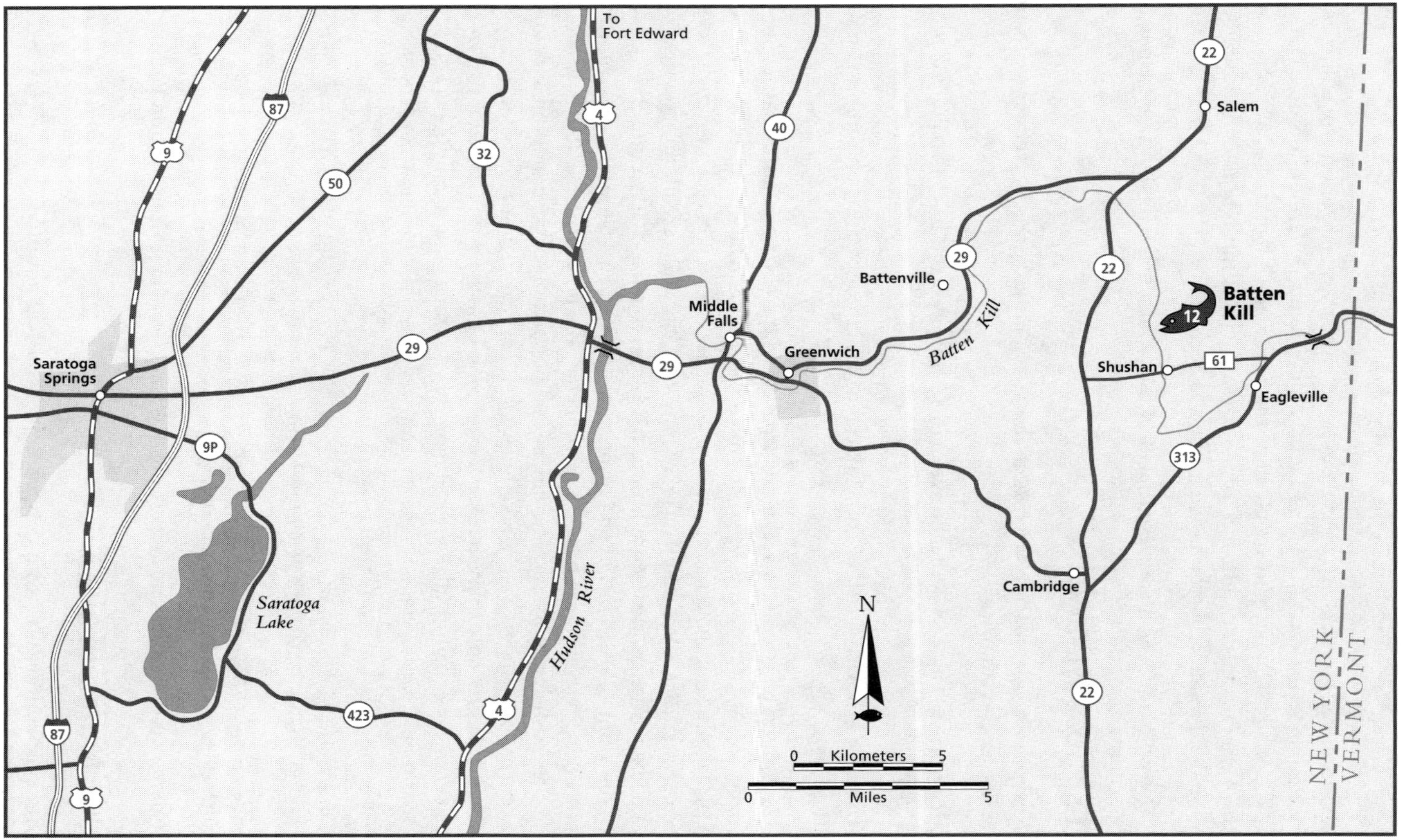

NEW YORK
VERMONT

Salem

Batten
Kill

61

Eagleville

313

22

22

Shushan

Cambridge

Battenville

Batten Kill

29

Greenwich

40

Middle Falls

29

To Fort Edward

4

32

N

Hudson River

29

4

50

423

87

9P

Saratoga Lake

9

Saratoga Springs

87

9

0 Kilometers 5

0 Miles 5

Directions: NY 313 parallels the river for its easternmost 5 miles. NY 29 parallels it from Greenwich Junction all the way to Middle Falls.

Additional information: A formal public fishing access and parking for about twenty cars is located on NY 313, about 0.25 mile from the Vermont border. The state owns public fishing rights on much of the river stretching for about 15 miles from the Vermont border. Informal access is available at most bridges and along the shoulder, particularly around Eagleville and Shushan.

Contact: New York State Department of Environmental Conservation Region 5.

13. Cossayuna Lake

Key species: Tiger muskie, largemouth bass, smallmouth bass, northern pike, brown bullhead, and sunfish.

Description: This 659-acre lake averages 12 feet deep and has a maximum depth of 25 feet.

Tips: Fly fish with wet flies and 0.32-ounce Hula Poppers for bluegills and pumpkinseeds.

The fishing: Each year, this lake gets stocked with 2,600 tiger muskies averaging 9.5 inches. Most that are caught go around 25 inches, 5 inches short of the minimum legal length. Still, enough keeper 30- to 36-inchers are caught each year to draw their fans back for more. They take Mepps Muskie Killers and minnow-imitating crankbaits such as MirrOlure Lipped 52Ms and Rapalas. Largemouth bass typically run from 12 to 18 inches and respond to spinnerbaits. So do the lake's northern pike. Ranging anywhere from 18 to 36 inches, the northerns also like large shiners suspended below bobbers. There is a good population of smallmouth bass ranging from 12 to 16 inches. They take bucktail jigs fished plain or tipped with scented tubes and curly tails. Sunfish reach a whooping 12 inches. Most are taken on worms, but they hit equally well—and are more fun to catch—on small poppers and flies. Brown bullheads average 14 inches. They are targeted with nightcrawlers fished on bottom at night or during a rain.

Directions: Head east out of Fort Edward on NY 197 for about 11 miles to South Argyle, then go east on CR 49 for 3 miles.

Additional information: The state boat launch on East Shore Road has a hard-surface ramp and parking for thirty rigs.

Contact: New York State Department of Environmental Conservation Region 5.

14. Moreau Lake

Key species: Rainbow trout, largemouth bass, smallmouth bass, chain pickerel, and panfish.

Cossayuna Lake · Moreau Lake

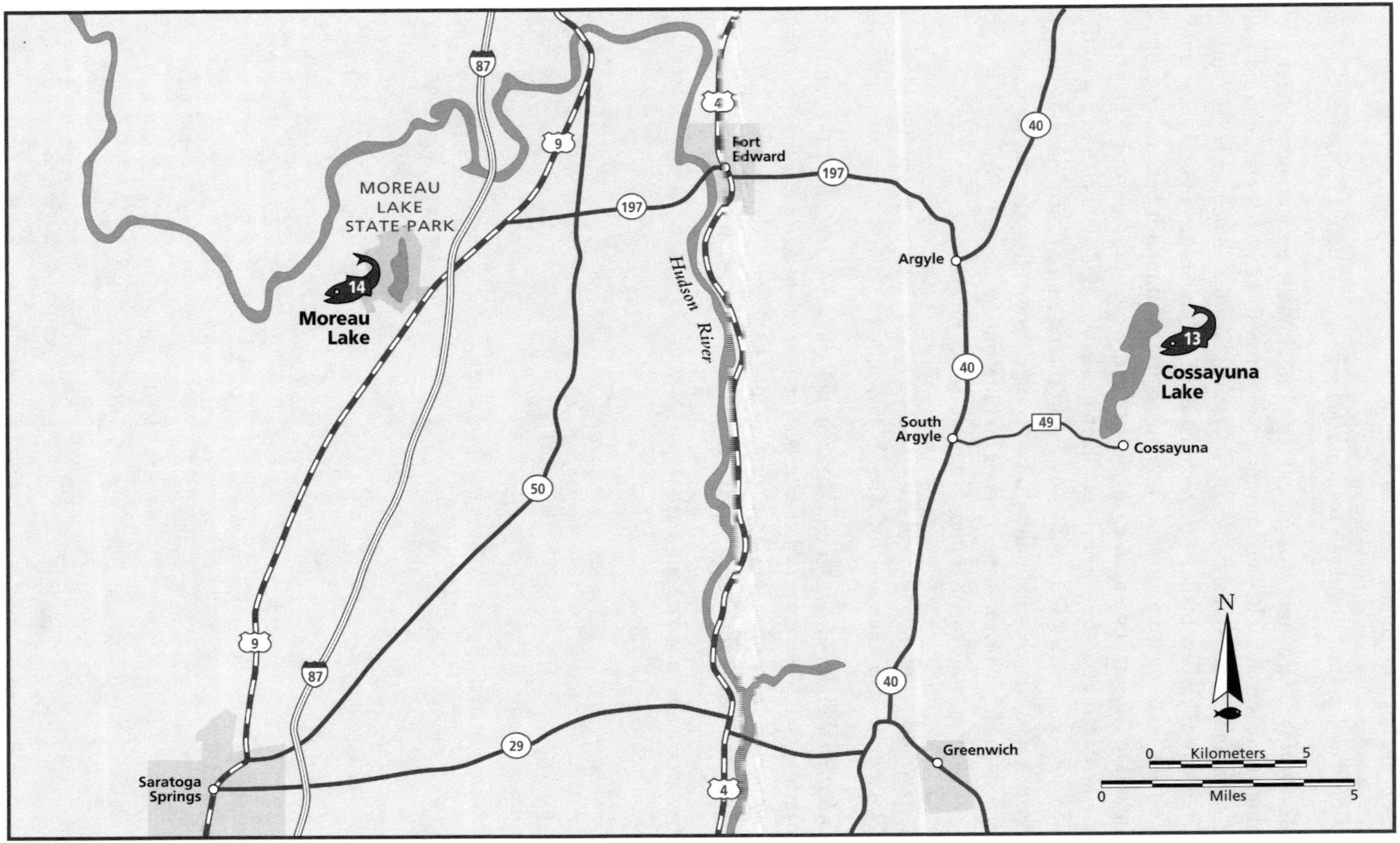

Cossayuna Lake

Cossayuna

49

40

Argyle

40

South
Argyle

40

197

Fort
Edward

4

Hudson River

197

9

87

50

MOREAU
LAKE
STATE PARK

Moreau
Lake

87

9

29

4

Greenwich

Saratoga
Springs

N

Kilometers
0   5

Miles
0   5

Description: Totally surrounded by a state park, this 128-acre lake averages 32 feet deep and has a maximum depth of 50 feet.

Tips: Paddle lightly and don't make noise by dropping things in the boat.

The fishing: The county stocks rainbow trout annually (exact figures weren't available at press time). They end up ranging from 8 to 12 inches and respond well to worms and kernels of canned corn. This small lake has some nice largemouth bass. They run anywhere from 2 to 4 pounds, and 5-pounders are present. They respond well to Texas-rigged worms and spinnerbaits. Smallmouth bass range from 0.75 pound to 2.5 pounds and like Carolina-rigged Exude finesse worms, crayfish, and minnows worked along drop-offs. Chain pickerel ranging from 0.5 to 2 pounds can be taken on Rooster Tails and scented, soft plastic slugs. Panfish include pumpkinseeds, yellow perch, and bullheads. Each ranges from 6 to 10 inches; all are favorites of kids fishing worms off bobbers or on bottom.

Trout season is year-round. No motors are allowed.

Directions: Head north out of Saratoga Springs on I–87 for about 10 miles to exit 17. Get onto US 9 and go south for about 1 mile.

Additional information: Moreau Lake State Park, a fee area, offers 148 campsites, a beach launch, showers, picnic facilities, a swimming beach, and a playground. The campgrounds are open mid-May through mid-October. A day-use fee is charged to noncampers during the season. Free day use is permitted off-season.

Contact: Moreau Lake State Park.

CATSKILL MOUNTAIN REGION

H ome to ninety-eight peaks rising more than 3,000 feet above sea level—each of which seems to be crowned in fog or mist as often as not—this magical mountain range has been stirring humankind's emotions since history began. The Indians believed the Great Spirit Manitou lived here and, fearing his wrath, pretty much stayed away. On the other hand, the lofty escarpments, scenic waterfalls, and mysterious hollows lured wagonloads of Europeans and watered their imaginations, spawning everything from literary characters such as Leatherstocking and Rip Van Winkle to cultural movements like the Hudson River School of landscape painting and American fly fishing.

Boasting one of the world's greatest urban populations, the Big Apple has a fierce thirst, and a series of reservoirs was built to quench it. The largest are in the Catskills. They are fed and drained by some of the world's most famous trout streams. For continuity's sake, the descriptions below will tie tributaries, reservoirs, and outlets into a web of related parts.

The September 11, 2001, terrorist attacks forced authorities to suspend public access to all the city's water supplies. According to Geoffrey Ryan of the New York City Department of Environmental Protection's Bureau of Public Affairs, however, by the following October, "the Army Corps of Engineers was given thirty million dollars to develop and implement a security program aimed at reopening these fabulous resources to public recreation."

15. Neversink Reservoir (see map on page 48)

Key species: Brown trout, landlocked Atlantic salmon, and smallmouth bass.

Description: Part of the New York City reservoir system, this 1,472-acre impoundment is completely surrounded by forest, averages 72 feet deep, and has a maximum depth of 164 feet.

Tips: Fish tributary mouths in spring with worms.

The fishing: This reservoir has a population of wild brown trout. They generally range from 1 to 5 pounds and respond to silver spoons, minnows, and worms fished at tributary mouths in spring and fall. The state annually stocks about 3,000 7-inch landlocked Atlantic salmon, which grow to average 18 inches on the reservoir's rich forage of alewives and smelt. They are mostly targeted in spring and autumn at tributary mouths, where they take worms and streamers. Smallmouth bass range from 12 to 15 inches and take crayfish, scented tubes, and diving crankbaits.

The minimum length for trout is 12 inches. Smelting is prohibited, as are motors. A New York City permit is required.

Neversink Reservoir · Lower Neversink River

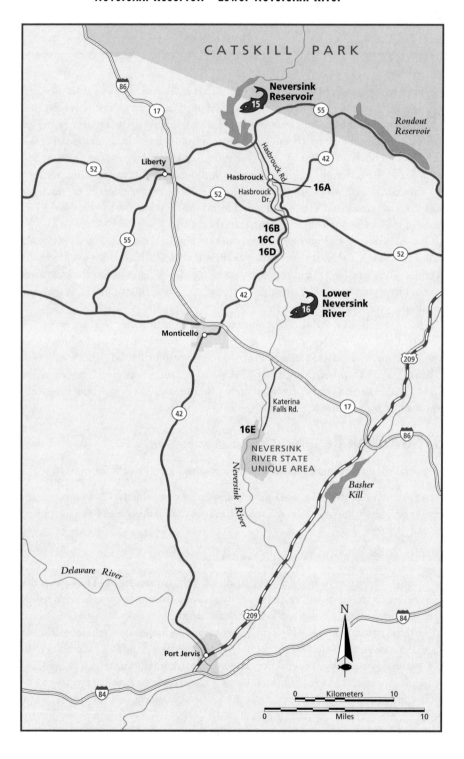

CATSKILL PARK

Neversink Reservoir

15

Rondout Reservoir

55

42

Hasbrouck Rd.

Liberty

52

52

Hasbrouck

16A

Hasbrouck Dr.

55

16B
16C
16D

52

42

Lower Neversink River

16

209

Monticello

Katerina Falls Rd.

17

86

42

16E

NEVERSINK RIVER STATE UNIQUE AREA

Basher Kill

Neversink River

Delaware River

209

N

84

Port Jervis

84

0   Kilometers   10

0   Miles   10

Directions: Head east out of Liberty on NY 55 for about 4.5 miles.

Additional information: Camping is prohibited on New York City property.

Contact: New York State Department of Environmental Conservation Region 3, and New York City Department of Environmental Protection.

16. Lower Neversink River

Key species: Brown trout and brook trout.

Description: This river's two branches and upper main stem run through private property and are heavily posted. Still, the tailwater snaking south from the Neversink Reservoir has some sizable stretches with public fishing rights.

Tips: Work streamers through the flatwater.

The fishing: The state annually stocks about 6,300 brown trout averaging 8 inches. Those that aren't caught out early in the season by locals still-fishing with worms end up migrating to shady areas in the gorge. They grow to average about 10 inches and respond to worms and nymphs. Wild brookies up to 14 inches are available about a mile downstream of the Neversink Reservoir Dam. They can be taken on worms, nymphs, and small lures.

The minimum size for trout is 9 inches. The Neversink River State Unique Area is restricted to catch-and-release fishing with artificial lures only. Private interests own fishing rights to portions of the river in the gorge. These areas are posted on shore, and the rights extend halfway out into the river.

Additional information: The state provides free maps showing all stretches of public fishing rights and parking areas. Fishing is prohibited in the posted areas upstream of the NY 55 bridge. There is no public camping on the river, but there are several motels and campgrounds nearby.

Contact: New York State Department of Environmental Conservation Region 3, and Sullivan County Visitors Association.

16A. Public Access

Description: This site has parking for about ten cars.

Directions: Head east out of Liberty on NY 55 for about 4.5 miles, cross the bridge downstream of the dam, and turn south onto Hasbrouck Road. Travel for about 2.5 miles to the hamlet of Hasbrouck, cross the bridge on Hasbrouck A Road, and turn south onto Hasbrouck Drive. Travel a little over 0.5 mile.

16B. Public Access

Description: This site has parking for about five cars.

Directions: Head south out of the hamlet of Hasbrouck on Hasbrouck Road for about a mile to its confluence with NY 42. Follow NY 42 south for about 2 miles.

16C. Public Access *(see map on page 48)*

Description: This site has parking for about five cars.

Directions: Continue down NY 42 from the above site for about 0.5 mile.

16D. Public Access *(see map on page 48)*

Description: This site has parking for five cars.

Directions: Continue down NY 42 from the above site for about 1 mile.

16E. Wolf Brook Multiple Use Area *(see map on page 48)*

Description: This public holding is adjacent to the north end of the Neversink River State Unique Area. Its namesake feeds the river in the gorge.

The fishing: Wolf Brook has wild brook trout ranging from 4 to 10 inches. They like worms and flies.

Directions: Head east out of Monticello on NY 17 (soon to become I–86) for about 4 miles to exit 109. Get on Katerina Falls Road and head south for about 2 miles.

Additional information: Primitive camping is allowed.

17. Swinging Bridge Reservoir

Key species: Walleye, smallmouth bass, brown trout, redbreast sunfish, pumpkin-seed, and bluegill.

Description: This 888-acre impoundment is moderately developed with private residences, averages 37 feet deep, and has a maximum depth of 120 feet.

Tips: Walleyes suspend in this reservoir.

The fishing: Before the turn of the last century, the state stocked fingerling walleyes for several years. A couple of the classes managed to spawn, and their offspring avoided predation by alewives. Currently the walleyes range from 18 to 25 inches. They hit bladebaits, diving crankbaits, and worms drifted or trolled on spinner harnesses. Smallmouth bass typically range from 12 to 16 inches and prowl drop-offs, where they'll take 3-inch plastic minnows and curly-tailed grubs fished on drop-shot rigs. Brown trout averaging 1 pound are also available and respond to worms and minnows. This reservoir has good numbers of sunfish ranging from 5 to 8 inches. They strike on surface poppers, wet flies, and worms.

The minimum length for walleyes is 18 inches, and the daily limit is three.

Swinging Bridge, Mongaup Falls, and Rio Reservoirs

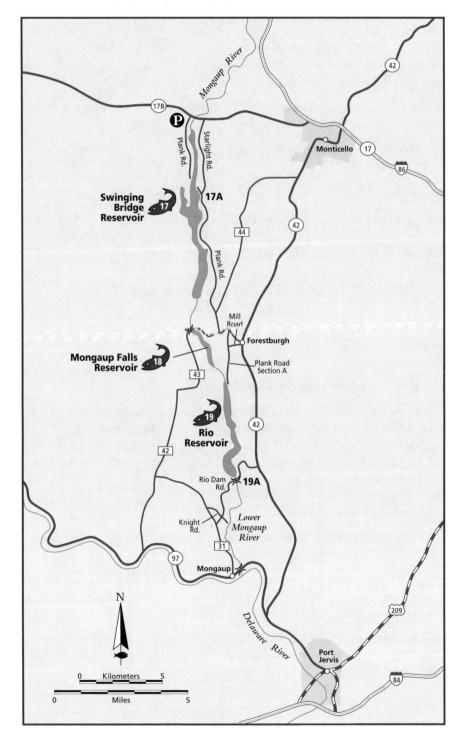

Directions: Head west out of Monticello on NY 17B for about 3 miles, then turn south onto Plank Road and continue for about 0.3 mile.

Additional information: A beach launch on Plank Road, about 0.5 mile south of its intersection with NY 17B, is suitable for small trailered craft and has parking for three rigs. There is no public camping on the reservoir. Private campgrounds, motels, and Borscht Belt resorts are found in the area.

Contact: New York State Department of Environmental Conservation Region 3, and Sullivan County Visitors Association.

17A. Fishing Access *(see map on page 51)*

Description: This site, provided by the utility, offers a hard-surface ramp and parking for about twenty-five rigs.

Directions: Head west out of Monticello on NY 17B for about 2.75 miles (if you cross the bridge over the Mongaup River, you've gone too far). Then turn south onto Starlight Road and travel for about 4 miles.

18. Mongaup Falls Reservoir *(see map on page 51)*

Key species: Brown trout, smallmouth bass, and largemouth bass.

Description: This 102-acre impoundment averages 10 feet deep and has a maximum depth of 32 feet.

Tips: Fly fish with large streamers scented with herring oil.

The fishing: The state stocks about 1,500 brown trout averaging 8 inches annually. They typically grow to between 1 and 3 pounds and hit worms, minnows, and Bomber Long "A"s. Smallmouth bass run from 12 to 15 inches and take the same baits, as well as YUM Walleye Grubs dragged or jigged on bottom. Largemouths ranging from 12 to 18 inches are also available and respond to diving baits such as the Cotton Cordel Rattlin' Shad and walking lures like MirrOlure's She Dog.

Outboard motors are prohibited.

Directions: Take NY 42 south out of Monticello for about 6 miles to Forestburgh, then take NY 43 west for about 1.5 miles.

Additional information: The hard-surface launch on CR 43 has parking for ten rigs. There is no public camping on the reservoir, but private campgrounds, motels, and Borscht Belt resorts are found in the area.

Contact: New York State Department of Environmental Conservation Region 3, and Sullivan County Visitors Association.

19. Rio Reservoir *(see map on page 51)*

Key species: Brown trout, smallmouth bass, and largemouth bass.

Description: Part of the Mongaup Valley Wildlife Management Area, this 422-acre impoundment averages 31 feet deep and has a maximum depth of 80 feet. Its shoreline is forested, prompting state aquatic biologist Robert Angyal to say, "Rio is the most aesthetically pleasing reservoir on the Mongaup River. It's a place where you might just see a bald eagle."

Tips: Brown trout are easiest to catch in May.

The fishing: This reservoir's wild browns usually go from 2 to 5 pounds. Most are taken on minnows and crankbaits in spring. Smallmouth bass range from 12 to 15 inches and respond well to crayfish and Exude Poc'it Fry dragged on Carolina rigs. A fairly large population of largemouths in the 12- to 18-inch range prowls the northern shallows. They respond to 7- to 10-inch worms fished wacky style and noisy surface baits such as Jitterbugs, propbaits, and poppers.

Outboard motors are prohibited.

Directions: From Forestburgh, take Mill Road southwest for about 0.3 mile to its end, then turn south onto Plank Road Section A and travel for about 3 miles.

Additional information: A cartop launch with parking for about five cars is located on Plank Section A Road.

19A. Public Access

Description: This site has a beach launch and parking for five cars.

Directions: Head west on NY 97 out of Port Jervis for about 4 miles to Mongaup. Turn north onto CR 31 (Upper Mongaup Road), travel for 2 miles, and take a right onto Knight Road. Take another right a few hundred feet later onto Rio Dam Road and continue for about 1 mile.

20. Lower Mongaup River *(see map on page 54)*

Key species: Brown trout and brook trout.

Description: Downstream of the Rio Reservoir powerhouse, the river flows through a scenic, 3-mile-long valley before feeding the Delaware River. Power generation causes its levels to fluctuate wildly.

Tips: Fish bite best when water is being released. Wear cleats or felt soles for traction.

The fishing: While the upper reaches contain trout, finding your way through the posted signs can be frustrating. Downstream of the Rio Dam, however, the river is open to the public (with the exception of a small strip just below the dam). Wild brown trout are the bread-and-butter fish here. They typically range from 12 to 15

Lower Mongaup River Public Access Points

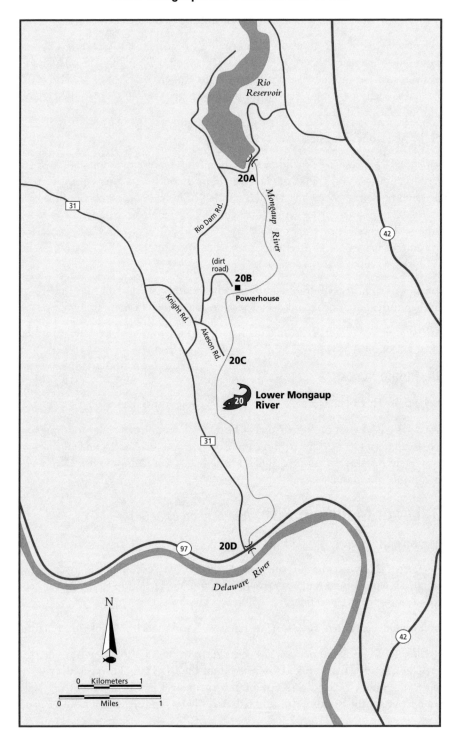

inches. Brook trout of about the same size are also present, especially in highly oxygenated pocket water. Both species take flies and in-line spinners.

The river from the Rio Dam to the NY 97 bridge is a special-regulations section. Baits are restricted to artificial lures. The minimum length for trout is 12 inches, and the daily limit is three.

Directions: About 4 miles west of Port Jervis on NY 97.

Additional information: There is no public camping along the river. Several private campgrounds, motels, and Borscht Belt resorts are found nearby.

Contact: New York State Department of Environmental Conservation Region 3, and Orange County Tourism.

20A. Public Access

Description: This site is at the Rio Dam; you have to walk down a steep trail to get to the river. There's parking for about five cars.

Directions: Head west on NY 97 out of Port Jervis for about 4 miles to Mongaup. Turn north onto CR 31 (Upper Mongaup Road), travel for 2 miles, and take a right onto Knight Road. Take another right a few hundred feet later onto Rio Dam Road and continue for about 1 mile.

20B. Public Access

Description: This site is at the powerhouse and is a launch for whitewater kayakers. There's parking for about five cars.

Directions: Follow the directions to site 20A above, but when you turn onto Rio Dam Road, take the next right onto a dirt road and follow it to the end.

20C. Public Access

Description: This site has parking for about three cars.

Directions: Follow the directions above to Knight Road, take a right, and follow it for a couple hundred feet to Akeson Road.

20D. Public Access

Description: This pull-off features parking for about five cars.

Directions: On CR 31, just a little north of its intersection with NY 97.

21. Esopus Creek *(see map on page 56)*

Key species: Rainbow trout and brown trout.

Description: Springing from Winnisock Lake, just a few yards north of the divide separating the Delaware and Hudson River drainages, this creek flows for about 20

Esopus Creek · Ashokan Reservoir

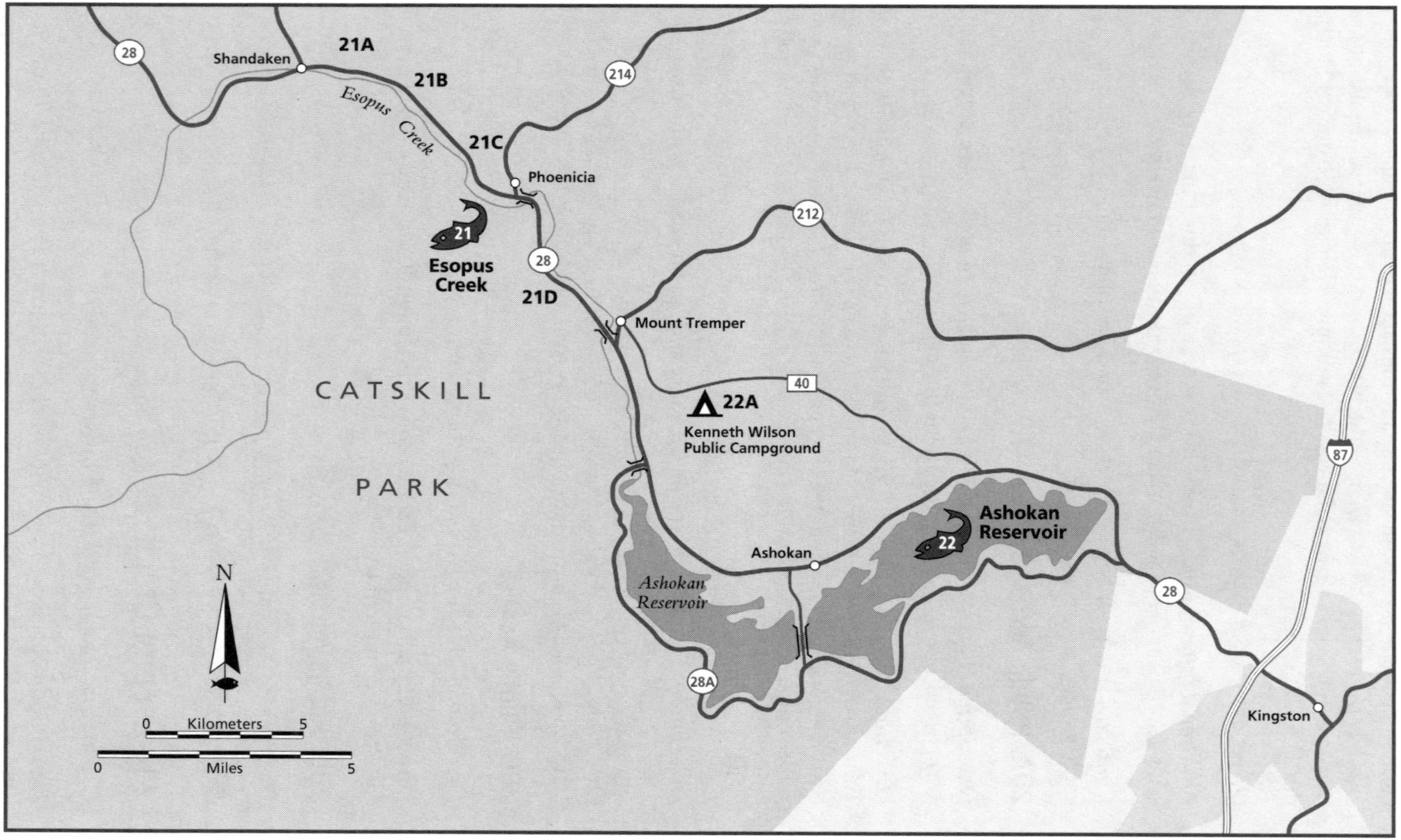

Shandaken

28

214

Esopus Creek

21A

21B

21C

Phoenicia

28

21D

Mount Tremper

212

40

22A

Kenneth Wilson
Public Campground

21

Esopus
Creek

CATSKILL

PARK

Ashokan

28A

Ashokan
Reservoir

Ashokan
Reservoir

22

28

Kingston

87

N

0   Kilometers   5

0   Miles   5

miles and feeds the Ashokan Reservoir. About a third of the way along, its volume quadruples with the water entering it from Schoharie Reservoir via the Shandaken Tunnel, locally called the portal. From here to the reservoir, the creek's personality changes utterly, from a free-flowing stream to a managed tailwater.

Tips: Use beadhead nymphs and conehead streamers.

The fishing: This creek is annually stocked with about 20,000 8-inch brown trout and almost 2,000 two-year-olds averaging 13.5 inches. Still, the average brown only reaches 8 inches. In autumn, however, Ashokan Reservoir browns ranging from 2 to 5 pounds run upstream. In addition, the creek is internationally famous for wild rainbow trout. Some experts claim this is the state's most productive wild rainbow trout fishery. Although they only range from 6 to 12 inches most of the year, some 5-pounders, spawners from Ashokan Reservoir, are taken each spring. Both species of trout respond well to worms, egg sacs, and wet flies.

Since the Ashokan's water is diverted to New York City, the Esopus below the dike has to start all over again. It gathers several tributaries and slowly travels north to feed the Hudson River in Saugerties. This lower stretch is warm-water habitat, and access is iffy. The tidal section below the dam is included in the Hudson River section (site 7).

A New York City permit is needed to fish downstream of the Five Arches Bridge in Boiceville and the reservoir. Trout season extends to November 30.

Directions: NY 28 parallels most of the stream.

Additional information: Numerous informal pull-offs line NY 28 from Boiceville to Shandaken.

Contact: New York State Department of Environmental Conservation, and New York City Department of Environmental Protection.

21A. Public Access

Description: Parking for about ten cars.

Directions: On NY 28, 0.5 mile east of Shandaken.

21B. Public Access

Description: This state site has parking for about twenty cars.

Directions: On NY 28, 2.5 miles west of Phoenicia.

21C. Public Access

Description: This formal state site has parking for about twenty cars.

Directions: On NY 28, 1.2 miles west of Phoenicia.

21D. Public Access *(see map on page 56)*

Description: This formal site has parking for twenty-five cars, picnic tables, and an antique caboose.

Directions: On NY 28, 2.1 miles east of Phoenicia.

22. Ashokan Reservoir *(see map on page 56)*

Key species: Brown trout, rainbow trout, smallmouth bass, largemouth bass, walleye, and black crappie.

Description: This 8,300-acre impoundment averages 47 feet deep and has a maximum depth of 190 feet. The largest body of water in the Catskills, it is halved by the "Dividing Weir," a dam that separates it into upper and lower basins, with an 18-inch difference in elevation between them.

Tips: In autumn, when water spills over the Dividing Weir, the current below is a hot spot.

The fishing: The 18,000 browns averaging 9 inches that are stocked here annually quickly grow to average 2 pounds, and some reach up to 15 pounds. Most are taken on live shiners or alewives. A good population of wild rainbows ranging from 1 to 8 pounds is also present. They take flatlined spoons, streamers, and crankbaits scented with herring oil. Walleyes average 4 pounds, but behemoths ranging from 8 to 11 pounds are caught occasionally. Most are taken on alewives and worms still-fished on bottom, or trolled slowly on spinner-rigged harnesses. Smallmouth bass ranging from 0.6 to 2.5 pounds are about equally distributed in both basins and respond well to crayfish worked over rock fields, minnows drifted along breaks, and Carolina-rigged finesse worms dragged in 20 to 30 feet of water. Largemouth bass aren't as plentiful as bronzebacks, but there are enough in the 2- to 5-pound range to make targeting them worthwhile. The heaviest concentrations are in the shallow east and south bays of the upper basin. Black crappies average a whopping 0.75 pound, and fish of more than 1 pound are common. Most are targeted with small lures such as Cotton Cordell Spot Minnows, Yo-Zuri Snap Beans, and Beetle Spins.

A New York City permit is required to fish this reservoir. If you want to use a boat, it must be registered as well. The minimum length for trout is 12 inches, and the daily limit is three. For walleyes, the minimum length is 18 inches and the daily limit is three. No motors are allowed.

Directions: Take NY 28 for about 5 miles east of I-87 exit 19 (Kingston).

Additional information: Primitive camping is permitted in the Bluestone Wild Forest, which brushes up against NY 28 in several spots due east of the reservoir. The state offers a free brochure on the forest containing maps and important information.

Contact: New York State Department of Environmental Conservation Region 3, and New York City Department of Environmental Protection.

22A. Kenneth Wilson Public Campground

Description: This fee area offers seventy-six no-frills sites, a beach launch, picnic areas, playing fields, a mountain biking trail, a swimming beach, and boat rentals. It's open mid-May through Columbus Day.

The fishing: This site's Upper and Lower Ponds are only about 3 acres each. They contain largemouth bass ranging from 1 to 3 pounds, and 5-pounders are possible.

Directions: From Ashokan, head west on NY 28 for about 8 miles to Mount Tremper. Turn right onto NY 212, then right again 0.5 mile later onto CR 40 (Wittenberg Road). Continue for about 4 miles.

23. Upper East Branch Delaware River *(see map on page 60)*

Key species: Brown trout and brook trout.

Description: This naturally flowing stretch of the river springs out of the hills a couple of miles west of Grand Gorge and runs southwest for about 20 miles to feed Pepacton Reservoir.

Tips: Blue-Winged Olives in sizes 18 through 28 produce all summer long.

Author holding brown trout caught at Upper East Branch Delaware River.

Upper and Lower East Branch Delaware River - Pepacton Reservoir

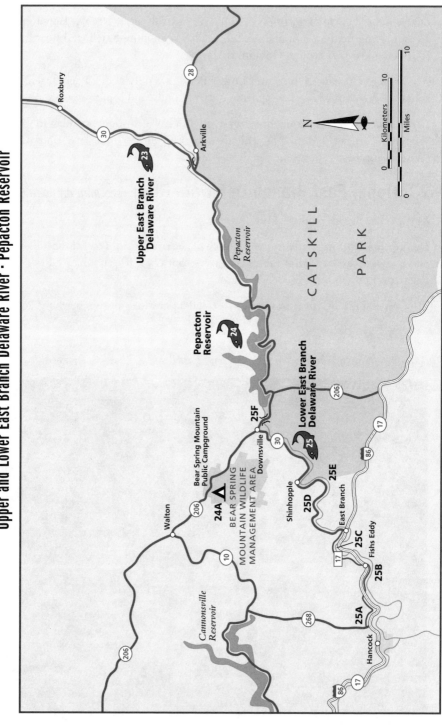

The fishing: The state stocks approximately 5,000 brown trout averaging 9 inches and 580 14-inch two-year-olds annually. Combined with winter holdovers and spawners entering the creek from Pepacton each fall, the average brown is about 12 inches. They hit best on worms and salted minnows until June, nymphs and dry flies matched to the hatch the rest of the season. Some trophies are usually present below Margaretville the first week or two of the season. Native brook trout spawned in tiny tributaries are also available. Ranging from 5 to 12 inches, they take the same baits the browns do.

The minimum length for trout is 9 inches and the season ends September 30.

Directions: NY 30 parallels this section.

Additional information: The only place where the public has formal fishing rights is at the confluence of the Bush Kill on the west side of the village of Arkville. Few farmers in the area, however, post their land and numerous informal pull-offs exist along NY 30. Still, if someone asks you to leave the stream, you should obey. No public camping is available along the river. A New York City permit is needed to fish the posted area upstream of Pepacton Reservoir.

Contact: New York State Department of Environmental Conservation Region 4, and New York City Department of Environmental Protection.

24. Pepacton Reservoir

Key species: Brown trout and smallmouth bass.

Description: Fed and drained by the East Branch of the Delaware River, this 5,763-acre reservoir averages 74 feet deep and has a maximum depth of 160 feet. Built in 1955, completely surrounded by woods, it is named for the town it inundated under 120 feet of water.

Tips: In the opening weeks of trout season, before ice-out, find an opening, cast a silver Krocodile onto the ice, pull it off the edge, and twitch the rod tip lightly so it flutters down.

The fishing: While this impoundment's greatest draw is trophy wild brown trout, these critters are savvier than most anglers, so each year the state stocks 10,000 averaging 9 inches to keep frustration levels manageable. The stockies, spirited little idealists that they are, eagerly take dry flies; most are removed by June. Serious trout anglers fish for wild browns ranging from 1 to 20 pounds (the average is 2.5 pounds) in open water all summer long with minnows, and with worms at tributary mouths and culverts after a rain. Come autumn, they ascend tributaries to spawn; precocious individuals start running upstream as early as the last week of the season and can be taken on worms and nymphs. Smallmouth bass find the alewives forage to their liking, too, and 2-pounders are typical. Crayfish is their preferred dish, but the impoundment's large population of small perch and rock bass can turn using live bait into a frustrating experience. Avoid the panfish by using diving plugs such as Poe's Super Cedar series 1100s, and vertical-jigging Heddon Sonar Flashes.

Trout season runs only from April 1 through September 30. The minimum length is 15 inches and the daily limit is two, of which only one can be more than 21 inches. A free fishing permit is required. Boats must be left on site. No motors are allowed.

Directions: Head east out of Hancock on NY 17 (soon to become I–86) for about 8 miles to the village of East Branch, then get onto NY 30 east for about 11 miles.

Additional information: Camping is prohibited on New York City property. Primitive camping is allowed on state property, however, and there's a big parcel bordering both sides of NY 206, about 3 miles south of its intersection with NY 30. In addition, several private campgrounds are found on NY 30, downstream of the reservoir.

Contact: New York State Department of Environmental Conservation Region 4, New York City Department of Environmental Protection, and Delaware County Chamber of Commerce.

24A. Bear Spring Mountain Public Campground *(see map on page 60)*

Description: This fee area offers forty no-frills sites, picnic areas, boat and canoe rentals, and trout fishing on Launt Pond. A day-use fee is charged to noncampers during the season, mid-May through Columbus Day. Free day use is permitted off-season.

The fishing: Covering 11 acres, averaging 6 feet deep, and dropping to a maximum depth of 10 feet, Launt Pond is stocked annually with 1,300 6-inch rainbows. They provide spirited action, especially for family groups still-fishing with worms and Berkley Trout Bait. The pond's source and outlet, East Brook, gets stocked with 700 yearling brook trout averaging 8 inches. They take worms and nymphs.

Directions:. Off NY 206, about 2.5 miles northwest of Downsville.

25. Lower East Branch Delaware River *(see map on page 60)*

Key species: Brown trout and rainbow trout.

Description: This tailwater portion of the river is spawned at the base of the Pepacton Reservoir and winds for about 30 miles (19 as the crow flies) to Hancock, where it joins the West Branch to form the main stem.

Tips: Don't be afraid to use nymphs larger than size 10.

The fishing: The state annually stocks about 11,000 9-inch browns and 750 two-year-olds averaging 14 inches. Generally, the browns average 10 inches, and a lot of fish are caught each year that are more than 20 inches. Browns like nymphs, streamers, salted minnows, and worms. Rainbow trout begin appearing more and more frequently the farther you go downstream of the Beaver Kill's mouth. Ranging from 8 to 18 inches, they take the same lures as the browns.

From the dam to the Shinhopple Bridge, the minimum size for trout is 12 inches, the daily limit is two, and the regular season ends September 30. Downstream of the Shinhopple Bridge to the junction with the West Branch, the minimum length is 12 inches and the daily limit is two—but trout season doesn't end until October 15. In addition, the stretch downstream of Shinhopple is open to catch-and-release fishing from October 16 to November 30. (Now you see why average anglers complain that you have to be an attorney and surveyor to fish the Delaware River.)

Directions: NY 30 parallels the river from the reservoir to NY 17 (also known as the Quickway, it is soon to become I–86), and NY 17 parallels it to Hancock.

Additional information: Fishing is prohibited in the posted stretch downstream of the dam. No public campgrounds exist on the river, but several private campgrounds are right on the water. The state owns public fishing rights to nearly half the stream. There are numerous parking areas on NY 30 and NY 17 (the future I–86). The county chamber of commerce publishes a free map showing locations of public fishing rights and access sites.

Contact: New York State Department of Environmental Conservation, and Delaware County Chamber of Commerce.

25A. Public Access

Description: This informal site offers parking for about five cars.

Directions: Take CR 17/NY 268 east out of Hancock for about 0.5 mile. The site is just before the NY 17 overpass.

25B. Public Access

Description: This site has parking for about fifteen cars and overflow parking for about twenty more nearby.

Directions: Head east out of Hancock on NY 17 for about 5 miles to Fishs Eddy (exit 89), then take CR 28 for 0.1 mile.

25C. Parking Area

Description: This highway parking area offers access to the river on its west end, just beyond the ramp back to the highway. There are bathrooms and picnic facilities.

Directions: On the westbound lane of NY 17, about 7.5 miles east of Hancock (2 miles east of Fishs Eddy).

25D. Public Access

Description: Parking for thirty cars right on the river.

Directions: Take NY 30 north from East Branch for 4.5 miles.

25E. Public Access *(see map page 60)*

Description: Parking for about five cars at the edge of a cornfield.

Directions: Head north out of East Branch on NY 30 for 5 miles.

25F. Public Access *(see map page 60)*

Description: This village park is at the foot of a covered bridge and offers parking for thirty cars, along with picnic facilities and a gazebo.

Directions: Head east out of Hancock on NY 17 for 6 miles to East Branch, then take NY 30 for about 11 miles to Downsville.

26. Upper West Branch Delaware River

Key species: Brown trout and brook trout.

Description: This section springs up near Stamford, quickly reaches creek size, and gently snakes through farm country for about 40 miles before coming to rest in Cannonsville Reservoir. Unburdened by the litany of special regulations imposed on its lower arm, this water doesn't attract as much attention and remains uncrowded, offering wide-open, gentle flows steeped in peaceful scenery punctuated with covered bridges.

Tips: Use terrestrial patterns.

The fishing: Roughly 14,000 yearling browns averaging 9 inches and 1,360 two-year-olds averaging 14 inches are stocked by the state annually. Growth is good, and the little browns end up growing to average 12 inches—the larger stockies are much dumber and get caught almost immediately after release. Fish of up to 20 inches are available, however. They are mostly taken on worms, salted minnows, and nymphs. A few wild brook trout ranging from 6 to 10 inches migrate to the river from tributaries. Most are caught early in the season on worms and salted minnows.

The minimum size for trout is 9 inches. The season ends September 30.

Directions: NY 10 parallels the river from Stamford to Cannonsville Reservoir.

Additional information: There are no campgrounds near the river. Most folks stay at nearby Bear Spring Mountain Public Campground (site 24A above). A New York City permit is required to fish in the posted areas just above the reservoir. The state owns public fishing rights to more than 70 percent of the shoreline. Numerous formal parking areas and informal shoulder pull-offs are found on NY 10. The county chamber of commerce provides a free fishing map highlighting the locations.

Contact: New York State Department of Environmental Conservation Region 4, New York City Department of Environmental Protection, and Delaware County Chamber of Commerce.

Upper and Lower West Branch Delaware River · Cannonsville Reservoir

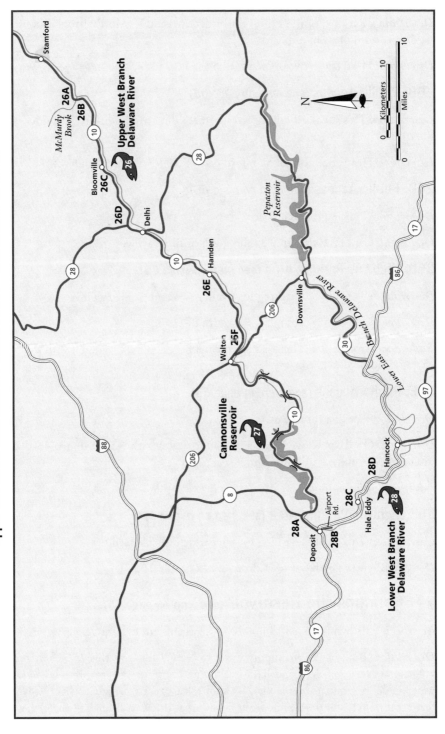

Stamford

26A
26B
Route 10
McMurdy Brook
Bloomville
26C
26
Upper West Branch
Delaware River

26D
Delhi
Route 28

Hamden
Route 28
Route 10
26E

Pepacton
Reservoir
Route 28

Route 206
Walton
26F

Downsville
Branch Delaware River
Route 30
Lower East

Route 17
Route 86

Route 88

Cannonsville
Reservoir
27
Route 206
Route 10

Deposit
28A
28B
Airport Rd.
Route 8
28C
Hale Eddy
28D
Hancock
28
Lower West Branch
Delaware River

Route 97
Route 17
Route 86

N

Kilometers
0   10
Miles
0   10

26A. Public Access *(see map on page 65)*

Description: Parking for five cars at the bridge crossing McMurdy Brook, about 100 yards upstream of its mouth.

Directions: Head south out of Stamford on NY 10 for 4.5 miles.

26B. Public Access *(see map on page 65)*

Description: This site is 0.2 mile down a farmer's dirt road leading to his bridge over the river.

Directions: Head south out of Stamford on NY 10 for about 5.5 miles.

26C. Public Access *(see map on page 65)*

Description: Parking for eight cars.

Directions: On NY 10, about 0.5 mile south of Bloomville.

26D. Highway Parking Area *(see map on page 65)*

Description: This site has parking for twenty cars and picnic facilities.

Directions: On NY 10, about 0.7 mile north of Delhi.

Additional information: There is a steep bank here about 20 feet high with a couple of trails leading down.

26E. Public Access *(see map on page 65)*

Description: Parking for five cars.

Directions: On Basin Clove Road, at the intersection with NY 10, on the north end of Hamden (7 miles south of Delhi).

Additional information: This site is at a covered bridge.

26F. Highway Parking Area *(see map on page 65)*

Description: This site has parking for ten cars and picnic facilities.

Directions: Head north out of Walton on NY 10 for 0.8 mile.

27. Cannonsville Reservoir *(see map on page 65)*

Key species: Brown trout, smallmouth bass, largemouth bass, and yellow perch.

Description: Built in 1967 to supply water to New York City, this 4,800-acre reservoir averages 61 feet deep and has a maximum depth of 140 feet. Besides sending water underground to the big city, its cool releases into the ancient river channel below the dam foster the terrific trout fishery that the West Branch of the Delaware River is famous for.

Tips: Anchor at night and suspend minnows under a Coleman lantern light.

The fishing: This is one of the few truly wild reservoir fisheries left in the Catskills. Although the state stocks roughly 15,000 brown trout into the West Branch of the Delaware River upstream of the dam annually, none are released into the impoundment. They have to make it on their own, through the gauntlet of anglers. By the time they reach the reservoir, they are totally relieved of trust and faith in man. They are even savvier than truly wild fish because they learned a thing or two about man in the hatchery, too. Still, anglers manage to land enough browns of up to 20 pounds to qualify this reservoir as the best-kept fishing secret in the Catskills. Most are taken in spring and early autumn on live minnows. In addition, they will hit Rapalas and Red Fins treated with scent to remove human stink. Smallmouth bass ranging from 2 to 4 pounds are abundant, and 5-pounders are possible. They hang out off the numerous points until mid-July, then mill around in 15 to 25 feet of water until fall, when they head closer to shore. They eagerly hit crayfish, minnows, yo-yoed spinnerbaits, and diving crankbaits. Although not plentiful, largemouth bass are available, with some better than 6 pounds. Search for them in shallow bays with surface lures and soft and hard jerkbaits. According to the free state brochure on the reservoir, yellow perch are abundant and underfished. Ranging from 6 to 10 inches, they travel in such large schools that when you locate one and fish it with small minnows, 2-inch scented curly-tailed grubs, or wet flies, you can catch so many, your arms will hurt.

The minimum length for trout is 12 inches and the daily limit is three. A permit is required to fish here. Boats must be registered; no motors are allowed.

Directions: On NY 10, a couple of miles east of Deposit.

Additional information: There are numerous formal and informal parking sites along NY 10. No camping is allowed near the impoundment, but primitive camping is permitted in the state land on Columbia Lake Road, about 1 mile east of Deposit. Several motels and private campgrounds are located in the area as well.

Contact: New York City Department of Environmental Protection (for permits), New York State Department of Environmental Conservation Region 4, and Delaware County Chamber of Commerce.

28. Lower West Branch Delaware River *(see map on page 65)*

Key species: Brown trout and rainbow trout.

Description: This tailwater fishery jets from Cannonsville Reservoir and flows about 9 miles to join the East Branch in Hancock and create the main stem.

Tips: The farther you can cast, the better.

The fishing: This stretch of the Delaware is famous as a wild trout fishery. Brown and rainbow trout averaging 14 inches draw anglers from throughout the Northeast. Fish of up to 10 pounds are allegedly caught each year. State aquatic biologist Norman McBride suggests that they probably escape from Cannonsville Reservoir. Light Cahills generate some exciting topwater action from mid-May through mid-July, but the largest trout are taken on streamers, in-line spinners, and crankbaits.

This section is known locally as a stream only a lawyer and surveyor can love. Fishing is prohibited in the 1.4 miles stretching from the Cannonsville Dam to the Stilesville Dam. Downstream from the Stilesville Dam to the NY 17 overpass, the minimum length for trout is 12 inches, and the daily limit is two. The stretch from the NY 17 overpass for 2 miles downstream is a special no-kill, artificial-lures-only section. From the lower limit of the no-kill section to the New York–Pennsylvania border water 1.7 miles downstream of the Hale Eddy Bridge, the minimum length for trout is 12 inches, and the daily limit is two. The section of the West Branch totally within New York's border is closed to fishing from October 1 through March 31. In the portion of the West Branch forming the New York–Pennsylvania border, the regular trout season runs from the first Saturday after April 11 to September 30, the minimum size is 12 inches, and the daily limit is two. No-kill fishing with artificial lures only is allowed in the boundary water from October 1 through the first Saturday after April 11.

Directions: NY 17 (also known as the Quickway, it is soon to become I–86) parallels this branch from Deposit to Hancock.

Additional information: Most of this branch runs through private property, and there are no public campgrounds. There are, however, several motels and private campgrounds nearby. Numerous informal pull-offs can be found along Airport Road in Deposit, and most of the folks living across the street are willing to give anglers access—if you ask.

Contact: New York State Department of Environmental Conservation Region 4, and Delaware County Chamber of Commerce.

28A. Public Access (see map on page 65)

Description: This site has parking for five cars.

Directions: On CR 48, on Deposit's north side.

28B. Public Access (see map on page 65)

Description: This site has parking for twenty cars.

Directions: On Airport Road, 0.8 mile downstream of the NY 17 overpass in the village of Deposit.

28C. Public Access (see map on page 65)

Description: This site has parking for seven cars and nearby overflow parking for ten more.

Directions: Head east out of Deposit on NY 17 for about 4 miles to Hale Eddy, then turn right onto River Road and travel for 0.1 mile.

28D. Public Access *(see map on page 65)*

Description: This informal site has parking for five cars on the bank of the river.

Direction: Roughly 2.5 miles east of Hale Eddy on NY 17.

Additional information: Though it's nothing more than a break in the guardrail, anglers have long used this railroad service road access without any problems. NY 17 is in the process of being turned into I–86, however, and chances are this access will be closed when the road officially changes to an interstate, probably by 2005.

29. Main Stem Delaware River *(see map on page 70)*

Key species: Brown trout, rainbow trout, smallmouth bass, walleye, American shad, pickerel, muskellunge, and striped bass.

Description: Formed by the union of the West and East Branches on the southern tip of Hancock, this mighty river flows southeast, forming the New York–Pennsylvania border all the way to Port Jervis, a distance of about 70 miles.

Tips: Float-fishing is the only way to reach all the spots in any section

The fishing: The state doesn't stock any trout into the main stem. Some stockies migrate from the East Branch, but by the time they get here they have lost their trust in humankind and, according to one local, "are harder to catch than wild trout because they know a thing or two about us." Brown and rainbow trout average 14 inches and are normally targeted in spring and fall with streamers, crankbaits, spinners, and worms, and in summer with large nymphs during the day and dry flies around dawn and dusk. While trout can show up just about anywhere, most experts consider Callicoon the transition to a warm-water fishery. Walleyes ranging from 18 to 23 inches can be caught in deep pools on lamprey eel larvae, bucktail jigs (fished plain or tipped with minnows or worms), and crankbaits such as Bomber Long "A"s. Smallmouth bass range from 12 to 14 inches and respond to worms, minnows, and crayfish. Huge schools of American shad swarm into the river each May to spawn, generally ranging from 2 to 5 pounds, though monsters of up to 7 pounds are possible. The best baits are red-and-white and red-and-yellow shad darts. Pickerel range from 12 to 20 inches and respond to inline spinners. Pennsylvania stocks 8,000 muskies averaging 5 inches annually into the border water. They typically range from 30 to 40 inches, but 40-pounders are possible. They take large minnows, jerkbaits, and crankbaits. In spring, striped bass make it upriver as far as the East Branch. Mostly undersized two-year-olds, they are taken serendipitously on streamers and crankbaits.

Trout season runs from the first Saturday after April 11 to September 30. The minimum length is 14 inches, and the daily limit is one. Catch-and-release fishing is

Main Stem Delaware River

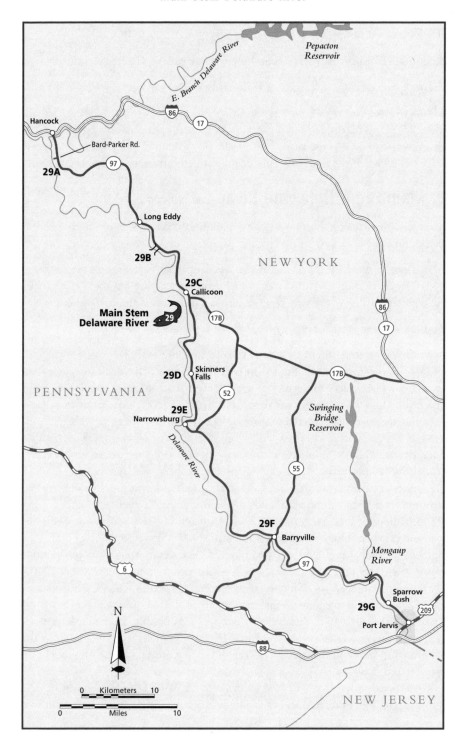

allowed for trout from October 1 through the first Saturday after April 11. There is no closed season for black bass. The minimum length for walleyes is 18 inches, the daily limit is three, and the season ends on March 14. The minimum size for pickerel is 12 inches; they can be taken year-round. For muskellunge the minimum size is 30 inches and it's 28 inches for striped bass. Both can be taken year-round with a daily limit of two.

The entire main stem is a border water, and a New York State license entitles the holder to fish the Pennsylvania side of the river.

Directions: NY 97 parallels the river.

Additional information: Numerous motels, private campgrounds, and canoe and rubber raft rental outfits operate along NY 97.

Contact: New York State Department of Environmental Conservation Regional Offices 3 and 4, Delaware County Chamber of Commerce, Sullivan County Visitors Association, and Orange County Tourism.

29A. Public Access

Description: This site, about 200 yards below the Junction Pool, has parking for forty cars, overflow parking for twenty-five more, and toilets.

Directions: Take NY 97 south out of Hancock for 1 mile to Bard-Parker Road. Cross the railroad tracks, turn left, then bear left again at the gate and travel about 0.25 mile.

29B. Kellums Bridge Public Access

Description: Parking for six cars and a beach launch for cartop craft.

Directions: Head south out of Long Eddy for about 2 miles on NY 97, then turn at Kellums Bridge.

29C. Callicoon Public Access

Description: Launch for cartop craft and parking for forty cars.

Directions: On NY 97, in the hamlet of Callicoon.

29D. Skinners Falls Public Access

Description: Launch for cartop craft and parking for fifty cars.

Directions: Off Main Street in the hamlet of Skinners Falls, 6.5 miles north of Narrowsburg on NY 97.

29E. Narrowsburg Public Access

Description: This access is at a long pool with a maximum depth of 113 feet. It offers a paved ramp and parking for twenty-four rigs.

Delaware River walleye taken in the Narrowsburg area.

Directions: On Main Street in the village of Narrowsburg.

29F. Highland Public Access *(see map on page 70)*

Description: Cartop launch and parking for forty cars.

Directions: On NY 97, 1.5 miles north of Barryville.

29G. Sparrow Bush Public Access *(see map on page 70)*

Description: Launch for cartop craft and parking for ten cars.

Directions: Head north on NY 97 out of Port Jervis for about 4 miles to the NY 97/NY 42 junction in Sparrow Bush, and turn west at the sign.

30. Willowemoc Creek *(see map on page 74)*

Key species: Brown trout, rainbow trout, and brook trout.

Description: Starting at the confluence of a couple of small mountain brooks just south of the Ulster and Sullivan County line, this creek flows for about 24 of the most exciting fly-fishing miles imaginable and feeds the Beaver Kill.

Tips: Blue-Winged Olives provoke surface strikes as early as late April.

The fishing: This stream's close relationship to the Beaver Kill and its miles of wide-open spaces make it one of the most popular trout streams in the country. The state helps it handle the pressure by stocking more than 10,000 8-inch brown trout and about 1,000 14-inch two-year-olds annually, and by setting aside a 3.5-mile no-kill zone restricted to fishing with artificial lures only. Overall, the browns average about 12 inches—and quite a few reach 16 inches and better. They respond best to worms and salted minnows early in spring, nymphs in summer, and egg-eating Woolly Buggers in fall. Wild brook trout ranging from 6 to 12 inches are present in the upper reaches and hit all the above baits.

Downstream of the iron bridge in Parkston, the minimum length for trout is 9 inches. The portion of creek stretching from 1,200 feet above the mouth of Elm Hollow Brook downstream for 3.5 miles to the second NY 17 bridge east of Roscoe is open year-round to catch-and-release fishing with artificial lures only. This special section is clearly marked with numerous signs.

Directions: NY 17 (also known as the Quickway, it is soon to become I–86) parallels most of the stream.

Additional information: There are several private campgrounds, motels, and restaurants in the area.

Main stem Delaware River near Sparrow Bush (site 29G).

Willowemoc Creek

Contact: New York State Department of Environmental Conservation Region 3, and Sullivan County Visitors Association.

30A. Hazel Bridge Pool Public Access

Description: This site has parking for fifteen cars.

Directions: Head east out of Roscoe on Old Route 17 (CR 179) for about 2 miles, then turn right onto Hazel Road and travel for 0.1 mile.

30B. Public Access

Description: This site has parking for five cars.

Directions: Continue down Hazel road for 0.5 mile from the above site.

30C. Quickway Pool Public Access

Description: This site has parking for ten cars.

Directions: Continue down Hazel Road for about 0.8 mile from the above site.

30D. Livingston Manor Covered Bridge Park

Description: This site offers parking for twenty cars, picnic facilities, and toilets at the foot of a scenic covered bridge.

Directions: Head east out of Roscoe on CR 179 (Old Route 17) for about 5 miles and turn right onto Covered Bridge Road.

30E. Public Access

Description: This site has parking for twenty cars.

Direction: On CR 179 (Old Route 17), 3.5 miles east of Roscoe.

30F. Public Access

Description: This site has parking for about forty cars.

Directions: On CR 179 (Old Route 17), 4.5 miles east of Roscoe.

Additional information: The entrance to the Catskill Fly Fishing Center & Museum is about 50 yards west.

30G. Public Access

Description: This site has parking for about ten cars.

Directions: Head east out of Roscoe on NY 17 for about 5 miles to Livingston Manor (exit 96), then continue east on CR 81 for about 0.75 mile.

Livingston Manor Covered Bridge over Willowemoc Creek (site 30D).

30H. Public Access *(see map on page 74)*

Description: This site has parking for ten cars.

Directions: Continue east on CR 81 (which turns into CR 82) for 1.5 miles from the above site.

30I. Willowemoc Wild Forest *(see map on page 74)*

Description: The upper Willowemoc runs through this 14,800-acre forest where primitive camping is allowed.

Directions: Take NY 17 east out of Roscoe for 5 miles to Livingston Manor (exit 96). Turn left onto CR 81 (which turns into CR 82), travel for 6 miles to Debruce, and take Mongaup Road north for about 1 mile.

30J. Mongaup Pond Public Campground *(see map on page 74)*

Description: This fee area isn't on the creek, but it's close. It offers 163 no-frills sites, picnic areas, hot showers, a 95-acre pond, a handicapped fishing pier, and a boat launch with parking for ten cars. A day-use fee is charged to noncampers when the campground is open, mid-May through Columbus Day.

The fishing: The campground totally surrounds 95-acre Mongaup Pond. State biologist Bob Angyal describes it as a "high-altitude warm-water fishery populated primarily by largemouth bass, chain pickerel, and yellow perch. A few brook trout enter it from a tributary." Bass ranging from 12 to 15 inches and chain pickerel up to 22 inches respond to spinnerbaits, soft plastic jerkbaits, and 7- to 10-inch plastic worms dragged rapidly across the surface. Yellow perch running from 6 to 10 inches and brook trout from 5 to 8 inches take worms, streamers, and in-line spinners.

The pond has a year-round trout season. Gas motors are prohibited.

Directions: Follow the directions to site 30I above. The campground is about 3 miles farther up Mongaup Road.

31. Beaver Kill *(see map on page 78)*

Key species: Brown trout, rainbow trout, and brook trout.

Description: Mentioned in every book ever written about fly fishing in the Catskills, and in just about every study ever done on fly fishing, this legendary river is arguably the most popular trout stream in the world. A wide, freestone stream, it is considered quintessential fly-fishing habitat. Much of the 26-mile stretch above Roscoe is controlled by fishing clubs. The 15 miles below the village are open to everyone, including members of the fishing clubs.

Tips: The best way to avoid the crowds is to stay away from legendary pools and the special-regulation sections.

The fishing: The state stocks roughly 18,000 9-inch and 1,800 16-inch two-year-old brown trout annually. In addition, the river has native brook trout in its upper reaches and wild rainbows that migrate down from tributaries or up from the Delaware River. Since this water is considered sacred by purists and wannabes, live bait, though legal on much of the stream, is shunned as sacrilegious; most trout are taken on nymphs and streamers. Many are taken at dusk by anglers matching the river's incredible hatches, however, and many others are taken on the worms that manly anglers keep hidden in their neoprenes.

Downstream of the NY 206 bridge in Delaware County (just before the river flows back into Sullivan County), the minimum length for trout is 9 inches and the season is extended to November 30. From the Sullivan County line in Roscoe downstream for 2.5 miles, and from 1 mile upstream to 1.6 miles downstream of the iron bridge at Horton, catch-and-release fishing with artificial lures only is permitted year-round.

Directions: CR 17 hugs the river's widest, deepest, and most famous water.

Additional information: Beaverkill Public Campground has 109 no-frills sites, picnic areas, and hot showers. A wooden bridge more than 150 years old crosses the stream here, and the pool below is one of the river's most famous. A day-use fee is charged to noncampers when the campground is open, mid-May through Labor Day. Free day use is permitted off-season. Numerous campgrounds, motels, fly shops, and restaurants are located in the area around Roscoe and East Branch. Numerous informal pull-offs line CR 17 in Delaware County.

Beaver Kill

Contact: New York State Department of Environmental Conservation Regions 3 and 4, Delaware County Chamber of Commerce, and Sullivan County Visitors Association.

31A. Public Access

Description: This site has parking for ten cars.

Directions: Head north out of Roscoe on CR 91 (NY 206) for about 0.5 mile to Rockland.

31B. Public Access

Description: This site has parking for ten cars.

Directions: About 0.5 mile farther north on CR 91 from the above site.

31C. Public Access

Description: This site is just downstream of the Junction Pool and has parking for twenty cars.

Directions: On Old Route 17 (CR 179A) in the village of Roscoe.

31D. Public Access

Description: This site has parking for thirty cars.

Directions: Head west out of Roscoe for 4.5 miles on Old Route 17 (the sign says 179A in Roscoe; it turns to CR 17 in Delaware County, about 1.5 miles later).

31E. Public Access

Description: This site has parking for fifteen cars.

Directions: Head west out of Roscoe on Old Route 17 for about 5 miles, then turn left onto Cooks Mills Road. The site is 0.1 mile later.

31F. Public Access

Description: This site has parking for ten cars.

Directions: Head east from the hamlet of East Branch on CR 17 for a little more than 7 miles to the bridges. This site is at the foot of the bridge on the other side of the stream.

32. Upper Schoharie Creek *(see map on page 80)*

Key species: Brown trout, rainbow trout, brook trout, and smallmouth bass.

Description: This stream slices through some of the prettiest scenery in the Catskills. Even when it leaves the park, it manages to cut a spellbinding valley.

Upper Schoharie Creek · Schoharie Reservoir · Batavia Kill

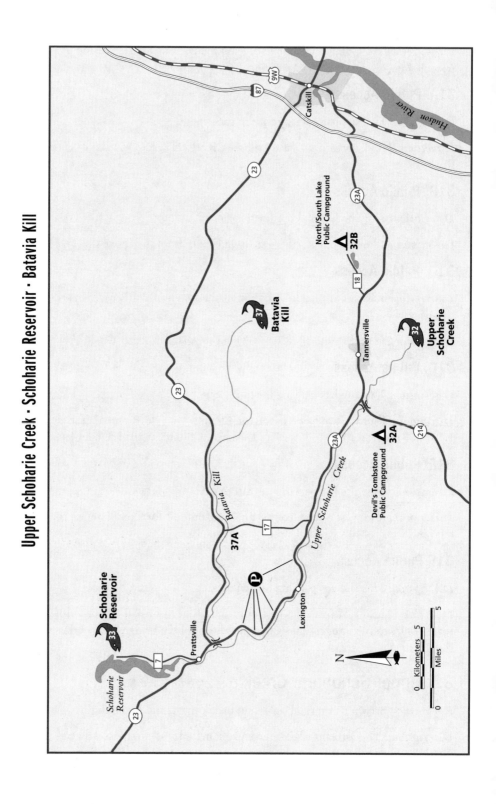

Tips: The best time to fish for trout is in spring.

The fishing: Wild brook trout running from 4 to 8 inches thrive in the cool headwaters paralleling CR 16, south of Haines Falls. They respond enthusiastically to worms and nymphs. The state stocks 16,820 yearling brown trout averaging 9 inches and 1,650 14.5-inchers annually in the 11 miles stretching from about a mile upstream of the NY 214 bridge to Lexington. The vast majority are caught by June on worms and salted minnows. Some pretty decent summer fly fishing is available, however. Since the creek flows east to west, the farther west you go, the warmer the water gets—a factor that can make or break a hot-weather fishing trip. The rule of thumb is that the closer you are to Hunter, the more productive the fishery. Still, a few spring holes moderate temperatures in the flow west of South Jewett, and if you can find one, you'll likely find trout. Nymphs, streamers, and dry flies all take summer trout. A few rainbows are also present. While some may be escapees from private trout ponds, most are truly wild scions of former stockings. They range from 6 to 10 inches, but their wildness and brilliant colors provide the kind of satisfaction normally derived only from trout twice that size. They hit worms, flies, and minnows. Smallmouth bass begin showing up downstream of Hunter and become increasingly available the closer you get to the reservoir. They typically range from too small to about 12 inches and take worms and spinners.

Directions: Head west out of Catskill on NY 23A for about 16 miles. The highway parallels the stream for most of its length.

Additional information: There are five public fishing access sites and numerous informal pull-offs on NY 23A. This stretch runs entirely through private property, and camping is prohibited. There are several motels and private campgrounds in the area. A New York City permit is required to fish downstream of the NY 23A bridge in Prattsville.

Contact: New York State Department of Environmental Conservation Region 4, New York City Department of Environmental Protection, and Greene County Promotion Department.

32A. Devil's Tombstone Public Campground

Description: This fee area offers twenty-four no-frills sites and picnic areas. It's open late May through Labor Day.

Directions: Take NY 23A west out of Tannersville for about 1.5 miles, turn south onto NY 214, and continue for 3 miles.

32B. North/South Lake Public Campground

Description: This fee area offers 219 no-frill sites, hot showers, two small lakes, two swimming beaches, boat rentals, and a spectacular web of hiking trails. A day-use fee is charged to noncampers when the campground is open, from early May through late October.

Directions: Get on CR 18 in Haines Falls and travel east for 2 miles.

The fishing: North and South Lakes collectively cover 84 acres. A channel connects them. Largemouth bass up to 3 pounds and pickerel up to 25 inches are available and hit soft jerkbaits, spinnerbaits, and rattling crankbaits. Yellow perch up to 12 inches, pumpkinseeds from 4 to 7 inches, and bullheads up to 2 pounds are plentiful and take worms.

Outboard motors are prohibited.

Additional information: This campground comes right to the edge of the fabulously scenic Catskill Escarpment, made famous by the Hudson River School of landscape painting and by such fictional characters as Leatherstocking in James Fenimore Cooper's novels.

33. Schoharie Reservoir *(see map on page 80)*

Key species: Brown trout, walleye, smallmouth bass, and largemouth bass.

Description: This 1,159-acre reservoir averages 56 feet deep and has a maximum depth of 120 feet.

Tips: After catching a walleye, cast back to the same spot immediately.

The fishing: The state stocks about 2,000 brown trout averaging 9 inches annually. They end up averaging 3.5 pounds and respond well to Bomber "A"s and Junior ThunderSticks cast along the shore in spring and fall, and alewives drifted over deep water in summer. Formerly one of the state's best walleye hot spots, this reservoir's walleye population ebbs and flows with the availability of alewives, which prey on their fry. Alewives numbers nose-dived after a storm in 1996, and the walleyes rebounded. As of this writing, they seem to be holding their own; frying-pan-sized "eyes" ranging from 16 to 18 inches are plentiful and respond well to worms that are trolled, drifted, or used to tip jigs. Smallmouths range from 1 to 2.5 pounds and are primarily targeted with crayfish, worms, and minnows. Largemouths run 12 to 20 inches and take buzzbaits and spinnerbaits.

The trout season runs year-round, the minimum length is 12 inches, and the daily limit is three.

Directions: Located 2 miles north of Prattsville on CR 7.

Additional information: A New York City permit is required to fish the reservoir. No camping is allowed on New York City property. Several private campgrounds and motels are found in the area.

Contact: New York State Department of Environmental Conservation Region 4, New York City Department of Environmental Protection, and Schoharie County Chamber of Commerce.

34. Blenheim-Gilboa Power Project Lower Reservoir
(see map on page 84)

Key species: Walleye, smallmouth bass, and rainbow trout.

Description: This 430-acre reservoir averages 100 feet deep and has a maximum depth of 125 feet. It's filled and lowered according to power needs; daily fluctuations in water levels can be as much as 25 feet.

Tips: Cast diving crankbaits along the shoreline at dawn and dusk.

The fishing: This impoundment has a good population of native walleyes. They range from 20 to 26 inches, and 36-inchers have been documented. Most are taken by casting or flatlining crankbaits or drifting worms. Smallmouths of up to 20 inches are available. They are especially fond of the impoundment's richest food source, crayfish. The New York Power Authority stocks roughly 7,000 6-inch rainbows and 400 24- to 26-inch lunkers annually. Most are taken incidentally by anglers targeting walleyes or bass, but a small group of fly fishers gets them with streamers, with terrestrials, and by matching evening hatches.

Directions: Head west out of Prattsville on NY 23 for about 4 miles, then turn north onto NY 30 for 6 miles.

Additional information: Mine Kill State Park, a fee area on NY 30, offers a paved ramp, parking for about ten rigs, picnic areas, three swimming pools, playing fields, and hiking trails. A day-use fee is charged mid-May through Labor Day. Camping is prohibited around the reservoir, but several private campgrounds are found nearby. Fishing from the dam or from shore on the power-plant side (east bank) is prohibited. Ice fishing is prohibited.

Contact: Blenheim-Gilboa Pumped Storage Power Project.

35. Blenheim-Gilboa Power Project Upper Reservoir
(see map on page 84)

Key species: Walleye, smallmouth bass, and rainbow trout.

Description: This 360-acre impoundment averages 100 feet deep and has a maximum depth of 125 feet. Filled and lowered according to power needs, its daily fluctuations in water levels can be as much as 25 feet.

Tips: Use bladebaits such as Heddon Sonars.

The fishing: Walleyes are the fish of choice up here. Unlike the lower reservoir, however, the upper is underutilized, a fact savvy locals would like to keep that way. Still, word is getting out about this honey hole's walleyes—they average 23 inches. Try crankbaits toward evening and in the morning, or vertical-jig bladebaits during daylight. Smallmouth bass reaching up to 20 inches are available and respond well

Blenheim-Gilboa Power Project Lower and Upper Reservoirs

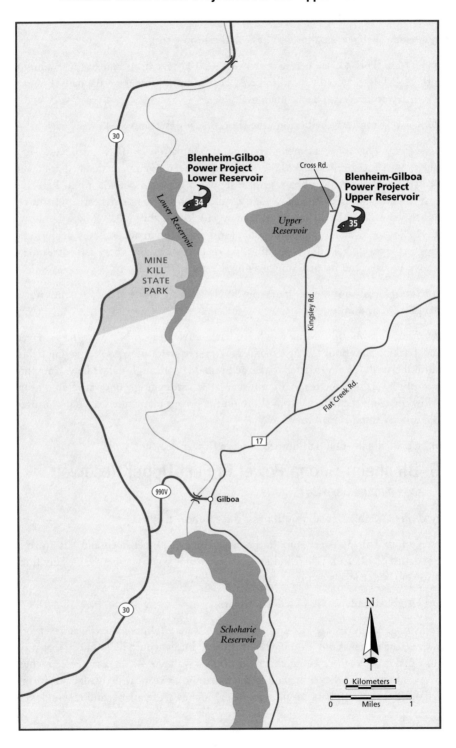

to crayfish and 4- to 7-inch scented, soft plastic worms swum deep on Slider Heads. Rainbow trout average 12 inches and respond at dusk and dawn to terrestrials. Motors are prohibited—except for the handicapped. Ice fishing is prohibited.

Directions: Take NY 23 west out of Prattsville for about 4 miles and turn north onto NY 30. Travel for 3 miles, turn east onto NY 990V, cross the bridge about 0.5 mile later, and turn left onto Flat Creek Road (CR 17). Travel a little over 0.5 mile, turn left onto Kingsley Road, then go left again, a little over 1 mile later, onto Cross Road.

Additional information: No camping on reservoir grounds.

Contact: Blenheim-Gilboa Pumped Storage Power Project.

36. Lower Schoharie Creek *(see map on page 86)*

Key species: Smallmouth bass, walleye, and northern pike.

Description: Called the devil's piss pot in the old days because of its tendency to flood, this stretch trickles out of the Blenheim-Gilboa Power Project Lower Reservoir, quickly picks up enough tributaries to float a canoe, and runs north to feed the Mohawk River at Fort Hunter. Although the creek has many long, deep pools, you will have to drag your canoe over numerous riffles.

Tips: Fly fish with crayfish imitations.

The fishing: Walleyes from 15 to 25 inches and smallmouth bass averaging 13 inches make this stretch a jealously guarded local secret. Both species hit worms, jigs, and crankbaits, and the smallmouths love crayfish to boot. Near Fort Hunter, northern pike of up to 26 inches can be taken on minnows, Lazy Ikes, and spinnerbaits.

Directions: NY 30 parallels most of the creek.

Contact: New York Department of Environmental Conservation Region 4, and Schoharie County Chamber of Commerce.

36A. Public Access

Description: This site lies between two long, deep pools located at the base of the dam. There's parking for fifteen cars.

Directions: Off NY 30, on the south side of the hamlet of North Blenheim.

36B. Max V. Shaul State Park

Description: This park offers twenty-eight no-frill campsites, hot showers, a picnic area, and trails leading to the creek. The campground is open mid-May through Labor Day.

Directions: Take NY 30 south out of Middleburgh for about 5 miles.

Lower Schoharie Creek

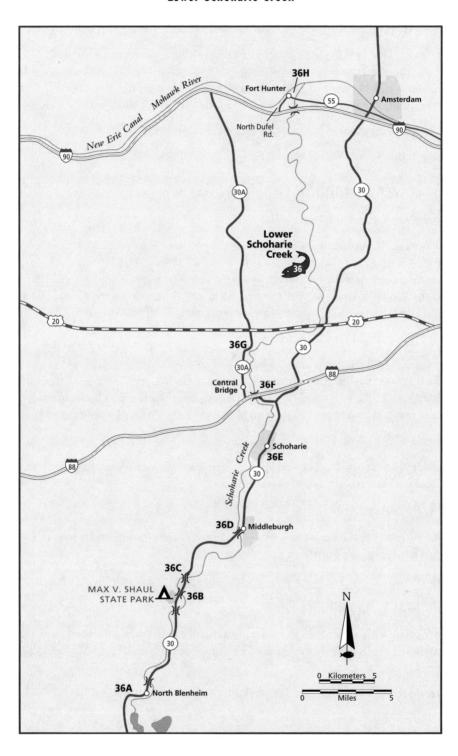

36C. Highway Parking Area

Description: This rest area has picnic facilities, parking for thirty cars, and stream access.

Directions: On NY 30, 0.2 mile from the park listed above.

36D. Public Access

Description: This village park has a canoe launch, parking for twenty cars, and picnic facilities.

Directions: Off NY 30, across the bridge, on the south side of the hamlet of Middleburgh.

36E. Public Access

Description: This site has parking for twenty cars and a picnic area.

Directions: In the hamlet of Schoharie.

36F. Public Access

Description: Provided by the Iroquois Pipeline Land Preservation & Enhancement Program, this site has parking for twenty cars and is located on a long, canoeable stretch of the creek.

Directions: At the NY 30A bridge in the hamlet of Central Bridge.

36G. Public Access

Description: This site has parking for twenty cars and a canoe launch.

Directions: On NY 30A, about 2 miles north of the above site.

36H. Schoharie Crossing Boat Launch

Description: Located at the mouth of Schoharie Creek, this site offers a double-wide paved ramp, parking for thirty rigs, 2.5 miles of shore-fishing access on the creek and the New Erie Canal, toilets, picnic tables, and a shelter.

Directions: Head west out of Amsterdam (NY Thruway exit 27) on NY 5S for about 4 miles. Cross the Schoharie Creek Bridge and make a right onto North Dufel Road.

Additional information: This is the only remaining site in the state where all three stages of the Erie Canal—the original, expanded, and new—exist side by side. Ruins of a cut-stone aqueduct dating back to the expansion in 1841 cross Schoharie Creek about 100 yards upstream.

Aqueduct over Schoharie Creek at Schoharie Crossing (site 36H).

37. Batavia Kill *(see map on page 80)*

Key species: Brown trout, brook trout, and rainbow trout.

Description: About 20 feet wide on average, this tributary of Schoharie Creek flows for about 15 miles, squeezing through a valley overshadowed by the Blackhead, Windham, and Cave Mountains, and through the picturesque village of Windham. Mostly privately owned, lightly posted, it doesn't get too crowded.

Tips: A Gold Ribbed Hare's Ear works just about anytime.

The fishing: Annually, the state stocks about 6,300 9-inch brown trout and 340 two-year-old brown trout averaging 14 inches. They join winter's survivors to offer anglers decent fly fishing for 12- to 14-inchers all season long. Seven hundred rainbow trout averaging 9 inches and 400 8.5-inch brook trout are also stocked each year. The Batavia Kill's rich variety of insect life fosters good growth, offering anglers mixed bags of trout ranging from 10 to 14 inches all season long. Streamers, in-line spinners, wet flies, and worms are effective.

Directions: NY 23 parallels most of the stream.

Additional information: No public camping is allowed on the stream. Several motels are in the area. There are numerous informal pull-offs on the shoulder of NY 23.

Contact: New York State Department of Environmental Conservation Region 4, and Greene County Promotion Department.

37A. Public Access

Description: This site offers bridge access to a stretch of water open to public fishing and shoulder parking for about three cars.

Directions: Head west on NY 23 out of Catskill for about 24 miles to East Ashland, then turn south onto CR 17.

ADIRONDACK MOUNTAIN REGION

pread over six million acres, nearly 20 percent of the state, the Adirondack Park is the largest preserve totally contained within the borders of a single state in the lower forty-eight. One of the earth's oldest mountain ranges, experts claim its peaks towered more than 25,000 feet when the Earth was young. While its summits have been worn smooth by the ages, forty-three of them still rise above 4,000 feet. Geologic wonders such as veins of garnet flow through its tired old granite, and 100,000 acres of ancient forest crown its expansive new growth. Best of all, this fabulous marriage of public and private forests offers anglers roughly 2,800 lakes and ponds, 1,500 miles of rivers, and 30,000 miles of brooks and streams on which to cast your dreams. The most popular areas are the St. Regis Canoe Area, the Saranac Lakes Chain, the Bog River Flow, the Raquette River, the Beaver River Canoe Route, and the Fulton Chain.

The St. Regis River (sites 76 and 77) has three branches. The west branch is not included because it is difficult to access and runs through a lot of private property. The St. Regis Canoe Area (sites 82 through 100) is the most popular canoe route in the Adirondack Park. Many of its numerous ponds are connected by narrow channels. Those that are landlocked are normally less than 0.5 mile from neighboring ponds, down well-defined portages. The area's most prominent boundary is the Adirondack Scenic Railroad on the south side. The state publishes a free map.

The Saranac Lakes Chain (sites 114 through 121) is popular with canoeists and anglers alike. Its web of waterways contains the Saranac River, Upper Saranac Lake, Middle Saranac Lake, Lower Saranac Lake, Weller Pond, Oseetah Lake, Kiwassa Lake, Lake Flower, and several smaller ponds and feeder streams. All but Upper Saranac Lake are connected by navigable stretches of the Saranac River or lake outlets. There is no creel limit on sunfish or yellow perch in these waters.

The Bog River Flow (sites 142 through 146) is a popular canoe route boasting two lakes and two ponds connected by the Bog River and Horseshoe Lake's outlet. Its greatest draws for backwoods anglers, canoeists, and earth travelers are its deep wilderness setting close to the road and its numerous hardened campsites right on the water. The route owes its navigability to two dams on the Bog River. Lows Lake (aka Bog River Flow) is one of the state's most productive loon nesting sites. Other rare birds likely to be sighted include bald eagles, ospreys, and spruce grouse. The regional Department of Environmental Conservation office publishes a free "Bog River Flow: Adirondack Forest Preserve Map and Guide."

The Raquette River runs for 136 miles, mostly through the Adirondack Park. It bears two distinct personalities: free and controlled. The upper river (free) is covered by sites 152 to 158. The controlled section of the river is covered by sites 159 to 170. Downstream of the dam at Carry Falls Reservoir (site 159), the river's natural rambunctiousness is tamed by a series of dams that transform its usual killer rapids into a gentle staircase of impoundments (sites 159 to 169). When the lower river (site 170) breaks out of Norwood Lake on its final 15-mile stretch, it's running again, but so slowly that it's considered flatwater. Still, it boasts a few modest rapids that'll give you some cheap thrills if you're not expecting them and can even be dangerous during high water. The controlled section of the river is detailed in the state's free pamphlet, "The Raquette River in St. Lawrence County: Official Maps and Guide," available through the region 6 office.

From the Moshier Reservoir Dam (site 176) to the High Falls Reservoir Dam (site 182) downstream, the Beaver River enters Reliant Energy property. The privately owned power company regulates the river for profit, storing it in reservoirs, pushing it over dams, squeezing it through power pipes, and even allowing it to foam and froth in a couple of wild stretches. Reliant Energy has constructed canoe launches, parking areas, portage trails, canoe rests, primitive campsites, a couple of handicapped fishing platforms, a handicapped-accessible trail, and a fee campground along the 14-mile course. The company offers the "Beaver River Canoe Route," a free brochure containing a detailed map of this fabulous recreation area.

Comprised of a pond and eight lakes in Herkimer and Hamilton Counties, the Fulton Chain of lakes (sites 186 through 194) is one of the most popular canoe routes in the Adirondack Park. Old Forge Pond and First through Fourth Lakes are connected by navigable channels. Fifth Lake is connected to Fourth by a shallow channel suitable only for cartop craft. A 0.5-mile portage is required to get to Sixth Lake from Fifth, and a mile carry is required to get from Seventh Lake to Eighth.

38. Lake George (see map on page 92)

Key species: Lake trout, landlocked Atlantic salmon, smallmouth bass, largemouth bass, northern pike, chain pickerel, yellow perch, black crappie, and panfish.

Description: Set in forested mountains, freckled with islands, and boasting water so clean you can drink right out of it, this 28,200-acre lake averages 50 feet deep and has a maximum depth of 200 feet. Known as the Queen of American Lakes, it is divided into north and south basins, separated by an island-choked narrows.

Tips: In summer, jig for smallmouths on bottom in 50 feet of water or more.

The fishing: This lake has always been famed for lake trout. But DDT all but wiped them out in the 1960s. Massive stocking by the state, coupled with environmental protection laws, brought them back from the brink. Indeed, the lakers took so well that the state stopped stocking them in the 1980s. Currently, wild lakers in the 5- to 8-pound range are run-of-the-mill. They respond well to spoons and cut bait dragged in deep water on Seth Green rigs or behind Christmas trees. Landlocked Atlantic salmon are the lake's most popularly sought cold-water species. They range from 18 to 23 inches, and 25-inchers are common. Most target them by flatlining tandem streamers. Smallmouth bass typically range from 1.5 to 2.5 pounds, but a lot of fish of up to 4 pounds are available. This clear habitat sends them much deeper than in average lakes, forcing anglers to jig for them vertically with tubes, curly-

Lake George

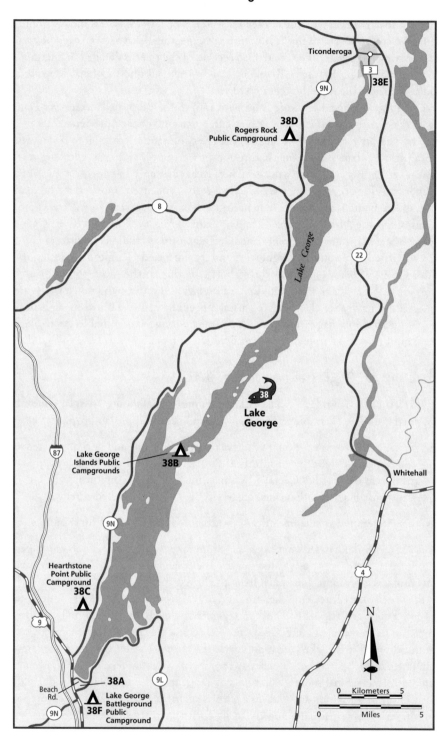

Ticonderoga

9N

3

38E

38D
Rogers Rock
Public Campground

8

Lake George

22

38
Lake
George

87

Lake George
Islands Public
Campgrounds

38B

9N

Whitehall

Hearthstone
Point Public
Campground

38C

4

9

N

38A

9L

Beach
Rd.

Lake George
Battleground
Public
Campground

38F

9N

0   Kilometers   5

0   Miles   5

tailed grubs, bucktail jigs, and bladebaits. Northern pike running from 22 to 30 inches and largemouth bass averaging 2.5 pounds are plentiful in the weedy bays. Both will take Zara Spooks when the lake is still, ThunderSticks, C. C. Shads, salted tubes, and minnows the rest of the time. Chain pickerel up to 30 inches are increasingly appearing in northern pike and largemouth bass territory. Known for their killer strikes and speed, they are especially fond of surface baits such as Jitterbugs, buzzbaits, and soft jerkbaits. Yellow perch averaging 9 inches, pumpkinseeds up to 8 inches, and bullheads up to 14 inches are plentiful and will take worms. Black crappies up to 12 inches are present and are targeted with Beetle Spins.

The possession of alewives or blueback herring as bait is prohibited. In addition, the use or possession of smelt as bait is prohibited. On all tributaries, up to the first barrier impassable by fish, fishing is prohibited from October 1 through March 31, and from 10:00 p.m. to 5:00 a.m. from April 1 through May 15. The lake has a special year-round season for lake trout and landlocked salmon. The minimum length is 23 inches for lakers, 18 inches for salmon; the daily limit is two of each.

Directions: Head north out of Saratoga Springs on I–87 for about 23 miles to the village of Lake George. NY 9N runs along the entire west bank.

Contact: New York State Department of Environmental Conservation Region 5, and Warren County Tourism.

38A. Million Dollar Beach Boat Launch

Description: This state facility has a double-wide hard-surface ramp and parking for 200 rigs. It's closed during the summer from the week before Memorial Day to the week after Labor Day. You'll have to go through an underpass whose clearance is only 7 feet.

The fishing: The deep middle, 1 mile due north of the launch, is a salmon hot spot in autumn. Flatline Junior ThunderSticks, Bomber Long "A"s, Red Fins, and tandem streamers on lead-core lines.

Directions: On Beach Road, in the village of Lake George.

38B. Lake George Islands Public Campgrounds

Description: This state-run fee operation offers 387 primitive, beach campsites on forty-four islands. These sites are accessible only by boat and are totally primitive with no treated water.

Directions: The islands are spread out all over the lake and are divided into three groups, each with its own headquarters.

Additional information: The state publishes a free brochure that includes a map.

38C. Hearthstone Point Public Campground

Description: This state-operated fee area offers 251 tent and trailer sites, hot showers, swimming, and shore-fishing access. The campground is open mid-May through

A pair of Lake George landlocked salmon.

Labor Day. Free day use is allowed off-season.

Directions: On NY 9N, 2 miles north of Lake George village.

38D. Rogers Rock Public Campground *(see map on page 92)*

Description: Located on the west bank, this state operated fee area offers 321 camp-sites, a paved boat launch, shore-fishing access, hot showers, picnic areas, a swimming beach, and a trailer dumping station. It's open May through Columbus Day. Free day use off-season.

Directions: On NY 9N, about 29 miles north of Lake George village.

38E. Mossy Point Boat Launch *(see map on page 92)*

Description: This site has a hard-surface ramp, parking for a hundred rigs, and a pump-out station.

Directions: Head south out of Ticonderoga on CR 3 for about 2 miles.

38F. Lake George Battleground Public Campground *(see map on page 92)*

Description: This fee area offers sixty-eight tent and trailer sites, hot showers, and a trailer dumping station. It's open mid-May through September.

Directions: On US 9, 0.25 mile south of Lake George village.

39. Lake Champlain *(see maps on pages 99 and 103)*

Key species: Lake trout, landlocked Atlantic salmon, walleye, largemouth bass, smallmouth bass, northern pike, sauger, pickerel, smelt, channel catfish, burbot, and panfish.

Description: Bordered by New York, Vermont, and the Canadian province of Quebec, this international waterway covers 452 square miles (289,280 acres)—an area so vast, local politicians have declared it the Sixth Great Lake. Averaging 64 feet deep, with a maximum depth of 403 feet, it has 587 miles of shoreline and seventy islands. Site of major battles during our wars with England, Lake Champlain's floor is littered with shipwrecks.

Tips: Scout the lake's numerous weed edges with red- and white-bladed spinnerbaits for huge northerns. After you catch the active pikasauruses, switch to a Texas-rigged worm or craw for the largemouth bass that always hangs out in the vegetation, too.

The fishing: The state stocks hundreds of thousands of salmonids annually. Lake trout range from 3 to 12 pounds. In spring and fall, they are taken from shore by casting silver crankbaits and spoons, or fishing on bottom with smelt. Come summer, they move into deep water, where they respond to cut bait and spoons trolled slowly anywhere from 50 to 150 feet down. Landlocked Atlantic salmon range from

2 to 9 pounds and are popularly sought in tributaries in spring and autumn, when they hit worms, egg sacs, and streamers. In summer, they suspend 5 to 40 feet over deep water and take flatlined, silver-colored, shallow-diving crankbaits such as MirrOlure's L52MRs, or floating-diving crankbaits like Rapalas and Junior ThunderSticks fished off downriggers. Smelt ranging from 5 to 7 inches are plentiful and many reach up to 12 inches. Come winter, ice-fishing villages go up along the deep channel in the Port Henry–Crown Point area. Anglers fish for them by using large dodgers to quickly lower strips of smelt belly down 20 to 40 feet, then swim the bait in a circular or figure-8 pattern.

Bucketmouths go from 2 to 7 pounds and are primarily taken in and around weed beds on jig-'n'-pigs, on spinnerbaits, and by slowly dragging Texas-rigged worms around old pilings and cribs. Bronzebacks range from 2 to 5 pounds and take jigs worked off points from opening day through mid-July and again in fall. The rest of summer, they hit Carolina-rigged Exude finesse worms worked along drop-offs and over boulder fields, as well as Zara Spooks and MirrOlure Top Dogs walked on the surface, over 10 to 20 feet of water, especially around dusk and dawn. Walleyes average 3 pounds, but 8-pounders are available. Trolling and casting crankbaits works well at night. Daylight anglers find that drifting minnows and spinner-rigged worm harnesses on bottom can be productive. Northerns run from 3 to 15 pounds and are targeted with minnowbaits and spinnerbaits along weed edges. The largest pike are caught through the ice with large minnows below tip-ups. Muskies in the 15-pound range are typical, but bruisers stretching the scale at more than 25 pounds are present. Most are caught incidentally by anglers targeting northerns. Chain pickerel normally range from 2 to 3 pounds. They take crankbaits, in-line spinners, and worms on spinner harnesses retrieved over weed beds. Channel cats of up to 20 pounds are targeted in the lake's southern narrows with minnows, cut bait, gobs of worms, and shrimp fished on bottom. Crappies of up to a pound, perch from 8 to 12 inches, and rock bass of up to 8 inches are commonly taken on small minnows and lures. Bluegills and pumpkinseeds range from 5 to 9 inches and readily take worms. Bullheads running from 8 to 14 inches congregate in spring on muddy flats, where they eagerly take worms. Burbot range from 1 to 3 pounds and are mostly taken through the ice on minnows. It is legal to snatch them in Scomotion Creek from December 1 through March 31.

Lake Champlain offers year-round seasons for more game fish than any other body of water. Muskellunge, northern pike, pickerel, landlocked salmon, rainbow trout, brown trout, and lake trout can be taken anytime. Black bass season opens the second Saturday of June.

Other differences from statewide regulations include: The minimum length for brown, brook, and rainbow trout is 12 inches, and the daily limit is three; the daily limit for landlocked salmon is two. The minimum length for lake trout is 15 inches; for walleye, 18 inches; for northerns, 20 inches; for black bass, 10 inches. There is no minimum length for pickerel, and the daily limit is ten. In Cumberland Bay, the daily limit for yellow perch and sunfish is fifty of each.

Since the only thing certain about these rules is that they will change, anglers are urged to check the special regulations for Lake Champlain in the state's *Fishing*

Two fishers admire a northern pike caught at Lake Champlain.

Regulations Guide. A Vermont fishing license is required to fish the eastern half of the lake.

While some sourpusses constantly harp on this lake's lamprey infestation, the states of Vermont and New York have been largely successful in controlling the parasites and a long-term management program is in place. Currently, however, all eyes are on the alewives, which threatens to invade from Vermont's Lake St. Catherine. This exotic, notorious for its reproductive capability, has a taste for walleye and perch fry, and has been known to wipe out indigenous populations of walleyes and greatly diminish perch numbers in some lakes.

Directions: I–87 parallels the lake.

Contact: New York State Department of Environmental Conservation Region 5, and Plattsburgh–North Country Chamber of Commerce.

39A. Rouses Point Municipal Boat Launch and Fishing Pier

Description: This facility offers a paved double-lane ramp, parking for forty rigs, and toilets. A fishing pier is located just south of the launch.

The fishing: The pilings crossing the lake here are remnants of an old railroad trestle, and are one of the best largemouth hot spots on the lake. Work Texas-rigged Exude Ribbon Tail worms around the supports.

Directions: Take I–87 north out of Plattsburgh for about 18 miles to Champlain (exit 42), then head east on US 11 for about 4 miles to Rouses Point. The launch is on Montgomery Street.

39B. Great Chazy River State Boat Launch

Description: This launch has two double-wide paved ramps, bulkheads, loading docks, parking for fifty rigs, and toilets.

The fishing: King Bay, directly north of the boat launch, is a hot spot for hawg bucketmouths all season long. On calm days, scout the weed edges with top-water lures such as Hula Poppers and buzzbaits. Then work the midlayer with Mister Twister RT Slugs and wacky-rigged nightcrawlers. Finish off the day by working Mister Twister Exude Salatubes and Super Craws on Texas rigs or jig-'n'-pigs.

Directions: Head north out of Plattsburgh on US 9 for about 15 miles to NY 9B and turn east. A little less than 2 miles later, turn south onto Lake Shore Road and travel about 1 mile.

39C. Point Au Roche State Boat Launch

Description: This facility offers a paved two-lane ramp, bulkheads, parking for sixty rigs, and toilets.

The fishing: Work spinnerbaits and crankbaits or drift minnows around this area's weed beds all summer long for scrappy smallmouth bass ranging from 1 to 3 pounds and northern pike of up to 8 pounds.

Directions: Head north out of Plattsburgh on US 9 for 6 miles, turn east onto Lake Shore Road (CR 22) for about 2 miles, then continue straight on Point Au Roche Road for about 2 miles.

39D. Point Au Rouche State Park

Description: This park offers a concrete launch, parking for twenty rigs, and toilets.

The fishing: Work the drop-offs of the shoal directly in front of the launch with crayfish for smallmouth bass ranging from 1 to 3 pounds. The drop-off along the east side of Long Point is notorious for holding good numbers of northern pike

Lake Champlain: Rouses Point to Willsboro

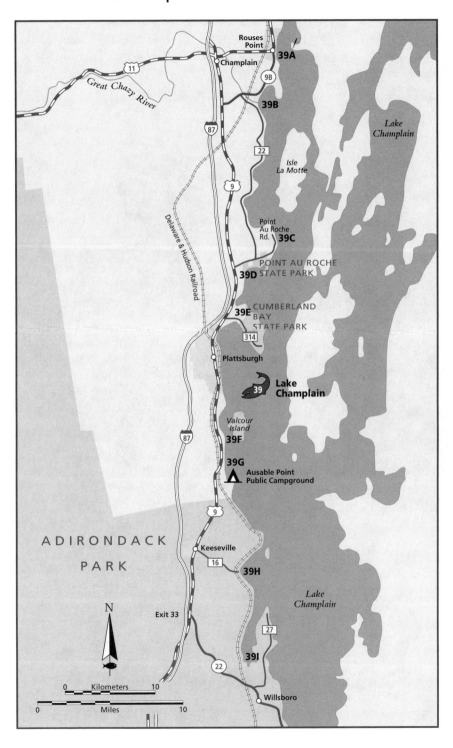

Working a Texas-rigged worm around the uprights of the old railroad trestle at Rouses Point (site 39A).

ranging from 4 to 8 pounds, and walleyes of up to 23 inches. The northerns will take spinnerbaits yo-yoed down the drop-off, and walleyes take Red Fins, C. C. Shads, and worms drifted on harnesses.

Directions: Head north out of Plattsburgh on US 9 for 6 miles, turn east onto Lake Shore Road (CR 22), and travel a little over 1 mile to the park entrance.

39E. Cumberland Bay State Park *(see map on page 99)*

Description: This 319-acre fee area boasts 134 primitive campsites (18 of them with electrical hook-ups), a bathhouse, a 2,700-foot sand beach, hot showers, picnic facilities, a dumping station, playgrounds, and ball fields. The campground is open from May through Columbus Day. Free day use is permitted off-season.

The fishing: Cumberland Bay is a popular ice-fishing spot for yellow perch and sunfish.

Directions: Head north out of Plattsburgh on US 9 for about 1 mile, then turn east onto NY 314 and travel for about 1 mile more.

Additional information: This area is popular with sailboarders.

39F. Peru Dock Boat Launch *(see map on page 99)*

Description: This site has a hard surface ramp, parking for fifty rigs, a pump-out, and toilets.

The fishing: Work the shoals around Valcour Island with slugs or a hard jerkbait for smallmouth bass.

Directions: Head south out of Plattsburgh on US 9 for about 4 miles.

39G. Ausable Point Public Campground *(see map on page 99)*

Description: This fee area is located on the mouth of the Ausable River. There is a cartop launch, parking for ten cars, shore-fishing access, 123 campsites (43 of them with electrical hook-ups), hot showers, a 0.25-mile sand beach, a bathhouse, playgrounds, and a basketball court. It's open from mid-May through mid-October. Free day use is permitted off-season.

The fishing: The upper and lower mouths of the Ausable River attract fish whenever they are swollen with runoff. Schools of landlocked salmon and trout converge on the spot and take flatlined streamers and silver floater-diver crankbaits. Walleyes are drawn to the river to spawn, and many hang out for a couple of weeks afterward, pigging out on everything from smelt to the worms carried by runoff. They hit Rattlin' Red Fins and Rattlin' C. C. Shads, Rat-L-Traps and Luhr Jensen's Sugar Shads, jigs tipped with scented curly-tailed grubs, and worms drifted or trolled on spinner harnesses.

Directions: Take US 9 south out of Plattsburgh for 9 miles.

Additional information: This area is popular with sailboarders.

39H. Port Douglas Public Boat Launch *(see map on page 99)*

Description: This site has a two-lane paved ramp, loading docks, parking for twenty rigs, and ten additional slots for cars.

The fishing: Port Douglas is smack in the middle of a 10-mile stretch of shoreline with a steep drop-off. In spring and fall, salmonids cruise the area within reach of shore anglers fishing smelt off slip bobbers or casting silver spoons and minnowbaits.

Directions: Take US 9 south out of Plattsburgh for about 13 miles to Keesville, turn east onto CR 16, and travel for about 3 miles.

39I. Willsboro Bay Public Boat Launch *(see map on page 99)*

Description: This site offers a hard-surface launch ramp, parking for a hundred rigs, toilets, and a pump-out station.

The fishing: Schools of landlocked salmon enter Willsboro Bay in summer and late fall to cruise the west bank and feast on smelt. They can be taken by trolling silver spoons and crankbaits, around dawn and dusk, in 25 to 65 feet of water. Come winter, this spot is transformed into shanty village by locals ice fishing for smelt along the drop-off with smelt bellies below large dodgers.

Directions: Head south out of Plattsburgh on I–87 for 17 miles to exit 33. Continue south on NY 22 for about 7 miles, then go north on CR 27 for about 2 miles.

39J. Westport Public Boat Launch

Description: Hard-surface ramp and parking for thirty-five rigs.

The fishing: Northwest Bay's gently sloping floor takes almost 2 miles to reach a depth of 150 feet. This results in ideal lake trout temperatures being present in some part of the bay year-round. From midfall through late spring, locals often take them by flatlining minnowbaits such as Red Fins and MirrOlure's Lipped 52Ms in 5 to 15 feet of water. Come winter, the bay is a popular ice fishing spot for lake trout.

Directions: Head south out of Plattsburgh on I–87 for 34 miles to exit 31. Head east on NY 9N for about 4 miles into Westport, then turn north onto NY 22.

39K. Port Henry Public Boat Launch

Description: This site has a hard-surface ramp and parking for forty-five rigs.

The fishing: Locals fish the northwestern part of Bulwagga Bay year-round with spinnerbaits and large minnows for northern pike ranging from 3 to 8 pounds. Ruins of an old railroad bridge at the mouth of the bay make this area one of the hottest bass spots on the lake. Largemouths of up to 5 pounds and smallmouths

Lake Champlain: Willsboro to Whitehall

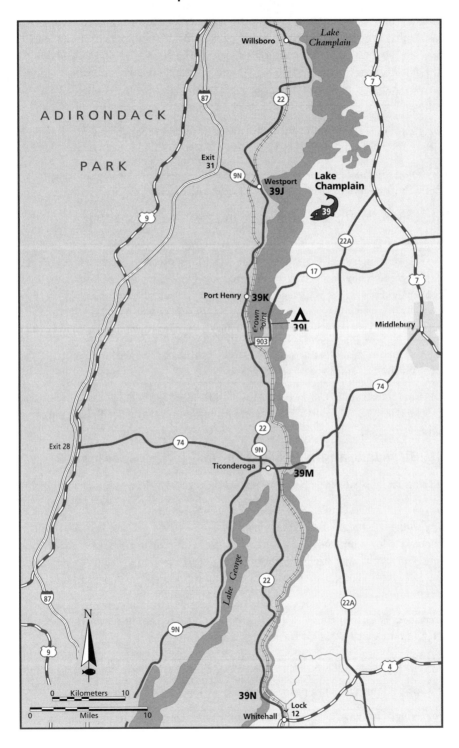

Willsboro

Lake Champlain

ADIRONDACK

PARK

87

22

7

Exit 31

9N

Westport 39J

Lake Champlain

39

9

22A

17

7

Port Henry 39K

Middlebury

Crown Point

39L

903

74

Exit 28

74

22

9N

Ticonderoga 39M

87

Lake George

9N

22

22A

9

N

4

39N

Lock 12

Whitehall

0 Kilometers 10

0 Miles 10

from 1.5 to 3 pounds are commonly taken by dragging Texas- and Carolina-rigged worms around the submerged pilings and cribs. Ice fishing is also hot here. Rich Preall, a senior aquatic biologist with the state, says that during normal winters a shanty village, complete with rentals, "springs up 0.75 mile north of the launch. These are the best smelt grounds on the lake." Preall adds that practiced anglers using smelt bellies on long-shanked gold hooks, and jigging or swimming them in a figure-8 pattern 20 to 40 feet deep, can catch fifty smelt ranging from 6 to 12 inches per hour.

Directions: Take I–87 south out of Plattsburgh for 34 miles to exit 31, then head south on NY 9N for 13 miles to Port Henry.

Additional information: Locals supplement their winter incomes by offering snow-mobile shuttle services from the launch out to the lake's hot spots.

39L. Crown Point Public Campground (see map on page 103)

Description: This fee area offers sixty-six sites, coin-operated hot showers, a trailer dumping station, a steel-grate launch ramp, parking for about ten cars, and shore-fishing access from a pier. The campground is open from April through mid-October. A day-use fee is charged from Memorial Day through Labor Day. Free day use is permitted off-season.

The fishing: The pier's concrete pilings hold northern pike and largemouth bass. Cast Carolina-rigged worms for hawg largemouth bass; scented tubes, curly-tailed grubs, and Rat-L-Traps for mixed bags.

Directions: Head south out of Plattsburgh on I–87 for 34 miles to exit 31, Westport. Head south on NY 9N for 16 miles, turn east onto NY 903 (Bridge Road), and travel for 4 miles.

39M. Ticonderoga Ferry Public Boat Launch (see map on page 103)

Description: This site has a paved ramp, parking for fifty-five rigs, and a pump-out station.

The fishing: This part of the lake is narrow. Ruins of an old pier just south of the launch are a local hot spot for taking large bucketmouths on Texas-rigged worms. Come winter, the spot holds northern pike up to 15 pounds, walleyes averaging 4 pounds, perch ranging from 6 to 12 inches, and black crappies up to a pound. Each takes minnows.

Directions: Head south out of Plattsburgh on I–87 for about 60 miles to exit 28, then continue east on NY 74 for about 19 miles.

39N. South Bay Public Boat Launch (see map on page 103)

Description: This site has a paved ramp and parking for fifty rigs.

The fishing: This bay is great walleye habitat and is one of the few spots in the state where sauger are taken regularly. Unfortunately, most anglers don't know a sauger from a walleye, and many 17-inchers are released because they are misidentified. Both species like minnows and worms drifted on bottom, and bladebaits yo-yoed and vertically jigged along drop-offs.

Directions: Head north on US 4 out of Hudson Falls for about 20 miles, then go north on NY 22 for about 3 miles.

40. Champlain Canal *(see map on page 106)*

Key species: Smallmouth bass and catfish.

Description: Stretching for 60 miles, this canal averages 12 feet deep and connects Lake Champlain with the Hudson River.

Tips: Use brightly colored spinners and plugs.

The fishing: The upper portion of the canal, from Whitehall to its junction with the Hudson River in Fort Edward, is mostly a stopgap fishery with anglers waiting to go through locks. It is a great spot to practice bass-fishing techniques on small-mouths in the 6- to 12-inch range. A few catfish in the 12- to 20-inch range are also available and will take worms fished on bottom.

Directions: US 4 parallels the canal.

Contact: New York State Department of Environmental Conservation Region 5.

41. Boquet River *(see map on page 108)*

Key species: Landlocked Atlantic salmon, brown trout, and brook trout.

Description: Tumbling down from the east slopes of the Adirondacks, this river flows for about 38 miles and feeds Lake Champlain east of Willsboro.

Tips: Use worms in spring.

The fishing: The state stocks this river with 80,000 salmon fry and 45,000 6-inchers annually. They invariably migrate into the lake but always return. While the fish ladder in Willsboro allows them to swim as far upstream as Wadhams, most are taken in the 2-mile stretch below the ladder. The river gets two major runs. The largest is in spring, when the fish range from 2 to 3 pounds. Come fall, the numbers are fewer, but the average size is about 6 pounds. In summer, a heavy rain will generally draw a small run. They take worms, streamers, and crankbaits in spring and summer, and will attack a streamer in autumn. The state also stocks roughly 8,000 brown trout averaging 9 inches and 400 two-year-olds averaging 14.5 inches. Released in both branches, throughout the length of the river, they join naturally spawned and holdover fish to provide anglers opportunities for fish ranging from 8 to 18 inches. They respond well to worms, nymphs, and streamers. Finally, about

Champlain Canal

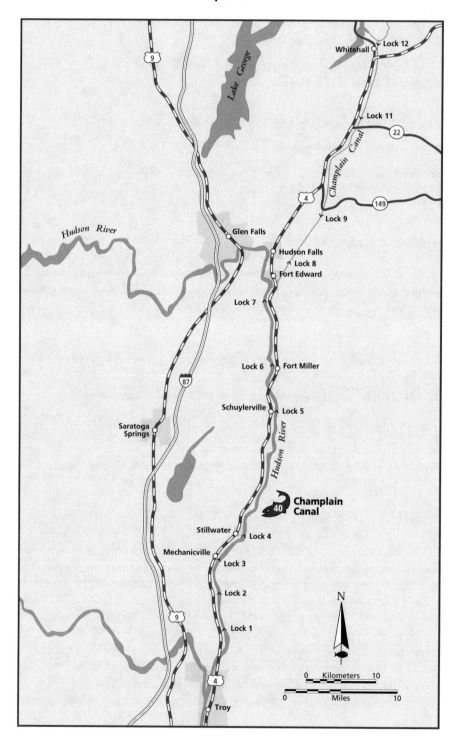

8,000 brook trout averaging 8.5 inches are stocked in the upper half. They grow to range between 9 and 11 inches and love worms, Mepps Spin Flies, and Panther Martins.

The lower part of the river, from the mouth to the first barrier impassable by fish, has its own regulations, including special fishing times and terminal tackle restrictions, all of which are listed in the Special Lake Champlain Regulations section of the *New York State Department of Environmental Conservation Fishing Regulations Guide*. From Wadhams Falls upstream to the NY 9N bridge in Elizabethtown, the minimum size for trout is 9 inches.

Directions: Head south out of Plattsburgh on NY 22 for about 28 miles to Willsboro. CR 68 parallels about 4 miles of the North Branch, and the main stem for a couple of miles upstream of Willsboro. NY 22 parallels the river between the hamlets of Wadhams and Bouquet, and US 9 parallels it from Elizabethtown upstream for about 10 miles.

Additional information: The river downstream of the weir in Willsboro is the most popular salmon stretch. There is parking on the side streets downstream of the NY 22 bridge, and an informal, hard-surface boat launch at the end of the road paralleling the river on the west side of the bridge.

Contact: New York State Department of Environmental Conservation Region 5.

42. Lincoln Pond (*see map on page 108*)

Key species: Tiger muskie, smallmouth bass, and yellow perch.

Description: This 643-acre pond averages 15 feet deep and has a maximum depth of 29 feet.

Tips: In spring, work the channel on the east side of the island with bucktail spinners.

The fishing: Recently the state has been annually stocking about 1,900 tiger muskies averaging 9 inches annually. Those that survive their first year eventually end up ranging from 30 to 40 inches. They like in-line spinners and large minnows. Smallmouth bass from 12 to 15 inches are present and are often taken on rattling crankbaits such as Rat-L-Traps and MirrOlure Shad Rattlers (91LSR). Yellow perch from 6 to 10 inches are plentiful and take worms and small minnows.

Directions: From I–87 exit 31(Elizabethtown), head west on NY 9N for 4 miles to Elizabethtown, then go south on CR 7 for about 6 miles.

Additional information: Lincoln Pond Public Campgrounds, a fee area, offers thirty-five campsites, coin-operated showers, a cartop boat launch, and canoe and rowboat rentals. The campground is open May through Labor Day. Free day use is permitted off-season.

Contact: New York State Department of Environmental Conservation Region 5.

Boquet River · Lincoln Pond

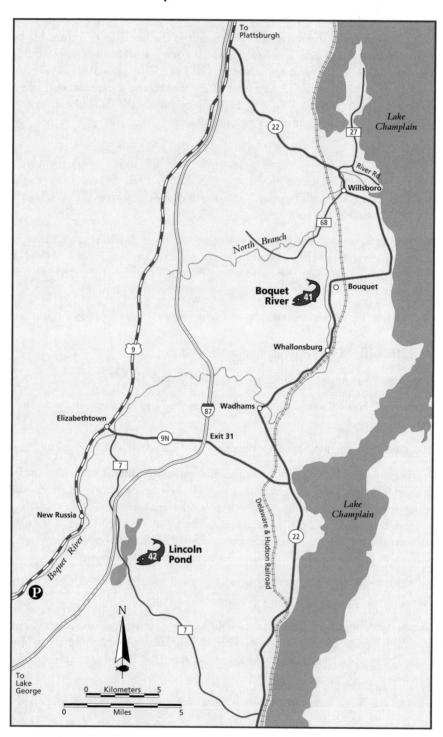

To Plattsburgh

22

27

Lake Champlain

River Rd.

Willsboro

68

North Branch

Boquet River 41

Bouquet

9

Whallonsburg

87 Wadhams

Elizabethtown

9N Exit 31

7

New Russia

Boquet River

Lincoln Pond 42

Delaware & Hudson Railroad

Lake Champlain

22

Ⓟ

N

To Lake George

0   Kilometers   5

0   Miles   5

43. Taylor Pond (see map on page 110)

Key species: Lake trout and landlocked Atlantic salmon.

Description: This 803-acre pond averages 44 feet deep and has a maximum depth of 95 feet. It is surrounded by the Taylor Pond Wild Forest.

Tips: In spring, cast spoons and crankbaits in the east and west basins.

The fishing: While the state stocks roughly 1,700 6.5-inch lake trout annually, a lot of the fish reported in angler surveys are wild. The average laker caught is a little too short, but fish of up to 36 inches are caught every year. They respond to spoons worked off downriggers or Seth Green rigs. About 600 6.5-inch landlocked Atlantic salmon are also stocked annually. Like lake trout, the average salmon is short—but fish of up to 9 pounds have been reported in surveys, and that's huge for such a small lake. They are targeted by high-lining spoons. Kokanees were first stocked in summer 2001, and current management plan calls for 100,000 fingerlings to be released annually. The minimum length for landlocked Atlantic salmon is 18 inches, and the daily limit is two.

Directions: From I–87 exit 34 (Keesville), take NY 9N west for about 9 miles to just before Au Sable Forks. Turn northwest onto Silver Lake Road and travel 8 miles.

Additional information: Taylor Pond Public Campground offers twenty-two no frills campsites, a hard-surface ramp, parking for ten rigs, boat and canoe rentals, and potable water. A day-use fee is charged to noncampers when the campground is open, mid-May through Labor Day. Free day use off-season. This area is popular with hikers because it has several well-defined trails to the scenic summits (there are two) of Catamount Mountain—allegedly so named because the state's last mountain lion was sighted here.

Contact: New York State Department of Environmental Conservation Region 5.

44. Chazy Lake (see map on page 115)

Key species: Lake trout, landlocked Atlantic salmon, rainbow trout, yellow perch, and pumpkinseed.

Description: Perched high in the northeastern corner of the Adirondacks in the shadow of Lyon, Johnson, and Ellenburg Mountains, this 1,606-acre lake averages 33 feet deep, drops to a maximum depth of 72 feet, and has water so squeaky clean you can drink it straight.

Tips: Flatline ⅛- to ¼-ounce spoons near shore in spring and fall.

The fishing: This lake has wild lake trout ranging from 2 to 6 pounds. Trolling Seth Green rigs (five spoons, each on a leader 5 to 10 feet long, staggered through the water column at 5- to 10-foot intervals) works well. The state annually stocks 1,200 landlocked Atlantic salmon averaging 6.5 inches. Enough make it to the 15-inch

Taylor Pond

keeper mark to make going after them worthwhile. They can be caught by flatlining tandem streamers. In autumn, cast silver minnowbaits such as MirrOlure's Lipped 52M and Rapalas around tributary mouths. Approximately 7,600 rainbow trout averaging 9 inches are also stocked each year. They end up ranging from 10 to 20 inches and take worms fished on bottom, near shore, in spring and fall, and spoons trolled in 20 to 40 feet of water in summer. Trout and salmon season is year-round and they can be taken through the ice by jigging minnows and Swedish Pimples. Yellow perch range from 6 to 12 inches and respond well to 2-inch curly-tailed grubs, small minnows, and worms. Pumpkinseeds average 6 inches and eagerly take worms, wet flies, and small surface poppers. Both panfish are popular targets with ice fishers using teardrop jigs baited with live grubs.

Use or possession of alewives or blueback herring as bait is prohibited

Directions: Take US 11 north out of Malone for about 11 miles to the village of Chateaugay. Turn south onto NY 374 and travel for 23 miles.

Additional information: A paved launch with parking for twenty rigs is located on NY 374. Primitive camping is allowed in the state forest preserve property on the southeast side, at the end of Wilfred King Road.

Contact: New York State Department of Environmental Conservation Region 5.

44A. Pump House Public Boat Launch (see map on page 115)

Description: This site has a paved ramp, parking for twenty rigs, and shore-fishing access.

Directions: Take NY 374 south out of the village of Chateaugay for about 27 miles, then turn right (south) onto Wilfred King Road and travel for 2.4 miles.

45. Great Chazy River (see map on page 115)

Key species: Brown trout, brook trout, walleye, muskellunge, and black crappie.

Description: Spawned by Chazy Lake, this stream starts out about the size of an average trout creek and heads northeast to feed Lake Champlain. On the way, it flows through Miner Lake and swallows several tributaries.

Tips: Fish large streamers downstream of Mooers Forks.

The fishing: This river is a two-story fishery. Its upper stretch contains prime trout water. Since access isn't great, it doesn't get stocked much and relies heavily on natural reproduction. Still, browns average 10 inches and hit worms, nymphs, and streamers. Brook trout go from 6 to 10 inches and take worms, nymphs, and dry flies.

Downstream of Mooers is primarily warm-water habitat. This area, known locally as the oxbow, is stocked annually with thousands of purebred muskellunge. They end up ranging from 5 to 15 pounds and provide explosive action for anglers fishing these slow, weedy waters with large, noisy surface baits like Jitterbugs and

Fisher with one of the typical bucketmouths caught at Great Chazy River (site 45).

Mister Twister Top Props. Lake Champlain's walleyes enter the stretch up to Perrys Mills in spring to spawn, and many remain for a couple of weeks afterward to fatten up after their ordeal. They range from 2 to 6 pounds and will take worms trolled on spinner harnesses and crankbaits such as MirrOlure Shad Rattlers. Black crappies congregate here in spring, too, and are popularly taken on small minnows fished below bobbers and on 2-inch scented curly-tailed grubs fished on spinner forms.

Fishing is prohibited from March 16 through the first Saturday in May from the NY 9B bridge in Coopersville upstream to the Perrys Mills Dam to protect spawning walleyes.

Use or possession of blueback herring or alewives as bait is prohibited.

Directions: Take I–87 north out of Plattsburgh for about 19 miles to exit 42 in Champlain and pick up US 11 west, which parallels a long stretch of the river.

Contact: New York State Department of Environmental Conservation Region 5.

45A. Great Chazy River State Boat Launch *(see map on page 115)*

Description: This launch has two double-wide paved ramps, bulkheads, loading docks, parking for fifty rigs, and toilets.

Directions: Head north out of Plattsburgh on US 9 for about 15 miles to NY 9B and turn east. A little less than 2 miles later, turn south onto Lake Shore Road and travel about 1 mile.

Additional information: The most convenient way to fish the Great Chazy River's highly productive lower reaches is by launching a boat here and heading upstream.

46. North Branch Great Chazy River *(see map on page 115)*

Key species: Brown trout and rainbow trout.

Description: Springing out of the northeastern corner of the Adirondack Mountains, this stream flows east for about 15 miles and feeds the Great Chazy River in Mooers Forks.

Tips: Work nymphs at a dead drift through rifts.

The fishing: The state annually stocks this river with 4,000 brown trout averaging 8 inches, 800 11-inchers, and 3,800 rainbows averaging 8.5 inches. Habitat is good, fishing pressure is moderate, and fish of more than 12 inches are common. The best bait is a juicy, fat worm. Fly fishers do well on light-colored, all-purpose nymphs, Muddler Minnows, and Woolly Buggers.

Directions: US 11 parallels the stream from the hamlet of Ellenburg to Mooers Forks.

Contact: New York State Department of Environmental Conservation Region 5.

46A. Public Access

Description: This state site has parking for fifteen cars.

Directions: About 0.5 mile east of Ellenburg on US 11.

47. Lower Chateaugay Lake

Key species: Northern pike, rainbow trout, smallmouth bass, and perch.

Description: This 568-acre lake averages 12 feet deep and has a maximum depth of 25 feet. The shoreline is heavily developed with private camps and homes.

Tips: Fish along the edges of the weed beds in the north and south basins for monster northern pike.

The fishing: Northern pike were illegally introduced into this lake recently, and the population is exploding. Fish of 15 pounds or better are caught regularly. They respond well to spinnerbaits and shallow-running crankbaits such as Red Fins. Smallmouth bass in the 1- to 2-pound range thrive along the rocky shoreline. They have a taste for scented and salted tube baits bounced along the rocks in 5 to 15 feet of water. The state discontinued stocking rainbows, but many run down from Upper Chateaugay Lake (site 48), especially in spring. They average about 10 inches and are mainly taken in the channel and pool above Forge Dam, on the lake's north side, with spinners, spoons, and flies. Yellow perch range from 6 to 12 inches and are targeted mostly by ice fishers jigging grubs.

Recently anglers have reported catching largemouth bass. Richard Preall, a state senior aquatic biologist, says this is an illegal introduction that has the potential for adversely affecting the fishery.

Use or possession of blueback herring or alewives as bait is prohibited.

Directions: Take US 11 north out of Malone for 12 miles to the village of Chateaugay, then turn right (south) onto NY 374 and travel for 7.8 miles.

Additional information: A public boat launch is found off NY 374, about 2.5 miles south of the lake. Located on the Narrows, a 3-something-mile-long navigable channel connecting Lower and Upper Chateaugay Lakes, it has a double-wide paved ramp, parking for about sixty rigs, and toilets. There is no public campground on the lake, but a few private ones are available in the area.

Contact: New York State Department of Environmental Conservation Region 5, and Plattsburgh–North Country Chamber of Commerce.

48. Upper Chateaugay Lake

Key species: Northern pike, landlocked Atlantic salmon, lake trout, rainbow trout, smallmouth bass, yellow perch, and pumpkinseed.

Chazy Lake · Great Chazy River · North Branch Great Chazy River · Lower and Upper Chateaugay Lakes · Chateaugay River

Description: This wide, windswept, 2,524-acre lake averages 33 feet deep and has a maximum depth of 72 feet. Its shoreline is mostly sand and silt, and heavily developed with camps.

Tips: Ice fish with minnows.

The fishing: Like its northern sister, this lake is suddenly producing numerous trophy northern pike. Richard Preall, a state senior aquatic biologist, says they were recently introduced illegally and took to their new, unsuspecting habitat like fire to kindling. Big northerns will be the norm until they exhaust the habitat's surplus biomass—which, incidentally, includes trout and salmon. And if the state continues stocking salmonids at the year 2000's levels (2,600 landlocked Atlantic salmon averaging 6.5 inches, 9,000 lake trout averaging 6.5 inches, and 7,700 rainbow trout averaging 9.5 inches), monster northern pike will remain the norm for a while.

Still, salmonids are holding their own. Landlocked Atlantic salmon reach their 15-inch legal size in a little more than two years. Indeed, a recent survey conducted by the state caught several ranging from 15 to 22 inches, indicating that the lake's salmon fishery is above average. They will hit worms and streamers. The lake trout fishery is totally dependent on stocking. A good number reach the 21-inch legal size limit. In spring and late fall, they can be taken near shore on crankbaits and even streamers. Come summer, try jigging spoons or still-fishing with smelt in deep water. Fish through the ice by suspending live minnows or jigging Swedish Pimples on bottom. Even though the rainbow trout that are stocked average almost 10 inches, their survival rates are nothing to write home to Mother about. Yet some get lucky, growing to range a respectable 4 to 7 pounds. They respond to worms and egg sacs in spring and fall; streamers, small spoons, and crankbaits trolled fast over deep water in summer.

Smallmouth bass do well, ranging from 12 to 19 inches. They respond to crayfish and minnows drifted along bottom. Yellow perch in the 6- to 12-inch range are typical, enthusiastically hitting small jigs. Pumpkinseeds of up to 7 inches can be taken on worms and wet flies.

Use or possession of blueback herring or alewives as bait is prohibited.

Directions: Take US 11 north out of Malone for 12 miles to the village of Chateaugay, then turn right (south) onto NY 374 and travel for about 11 miles.

Additional information: A public boat launch is located off NY 374, about 0.5 mile north of the lake. Located on the Narrows, a 3-something-mile-long navigable channel connecting Lower and Upper Chateaugay Lakes, it has a double-wide paved ramp, parking for about sixty rigs, and toilets.

Contact: New York State Department of Environmental Conservation Region 5.

49. Chateaugay River *(see map on page 115)*

Key species: Brown, rainbow, and brook trout.

Description: This river drains Lower Chateaugay Lake (site 47) and runs north for about 13 miles to Canada, cutting a fabulous chasm along the way.

Tips: Work Mepps XD Spinners through pockets.

The fishing: The state annually stocks 8,600 brook trout averaging 8.5 inches, 2,700 rainbow trout averaging 12 inches, and 480 brown trout averaging 14.5 inches. Survival is good in the favorable habitat, and the brook trout quickly grow to range from 9 to 12 inches, the rainbows to between 13 and 16 inches, and the browns to between 15 and 22 inches. They all eagerly take streamers fished at dusk and dawn, nymphs throughout the day, and worms after a rain. So many big trout in such a small area makes this one of the most exciting fishing streams in the North Country.

Additional information: The state Department of Environmental Conservation's Web site (www.dec.state.ny.us) has maps showing where the river's public fishing rights are located. A couple of commercial campgrounds are on the west side of the river, south of US 11.

Contact: New York State Department of Environmental Conservation Region 5, and Plattsburgh–North Country Chamber of Commerce.

49A. Public Fishing Rights

Description: This mile-long stretch of public fishing rights runs through a gorge, from the US 11 bridge upstream to High Falls. You'll have to park at the shoulder and climb down a steep slope into the gorge.

Directions: Take US 11 north out of Malone for about 14 miles to the bridge just before the hamlet of Chateaugay.

49B. CR 35 Bridge Public Access

Description: This site offers access to public fishing rights stretching from the mouth of the Marble River (a couple of hundred yards downstream of the bridge) upstream for about a mile. In addition, public fishing rights exist on the Marble River, from its mouth to about 0.5 mile upstream. Park on the shoulder.

The fishing: The Chateaugay River upstream of the Marble River's mouth is the most easily accessible, and one of this stream's most productive stretches. In addition, the Marble River is a very productive wild trout fishery. Its brook trout range from 6 to 10 inches, while rainbow trout range from 8 to 12 inches; brown trout reach up to 16 inches. Worms and flies work best.

Directions: Take US 11 north out of Malone for about 14 miles, then turn north onto CR 35 and travel for about 2 miles.

49C. Cooks Mills Public Access

Description: Access at the Sam Cook Road Bridge, parking on the shoulder.

Directions: Take US 11 north out of Malone for about 14 miles and turn north onto CR 35. Follow it for about 3 miles, continue straight on Simms Road for a few hundred yards then turn west onto Sam Cook Road.

Additional information: The state owns public fishing rights on the right bank (looking downstream), 1.5 miles from the bridge, to just about the Canadian border.

50. Schroon River

Key species: Landlocked Atlantic salmon, brook trout, brown trout, rainbow trout, and smallmouth bass.

Description: Starting out as a creek averaging 15 feet wide and 10 inches deep, this river flows gently south for about 65 miles through the eastern Adirondacks, growing to 85 feet wide and 4 feet deep by the time it feeds the Hudson River west of Warrensburg.

Tips: In spring and fall, work Gray Ghosts around the mouth at Schroon Lake.

The fishing: Historically, this river has been a spawning ground for landlocked salmon. Annually, the state stocks 20,000 fry to supplement natural reproduction. They migrate to Schroon Lake but return in fall and again in spring. Recently, according to state aquatic biologist Rich Preall, "Landlocked salmon have been making late-summer and early-fall runs up to the Palmer Pond Dam in the town of North Hudson." Overall, the salmon range from 1 to 4 pounds and hit salmon flies, streamers, and worms. Brook trout occur naturally in the tributaries, and many migrate to the river when they outgrow their home stream. In addition, the state annually stocks about 3,000 averaging 7.5 inches. Overall, brookies range from 6 to 14 inches and respond well to worms, minnows, flies, and spinners. The state also stocks about 1,300 brown trout averaging 9 inches in the area around North Hudson. They grow to average 12 inches and hit worms, streamers, and minnow crankbaits. More than 5,000 rainbows averaging 11 inches are stocked annually into the river below Schroon Lake. They end up averaging 12 inches and are mostly taken on worms, salted minnows, nymphs, and wet flies. Smallmouth bass begin appearing below Schroon Lake. While most are small, seldom exceeding 14 inches, they are notorious for violently striking streamers.

Trout, lake trout, landlocked salmon, and pickerel can be taken year-round in the river from Schroon Lake upstream to Alder Meadow Road. Downstream of Schroon Lake to Starbuckville Dam, landlocked salmon, lake trout, and trout can be taken year-round; lake trout only need to be 18 inches long. From Starbuckville Dam downstream, trout, lake trout, and landlocked salmon can be taken year-round, in any size, and the minimum length for black bass in this lower section is 10 inches. Use or possession of alewives or blueback herring as baitfish is prohibited.

Directions: I–87 parallels most of the river, and US 9 parallels its northern half.

Schroon River · Schroon Lake · Paradox Lake · Putnam Pond · Brant Lake · Loon Lake

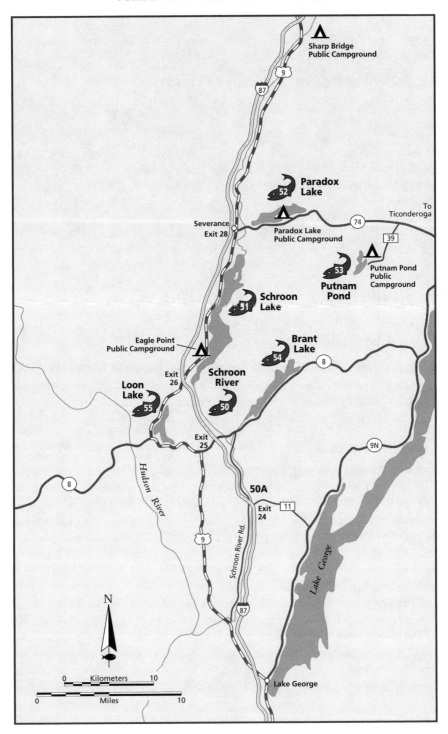

Additional information: Sharp Bridge Public Campground, on US 9, 6 miles south of I–87 exit 30, is a fee area offering forty no-frills campsites, shore-fishing access, showers, picnic areas, and water. Warren County Tourism's free publication "Grand Slam Fishing" has a map and tips.

Contact: New York State Department of Environmental Conservation Region 5, Lake Placid/Essex County Visitors Bureau, and Warren County Tourism.

50A. Public Fishing Rights *(see map on page 119)*

Description: The state owns 0.8 mile of public fishing rights on both sides of the stream. Shoulder parking.

The fishing: This stretch has a good mixture of wild and stocked brown trout. They typically range between 10 and 15 inches, but 20-inchers are available. Worms work best after a rain, spinners and nymphs during the height of day, dry flies and streamers at dawn and dusk.

Directions: Head north on I–87 out of the village of Lake George for about 12 miles to exit 24. Get on CR 11 toward Riverbank, cross the river, turn north onto Schroon River (Burnt Hill) Road, and travel about 1 mile.

51. Schroon Lake *(see map on page 119)*

Key species: Landlocked Atlantic salmon, lake trout, smallmouth bass, largemouth bass, northern pike, pickerel, and yellow perch.

Description: Wearing the Essex and Warren County line in the middle like a belt, this 4,128-acre lake averages 56 feet deep and has a maximum depth of 152 feet. Its shoreline is heavily developed with private cottages.

Tips: Flatline Rapalas in spring and fall for salmon and lake trout.

The fishing: Although this lake is stocked with 3,100 landlocked Atlantic salmon averaging 6.5 inches each year, surveys show that roughly 10 percent of the population is naturally spawned in the Schroon River and other tributaries. The salmon range from 15 to 20 inches and are commonly taken on smelt-imitating streamers and crankbaits trolled at about 3 miles per hour. Lake trout are the predominant cold-water predator. The state annually releases 6,600 of them averaging 7.5 inches. They easily reach 18 inches and respond to silver minnowbaits trolled slow and deep. The minimum length for lake trout is 18 inches, and the daily limit is two. Trout can be taken year-round.

Northern pike ranging from 20 to 30 inches are plentiful. They take large minnows and minnow-imitating crankbaits. Pickerel range from 15 to 22 inches and will take just about any bite-sized lure ripped rapidly along weed edges. Smallmouths from 12 to 16 inches are also abundant and are mostly taken on bottom with crayfish, minnows, and jigs. Largemouth bass in the 1- to 4-pound range are available in the weedy north and south ends, and are commonly targeted with Texas-rigged worms and buzzbaits. Yellow perch go from 8 to 13 inches. They respond to worms, minnows, and scented 2- and 3-inch curly-tailed grubs and tubes.

There is no daily limit on perch or sunfish. In addition, pickerel can be taken year-round, in any number and any size. The lake has high mercury and PCB levels, and the state advises against eating more than one meal a month of lake trout over 27 inches, perch over 13 inches, or smallmouth bass of any size. Use or possession of alewives or blueback herring as bait is prohibited.

Directions: Take I–87 north out of the village of Lake George for about 20 miles to exit 26, then head north on US 9, which parallels the lake.

Additional information: The state operates a boat launch on the south end of the lake, off CR 62, which has a paved launch ramp and parking for about forty-five rigs. Eagle Point Public Campground, on US 9, 2 miles north of Pottersville, is a fee area offering seventy-two no-frills sites, a cartop boat launch, showers, potable water, picnic areas, and a swimming beach. The campground is open May through Labor Day. A day-use fee is charged from mid-June through Labor Day. Free day use is permitted off season. Warren County Tourism's free publication "Grand Slam Fishing" has a map and tips.

Contact: New York State Department of Environmental Conservation Region 5, Lake Placid/Essex County Visitors Bureau, and Warren County Tourism.

52. Paradox Lake (see map on page 119)

Key species: Rainbow trout, lake trout, northern pike, and smallmouth and largemouth bass.

Description: During spring runoff, this lake's outlet is forced by the swollen Schroon River to flow in reverse, prompting it to be called Paradox—which, locals claim, means "water running backward" in Indian. Spread over 840 acres, the lake averages 19 feet deep and has a maximum depth of 55 feet.

Tips: Ice fish with large minnows in the bays on the north end.

The fishing: Every year, the state stocks roughly 1,500 lake trout averaging 6.5 inches. They do well on the abundant forage, and although they range only from 2 to 4 pounds, 20-pounders are available. They respond to spoons, streamers, and worms trolled deep and slow about a foot behind a wobbler or dodger. Rainbow trout are stocked to the tune of about 5,300 annually. Averaging 9 inches upon release, they quickly grow to range from 12 to 18 inches, and some of up to 8 pounds are taken annually. In spring and fall, and at dusk and dawn all summer long, they will take small spoons flatlined parallel to shore in 5 to 15 feet of water. Northern pike range from 4 to 8 pounds, but 20-pounders are regularly taken in winter. They hit large minnows and crankbaits. Smallmouth bass thrive along the lake's drop-offs where they can be taken all day long on Carolina-rigged Exude finesse worms and by drop-shotting 2- and 3-inch curly-tailed grubs and Mister Twister Poc'it Fry.

Largemouth bass up to 6 pounds find the weed beds to their liking and can't seem to resist a scented slug or buzzbait ripped violently alongside or through their cover. Yellow perch ranging from 8 to 12 inches are targeted by ice fishers with minnows or teardrop jigs tipped with grubs.

Trout season is year-round, and the minimum size for lakers is 18 inches. Pickerel can be taken year-round, in any size and in any number. Use or possession of blueback herring or alewives as bait is prohibited.

Directions: Head east out of Severance (exit 28 off I–87) on NY 74 for 2 miles.

Additional information: Paradox Lake Public Campground offers fifty-eight no-frills sites, coin-operated showers, a launch site, canoe and boat rentals, a sand beach and bathhouse, and picnic areas. A day-use fee is charged to noncampers when the campground is open, from May through Columbus Day. Free day use is permitted off-season. The grounds are plowed in winter.

Contact: New York State Department of Environmental Conservation Region 5.

53. Putnam Pond (see map on page 119)

Key species: Northern pike, largemouth bass, and brown bullhead.

Description: Set in the east side of the Pharaoh Lake Wilderness, this 172-acre pond averages 10.5 feet deep and has a maximum depth of 34 feet.

Tips: Cast a spinnerbait to weed edges or timber and yo-yo it back.

The fishing: Northern pike in the 18- to 26-inch range and largemouth bass up to 20 inches are plentiful. Both will take a scented slug worked in weeds and timber, a buzzbait ripped over water lilies, and spinnerbaits worked along weed edges and breaks. Brown bullheads ranging from 8 to 12 inches are taken on worms fished on bottom, particularly in spring.

The use or possession of blueback herring or alewives as bait is prohibited.

Directions: Take NY 74 west out of Ticonderoga for about 6 miles to CR 39, then head south for about 3 miles.

Additional information: Putnam Pond Public Campground is a fee area offering seventy-two campsites, a hard-surface launch ramp, boat rentals, a sand beach, play areas, picnic facilities, and coin-operated showers. It's open May through Labor Day. Free day use is permitted off-season.

Contact: New York State Department of Environmental Conservation Region 5.

54. Brant Lake (see map on page 119)

Key species: Largemouth bass, smallmouth bass, pickerel, pumpkinseed, brown bullhead, and brown trout.

Description: Considered one of the prettiest lakes in the North Country, this 1,376-acre gem, set in a mountain valley, averages 30 feet deep and has a maximum depth of 65 feet. Its shoreline is heavily ringed with cottages.

Tips: Cast Texas-rigged worms under docks, making sure to hit the stanchions with the lead.

The fishing: This lake offers largemouth bass up to 6 pounds and smallmouths of better than 4 pounds. The bucketmouths like shallow water and structure, and respond well to buzzbaits, beaded spoons, and shallow-diving minnowbaits. Smallmouths congregate in deeper water, over rocks and boulders, especially off points. They always respond to crayfish, minnows, and plugs such as Big O's and C. C. Shads. Pickerel range from 18 to 30 inches and respond to Rooster Tails, Dardevle spoons, and worms dragged along weed edges on spinner harnesses. Brown bullheads from 10 to 14 inches are plentiful, especially in the southern basin, where they hit worms and stinkbaits still-fished on bottom. The lake's numerous pumpkinseeds grow up to 0.5 pound and take worms, wet flies, and tiny surface poppers. Some brown trout, scions of former state stocking programs, are also available. There aren't many but when you get one, it is generally over 3 pounds—and can go as big as 6 pounds. Folks target them by trolling small spoons and minnowbaits scented with herring oil.

There is no closed season for trout. Use or possession of blueback herring or alewives for bait is prohibited.

Directions: Head north on I–87 out of the village of Lake George for about 16 miles to exit 25, then continue east on NY 8 for a couple of miles.

Additional information: The state boat launch on NY 8, on the south tip of the lake, has a hard-surface ramp and parking for eleven rigs. Primitive camping is permitted in the Lake George Wild Forest, which touches NY 8 on the lake's northeastern end.

Contact: New York State Department of Environmental Conservation Region 5, and Warren County Tourism.

55. Loon Lake *(see map on page 119)*

Key species: Largemouth bass and northern pike.

Description: Covering almost 600 acres, this lake is shaped like a crooked H, averages 15 feet deep, and has a maximum depth of 33 feet. Completely encircled by good roads, what it lacks in silence it more than makes up for with great fishing.

Tips: Cast spinnerbaits at right angles to weed edges and yo-yo them back.

The fishing: Bucketmouths of up to 7 pounds are the main draw. They respond well to surface baits, fat-bodied crankbaits such as Mann's 1-Minus, and diving crankbaits like MirrOlure's 92LSR. Northern pike range from 3 to 6 pounds. While

Lake Placid from atop Whiteface Mountain.

not huge, these scrappy fighters can be expected to provide heart-stopping strikes on buzzbaits, following through with spectacular aerial displays.

Directions: Head north out of the village of Lake George on I–87 for about 16 miles to exit 25, then go west on NY 8/US 9 for 5 miles.

Additional information: The town boat launch on NY 8/US 9 has a paved launch and parking for five rigs.

Contact: New York State Department of Environmental Conservation Region 5, and Warren County Tourism.

56. Lake Placid *(see map on page 126)*

Key species: Lake trout, rainbow trout, smallmouth bass, and yellow perch.

Description: Known worldwide for the winter Olympic games held nearby in 1932 and 1980, this spring-fed, 2,173-acre lake averages 52 feet deep and has a maximum depth of 151 feet. There are two huge islands in the middle; the lake's floor is rocky with little vegetation.

Tips: Troll spoons for lakers.

The fishing: This lake trout fishery is legendary. Although 30-something-pound fish have been taken in the past, and 15-pounders are landed each year, the typical laker is 2 pounds. Flatlining spoons slowly in spring and fall is the technique favored by locals. The state annually stocks 8,500 rainbow trout averaging 9 inches, and most reach between 12 and 18 inches. Rich Preall, senior aquatic biologist with the state, considers Lake Placid the county's best open water for rainbows. He says, "Impressive *Hexagenia* mayfly hatches occur most evenings from the last week of June through the first week of July, drawing hundreds of rainbows to the surface, where anglers spot-fish for them with Green Drake variations." Smallmouth bass go anywhere from 1 to 4 pounds and respond well to crayfish and minnows fished on bottom. The lake doesn't have many yellow perch but the ones it has average 12 inches, with some reaching 14 inches. They take minnows and jigs.

The minimum length for lake trout is 15 inches.

Directions: Head south out of Plattsburgh on I–87 for about 15 miles. Get off at exit 34, head west onto NY 9N for about 15 miles to Jay, then get on NY 86 and head south for about 16 miles.

Additional information: Hopping Bear Point, on the northeastern corner of the north island, has two lean-tos available on a first-come, first-served basis. In addition, primitive camping is allowed on state land on both islands—but suitable sites are rare because the banks are steep and heavily wooded. The public launch on Mirror Lake Drive, in the village of Lake Placid, has a hard-surface ramp and parking for 25 rigs.

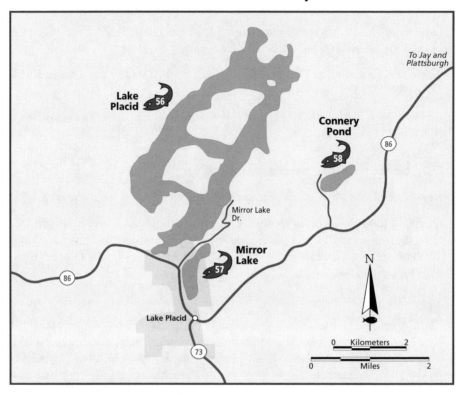

Contact: New York State Department of Environmental Conservation Region 5, and Lake Placid/Essex County Tourism.

57. Mirror Lake

Key species: Rainbow trout, lake trout, smallmouth bass, and perch.

Description: This lake covers 128 acres, averages 14 feet deep, and has a maximum depth of 60 feet. The shoreline is totally developed with marvelous homes, hotels, and the backyards and balconies of Main Street's shops.

Tips: Drift and bounce jigs tipped with minnows off bottom for lake trout.

The fishing: This lake gets surprisingly little fishing pressure considering that it comes right to the road of one of New York's most popular resort towns. But the fish are there. The state annually stocks more than 1,000 rainbow trout averaging 9 inches and about 500 lake trout averaging 7 inches. Both grow to range from 10 to 16 inches. Natural populations of smallmouth bass, ranging from 8 to 14 inches, and perch, ranging from 6 to 8 inches, hang out on drop-offs and are taken mostly on worms and crayfish. The minimum length for lake trout is 15 inches.

Directions: Located in the heart of Lake Placid village, site of the 1932 and 1980 winter Olympic games, a stone's throw from NY 86.

Additional information: Lake Placid Village Park and Beach, on the southern tip of the lake, allows launching of cartop craft; there's also a beach launch on Mirror Lake Drive, on the north shore, with parking for five cars. No motors are allowed on the lake. Numerous motels are located in the village.

Contact: Lake Placid/Essex County Visitors Bureau, and New York State Department of Environmental Conservation Region 5.

58. Connery Pond

Key species: Brown trout and splake.

Description: Nestled in a combination of wilderness, wild forest, and private land, this 75-acre pond averages 17 feet deep and has a maximum depth of 50 feet. Two private camps and a small sandy beach punctuate the forested shoreline.

Tips: Jig minnows through the ice.

The fishing: The state has been stocking splake averaging 10 inches into the pond since the 1950s. The fish reach between 2 to 5 pounds and can be taken by trolling streamers or worms behind wobblers, or jigging spoons and minnows on bottom. Brown trout were initially stocked in error but took so well, and proved so popular with ice anglers, the state now annually stocks about 1,000 browns averaging 8 inches. They grow to range from 9 to 18 inches and take worms, minnows, and wet flies. Trout season is year-round. Motors of up to 7.5 horsepower are allowed.

Additional information: Primitive camping is allowed in the McKenzie Mountain Wilderness Area on the pond's north shore.

Directions: Head north on NY 86 out of Lake Placid village for about 2.5 miles and turn west onto the hard-surface, unnamed road. Follow it for about 0.5 mile and park in the unpaved lot. You'll have to cross private land to get to the pond, but getting permission isn't necessary because of an agreement between the state and the owners.

Contact: New York State Department of Environmental Conservation Region 5.

59. West Branch Ausable River *(see map on page 128)*

Key species: Brook trout, brown trout, and rainbow trout.

Description: Spawned in the shadow of Mount Marcy, the highest peak in the Adirondack Mountains, this splendid river runs independently for about 30 miles before linking up with the East Branch at Au Sable Forks. Along the way it undergoes many changes in character—everything from flowing quietly and gently through fertile mountain meadows to raging whitewater squeezed between austere mountain cliffs. Every trout habitat imaginable can be found in its path, earning the

Ausable River

West Branch a reputation as one of the greatest trout streams in the Northeast.

Tips: In the opening weeks of the season, fish worms and minnows slowly on bottom in pools and deep channels.

The fishing: Brook trout of up to 10 inches occupy the wilderness portion of the river a few miles south of the village of Lake Placid. In addition, a few lunker speckled trout, refugees from the numerous tiny feeders, are caught each year in other sections of the river. They are mostly taken with worms and small spoons such as Dardevles.

One of the most heavily stocked streams in the state, the West Branch is loaded with browns and rainbows from the Olympic ski jumps towering over the south side of Lake Placid village all the way to Au Sable Forks. A combination of plentiful cover (boulder fields, blowdowns, undercut banks), cool water temperatures (maintained by cold mountain springs, shady banks, and sun-blocking cliffs), and a good food supply (abundant populations of aquatic and terrestrial insects, crayfish, and minnows) conspire to make the river ideal trout habitat. Fish between 12 and 16 inches are common, and browns and rainbows tipping the scale at slightly more than 8 pounds are caught each year. The fish can be taken on everything from minnows and worms to spoons, in-line spinners, streamers, and flies.

Like all of New York's famous streams in the age of affirmative action, the West Branch has a section set aside for special populations. A no-kill, artificial-lures-only section stretches from the mouth of Holcomb Pond Outlet, off River Road (CR 21), to the marked boundary 2.2 miles downstream of Monument Falls. This section is open to year-round fishing.

Directions: NY 86 parallels the river from the bridge just north of the village of Lake Placid, all the way to Wilmington.

Additional information: Lake Placid village, site of the 1936 and 1980 Olympic games, is a classy little town offering food and lodging spanning the price spectrum. Primitive camping is allowed on forest preserve lands skirting the stream.

Contact: New York State Department of Environmental Conservation Region 5.

59A. Wilmington Notch Public Campground

Description: A fee area on the east edge of the Wilmington Notch, a deep canyon carved out of the granite mountain by the river, this scenic campground offers fifty-four sites, showers, toilets, and a trailer dumping station. It's open from April through October.

Directions: Head north on NY 86 out of Lake Placid village for 8 miles.

Additional information: The campground's west side sits 300 feet above the river. A steep, difficult trail leads down. The entrance to Whiteface Mountain Ski Area, site of the 1980 winter Olympic games, is about 100 feet north of the campgrounds.

60. East Branch Ausable River (see map on page 128)

Key species: Brown trout and rainbow trout.

Description: The outlet of Upper and Lower Ausable Lakes, this river flows north for about 25 miles to join the West Branch at Au Sable Forks. Relatively mild mannered compared to its sibling, the East Branch is far safer and easier to wade.

Tips: Fish the runs and pools around tributary mouths.

The fishing: The state stocks several thousand rainbow trout averaging 9 inches and about 15,000 browns averaging 8 inches annually. From mid-May through early June, when water temperatures are rising and the river is downsizing from meltwater to summer level, it becomes wonderful dry-fly water through most of its length; large patterns such as the Irresistible and Ausable Wulff can be productive. Come July and August, the pickings turn slim as trout hole up in the river's few, widely scattered pools and runs or migrate into small feeders that are difficult to fish.

Directions: NY 73 parallels the river through the Keene Valley, and NY 9N follows it from the hamlet of Keene to Ausable Forks.

Additional information: Most of the East Branch flows through private property. The 2-mile stretch of west shore just south of the hamlet of Upper Jay is in the Sentinel Range Wilderness Area, and primitive camping is allowed.

Contact: New York State Department of Environmental Conservation Region 5.

61. Main Stem Ausable River (see map on page 128)

Key species: Brown trout, steelhead, and landlocked Atlantic salmon.

Description: Formed by the union of the East and West Branches in Au Sable Forks, this wide, shallow river runs northeast for about 16 miles to feed Lake Champlain.

Tips: Fish around the US 9 bridge in spring and autumn.

The fishing: Wide and shallow, this river's upper reaches nonetheless support brown trout in the 12- to 18-inch range. They are mostly caught on live bait and flies by locals who know the locations of spring pools. The fishing peters out, however, when July and August heat the water to barely tolerable temperatures. Add to that the fact that most of the stream flows through private property and you come up with a less-than-perfect fishery.

The stretch of river from the mouth upstream to the falls at Ausable Chasm is a different story. The state stocks more than 40,000 landlocked Atlantic salmon and several thousand steelhead into the lower portion each year. The fish return in spring and fall. Ice-out sees runs of landlocked Atlantic salmon and steelhead in the 15- to 21-inch range. They return in fall, only this time they average a couple of inches longer, and their numbers include spawn-heavy brown trout of equal size. Worms and smelt are the most popular bait. Fly fishers do well on streamers imitating perch (Mickey Finns and Black Ghosts) and smelt (Gray Ghosts and Black Nose Dace). Spin casters find success with silver Dardevles, blue-and-silver Little Cleos, and white Rooster Tail spinners.

From its mouth upstream to the falls at Ausable Chasm, the river is governed by Lake Champlain regulations.

Directions: NY 9N and US 9 parallel the river.

Additional information: A cartop boat launch and shore-fishing access is located at Ausable Point Public Campground, on the mouth of the river. This state-run fee area has 123 campsites (43 of them with electrical hook-ups), hot showers, a 0.25-mile sandy swimming beach, a bathhouse, playgrounds, and a basketball court. It's open from mid-May through mid-October. A day-use fee is charged to noncampers during summer. This area is popular with sailboarders.

Contact: New York State Department of Environmental Conservation Region 5.

62. Moose Pond (see map on page 132)

Key species: Brook trout, rainbow trout, lake trout, landlocked salmon, and small-mouth bass.

Description: Set between the Saranac Lake Wild Forest and the McKenzie Mountain Wilderness, this 140-acre pond averages 28.5 feet deep and has a maximum depth of 70 feet. More than half of its shoreline is rocky.

Tips: Silver crankbaits are productive early in the season.

The fishing: This pond has wild brook trout ranging from 6 to 15 inches. They take wet flies and worms. Naturally spawned lake trout are also present. They range from 2 to 8 pounds and take silver spoons jigged on bottom. Each year the state stocks 1,300 rainbow trout averaging 8 inches. Most reach 12 inches or a little better and take dry flies all summer long. A couple hundred of landlocked Atlantic salmon averaging 6 inches are also stocked annually. Survival is good, and they grow to between 15 and 20 inches. They like streamers and shallow-running minnow-baits. Smallmouth bass are plentiful but not big. Ranging from 6 to 12 inches, they are a lot of fun to catch on spinners and Z-Ray spoons worked on ultralight tackle.

The minimum length for lake trout is only 15 inches. Black bass season opens April 1; they can be taken in any size and any number. Possession or use of baitfish is prohibited. This is one of the few ponds in which the state releases spent land-locked Atlantic salmon brood stock up to 38 inches long. Stocked in autumn, they overwinter, growing savvy, providing challenging sport for anglers the following season. Try silver Rapalas.

Directions: Take NY 3 north out of the hamlet of Saranac Lake for 6 miles to Bloomingdale. Turn east onto CR 18, then south, 1.5 miles later, onto Moose Pond Road and continue for about 1 mile.

Moose, Buck, Jones, and Osgood Ponds · Lake Kushaqua · Rainbow Lake

Moose Pond 62

Moose Pond Rd.

18

3

Bloomingdale

55

To Saranac Lake

3

30

Buck Pond Public Campground

Buck Pond 64

Onchiota

Lake Kushaqua 63

Rainbow Lake Rd.

Rainbow Lake 65

Jones Pond 66

Gabriels

30

86

White Pine Rd.

31

86

Osgood Pond 67

Mountain Pond

Barnum Pond

Paul Smiths

Upper Saint Regis Lake

30

N

Kilometers
0   4

Miles
0   4

Additional information: There are several campsites around the pond. The boat launch at the end of Moose Pond Road is rather steep, but small trailers can make it. There's parking for about five cars.

Contact: New York State Department of Environmental Conservation Region 5.

63. Lake Kushaqua

Key species: Lake trout, largemouth bass, smallmouth bass, and northern pike.

Description: This 377-acre lake averages 20 feet deep and has a maximum depth of 91 feet. Almost totally surrounded by state land, the shoreline is mostly forested.

Tips: Walk Zara Spooks around emergent vegetation.

The fishing: The state annually stocks about 1,300 lake trout averaging 7 inches. They hang out in the deep, cold middle and grow to range from 2 to 5 pounds. They take worms or tinsel flies trolled behind attractors in 40 to 60 feet of water. In summer, you'll catch more lakers by bumping bottom, but the larger ones suspend. Largemouth bass ranging from 1 to 3 pounds thrive all along the shoreline but are especially numerous in the southern end. During hot weather, they seek shade in the shadow of lily pads, weed beds, and under banks and logs. Buzzbaits retrieved quickly over their heads provoke explosive reactions. Smallmouths ranging from 8 to 14 inches can be found over drop-offs in 15 to 30 feet of water. During the heat of the day, cast diving crankbaits such as MirrOlure's 91LSRs and Cotton Cordell's Spot Minnows. On calm evenings, however, twitch a MirrOlure Prop Bait off points and over drop-offs at the mouths of bays.
Use or possession of blueback herring or alewives for bait is prohibited.

Directions: From its intersection with NY 30 in Paul Smiths, head east on NY 86 for 4.5 miles to Gabriels and turn north onto CR 30. Continue 6.3 miles to the Buck Pond Public Campground.

Additional information: Buck Pond Public Campground operates a paved launch ramp on the lake's southeastern bank with parking for about ten rigs. A day-use fee is charged to noncampers from Memorial Day through Labor Day. The campground offers 116 sites, including several on the beach and a couple on a nearby island, as well as hot showers, a dumping station, a sand beach, and boat and canoe rentals.

Contact: New York State Department of Environmental Conservation Region 5, and Franklin County Tourism.

64. Buck Pond

Key species: Northern pike, largemouth bass, smallmouth bass, yellow perch, pumpkinseed, and brown bullhead.

Description: The only development on this 130-acre pond's shoreline is campsites. It averages 7.5 feet deep and has a maximum depth of 15 feet.

Tips: Cast red-and-white Dardevle spoons over 5 to 15 feet of water.

The fishing: This pond contains a healthy population of northern pike. Ranging from 18 to 28 inches, they hit minnows, crankbaits, and spoons. Bronzebacks range from 10 to 16 inches and hit Carolina-rigged YUM Rib Worms. Bucketmouths grow to 20 inches and like Mystic 5-inch Fingerlings and YUM Vibra King Tubes. Yellow perch and bullheads run between 6 and 12 inches. Both hit worms fished on bottom. Bullheads are especially active in the evening. Perch will also hit wet flies and small lures.

Use or possession of blueback herring or alewives is prohibited. No motors are allowed.

Directions: From its intersection with NY 30 in Paul Smiths, head east on NY 86 for 4.5 miles to Gabriels and turn north onto CR 30. Continue 6.3 miles to the Buck Pond Public Campground.

Additional information: Buck Pond Public Campground, a fee area, is on the pond's west bank. It offers 116 sites, hot showers, a cartop boat launch, and boat and canoe rentals. Day use is permitted year-round, with a fee charged to noncampers when the campground is open, Memorial Day through Labor Day.

Contact: New York State Department of Environmental Conservation Region 5, and Franklin County Tourism.

65. Rainbow Lake (see map on page 132)

Key species: Largemouth bass, northern pike, walleyes, yellow perch, and brown bullhead.

Description: Averaging 15 feet deep and dropping to a maximum depth of 58 feet, much of this 354-acre lake's southern and western shores are bordered by private dwellings. An esker runs along most of its north shore, separating it from Clear Pond, a backwater popular with canoeists and campers but not anglers.

Tips: Cast floating-diving perch-colored crankbaits during low-light conditions.

The fishing: This lake is loaded with stunted perch averaging 6 inches. Their massive number has caused a terrible imbalance, resulting in even the pumpkinseeds and rock bass being stunted. Largemouth bass were introduced in the 1940s, followed by northern pike around 1960. While recent surveys show that the largemouths range from 10 to 14 inches and northern pike go from 18 to 32 inches, their numbers aren't great. In an attempt to manage the perch, the state began stocking walleyes in 1990s. Richard Preall, the state aquatic biologist charged with managing the fishery, says a 1997 survey caught healthy five- and six-year-olds averaging 21.5 inches. Pleased, Preall has recommended to his superiors that walleyes continue being stocked. "Eyes" respond to drifted minnows and worms, as well as bucktail jigs fished plain or tipped with scented curly tails. Brown bullheads do well, too, averaging a respectable 10 inches. They are a popular rite of spring among locals, who fish for them with worms at night. Few fish for bullheads in daylight because of all the stunted perch and sunfish.

The use and possession of blueback herring or alewives as bait is prohibited.

Directions: Head north out of Gabriels for about 2 miles on CR 30 (Rainbow Lake Road).

Additional information: The south shore is largely on private property, and access from land can be iffy. The easiest way to get here is from Lake Kushaqua (site 63), by paddling or motoring up its inlet, through the scenic Rainbow Narrows. You'll need a low-deck craft such as a canoe or small motorboat to make it under a bridge. Several primitive beach campsites are located on the esker on the north side of the lake.

Contact: New York State Department of Environmental Conservation Region 5, and Franklin County Tourism.

66. Jones Pond *(see map on page 132)*

Key species: Northern pike, yellow perch, and brown bullhead.

Description: Bordered on its west end and southern tip by vast, weedy bays, this 140-acre pond is a warm-water fishery that averages only 4.3 feet deep and has a maximum depth of 8.9 feet. The vast majority of its shoreline is evergreen forest, but there is also some light development.

Tips: Cast red-and-white Daredevle spoons along the edges of the marshes in early spring and late fall.

The fishing: Northern pike are the main predator. They range from 18 to 32 inches and respond well to artificials resembling life-forms ranging from minnows, mice, frogs, and snakes to ducklings and baby muskrats. Bullheads average 9 inches and hit worms fished on bottom. Perch go from 5 to 10 inches and hit 1- to 2-inch curly-tailed grubs swum 1 to 2 feet below the surface and jerked periodically—say, every 10 feet or so.

The use or possession of blueback herring or alewives as bait is prohibited.

Directions: Head east out of Paul Smiths for about 1 mile on NY 86, then turn left onto CR 31 for about 1.5 miles.

Additional information: A couple of informal cartop launches are found on CR 31. Adventurers get here by paddling up the outlet from Osgood Pond (site 67). If you decide to take this route, be prepared to pull the canoe through shallow spots. Primitive camping is allowed on the state land surrounding three-quarters of the pond.

Boardwalk at White Pines Camp, Osgood Pond (site 67).

Contact: New York State Department of Environmental Conservation Region 5, and Franklin County Tourism.

67. Osgood Pond (see map on page 132)

Key species: Northern pike and largemouth bass.

Description: Ringed mostly by woods, this 508-acre pond has a few private residences and two Adirondack Great Camps. It averages 13 feet deep and has a maximum depth of 25 feet. Bald eagles nest in the surrounding forest and are often spotted swooping down for fish.

Tips: Rattling crankbaits are productive.

The fishing: This place is notorious for northerns ranging from 18 to 24 inches. They are mostly targeted by ice fishers using shiners on tip-ups. Largemouth bass range from 1 to 4 pounds and take Texas-rigged worms tossed into the fallen timber, weed beds, lily pads, and any other cover you can find.

Use or possession of blueback herring or alewives for bait is prohibited.

Directions: Head east out of Paul Smiths on NY 86 for 0.6 mile to White Pine Road. Turn left and travel for 0.3 mile.

Additional information: A beach launch with parking for five rigs is found on White Pine Road. Primitive camping is allowed on the state land on the north shore. This pond has two majestic Adirondack Great Camps, massive private estates that are open to the public. Northbrook Lodge, one of the best-kept secrets in the Adirondacks, is a summer resort. It was built in the 1920s by a politician or bootlegger (it depends on who you talk to). White Pines Camp, built in 1907, served as the White House when President Calvin Coolidge spent the summer here in 1926.

Contact: Franklin County Tourism and New York State Department of Environmental Conservation Region 5.

68. Boy Scout Clear Pond (Clear Pond) *(see map on page 138)*

Key species: Splake.

Description: Almost totally undeveloped, this 81-acre pond is skirted by marsh and woods. It averages 28 feet deep and has a maximum depth of 63 feet.

Tips: Stay away from the Boy Scout camp on the north end in summer.

The fishing: The splake in this pond can reach 6 pounds. A cross between brook trout and lake trout, this species gets confused a lot with one or the other—but here, splake are the only trout in the pond. Fish for them on bottom with worms, jigs, and spoons.
   Use or possession of blueback herring or alewives as bait is prohibited.

Directions: Head north out of Paul Smiths for about 10 miles on NY 30 and turn east at the northern Meacham Lake Public Campground entrance. A beach launch is about 100 yards down the road.

Additional information: Electric motors up to 5 horsepower are allowed.

Contact: New York State Department of Environmental Conservation Region 5, and Franklin County Tourism.

69. Meacham Lake *(see map on page 138)*

Key species: Northern pike, smallmouth bass, splake, brown trout, landlocked Atlantic salmon, and yellow perch.

Description: This lake covers 1,203 acres, averages 36 feet deep, and has a maximum depth of 63 feet. Its only development is a public campground on the north end.

Tips: Use large minnows over deep structure in winter for huge northern pike.

The fishing: This lake is known for producing northerns of pikasaurus proportions. Each year, pike of more than 15 pounds are taken by ice fishers using minnows. Summer anglers get in on the action by throwing crankbaits and spoons for fish of

From East Branch St. Regis River to Lake Clear Outlet, with Nearby Lakes and Ponds

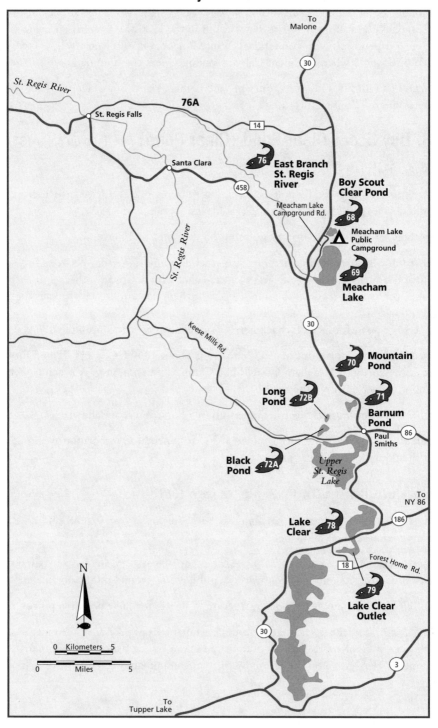

up to 10 pounds. Smallmouth bass reach a whopping 5-something pounds. They prefer the rocky east shore between Winnebago Creek and Roaring Brook, and respond to crayfish and scented craws worked on bottom. The state stocks 2,500 splake averaging 10 inches annually. They typically reach 2 to 4 pounds. Bottom oriented, they hit deep-diving minnowbaits and suckers fished on bottom. About 250 brown trout averaging 14 inches are stocked annually. Most are caught in spring and fall on worms or through the ice by anglers suspending golden shiners a few feet below bobbers. Landlocked Atlantic salmon range from 15 to 20 inches and will hit small silver spoons and crankbaits, especially near tributary mouths from mid-April through mid-May. This lake has some of the largest perch in the Adirondack Mountains. Unfortunately, they have high mercury levels; the state has issued a health advisory against eating any over 12 inches, and recommending that you eat no more than one meal (8 ounces) a month of perch under 12 inches. They take minnows and curly-tailed grubs.

Trout and salmon can be taken year-round. Use or possession of alewives or blueback herring as bait is prohibited.

Directions: Head north out of Paul Smiths on NY 30 for about 8 miles.

Additional information: Meacham Lake Public Campground, a fee area, has 224 no-frill sites, a boat launch, coin-operated showers, a sand beach, a bathhouse, and canoe and boat rentals. Each of the twenty-five beach campsites has its own outhouse. A day-use fee is charged to noncampers while the campground is open, from mid-May through Columbus Day. Free day use off-season. The park road is plowed in winter.

Contact: New York State Department of Environmental Conservation Region 5, and Franklin County Tourism.

70. Mountain Pond

Key species: Brook trout.

Description: Located within the Debar Mountain Wild Forest, this 56-acre pond averages 9 feet deep and has a maximum depth of 29 feet.

Tips: Use lures with barbless hooks to facilitate easy release.

The fishing: This pond is managed for New York's native Windfall-strain brook trout. "Our policy is to supplement the pond's naturally reproducing population by stocking 2,000 brook trout annually for two years, then no trout for two years," says Rich Preall, a state senior fisheries biologist. A state survey taken in November 2000 revealed that the average trout measured 10.8 inches; many were more than 16 inches.

This pond is for catch-and-release fishing with artificial lures only. No motors are allowed.

Directions: Head north out of Paul Smiths on NY 30 for about 2.5 miles, then turn right onto Mountain Pond Road.

Contact: New York State Department of Environmental Conservation Region 5, and Franklin County Tourism.

71. Barnum Pond *(see map on page 138)*

Key species: Largemouth bass and brown trout.

Description: Averaging about 3 feet deep and having a maximum depth of 10 feet, this pond covers 89 acres and has sprawling wetlands equal its size along the south shore.

Tips: Wash your hands with a scent-eliminating soap before handling lures.

The fishing: This lake has a lot of largemouth bass ranging from 6 to 14 inches. They respond best to worms and crayfish. The state annually stocks 250 two-year-old brown trout averaging 14 inches. Although the pond is shallow, springs keep it cool; trout survival is good, and browns of up to 20 inches are caught each spring with live bait. Come summer, they are heavier and smarter. Still, some are taken on worms fished on bottom after a rain. In addition, some are taken on minnowbaits treated with a fish scent such as herring oil. Use or possession of baitfish is prohibited.

Directions: From Paul Smiths, head north on NY 30 for about 1 mile.

Additional information: This lake is an example of the damage that informal stocking can do to native species. A few years back, this was one of the best roadside brook trout ponds in Franklin County. Then someone threw in a couple of largemouths, and they wiped out the brookies. Chemical reclamation is out of the question because of the massive wetlands. A beach launch for cartop craft is on NY 30. A couple of primitive campsites are located north of the launch.

Contacts: New York State Department of Environmental Conservation Region 5, and Franklin County Tourism.

72. Black and Long Ponds Recreation Area
(see map on page 138)

These two ponds are located north of the St. Regis Canoe Area. They are popular destinations with hikers and canoeists. Both were reclaimed with chemicals in 1997 and now support Windfall-strain brook trout indigenous to New York.

72A. Black Pond

Key species: Brook trout.

Description: This 73-acre pond is completely surrounded by forest and has an esker running along its west bank. Its average depth is 20 feet and the maximum is 45 feet deep.

Tips: If the fish aren't hitting in the main pond, canoe up the east side and try the big bay some call Little Black Pond.

The fishing: Since being chemically reclaimed in 1997, this pond has been stocked twice, each time with roughly 2,600 Windfall-strain brook trout averaging 3 inches. Currently most of the trout are wild, and the state feels future stocking probably won't be necessary. They range from 6 to 16 inches and eagerly hit almost any fly early in the season but clam up as summer progresses. Still, a few can be coaxed at dawn and dusk to take a tiny, gently presented spinner or caddis.

Use or possession of baitfish is prohibited.

Directions: Head west out of Paul Smiths on Keese Mills Road for about 2 miles.

Additional information: Located on Adirondack Visitors Interpretive Center property, this pond's lean-tos are for day use only; camping is prohibited on the property.

Contact: New York State Department of Environmental Conservation Region 5, and Franklin County Tourism.

72B. Long Pond

Key species: Brook trout.

Description: Spread over 14 acres, this pond is completely surrounded by forest, shrubs, and wetland. Averaging 9.5 feet deep and dropping to a maximum depth of 20 feet, it feeds Black Pond. Two dams—one at the canoe launch on the pond's outlet, the other on the channel halfway to Black Pond—prevent fish movement between the two.

Tips: Cast a light-colored fly such as a Yellow Humpy near beaver lodges.

The fishing: Since being chemically reclaimed in 1997, this pond has been stocked a couple of times with about 550 3-inch brook trout each time. Currently most fish are wild and average 10 inches—but 2-pounders are reported taken each year. They hit worms, streamers, and in-line spinners.

Use or possession of baitfish is prohibited.

Directions: Head up Black Pond's inlet (site 72A) for about 0.5 mile; you will have to carry for about 0.25 mile

Additional information: This pond is located on Adirondack Park Visitor Interpretive Center property, and the lean-tos are for day use only. Camping is prohibited on the property.

Contact: New York State Department of Environmental Conservation Region 5, and Franklin County Tourism.

73. Lower St. Regis Lake *(see map on page 142)*

Key species: Northern pike, largemouth bass, smallmouth bass, yellow perch, and panfish.

Upper and Lower St. Regis Lakes · Spitfire Lake

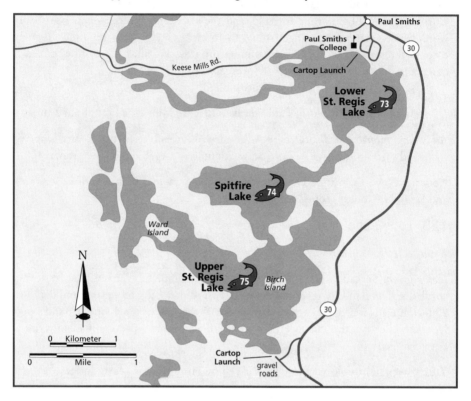

Description: Covering 350 acres, this lake has an average depth of 17 feet and drops to a maximum depth of 38 feet.

Tips: Rip jerkbaits around the marshy east and south banks.

The fishing: This pond has a good warm-water fishery. Northern pike ranging from 18 to 30 inches, largemouth bass from 1 to 3 pounds, and smallmouth bass from 0.75 pound to 2 pounds are plentiful. Each responds well to spinnerbaits and crankbaits worked in 10 to 20 feet of water. In addition, smallmouths hang out on the drop-offs in up to 30 feet of water in summer and take bucktail jigs, scented 3-inch curly-tailed grubs, and salted tubes. Yellow perch running from 6 to 12 inches are numerous and take small minnows and lures, especially 2-inch scented curly-tailed grubs. There are good populations of 5- to 8-inch pumpkinseeds and bullheads of up to 14 inches. They like worms.

Use or possession of blueback herring or smelt as bait is prohibited.

Directions: Located on the south side of the hamlet of Paul Smiths.

Additional information: Paul Smiths College occupies much of the north shore, and there is a small, public cartop launch on campus—you will have to carry for about

100 yards. Parking is limited to six cars. The college has a forestry and environmental science program, and the ramp is closed to the public when students are doing field work.

Contact: Franklin County Tourism, and New York State Department of Environmental Conservation Region 5.

74. Spitfire Lake

Key species: Northern pike, largemouth bass, and smallmouth bass.

Description: This 260-acre lake averages 16 feet and has a maximum depth of 31 feet.

Tips: Active smallmouths hang around boathouses at dusk.

The fishing: Northern pike range from 2 to 5 pounds, largemouth bass run between 1.5 and 4 pounds, and smallmouths go from 1 to 2.5 pounds. Each takes loud crankbaits. The largest northerns are caught through the ice on large minnows.

Directions: This lake is nestled between Upper and Lower St. Regis Lakes. There is no shore access; the only way to get to it is through the channels connecting it to the St. Regis Lakes. Normally, the channels are deep enough to accommodate motorboats.

Contact: Franklin County Tourism, and New York State Environmental Conservation Region 5.

75. Upper St. Regis Lake

Key species: Lake trout, landlocked Atlantic salmon, northern pike, largemouth bass, and smallmouth bass.

Description: This 742-acre lake's average depth is 25 feet; it has a maximum depth of 90 feet. One of the world's classiest lakes, it boasts a wooded shoreline decked in beautiful Great Camps and numerous lesser mansions.

Tips: Bump spinnerbaits off the exposed branches of submerged timber.

The fishing: The state stocks several hundred yearling landlocked salmon annually. They normally reach 15 to 19 inches and are mostly caught on streamers. A little more than 1,000 yearling lake trout are also stocked annually. They end up ranging from 2 to 5 pounds and respond to spoons trolled on Seth Green rigs. Northern pike range from 5 to 10 pounds, and 15-pounders are possible. They hit large minnows and spinnerbaits. Largemouth bass range from 2 to 4 pounds and share the shallow, heavily wooded areas with the northerns. They also take the same baits, as well as crayfish. Smallmouths range from 1 to 3 pounds and prefer rocky points, where they can be taken on Carolina-rigged finesse worms and 3-inch, soft plastic minnows fished on drop-shot rigs.

Directions: At the other end of the channel on Spitfire Lake's south end.

Additional information: Primitive camping is allowed on the state land midway up the lake's west bank. A beach launch for cartop craft is located on the south end. Head south on NY 30 from its intersection with NY 86 in Paul Smiths. Turn right 3.2 miles later onto a gravel road and keep bearing right; skirt the private club grounds, and the small launch is at the tip of the point. There's parking for about five cars.

Contact: Franklin County Tourism, and New York State Environmental Conservation Department's Region 5.

76. East Branch St. Regis River (see map on page 138)

Key species: Brook trout.

Description: This branch starts in Meacham Lake, meanders for 11 miles, and joins the main branch a couple of miles north of the village of Santa Clara. Although it has some rapids, it is mostly mild-mannered, flowing through fabulous forest; it's best float-fished in a canoe.

Tips: Wear hip boots to facilitate carrying around beaver dams.

The fishing: Native brook trout rule this stream. They migrate into it when they outgrow their natal waters but seldom stray more than a couple of hundred feet beyond the mouths. Although most range from 7 to 12 inches, 14-inchers are possible. Wet flies and worms work best.

Directions: Head north out of Paul Smiths on NY 30 for about 8 miles then turn west onto NY 458, which parallels the upper half of the river.

Contact: New York State Department of Environmental Conservation Region 5, and Franklin County Tourism.

76A. Public Access

Description: This site is owned by The Nature Conservancy. There's parking for five cars.

Directions: Take NY 458 into the hamlet of St. Regis Falls. Head north on CR 5 for a couple of blocks, then turn east onto CR 14 and travel for about 6 miles.

77. St. Regis River (see map on page 146)

Key species: Brook trout, brown trout, rainbow trout, northern pike, walleye, smallmouth bass, largemouth bass, and muskellunge.

Description: This river pours out of Lower St. Regis Lake (site 73) and meanders north for about 80 miles to feed the St. Lawrence, gathering the East Branch along the way. Starting out as good trout habitat, its cold-water environments steadily deteriorate until Nicholville, where it becomes a warm-water fishery.

Tips: The most productive trout water is from the mill dam in the hamlet of St. Regis Falls, and downstream for about 2 miles.

The fishing: The upper reaches have natural brook trout ranging from 4 to 12 inches. The state annually supplements this fishery by stocking about 6,000 rainbow trout averaging 8 inches, roughly 2,600 brown trout averaging 8 inches, and 500 two-year-old browns averaging 14 inches. All are stocked in the townships of Santa Clara and Dickinson. Unfortunately, this water quickly heats up in summer, and holdover trout are rare. They respond to worms, in-line spinners, and small crankbaits such as Junior ThunderSticks.

Northern pike ranging from 18 to 22 inches, locally referred to as ax handles, are present in the impoundments at Santa Clara and St. Regis Falls. They respond to minnows, streamers, spinnerbaits, and buzzbaits. Smallmouth bass begin appearing in the impoundment at St. Regis Falls. Ranging from 0.5 to 1.5 pounds, they hit minnows, crayfish, worms, small crankbaits like Mister Twister's BigySmals, and spinnerbaits. The area a couple of miles downstream of St. Regis Falls sees bigger northern pike, up to 28 inches, and smallmouth bass from 12 to 16 inches. Walleyes of up to 20 inches begin appearing around Nicholville and have a taste for spinner-rigged worms, jigs, and crankbaits. Great Lakes–strain muskellunge are available from Helena downstream. They range from 5 to 15 pounds and respond best to large minnows, Jitterbugs, Super Top Props, and hard jerkbaits. Largemouth bass also become abundant in the last 10 miles or so of the river and have a taste for soft jerkbaits and plastic worms.

Trout can be taken year-round from Fort Jackson upstream to Days Mill Road in Hopkinton. The minimum length for muskies is 30 inches. For black bass in the section flowing through St. Lawrence County (the county line is a couple of miles upstream of Nicholville), the minimum length is 10 inches.

Additional information: The state offers the free brochure "Fishing and Canoeing the St. Regis River in St. Lawrence County." The 3-mile stretch of river below the Canadian border is on the St. Regis Indian Reservation; you need permission from the tribe to fish here.

Contact: New York State Department of Environmental Conservation Regions 5 and 6, and the Mohawk Council of Akwesasne Conservation Department.

77A. Public Access

Description: This state site had a road leading down to a parking lot on the riverbank. At press time, the road was washed out. If it gets repaired, there is parking for ten cars on the landing at the river. Otherwise, park on the shoulder and walk down about 100 feet.

The fishing: In this stretch, the river is littered with huge boulders and flows

St. Regis River

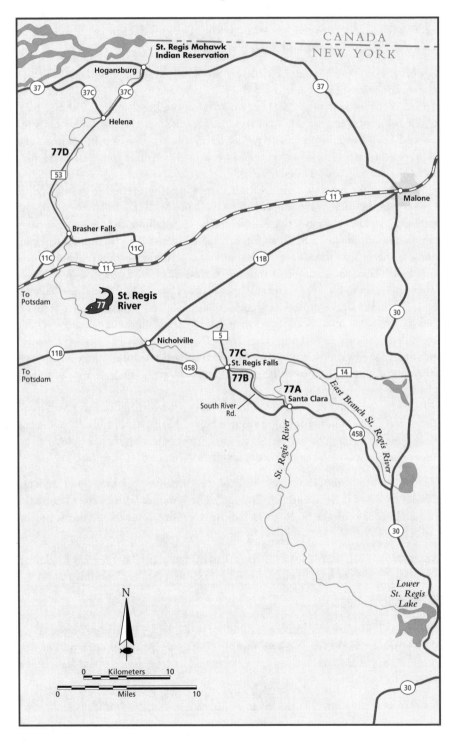

through spellbinding woods. The area is prime trout water from spring through early summer. Come August, you'll find the fish holing up in spring pools and tributary mouths.

Directions: Head north out of Paul Smiths on NY 30 for about 8 miles and turn west onto NY 458. Travel for 10.8 miles, bearing right onto South River Road. The access is 0.1 mile farther.

77B. Public Access

Description: This town of Waverly park is located on the impoundment in St. Regis Falls. The grounds offer a paved ramp, a loading dock, formal parking for three cars, shoulder parking for about twenty more, shore-fishing access, and picnic facilities.

The fishing: This impoundment has trout, northern pike, and smallmouth bass.

Directions: From the above site, continue west on South River Road for about 5 miles to the east side of the village of St. Regis Falls.

77C. St. Regis Falls Scenic Campsite

Description: Run by the town of Waverly, this fee area is right at the waterfall and offers numerous waterfront sites with and without hook-ups, several cabins, playgrounds, and a museum. It's open May 1 through October 15

The fishing: The stretch from the falls and about 2 miles downstream is the best trout water on the river.

Directions: From the above site, continue west on South River Road for about 100 yards to the stop sign. Turn right, cross the bridge, and turn left.

77D. Brasher Falls State Forest Public Access

Description: This site has an unpaved ramp for cartop craft and parking for five cars.

The fishing: The water here is slow and fairly deep—good habitat for bass, northern pike, walleyes, and an occasional muskie.

Directions: From the US 11/NY 11B intersection in Pottsdam, head north on US 11 for 10 miles, then turn north onto NY 11C for 4 miles. Get on CR 53 in Brasher Falls and head north for 5.5 miles.

Additional information: Primitive camping is allowed across the road in the state forest.

78. Lake Clear (see map on page 138)

Key species: Landlocked Atlantic salmon, northern pike, largemouth bass rainbow smelt, yellow perch, and pumpkinseed.

St. Regis River in the village of St. Regis Falls.

Description: This 979-acre lake averages 28 feet deep and has a maximum depth of 60 feet. Its shoreline is partly developed with private homes and camps.

Tips: Cast streamers around tributary mouths in September.

The fishing: The state maintains a landlocked Atlantic salmon presence through stocking. Most anglers take them in mid-September (autumn comes early in the Adirondacks) by wading out into the surf and casting small spinners and wet flies into the mouth of the little brook just north of the access trail. Largemouth bass range from 1 to 3 pounds and respond well to live minnows and crayfish. Northern pike range from 2 to 6 pounds and are usually taken through the ice on large minnows. Smelt numbers have been dropping recently, but enough ranging from 6 to 10 inches are around to attract a loyal following of anglers who go for them through the ice by jigging fish bellies worked 6 to 12 inches below a Swedish Pimple, which acts as an attractor. If populations don't rebound soon, Rich Preall, the state's regional aquatic biologist, says the authorities may intervene to reestablish the species. Yellow perch ranging from 6 to 10 inches and pumpkinseeds from 6 to 8 inches are commonly targeted through the ice with flies or tiny jigs baited with grubs and perch eyes. Residual populations of naturally reproducing lake trout and brown trout, scions of former stocking programs, are also present. They go anywhere from 1 to 6 pounds and are usually caught incidentally on minnows targeting bass and pike.

Use or possession of blueback herring or alewives as bait is strictly prohibited.

Directions: Take NY 30 south from the hamlet of Paul Smiths for 5.5 miles.

Additional information: Lake Clear Public Access Site has parking for about fifty cars and a long sandy beach suitable for launching cartop craft. A barrier blocks vehicles from driving down to the lake, however, so you have to carry your craft 80 yards. Primitive camping is allowed in the state forest on the west bank.

Contact: Franklin County Tourism, and New York State Department of Environmental Conservation Region 5.

79. Lake Clear Outlet *(see map on page 138)*

Key species: Northern pike, largemouth bass, and yellow perch.

Description: Also known as Mill Pond, this 103-acre impoundment averages 3.6 feet deep and has a maximum depth of 8.5 feet. It is a weedy place, and its north shore is lightly developed with private residences.

Tips: Work drop-shot rigs baited with plastic worms and minnows in channels and weed openings.

The fishing: This warm-water fishery supports a good population of northern pike ranging between 18 and 24 inches. They hit minnows and their imitations. Largemouth bass in the 0.75- to 3-pound range take the same baits as northerns, but strike most violently at 7- to 10-inch worms bounced in front of their noses. Perch are usually 6 to 9 inches, but larger ones are present. They can be taken on worms and small minnows.

Directions: Head south out of Paul Smiths on NY 30 for about 6 miles.

Additional information: An informal canoe launch with shoulder parking for about six cars is found on the Lake Clear outlet at the NY 30 bridge. Several informal shore access sites and a canoe launch are located off Forest Home Road (head west on NY 30 for about 1 mile from the outlet stream, then turn left and travel about 0.75 mile).

Contact: New York State Department of Environmental Conservation Region 5, and Franklin County Tourism.

80. Rat Pond *(see map on page 150)*

Key species: Brown trout.

Description: This 29-acre pond averages 12 feet deep and has a maximum depth of 29 feet. The Adirondack Scenic Railroad runs along its north shore.

Tips: Apply herring oil or a similar masking scent to crankbaits.

The fishing: This pond is annually stocked with about 500 8-inch brown trout. Most are taken on dry flies by mid-June. The survivors become the low end of a

Rat Pond · Hoel Pond

Map showing Rat Pond (80) and Hoel Pond (81) in the Adirondack region, with Upper St. Regis Lake, Lake Clear, Lake Colby, Upper Saranac Lake, and Saranac Lake. Roads include Routes 86, 186, 30, 46, and 3, along with the Adirondack Scenic Railroad, Hoel Rd., and Floodwood Rd. Directions noted To Malone, To Tupper Lake, with Saranac Inn marked.

trout population notorious for ranging from 12 to 18 inches. They take worms, silver spoons, and crankbaits such as Bomber Long "A"s.

Motors are prohibited.

Directions: The pond is located about 0.5 mile due north of Saranac Inn. Take the first dirt road on the north side of NY 30, just east of the eastern terminus of CR 46, and travel north about 0.25 mile.

Additional information: There are several primitive campsites on the west and east banks.

Contact: New York State Department of Environmental Conservation Region 5, and Franklin County Tourism.

81. Hoel Pond

Key species: Lake trout, landlocked Atlantic salmon, smallmouth bass, largemouth bass, and yellow perch.

Description: Located off one of the greens of the Saranac Inn Golf Course, 25 percent of this 445-acre pond's shoreline, mainly on the west bank, is developed with private homes. Averaging 26 feet deep, its maximum depth is 80 feet and it has good levels of dissolved oxygen throughout the water column.

Tips: In spring, flatline Sutton spoons.

The fishing: Lake trout are the primary predator and range from 2 to 10 pounds. They can be caught in spring by flatlining crankbaits and spoons, and in summer by taking these baits deep with Seth Green rigs. Atlantic salmon have been stocked since 1996, and anecdotal evidence indicates that they are doing well—easily reaching 15 to 21 inches in length. A few 8-pounders have been caught. Fish for them in spring and fall by flatlining Gray Ghosts and small Rapalas at a relatively fast clip. Smallmouth bass outnumber largemouths in the main lake and take worms and crayfish. Largemouths claim the shallows along the shoreline and the northeastern bay, where they like floating crankbaits twitched on the surface. Perch range a decent 7 to 10 inches and hit worms and small lures.

Directions: From the NY 30/CR 46 intersection at Saranac Inn, head west on Floodwood Road for 0.4 mile and bear right onto Hoel Road. Turn left onto the dirt road that parallels the golf course fairway 0.2 mile later and follow it to the cartop launch.

Additional information: Primitive camping is allowed on public land near the launch site. There is no creel limit on perch.

Contacts: Franklin County Tourism, and New York State Department of Environmental Conservation Region 5.

82. Bear Pond

Key species: Brook trout.

Description: This 54-acre pond's shoreline is totally forested, and its bottom is rocky. It averages 22 feet deep and drops to a maximum depth of 60 feet.

Tips: Use a sinking line to get a Montana nymph to the bottom. Run it at least 100 feet behind the boat and troll slowly by paddling around in a figure-8 pattern.

The fishing: This pond has some wild brook trout. In addition, the state stocks several thousand brookies averaging 4 inches annually. In this ideal habitat, they range from 8 to 18 inches—some even bigger. The water is exceptionally clear and if one trout spots you, it seems they all clam up. It is essential you work the bait as far away from the boat as possible, make no unnecessary moves, and wear camo. The most productive patterns imitate burrowing insects and leeches.

Use or possession of baitfish is prohibited.

Directions: Located about 0.5 mile west of Upper St. Regis Lake (site 75). Take the portage on the southwestern end of Upper St. Regis Lake for a couple of hundred yards to Bog Pond. Paddle to the west side of Bog Pond and take the portage southwest for about 150 yards to Bear Pond.

Additional information: Primitive camping is allowed in the state forest on the west bank.

Contact: New York State Department of Environmental Conservation Region 5.

83. Little Long Pond (east)

Key species: Brook trout, rainbow trout, and splake.

Description: The larger of the St. Regis Canoe Area's two Little Long Ponds, this body of water covers 82 acres, averages 19 feet deep, and has a maximum depth of 60 feet.

Tips: Cast small minnow-imitating crankbaits around the islands at dusk.

The fishing: This pond is managed as a cold-water fishery. Extensive stocking and good habitat make it one of the St. Regis Canoe Area's top producers of large trout. Annually, the state stocks about 1,200 fingerling brook trout averaging 4.5 inches. Those that survive the drop from the airplane end up ranging from 8 to 12 inches. They'll hit worms and flies. Roughly 1,000 rainbow trout averaging 9 inches are also stocked by airplane each year. They end up growing to between 12 and 16 inches and provide good sport all summer long on dry flies and in-line spinners. Several hundred 10-inch splake are thrown into the mix annually. They end up 2 to 4 pounds and are targeted with streamers trolled deep, 8 inches or so behind attractors.

Use or possession of baitfish is prohibited.

Directions: Take the 0.25-mile portage on the south end of Bear Pond (site 82).

St. Regis Canoe Area

Additional information: There are a couple of primitive campsites at the portages on the north and south end of the pond. Motors are prohibited.

Contact: New York State Department of Environmental Conservation Region 5.

84. Green Pond (St. Regis Canoe Area) *(see map on page 153)*

Key species: Brook trout.

Description: This 22-acre pond averages 18 feet deep and has a maximum depth of 30 feet. Completely surrounded by a forest pretty evenly mixed with hardwoods and evergreens, its floor is 50 percent sand and 40 percent pebbles and rock.

Tips: Cast small spinners and spoons over and along the northeastern shoal.

The fishing: This pond is a decent cold-water fishery. It has a good population of naturally reproducing brook trout averaging 8 inches. Fish for them with worms or by drifting wet flies such as March Browns. Use or possession of baitfish is prohibited.

Directions: Located directly south of Little Long Pond (east—site 83). Get there by taking the 0.25-mile portage on Little Long Pond's south end.

Additional information: There is a primitive campsite on the beach at the portage from Little Long Pond, and another on the south side, at the portage to Little Clear Pond. Motors are prohibited.

Contact: New York State Department of Environmental Conservation Region 5.

85. St. Regis Pond *(see map on page 153)*

Key species: Brook trout, lake trout, and splake.

Description: The largest of the ponds along the highly popular Seven Carries Route of the St. Regis Canoe Area, this 401-acre body of water averages 15 feet deep and has a maximum depth of 31 feet. Its wonderfully irregular shoreline is wooded; it has several islands.

Tips: Deep-troll Muddler Minnows on a sinking line.

The fishing: This pond is managed as a diverse cold-water fishery. The state annually stocks a couple of thousand splake averaging 10 inches. They find the pickings good and easily grow to 20 inches; 25-inchers have been reported. They orient toward bottom and will take a large streamer. Brook trout occur naturally and range from 6 to 12 inches. They'll take a worm early in the season and flies in late May and June. Lake trout range from 12 to 25 inches. They will take a spoon or scented bait such as D.O.A.'s TerrorEyz minnow jigged on bottom in deep water.

The minimum length for lake trout is 15 inches. Use or possession of baitfish is prohibited.

Directions: Located 0.25 mile west of Green Pond (site 84) via portage.

Additional comments: The pond has several beach campsites, including one on each of its two largest islands. Motors are prohibited.

Contact: New York State Department of Environmental Conservation Region 5.

86. Ochre Pond *(see map on page 153)*

Key species: Brook trout and lake trout.

Description: This 22-acre pond is completely surrounded by wild forest, averages 18 feet deep, and has a maximum depth of 52 feet.

Tips: Work a beadhead Woolly Bugger slowly on bottom with a sinking line.

The fishing: This lovely pond is managed for brook trout. The state stocks about 800 annually that average 4.5 inches. A survey conducted in July 2001 found that the pond's average speckled trout is a whopping 12 inches, with a few reaching 16 inches. There aren't many and they are supersavvy, but they will respond to a properly presented wet fly or streamer. Lake trout typically range from too small to 23 inches. Keepers are hard to come by. Most are taken after ice-out on spoons cast near shore. Come summer, a few are taken on streamers such as Gray Ghosts and Black Nose Dace tied about a foot behind a wobbler or similar attractor and trolled deep at paddling speed.

The use or possession of baitfish is prohibited.

Directions: Head west for 0.3 mile on the northernmost portage, on the west end of St. Regis Pond (site 85).

Additional information: A campsite is located on the east shore, several hundred feet north of the portage to St. Regis Pond. No motors are allowed.

Contact: New York State Department of Environmental Conservation Region 5.

87. Fish Pond *(see map on page 153)*

Key species: Brook trout and lake trout.

Description: This 116-acre pond averages 23 feet deep and has a maximum depth of 50 feet. Underwater springs keep it cool. Its outlet feeds Little Fish Pond.

Tips: Use Black Nose Dace or Black Ghost streamers just after ice-out.

The fishing: This pond's natural brookies average 8 inches, and lakers average 17 inches. Recent studies showed the lake trout doing better than the brookies—possibly because they were feeding on the brookies. This caused the state to discontinue stocking brook trout. The best time to fish is the first two weeks after ice-out. Both species respond to streamers stripped slowly and jerked periodically to imitate the erratic behavior of a fleeing baitfish. Spinners and crankbaits treated with fish scent also work in the early season. As summer comes around, pickings get slim. Still, some lakers can be coaxed out of hiding on spoons jigged in deep water.

The minimum length for lake trout is 15 inches. Use or possession of baitfish is prohibited.

Directions: Take the portage on Ochre Pond's (site 86) northwestern end for about 0.75 mile (you'll pass tiny Mud Pond).

Additional information: Camping is allowed in the lean-to on the north shore and the beach campsites along the south shore. Motors are prohibited.

Contact: New York Department of Environmental Conservation Region 5.

88. Little Fish Pond *(see map on page 153)*

Key species: Brook trout and lake trout.

Description: This 24-acre pond averages 14 feet deep and has a maximum depth of 30 feet.

Tips: Cast silver spoons after ice-out.

The fishing: This pond has a few brook trout. They average 9 inches and are usually caught on worms early in the season. Lake trout are much more plentiful and reach up to 23 inches. Early in the season they can be caught near shore on spinners and spoons. Come summer, they go deep, where they will take spoons and scented, soft plastic minnows jigged on bottom.

The minimum length for lake trout is only 15 inches. Possession or use of baitfish is prohibited.

Directions: Head southwest for about 150 yards on the portage running along Fish Pond's (site 87) outlet (northwestern corner).

Additional information: A primitive campsite is off the portage from Fish Pond. Motors are prohibited.

Contact: New York State Department of Environmental Conservation Region 5.

89. Little Long Pond (west) *(see map on page 153)*

Key species: Brook trout.

Description: This pristine, 40-acre pond's extremely clear water averages 19 feet deep and has a maximum depth of 41 feet.

Tips: Move carefully and wear camouflage.

The fishing: This pond's water ranks among the clearest in the Adirondacks. Living in such lucid environs makes the fish superspooky. If one spots you and panics, every trout in the drink takes cover and clams up. Indeed, during one survey, sloppy state

Canoe fishing in the Adirondacks.

personnel spooked the pond and only two brookies averaging 3.7 inches were netted. In a later survey, the experts were a little more careful and netted three brookies averaging 15 inches. Rich Preall, a biologist for the state, says the more flattering survey is the accurate one. The state stocks about 1,000 brook trout annually averaging 4.5 inches. They grow to range anywhere from 6 to 20 inches. The 20-inchers are few but they're definitely there and will drive you crazy by rushing your dry fly, getting a look at it, then simply swimming away. Some are taken by anglers running Woolly Buggers, on sinking lines, 100-something feet behind the canoe and trolling in a figure-8 pattern.

Use or possession of baitfish is prohibited.

Directions: Due south of Little Fish Pond (site 88), via either of the two 150-yard portages.

Additional information: There is a campsite on the east shore. Motors are prohibited.

Contact: New York State Department of Environmental Conservation Region 5.

90. Lydia Pond *(see map on page 153)*

Key species: Brook trout.

Description: This 20-acre pond averages 21 feet deep and has a maximum depth of 38 feet.

Tips: Paddle slowly and troll a conehead Woolly Bugger.

The fishing: The state manages this pond as a brook trout fishery and dumps 700 of them, averaging 4.5 inches, out of airplanes each year. Those that hit the water and survive the plunge end up growing to range from 6 to 12 inches. They hit slowly drifted worms in spring, in-line spinners and small spoons the rest of the year.

Use or possession of baitfish is prohibited.

Directions: Portage along the channel on the northwestern tip of Little Long Pond (west—site 89) for about 100 yards.

Additional information: There is a primitive campsite on the beach, at the end of the portage from Little Long Pond. Motors are prohibited.

Contact: New York State Department of Environmental Conservation Region 5.

91. Kit Fox Pond *(see map on page 153)*

Key species: Brook trout.

Description: Covering a little less than 10 acres, this pond averages 14 feet deep and has a maximum depth of 38 feet. This is another of the clearest ponds in the mountains, and its water is borderline acidic.

Tips: Stay as invisible as possible. If you are fishing out in the middle, wear sky colors (blue hat, white T-shirt); green camouflage if you're fishing near shore.

The fishing: The state drops 500 brook trout averaging 4.5 inches into this pond from aircraft each year. The experience instills in them a healthy fear of humankind. When the place was surveyed in July 2001, all that was caught in the researcher's nets were a few fish under 12 inches. Still, state biologist Rich Preall says he's seen "some absolutely huge trout here, up to 20 inches." Use or possession of baitfish is prohibited.

Directions: Head due south for a couple of hundred yards on the portage at the southeastern tip of Little Long Pond (west—site 89).

Additional information: Motors are prohibited.

Contact: New York State Department of Environmental Conservation Region 5.

92. Nellie Pond *(see map on page 153)*

Key species: Brook trout.

Description: This 13-acre pond averages 11 feet deep and has a maximum depth of 19 feet.

Tips: Work Woolly Worms along the shore from mid-August through September.

The fishing: This water contains brood stock of native Horn Lake–strain brook trout. They average about 6 inches, with a few going more than twice that. Totally wild, these fish clam up at the slightest indication something isn't right. Present tiny dry flies gently in summer. Use or possession of baitfish is prohibited.

Directions: Take the portage on the western end of Kit Fox Pond (site 91) for about 0.25 mile.

Additional information: There are two campsites at the end of the portage from Kit Fix Pond. No motors are allowed.

Contact: New York State Department of Environmental Conservation Region 5.

93. Bessie Pond *(see map on page 153)*

Key species: Brook trout.

Description: This 16.5-acre pond averages 15 feet deep and has a maximum depth of 50 feet.

Tips: Fish maggot patterns at a dead drift.

The fishing: This pond contains brood stock of the Horn Lake strain of brook trout native to the Adirondacks. The fish range from 6 to 12 inches and will take wet flies worked at a dead drift and leech-imitating streamers trolled deep on a sinking line. Use or possession of baitfish is prohibited.

Directions: Head due south for a few hundred yards on the portage from Nellie Pond (site 92).

Additional information: A primitive campsite is located on the west side, along the portage from Nellie Pond. Motors are prohibited.

Contact: New York State Department of Environmental Conservation Region 5.

94. Clamshell Pond *(see map on page 153)*

Key species: Brook trout.

Description: This 35-acre pond averages 13 feet deep and has a maximum depth of 28 feet. A wetland clings to its southern tip.

Tips: Use terrestrial fly patterns at dawn and dusk.

The fishing: The state manages this pond for brook trout. Springs keep it at just the right temperature year-round, and the brookies average 8 inches—but 14-inchers are caught frequently. They hit worms fished close to shore in spring, and in-line spinners in summer.

Directions: Take the 0.5-mile portage at the tip of Fish Pond's (site 87) southwestern bay.

Contact: New York State Department of Environmental Conservation Region 5.

95. Grass Pond (west) *(see map on page 153)*

Key species: Brook trout.

Description: Spread over 22 acres, this pond averages 4.5 feet deep and has a maximum depth of 12 feet. It is bordered in equal measure by evergreens, shrubs, and wetland.

Tips: Use in-line spinners such as Panther Martins.

The fishing: Although it's rather shallow, springs keep this pond's temperature at ideal levels for brookies. The state annually airlifts more than 1,000 averaging 4.5 inches, and those that hit the pond eventually end up averaging 10 inches. They have a taste for worms and streamers. Use or possession of baitfish is prohibited.

Directions: Take the southern portage on the west bay of St. Regis Pond (site 85) for about 0.25 mile to the T. Head north for about 0.1 mile, then west for about 0.3 mile.

Additional information: A primitive campsite is on the beach, at the portage. Motors are prohibited.

Contact: New York State Department of Environmental Conservation Region 5.

96. Turtle Pond *(see map on page 153)*

Key species: Largemouth bass.

Description: This 68-acre pond averages 7 feet deep and has a maximum depth of 35 feet.

Tips: Fly fish among water lilies with bass bugs.

The fishing: This lake is loaded with largemouth bass ranging from 2 to 5 pounds. They hit Jitterbugs, Lazy Ikes, and Texas-rigged worms and craws. Possession or use of baitfish is prohibited.

Directions: The easiest way to get here is to go under the culvert or over the tracks at the channel connecting it to the northwestern side of Hoel Pond (site 81). Or you can head south on the mile-long portage at the southern end of Clamshell Pond (site 94).

Additional information: A short portage is necessary over the railroad culvert. A campsite is found just east of the culvert, and another one is at the tributary mouth on the north end. Motors are prohibited.

Contact: Franklin County Tourism, and New York State Department of Environmental Conservation Region 5.

97. Slang Pond *(see map on page 153)*

Key species: Largemouth bass.

Description: This 45-acre pond averages 10 feet deep and has a maximum depth of 19 feet.

Tips: Fish the large, southwestern bay for postspawn bucketmouths.

The fishing: This pond is loaded with largemouth bass that can range anywhere from 2 to 5 pounds, with larger fish possible. They find soft plastic jerkbaits irresistible. Use or possession of baitfish is prohibited.

Directions: About 100 yards up the channel on Turtle Pond's (site 96) northwestern tip.

Additional information: There is a primitive campsite on the north tip, and another one on the east point. Motors are prohibited.

Contact: Franklin County Tourism, and New York State Department of Environmental Conservation Region 5.

98. Long Pond *(see map on page 153)*

Key species: Largemouth bass and smallmouth bass.

Description: Totally surrounded by forest, this remote pond covers 338 acres, averages 12.5 feet deep, and has a maximum depth of 49 feet.

Tips: Cast C. C. Shads around shoreline structure.

The fishing: Largemouth and smallmouth bass are about equally represented. Smallmouths ranging from 12 to 16 inches occupy rocky and muddy floors in 10 to 20 feet of water, where they'll take a worm or crayfish drifted on bottom. Largemouths of up to 5 pounds claim shallower habitats near shore, especially around windfalls or emergent vegetation, where they respond well to noisy surface baits like Mann's Chug-N-Spits.
   Use or possession of baitfish is prohibited. No motors are allowed.

Directions: From the NY 30/CR 46 intersection west of Saranac Inn, head west on Floodwood Road for 5 miles and turn right at the sign. Or take the 0.25-mile portage on the west side of Slang Pond (site 97).

Additional information: This pond is about 0.25 mile from the parking area, down a developed path. Several campsites are right on the water, mainly on points. Loons like this pond, and their song fills the early evening.

Contact: New York State Department of Environmental Conservation Region 5.

A wilderness guide holds a typical Long Pond bucketmouth.

99. Mountain Pond *(see map on page 153)*

Key species: Brook trout and bullhead.

Description: Nestled in deep woods, this 12-acre pond feeds Long Pond. It averages 10 feet deep, and its maximum depth is 22 feet.

Tips: Small Panther Martin spinners produce for a couple of weeks after ice-out.

The fishing: This pond is managed as a brook trout fishery. Annually, the state stocks an average of 450 by dropping them out of an airplane. Those that survive the fall have a good chance of making it to 10 inches. Many fish up to 14 inches are present. Spinners and small plugs produce best in spring. Recently bullheads have been appearing. As their number and size increase, the brook trout population may decrease. Still-fish for these whiskered delicacies with worms on bottom. Use or possession of baitfish is prohibited.

Directions: Take the 0.25-mile portage at the north end of Long Pond's (site 98) middle (north-central) bay.

Additional information: A primitive campsite is found on the south side, just off the portage trail. A path runs along most of the pond, making shore fishing easy. In addition, it provides access to the surrounding woods in the event—which is likely—that the pond's lone campsite is occupied. Motors are prohibited

Contact: New York State Department of Environmental Conservation Region 5.

100. Pink Pond *(see map on page 153)*

Key species: Largemouth bass.

Description: Covering 13 acres, this pond averages 6 feet deep and has a maximum depth of 14 feet.

Tips: Use buzzbaits on still days.

The fishing: Largemouth bass run from 8 to 14 inches. Some get bigger. They hit crankbaits, bass bugs, and 4- and 7-inch worms, worked over the surface or on Texas rigs. Use or possession of baitfish is prohibited.

Directions: About 0.25 mile due north via the channel on Long Pond's (site 98) northwestern end.

Additional information: The area's beavers keep busy, so be prepared to lift your canoe over dams. Motors are prohibited.

Contact: New York State Department of Environmental Conservation Region 5.

Ponds Outside the St. Regis Canoe Area

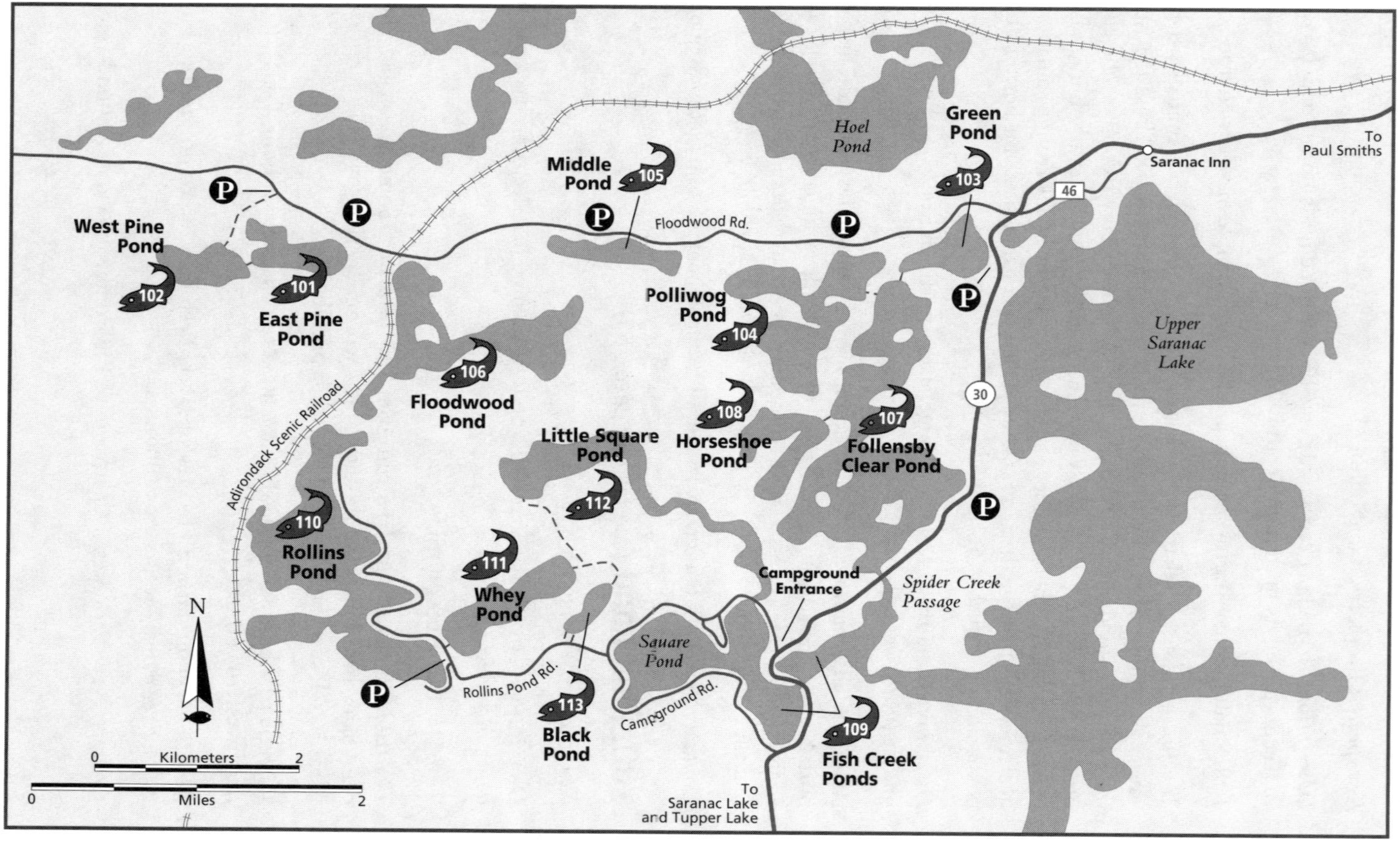

101. East Pine Pond

Key species: Largemouth bass.

Description: Nestled in deep forest, this 60.5-acre pond averages about 15 feet deep and has a maximum depth of 33 feet. Levels of dissolved oxygen are low below 20 feet.

Tips: Work deep-diving crankbaits such as C. C. Shads along breaklines.

The fishing: This pond has a good population of largemouth bass averaging 14 inches, a feisty size that seem to spend as much time in the air as in the water during their bid to shake a hook. The shallow northern bay contains the bulk of the pond's aquatic vegetation and is a great spot for working floating lures such as ¼-ounce Hula Poppers on fly-fishing equipment and Mann's Loudmouth Chug-N-Spits on spinning tackle. Possession or use of baitfish is prohibited.

Directions: On Floodwood Road, 0.5 mile west of Floodwood Pond (site 106).

Additional information: Several primitive campsites are located at the cartop boat launch off Floodwood Road.

Contact: New York State Department of Environmental Conservation Region 5.

102. West Pine Pond

Key species: Brook trout, lake trout, rainbow trout, and kokanee salmon.

Description: Primarily spring fed, this 62.5-acre pond averages 18 feet deep and has a maximum depth of 38 feet. A steep esker separates it from East Pine Pond.

Tips: Drift near shore with free-floating worms.

The fishing: This pond is best known for wild brook trout in the 4- to 6-inch range. The state stocks several hundred rainbows averaging 9 inches annually, and they easily reach 14 inches. A series of stocking mistakes added lake trout and kokanee salmon. Surprisingly, both are doing well. Indeed, the kokanees and lake trout maintain their numbers through natural reproduction. Kokanees range from 6 to 12 inches and take small worms slowly trolled behind attractors. Lake trout range from a whopping 6 to 10 pounds and take spoons jigged on bottom. The minimum size for lakers is 15 inches. Use or possession of baitfish is prohibited.

This pond was first reclaimed with rotenone, a chemical that kills all the fish, in 1975, and rainbow trout and brook trout were stocked. Since then, stocking mistakes by the state and individuals emptying their bait buckets have resulted in the introduction of several non-native species, including rainbow smelt. Now that the Boy Scout camp is closed and access requires a great degree of effort, the state is considering reclaiming the pond again and managing it as a rainbow and brook trout fishery.

One of the many brook trout ponds in the Adirondacks.

Directions: From the NY 30/CR 46 intersection west of the hamlet of Saranac Inn, head west on Floodwood Road for about 4.8 miles to the dirt road on the left. Park and hike down the trail for about 0.5 mile. You can also get there from East Pine Pond (site 101), via the 150-yard portage from the southwest corner.

Additional information: There is a beach campsite at the canoe launch on the north end of the lake. No motors are allowed.

Contact: New York State Department of Environmental Conservation Region 5.

103. Green Pond (see map on page 164)

Key species: Brown trout and splake.

Description: Located across the street from a golf course, this pond's shoreline is partially developed with summer cottages. Spread over 63 acres, it averages about 40 feet deep and has a maximum depth of 69 feet.

Tips: Work the edges of the shoal in the middle.

The fishing: About 150 splake averaging 6 inches are stocked each year. Many make it to 3 pounds, and some reach 8. The technique favored by locals is to bait a Lake Clear Wobbler with a worm gob and troll it slowly on bottom in deep water. Recently the state has also been annually stocking 150 brown trout averaging 14 inches. Although they're dumb upon release, it only takes one brush with a hook point to enlighten them to the ways of the real world; they clam up quick. Many are reaching 5 pounds plus and are being seduced to suck in the hooks of crankbaits such as Rapala Husky Jerks.

Use or possession of baitfish is prohibited.

Directions: Take the 0.25-mile portage from the north tip of Follensby Clear Pond (site 107).

Additional information: A fishing access site with a beach launch and parking for about ten cars is found on NY 30, a few hundred yards from its intersection with CR 46, west of Saranac Inn.

Contact: New York State Department of Environmental Conservation Region 5.

104. Polliwog Pond *(see map on page 164)*

Key species: Kokanee salmon and brown trout.

Description: This 185-acre pond comes about as close to wilderness as you can get alongside an improved dirt road. Pristine and cool, it averages 33 feet deep and drops to a maximum depth of 72 feet.

Tips: Chum a spot with oatmeal, then flatline slowly through it with a small garden worm a foot behind a wobbler.

The fishing: The state maintains a kokanee salmon presence by stocking 20,000-something fry annually. Growing to between 8 and 10 inches, primarily by feeding on plankton, they have extremely delicate mouths. They will take a small worm occasionally, and anglers avoid ripping the hook out of their mouth by keeping it tiny (size 14 to 20) and tying a rubber band on to the line as a shock absorber. The state also annually stocks about 2,300 brown trout averaging 8 inches, with a couple of hundred mixed in that stretch the tape to more than 14 inches. They hit streamers, crankbaits, and worms.

Use or possession of baitfish is prohibited. Trout and salmon season is year-round; the daily limit is five trout and ten salmon of any size.

Directions: Take Floodwood Road for 1.1 miles from its intersection with CR 46/NY 30, west of Saranac Inn.

Additional information: There are two cartop boat launches, each with several primitive campsites. Numerous campsites line the shore.

Contact: Franklin County Tourism, and New York State Department of Environmental Conservation Region 5.

105. Middle Pond (see map on page 164)

Key species: Bullhead, largemouth bass, northern pike, yellow perch, and panfish.

Description: This 60-acre pond averages 5 feet deep and has a maximum depth of 11 feet. Circled by lily pads and carpeted with weeds, it is ideal warm-water habitat.

Tips: Still-fish worms on bottom for monster brown bullheads.

The fishing: Gallon for gallon, this pond harbors more bullheads stretching beyond 12 inches than most lakes a hundred times its size. Ranging from 11 to 14 inches, these tasty bottom dwellers are often sought in spring by local family groups teaching kids the pleasures of catching bullhead dinners. Fly fishers will find exciting action at the edges of lily pads with bass bugs. Cast into the middle of the bed and hop the offering from pad to pad to the edge of the water, and stop. Often this draws bass out of their cover to see what's bouncing on the roof. They sit impatiently, on the edge, waiting. Sometimes they will nose right up to the pad and tip it, hoping to slide the critter off. Twitch the rod gently to send the bug into the water and drive the bucketmouth to erupt through the surface like a submarine-based cruise missile. Northerns ranging from 18 to 22 inches are plentiful. They like buzzbaits and spinnerbaits. Perch from 6 to 8 inches and pumpkinseeds from 5 to 7 inches are plentiful and take worms suspended below tiny, marble-sized bobbers. Avoid using bobbers the size of softballs—they're too big for panfish to pull down. Use or possession of alewives or blueback herring as bait is prohibited.

Directions: On Floodwood Road, 1 mile west of Pollywog Pond's (site 104) westernmost launch.

Additional information: A beach launch for canoes with parking for about five cars, and several no-fee, primitive camping sites are located off the shoulder of Floodwood Road. Camp only in numbered sites.

Contact: New York State Department of Environmental Conservation Region 5.

106. Floodwood Pond (see map on page 164)

Key species: Northern pike, largemouth bass, smallmouth bass, and panfish.

Description: This 222-acre pond has several private dwellings along its shore. Easy access makes it one of the most popular canoeing ponds in the Saranac Lakes Wild Forest. Averaging 17 feet deep, it has a maximum depth of 36 feet.

Tips: Work jointed MirrOlures parallel to drop-offs.

The fishing: This pond is dynamite warm-water habitat. Northern pike range between 4 and 10 pounds and seem particularly disposed to violently attacking any rattling crankbait violating the pond's silence. Largemouth bass ranging from 1 to 4 pounds are equally prejudiced against Rat-L-Traps but seem to have an identical aversion for surface rattling baits like MirrOlure's Top Dog Juniors. Smallmouth bass go from 0.75 to 2 pounds and like deep-running baits such as MirrOlure's Shad Rattlers. Yellow perch up to 12 inches, pumpkinseeds up to 8 inches, and brown bullheads up to 10 inches are plentiful, and natives target them in spring with worms.

No motors are allowed. Possession or use of baitfish is prohibited.

Directions: On Floodwood Road, 0.75 mile west of Middle Pond (site 105).

Additional information: There are several numbered campsites on the pond's shore and its largest island. Beach camping is permitted in designated sites only. A canoe launch on the shoulder of Floodwood Road has parking for about ten cars.

Contact: New York State Department of Environmental Conservation Region 5.

107. Follensby Clear Pond (see map on page 164)

Key species: Northern pike, largemouth bass, smallmouth bass, landlocked Atlantic salmon, rainbow smelt, and panfish.

Description: Covering 491 acres, totally surrounded by state forest, this pond has several islands and numerous shoals, points, and bays. It averages about 21 feet deep and has a maximum depth of 60 feet. The shoreline is totally undeveloped except for several primitive campsites.

Tips: Work the weeds on the southeastern end of the pond for bucketmouths.

The fishing: Northern pike range from 22 to 36 inches. The large numbers of big fish send small northerns into deep cover, so you hardly ever catch a "pin-pike." They almost always react with extreme prejudice whenever a spinnerbait or rattling crankbait enters their space. Largemouth bass go from 12 to 16 inches and also hit spinnerbaits. Smallmouths range from 1 to 2 pounds and like deeper habitat. They hang out in the channels between the islands and hit minnows and crayfish. Landlocked salmon from 15 to 21 inches can be taken on 2- to 3-inch streamers and crankbaits like MirrOlure's Lipped 52Ms and original Rapalas worked over the deep water due west of the access site. Smelt averaging 8 inches are popularly targeted in this same deep area by ice anglers jigging smelt bellies. Panfish include yellow perch up to 10 inches, pumpkinseeds up to 8 inches, and brown bullheads up to 10 inches. They are plentiful and can be taken on worms.

Use or possession of alewives or blueback herring as bait is prohibited.

Directions: From the NY 30/CR 46 intersection west of the hamlet of Saranac Inn, head south on NY 30 for 1.7 miles to the fishing access site. Canoeists can access the pond from the west bank of Upper Saranac Lake (site 114) by paddling up Fish Creek Bay, hugging the east shore of Fish Creek Pond, and taking Spider Creek Passage.

Two fishers showing off a northern pike caught in the Adirondacks.

Additional information: The access site has a beach launch suitable for small trailered craft and parking for about seven rigs. Several campsites punctuate the shoreline and islands.

Contact: New York State Department of Environmental Conservation Region 5.

108. Horseshoe Pond *(see map on page 164)*

Key species: Brook trout, rainbow trout, and brown trout.

Description: Set entirely on forested state land, this 82-acre V-shaped pond averages 14 feet deep and has a maximum depth of 26 feet.

Tips: Shore fish right after ice-out.

The fishing: State aquatic biologist Rich Preall says this pond was reclaimed several times in the past century by killing all the fish with rotenone. It is managed as a brook trout fishery and boasts a naturally reproducing population. Still, the state annually stocks about 4,000 brookies averaging 4 inches. They grow to 8 to 15 inches, and 20-inch trophies are possible. Roughly 1,000 rainbows averaging 9 inches are also stocked annually, and many reach 12 to 16 inches. Brown trout were introduced accidentally a few years ago and the residual population, though not large, seems to be doing well on its own, with browns of better than 16 inches caught each year. Each species hits worms, flies, and in-line spinners such as Panther Martins and Rooster Tails.

    Use or possession of baitfish is prohibited.

Directions: Located a few hundred yards west of Follensby Clear Pond (site 107), via the portage at the end of the bay, midway down the lake. Both arms of Horseshoe Pond can be reached overland by taking the first trails striking north—at 0.5 and 0.75 mile, respectively—from the Fish Creek Public Campground (see site 109).

Additional information: The pond has several campsites on its east bank.

Contact: New York State Department of Environmental Conservation Region 5.

109. Fish Creek Ponds *(see map on page 164)*

Key species: Northern pike, smallmouth bass, largemouth bass, and panfish.

Description: These three ponds cover a combined total of 355 acres. The eastern two, separated by the NY 30 culvert, average 12 feet deep and drop to a maximum of 20 feet. The westernmost, Square Pond, is included in the group because it is connected by a wide neck and is surrounded by the Fish Creek Pond Public Campground. Square Pond averages 30 feet deep and has a maximum depth of 55 feet.

Tips: Work 3-inch scented grubs, on drop-shot rigs, along drop-offs.

The fishing: Relatively shallow, these ponds are ideal warm-water habitat. Northern pike range from 20 to 30 inches, and largemouth bass from 12 to 16 inches. Both can be found virtually anywhere and provide consistent action to anglers throwing rattling crankbaits and jerkbaits. Bronzebacks from 10 to 14 inches are also present, and the majority seem to migrate to Square Pond's drop-offs as the weather warms up. Vertical-jig rattling bladebaits such as Heddon's Sonar Flash. Yellow perch up to 12 inches and pumpkinseeds up to 8 inches are plentiful and hit worms.

In 2001 an experimental stocking of 200 7-inch landlocked Atlantic salmon took place in Square Pond, and the same number will be stocked annually until 2006. If they take, they should be keeper sized (15 inches) by 2003. Troll streamers and minnow-imitating crankbaits over deep water.

Directions: Head west out of Saranac village on NY 3 south for about 13 miles, then head north on NY 30 for about 4 miles to Fish Creek Ponds Public Campground.

Additional information: The Fish Creek Public Campground skirts the entire shoreline. This fee area offers 355 no-frill sites, mostly on the beach, along with canoe and boat rentals, coin-operated showers, potable water, a dumping station, picnic areas, a basketball court, playing fields, a swimming beach, and a wood truck that comes around in the evening. A day-use fee is charged when the campground is open, mid-April through mid-November.

Contact: New York State Department of Environmental Conservation Region 5.

110. Rollins Pond *(see map on page 164)*

Key species: Lake trout, landlocked salmon, northern pike, smallmouth bass, brown bullhead, and pumpkinseed.

Description: Covering approximately 442 acres, this pond averages 30 feet deep and has a maximum depth of 77 feet. Its west bank is completely forested.

Tips: Pitch slugs into snags.

The fishing: Lake trout averaging about 3 pounds thrive in the pond's deep holes. Jig scented, soft plastic minnows such as D.O.A. TerrorEyz on bottom. The state annually stocks several hundred landlocked Atlantic salmon. There aren't many, but those that are caught average 15 inches and are mostly taken on small minnow crankbaits such as Junior ThunderSticks and silver spoons. This pond is notorious for northern pike ranging from 30 to 40 inches. They respond to minnows, spinnerbaits, and spoons. Smallmouths in the 1- to 2-pound range are abundant and take deep-diving crankbaits such as Poe's Super Cedars. Brown bullheads reach 14 inches; pumpkinseeds range from 5 to 7 inches. Both take worms.

Motorboats of more than 25 horsepower are prohibited.

Directions: Head west out of Saranac village on NY 3 south for about 13 miles, then go north on NY 30 for about 4 miles to the Fish Creek Ponds Public Campground. Rollins Pond Campground borders the west side of Fish Creek Public Campground (see site 109).

Additional information: Rollins Pond Public Campground lines the entire east shore. This fee area offers 287 campsites suitable for everything from pup tents to RVs 40 feet long, coin-operated showers, a pumping station, canoe and rowboat rentals, and a paved boat launch with parking for ten rigs. A day-use fee is charged when the campground is open, mid-May through Labor Day.

Rollins Pond and Fish Creek Public Campgrounds honor each other's day-use tickets. Fish Creek charges a slightly higher fee, however, because it has a swimming beach. If all you want to do is fish, tell the attendant at the Fish Creek Campground gate that you're heading to Rollins Pond; you'll be allowed to go through to pay the cheaper rate up ahead.

Contact: New York State Department of Environmental Conservation Region 5.

111. Whey Pond *(see map on page 164)*

Key species: Brook trout and rainbow trout.

Description: This pond covers 108 acres, averages about 12 feet deep, and has a maximum depth of 20 feet. Its shoreline is completely undeveloped.

Tips: Cast terrestrial patterns at dusk.

The fishing: Easy access and a naturally reproducing population of Windfall-strain brook trout—one of the state's indigenous strains—make this one of the most popular trout ponds in the Adirondack Park. The state draws on this population for brood stock, and the fish are totally protected. They take streamers and wet flies at dusk. The state annually stocks about 1,100 9-inch rainbow trout, and they end up ranging from 12 to 18 inches. They like green streamers.

Fishing is restricted to artificial lures only. *All brook trout must be released.* The minimum length for rainbows is 12 inches, and the daily limit is three. Only electric motors are allowed.

Directions: Nestled in the southeastern corner of Rollins Pond Public Campground (see site 110), a 100-foot-long access trail, directly across the street from the campground's boat launch, leads to the pond.

Additional information: From Memorial Day to Labor Day, a day-use fee is charged to noncampers. The cost is cheaper at Rollins Pond because there's no swimming beach. Just tell the attendant at the Fish Creek Ponds gate you'll pay at Rollins Pond Campground, and you'll be allowed to go through.

Contact: New York State Department of Environmental Conservation Region 5.

112. Little Square Pond (see map on page 164)

Key species: Smallmouth bass, largemouth bass, and northern pike.

Description: This 117-acre pond averages 10 feet deep and has a maximum depth of 29 feet.

Tips: Cast buzzbaits on quiet evenings.

The fishing: This warm-water fishery has good populations of smallmouth and largemouth bass ranging from 10 to 16 inches. As in many Adirondack ponds, largemouths are becoming far more numerous, causing some to speculate that this is a sign of global warming. Both species can be taken on Texas- and Carolina-rigged worms. Northerns in the 22- to 32-inch range are also present. They hit large minnows and spinnerbaits. Possession or use of blueback herring or alewives as bait is prohibited.

Directions: Due north of Square Pond (see site 109). Paddle up Fish Creek about 1 mile from the western Fish Creek Pond.

Contact: New York State Department of Environmental Conservation Region 5.

113. Black Pond (see map on page 164)

Key species: Brook trout and rainbow trout.

Description: Completely surrounded by wild forest and a tiny wetland, this 20-acre pond averages 20 feet deep and has a maximum depth of 44 feet.

Tips: Suspend worms below bubble bobbers.

The fishing: This small pond is annually stocked with about 800 brook trout ranging from 2 to 3.5 inches. They grow quickly to between 5 and 7 inches and hit worms. In addition, the state annually stocks 400 rainbows averaging 9 inches. They grow to average about 11 inches and hit spinners and perch-colored spoons. Use or possession of baitfish is prohibited.

Directions: Located about 0.25 mile east of Whey Pond (site 111). Two footpaths lead there from the Rollins Pond Road. They strike off into the bush a few hundred feet north of the shower building just beyond the intersection on the west side of Square Pond.

Additional information: This pond is very susceptible to acid rain and is limed regularly.

Contact: New York State Department of Environmental Conservation Region 5.

114. Upper Saranac Lake *(see map on page 176)*

Key species: Lake trout, brown trout, rainbow trout, northern pike, smallmouth bass, largemouth bass, rainbow smelt, and yellow perch.

Description: This 4,776-acre lake averages about 15 feet deep and has a maximum depth of 103 feet. Although only about 7 miles long, its shoreline is highly irregular; if you stretched it out, it would measure more than 20 miles. Kick in the lake's islands and you get a couple more miles of beach.

Tips: Cast small streamers near shore in spring for trout and yellow perch.

The fishing: Lake trout averaging 8 pounds are abundant and can be taken on spoons trolled deep on Seth Green and Christmas tree rigs. Rainbows range from 10 to 18 inches and are mostly taken by fishing worms on bottom, or by matching summer hatches at dusk. Brown trout of up to 10 pounds are caught each year, many on minnows and worms fished near shore in spring, or on minnow-imitating crankbaits trolled 5 to 20 feet deep in summer. Smelt ranging from 4 to 8 inches are taken by jigging strips of smelt belly through the ice. Several islands and the irregular shoreline's bays and shallow flats conspire to make this lake northern pike and smallmouth bass friendly. Pike range from 22 to 30 inches and respond best to large minnows, Daredevles, and chartreuse spinnerbaits. Smallmouth bass average about 1.5 pounds and take live bait, Mister Twister Exude grubs, Carolina-rigged 4-inch finesse worms, and spinnerbaits. Largemouth bass somehow found their way into the system and are becoming increasingly common. They range from 2 to 4 pounds and take surface poppers and walking lures.

Trout season runs from April 1 to October 15. The minimum length for lake trout is 23 inches. Tip-ups are prohibited.

Directions: Take NY 3/NY 30 east out of the hamlet of Tupper Lake for about 6 miles. When the highways separate, NY 30 heads north and parallels the lake's west bank.

Additional information: A dam midway down its outlet (the Saranac River—site 115) blocks boats from accessing this lake from Middle Saranac Lake (site 116). A state boat launch with a double-wide paved ramp and parking for fifty rigs is found on CR 46, in the north-shore hamlet of Saranac Inn. Bank fishing is prohibited at the launch site.

Contact: Saranac Lake Area Chamber of Commerce, and the New York State Department of Environmental Conservation Region 5.

114A. Indian Carry Fishing Access Site

Description: This site has a beach launch for cartop craft and parking for fifteen cars.

Saranac Lakes Chain

Union Falls Pond

.123

Hough Brook

Franklin Falls
Pond

.122

48

P

18

3

Bloomingdale

Saranac River

Lake Placid

Lake Flower

.121

Saranac Lake Village

86

Lake Placid

Oseetah Lake

.119

Kiwassa Lake

.120

State Bridge
Fishing Access Site

Lake Colby

.124

86

Little Colby Pond

.125

186

Forest Home Rd.

18

Lower Saranac Lake

.118

Middle Saranac Lake

.116

Weller Pond

.117

Upper Saranac Lake

.114

116A

114A

Paul Smiths

30

Lake Clear

Upper St. Regis Lake

30

Saranac Inn

Floodwood Rd.

3

To Tupper Lake

30

N

Kilometers

Miles

0   5

0   5

Directions: Head west on NY 3 from Saranac Lake village for about 10 miles to the sign on Old Dock Road.

115. Saranac River *(see map on page 178)*

Key species: Northern pike, smallmouth bass, largemouth bass, walleye, brown trout, rainbow trout, landlocked salmon, yellow perch, and panfish.

Description: Spawned as the outlet of Upper Saranac Lake (site 114), this river flows northeast for about 60 miles to its mouth in Lake Champlain at Plattsburgh. Along the way, it feeds and drains several lakes and ponds and picks up its North Branch in Clayburg.

Tips: Jig salted tubes in rapids, in deep holes, and along outcrops, deadfalls, and undercut banks for smallmouths, walleyes, and northern pike.

The fishing: This river's greatest predator is the northern pike. They range from 22 inches all the way to 40-something inches. True to their reputation, they'll hit anything that moves, but locals specifically target them with large minnows in slow-moving pools, or tandem streamers and large bucktail spinners ripped rapidly across fast water. Smallmouth bass between 10 and 16 inches reign in deep channels and in the rapids at the heads and tails of pools, where they can be taken on live bait and soft plastic tubes, grubs, and jerkbaits. Probe the lily pads, weed edges at drop-offs, and slop lines where marsh and swamp meet the river with jig-'n'-pigs and jig-'n'-craws for bucketmouths ranging from 1 to 3 pounds. Walleyes ranging from 15 to 25 inches can be taken in deep channels, especially downstream of the Franklin Falls Dam, with bucktail jigs. Yellow perch hang out in slow sections of the river and take small minnows and lures. Panfish include pumpkinseeds between 6 to 8 inches and bullheads between 8 and 14. Both take worms.

Each year, the state stocks about 13,000 brown trout averaging 9 inches, with several hundred 14-inchers thrown in to make things interesting. Many overwinter, and numerous others enter the river from tributaries, making this one of the top brown trout streams in the Adirondacks. Also, a lot of Lake Champlain browns ranging from 16 to 20 inches run the lower river near the mouth in fall and spring and are primarily targeted by purists casting salmon flies, and by meat anglers floating worms off the bridges near the mouth. In addition, tens of thousands of landlocked salmon and thousands of rainbow trout are stocked annually into the river near its mouth in Plattsburgh. Landlocked salmon spend most of their time in Lake Champlain but stage two major runs each year. The largest numbers appear April through mid-May and average 18 inches. Autumn sees fewer fish, but they are bigger—up to 8 pounds. They seem hungriest in spring, but hit worms, lures, and streamers during both runs. While some rainbows in the 1- to 3-pound class run the river from autumn through spring, and take worms and egg sacs, most seem to gravitate to Vermont's streams.

The lower portion of the river, to the first barrier impassable by fish, has its own fishing regulations, including terminal-tackle restrictions and fishing hours, all

Saranac River: Union Falls Pond to Lake Champlain

of which are listed in the Special Lake Champlain Regulations section of the *New York State Department of Environmental Conservation Fishing Regulations Guide.*

In addition to the lower river, several upstream sections have special regulations. In the hamlet of Saranac Lake, trout season is open year-round from the Pine Street Bridge upstream to the Lake Flower Dam; access is easy along the Riverwalk. Fishing is prohibited from March 1 through May 15 from Hough Brook at Union Falls Flow upstream to Franklin Falls Flow Dam, to protect spawning walleyes. From the Kents Falls Dam upstream to Union Falls Dam, northern pike and black bass can be taken in any size and number from April 1 through November. Trout season is open year-round in the stretch from the Imperial Dam upstream to Kents Falls Dam; the minimum size is 12 inches.

Directions: NY 3 parallels much of the river, and informal pull-offs exist all along the shoulder.

Additional information: A fish ladder is on the drawing boards for the Imperial Dam in Plattsburgh. Upon completion, it'll extend the distance that trout and landlocked salmon can run up the river. Check the special regulations for Lake Champlain and Clinton County (Region 5) in the *New York State Department of Environmental Conservation Fishing Regulations Guide* for further information.

Contact: Saranac Lake Area Chamber of Commerce, Plattsburgh–North Country Chamber of Commerce, and New York State Department of Environmental Conservation Region 5.

115A. Fishing Access

Description: This site has parking for five cars.

Directions: Head east out of Saranac Lake village on NY 3 for 24 miles to Clayburg. Turn south onto CR 1 (Silver Lake Road).

115B. Fishing Access

Description: This site has parking for five cars.

Directions: About 1 mile south of site 115A.

115C. Fishing Access

Description: This site has parking for five cars.

Directions: About 1 mile south of site 115B.

115D. Fishing Access

Description: This site has parking for five cars.

Directions: Head east out of Clayburg on NY 3 for about 2.5 miles to Redford, then turn south onto Cane Road.

115E. Parking *(see map on page 178)*

Description: The State University of New York fieldhouse parking lot is huge and close to some of the best seasonal salmon and trout action on the river.

Directions: Off Ruger Street, Plattsburgh.

115F. Fishing Access *(see map on page 178)*

Description: This site has a handicapped fishing platform and shoulder parking for about five cars.

Directions: At the Mcdonough Monument, off City Hall Place, Plattsburgh.

115G. Fishing Access *(see map on page 178)*

Description: This site at the mouth of the river has a hard-surface ramp and parking for twenty cars. It's popular with surf anglers.

Directions: On Green Street (off US 9/Bridge Street), Plattsburgh.

116. Middle Saranac Lake *(see map on page 176)*

Key species: Northern pike, smallmouth bass, and yellow perch.

Description: Spread over 1,393 acres, this lake averages 9 feet deep and has a maximum depth of 21 feet. The shoreline is virtually undeveloped.

Tips: Drag Carolina-rigged finesse worms off points and around boulder fields for smallmouth bass.

The fishing: This warm-water fishery is loaded with northern pike ranging from 2 to 6 pounds. While they take minnows, they can't seem to keep their mouths shut around spinnerbaits. Smallmouth bass average 1.5 pounds and hit crankbaits such as Bomber Long "A"s. Perch average 7 inches and hit worms and small crayfish.

Directions: Nestled in the Adirondack High Peaks off NY 3, midway between the hamlets of Saranac Lake and Tupper Lake.

Additional information: Most folks get to this lake by launching on the Saranac River at the State Bridge Fishing Access Site (paved ramp, parking for seventy-five rigs, toilets), 6 miles west of Saranac Lake village on NY 3. Head upstream, turn west on Lower Saranac Lake, go to the end, reenter the river, and head upstream to Middle Saranac Lake. You'll have to go through a small, no-fee lock to get around a set of rapids. A lock operator is usually present, but if not, you'll have to operate the thing yourself. Instructions are posted on site.

This lake has several islands, and the larger ones have primitive campsites. Permits are needed to camp. They are available at the State Bridge Boat Launch Site.

Contact: Saranac Lake Area Chamber of Commerce, and New York State Department of Environmental Conservation Region 5.

A couple of anglers going through one of the Saranac River's hand-operated locks.

116A. South Creek Fishing Access Site

Description: Beach launch for cartop craft and parking for twenty cars.

Directions: Head west out of Saranac Lake village for 10 miles on NY 3.

117. Weller Pond *(see map on page 176)*

Key species: Northern pike and largemouth bass.

Description: This 180-acre wilderness pond averages 10 feet deep and has a maximum depth of 22 feet.

Tips: Ricochet a rattling crankbait such as a Luhr Jensen Sugar Shad off timber poking through the surface—and be prepared for a violent strike when it hits the water.

The fishing: This small pond has good numbers of northern pike between 18 and 24 inches. What these guys lack in size, they more than make up for in the viciousness of their strikes They like noisy baits such as Rat-L-Traps. Largemouth bass ranging from 1 to 2.5 pounds are plentiful. They react violently to soft and hard jerkbaits.

Directions: There are no roads to the pond. Boats can get there by heading up the slow-moving channel on the north side of Middle Saranac Lake (site 116).

Contact: Saranac Lake Area Chamber of Commerce, and New York State Department of Environmental Conservation Region 5.

118. Lower Saranac Lake *(see map on page 176)*

Key species: Northern pike, smallmouth bass, walleye, yellow perch, and pumpkinseed.

Description: This 2,214-acre lake averages 28 feet deep and has a maximum depth of 65 feet. Its shoreline is lightly developed with summer cottages and a couple of commercial establishments, including a marina.

Tips: Work 3-inch grubs on drop-shot rigs below island cliffs and along the shoals poking out of the waves in various parts of the lake.

The fishing: This lake's northern pike range from 4 to 10 pounds, but some monsters twice that size are caught through the ice on big minnows each year. Smallmouths range from 8 to 16 inches and hit fat-bodied crankbaits and 4-inch worms rigged wacky style. The state has been stocking about 40,000 advanced walleye fingerlings annually since 1999. If they take, anglers should be able to catch keepers (18 inches) by the 2004 season. Yellow perch range from 6 inches to a whopping 14 inches and love 2-inch scented grubs and small minnows. Pumpkinseeds grow to a respectable 8 to 10 inches and hit worms. Both the yellow perch and sunfish are popular with ice fishers, who catch them on ice jigs tipped with grubs.

Directions: On the west side of the village of Saranac Lake.

Additional information: The State Bridge Fishing Access Site on NY 3, 6 miles west of Saranac village, offers hard-surface ramps, parking for seventy-five rigs, and toilets. Lower Saranac Lake is peppered with undeveloped islands; the bigger ones make up the Saranac Lake Islands Public Campgrounds. A permit is needed to camp at the hardened sites and can be obtained at the ranger shack at the State Bridge Fishing Access Site.

Contact: Saranac Lake Area Chamber of Commerce, and New York State Department of Environmental Conservation Region 5.

119. Oseetah Lake *(see map on page 176)*

Key species: Largemouth bass, northern pike, yellow perch, and pumpkinseed.

Description: This 657-acre lake averages only about 3 feet deep and has a maximum depth of 7 feet. Its weedy flats are punctuated with ancient stumps and submerged snags. The shoreline is undeveloped, and a ring of high peaks towers over it.

Tips: Only run your outboard motor in the channel clearly marked with green-and-orange buoys.

The fishing: Largemouth bass grow big in this fertile habitat. They average 3 pounds, and 5-pounders are common. Topwater lures such as Zara Spooks and prop lures like the Smithwick Devil's Horse work even under windy conditions. Northern pike range from 3 to 6 pounds and are partial to spinnerbaits. Yellow perch easily reach 10 inches, and pumpkinseeds average 7 inches. Both take worms and wet flies.

Directions: This lake is connected to Lake Flower (site 121) by the Saranac River. Launch at the Lake Flower state ramp on NY 86 in the village of Saranac Lake and head due south.

Additional information: There is no public access site on the lake.

Contact: Saranac Lake Area Chamber of Commerce, and New York State Department of Environmental Conservation Region 5.

120. Kiwassa Lake *(see map on page 176)*

Key species: Smallmouth bass, northern pike, yellow perch, and panfish.

Description: This 282 acre lake has an average depth of 21 feet and a maximum depth of 45 feet. About 50 percent of its shoreline is developed with summer homes.

Tips: If you launch at the beach launch at the end of Kiwassa Lake Road, don't block private driveways when you park.

The fishing: This lake is a local favorite because the fish always seem to cooperate. Smallmouth bass range from 1.5 to 3 pounds and take everything from spinner-rigged curly-tailed grubs and 3-inch minnows on drop-shot rigs to jerkbaits and fat-bodied crankbaits. Northerns average about 4 pounds, but larger fish up to 10 pounds are taken regularly. They are particularly partial to spinnerbaits but also take minnows, large Flatfish, and minnow-imitating crankbaits. Yellow perch range from 6 to 12 inches, pumpkinseeds 6 to 8 inches, and rock bass 5 to 8 inches. Each species responds to a worm, suspended a couple of feet below a tiny bobber, cast into windfalls along the shore.

Directions: A couple of hundred yards up the channel on the northwest side of Oseetah Lake (site 119).

Additional information: A beach launch is at the end of Kiwassa Lake Road, 2.2 miles from its intersection with NY 3 in the village of Saranac Lake. You'll find parking for about five cars and shoulder parking for about three rigs.

Contact: Saranac Lake Area Chamber of Commerce, and New York State Department of Environmental Conservation Region 5.

121. Lake Flower *(see map on page 176)*

Key species: Northern pike, largemouth bass, smallmouth bass, and panfish.

Description: This 166-acre lake's average depth is 5 feet, and its maximum depth is 12 feet. Created by a dam built on the Saranac River to power sawmills, the area was quickly settled and the shoreline is heavily developed, and includes Saranac Lake village on its north shore.

Tips: Flatline Mepps bucktail spinners for northern pike.

The fishing: Northern pike range from 4 to 7 pounds, but 10-pounders are common and 15-pounders are possible. They take Daredevles, and minnows drifted or suspended below bobbers. This lake is loaded with bucketmouths weighing between 2 and 4 pounds. They hit well on buzzbaits worked around lily pads or Texas-rigged worms pitched under docks. Though not as common as their big-mouth cousins, there are still enough 1- to 2-pound smallmouths in the lake to make going after them worthwhile. Jigging salted tubes on bottom is a productive technique for these scrappy fighters. Perch averaging 8 inches are plentiful and mouth every small minnow and 2-inch curly-tailed grub they can. The lake's panfish include rock bass and pumpkinseeds averaging 7 inches and brown bullheads up to 14 inches. The sunfish can be taken by drifting along weed edges with free-floating worms. The bullheads like their worms still-fished on bottom.

Additional information: A two-lane paved boat launch is located on NY 86, in the heart of the village of Saranac Lake. There's parking for fifteen rigs and six slots exclusively for cars without rigs.

Contact: Saranac Lake Area Chamber of Commerce, and the New York State Department of Environmental Conservation Region 5.

122. Franklin Falls Pond *(see map on page 176)*

Key species: Northern pike, smallmouth bass, walleye, yellow perch, and brown bullhead.

Description: This 455-acre impoundment on the Saranac River averages 10 feet deep and has a maximum depth of 20 feet. Mostly forested, it has a few camps.

Tips: Fish the eddies along the mouth with jigs.

The fishing: Northern pike typically range from 18 to 22 inches and hit any spinnerbait or crankbait they can fit in their mouths. Smallmouths average 13 inches and like minnows and crayfish drifted along the old river channel. The state started a five-year walleye stocking program in 1998, adding 9,000 4-inchers annually. At the last survey, walleyes ranged from 16 to 25 inches. Drift for them with worms. Yellow perch averaging 7 inches and brown bullheads of up to 16 inches are plentiful. Both hit worms and the perch also like minnows and Beetle Spins.

The minimum length for walleyes is 18 inches and the daily limit is three.

Directions: Head north out of the village of Saranac Lake on NY 3 for about 6 miles to Bloomingdale, then go east on CR 18 for about 4 miles.

Additional information: The fishing access site on CR 18 has a beach launch for cartop craft, parking for eight cars, and shore-fishing access. Several hardened beach campsites are available on a first-come, first-served basis.

Contact: New York State Department of Environmental Conservation Region 5.

123. Union Falls Pond *(see map on page 176)*

Key species: Northern pike, smallmouth bass, walleye, yellow perch, and brown bullhead.

Description: This 1,704-acre Saranac River impoundment averages 10 feet deep and has a maximum depth of 22 feet.

Tips: Be on the lookout for eagles begging for fish.

The fishing: Northerns grow to a respectable 30 inches and like minnows and their imitations worked near heavy cover. Smallmouths range from 12 to 15 inches and also like minnows, but quite a few are taken on spinnerbaits with tandem blade as well. This is one of only two lakes in the mountains in which the authorities stock walleye fry—upward of 228,000 annually. Survival is decent, and those that can survive the first couple of years grow to anywhere from 1 to 3 pounds. They like worms, bladebaits, and jigs worked on bottom, in deep water. Yellow perch averaging 11 inches and brown bullheads of up to 14 inches are plentiful and take worms or crayfish fished on bottom.

Directions: Head north from site 122 on CR 18 (it turns to CR 48 when you cross the county line) for less than a mile.

Additional information: While there is no formal fishing access site, locals fish from shore and launch cartop craft from the shoulder of CR 48, on the east side of the Saranac River, just below the Franklin Falls Pond Dam. You'll have to float a few hundred feet to the lake. This area is a well-established bald eagle nesting site, and anglers are advised to stay out of the bay cordoned off by buoys on the east shore.

Contact: New York State Department of Environmental Conservation Region 5.

124. Lake Colby *(see map on page 176)*

Key species: Rainbow trout, brown trout, landlocked salmon, largemouth bass, smallmouth bass, yellow perch, and brown bullhead.

Description: Easy access off a major highway makes this 286-acre lake one of the most popular fisheries in the Saranac Lake region. It averages 20 feet deep and has a maximum depth of 46 feet. A railroad causeway runs across the south bay, separating it from the main lake, creating Little Colby Pond (site 125). Though too shallow and narrow for most motorboats, the channel is deep enough for the fish to go back and forth.

Tips: Suspend minnows a couple of feet below tip-ups for the surplus brood stock salmon that the state releases into the lake each fall.

The fishing: The state stocks this lake annually with more than 2,000 brown trout and more than 3,000 rainbow trout, averaging 8 inches. Additionally, about a hundred mature landlocked salmon, averaging 23.5 inches, and 750 brown trout more than 14 inches are stocked annually. Rainbows hit dry flies at dawn and dusk, and worms and small spoons by day. Browns like worms and minnows. In spring and summer, salmon that survived the winter (surplus brood stock is released each November) can be taken by flatlining spoons and crankbaits such as Red Fins. Trout and salmon season is year-round, resulting in the lake resembling an ice shanty village each winter. The lake is loaded with smallmouth and largemouth bass ranging from 10 to 14 inches. They eagerly hit live bait and rattling crankbaits such as Rat-L-Traps, the Excaliber Fat-Free family, and MirrOlure Shad Rattlers. Indeed, largemouth bass were first observed in research nets during a 1987 survey. By 1993 their population had increased to the point that authorities now electroshock occasionally to stock them into less fortunate waters. Yellow perch up to 12 inches and brown bullheads ranging from 8 to 14 inches are popular and popularly targeted with worms by locals fishing from the railroad causeway on the lake's south end.

Use or possession of alewives or blueback herring as bait is prohibited. Motors exceeding 10 horsepower are prohibited. There is no size limit for bass.

Directions: Half a mile north of the village of Saranac Lake on NY 86.

Additional information: The fishing access site on NY 86 has a single-lane gravel launch, parking for twenty-five rigs, and a toilet. Locals use the soft-surface ramp to launch small trailered craft and have rutted it terribly, making it hazardous for motor vehicles. In his current fisheries management report, state biologist Richard Preall suggests that the state revamp and pave the deteriorating facility. In addition, he suggests underwater platforms be constructed to give fly anglers a stable floor on which to wade while casting streamers to salmon and trout milling around the tributary mouth north of the access site each spring and fall. Use or possession of blueback herring or alewives as bait is prohibited.

Contact: Saranac Lake Area Chamber of Commerce, and New York Department of Environmental Conservation Region 5.

125. Little Colby Pond (see map on page 176)

Key species: Largemouth bass and brown bullhead.

Description: Separated from Lake Colby (site 124) by the Remsen–Lake Placid Railroad culvert, this 35-acre pond averages 5 feet deep and has a maximum depth of 15 feet. It is framed in bog mats and has massive weed beds.

Tips: Using a long rod, vertically jig a Texas-rigged scented worm along the under-cut banks of cattail and bog mats.

The fishing: Although some salmon and trout mill around the culvert in spring and fall, largemouth bass ranging from 2 to 4 pounds are the predominant game fish. The pond's vegetation makes it a spot fishery where you throw surface baits and rigged soft plastics into openings, channels, and holes. Brown bullheads of up to 14 inches are popular with locals, especially in late spring. Still-fish with worms and crayfish on bottom. Use or possession of blueback herring or alewives as bait prohibited.

Directions: Take Ampersand Avenue from the west side of Saranac Lake village to CR 18 (Forest Home Road).

Additional information: The railroad culvert is only tall enough for a canoe to pass under, provided its occupants slouch over. An informal small-craft launch is found on Forest Home Road.

Contact: Saranac Lake Area Chamber of Commerce, and New York State Department of Environmental Conservation Region 5.

126. Lewey Lake *(see map on page 188)*

Key species: Landlocked Atlantic salmon, brown trout, lake trout, and northern pike.

Description: This 361-acre lake's wonderfully symmetrical floor gently slides from the shoreline to a 50-foot-deep hole out in the middle. Averaging 25 feet deep with a maximum depth of 55 feet, its shoreline is mostly surrounded by wild forest. A navigable channel connects it to Indian Lake.

Tips: Ice fish with minnows at the mouth of its major tributary, the Miami River.

The fishing: Savvy locals ice fish the mouth of the Miami River for landlocked salmon ranging from 3 to 5 pounds. Most speculate that these fish were originally stocked into Indian Lake (site 127) but found the pickings and spawning in Lewey Lake and the Miami River more to their liking. Indeed, some are convinced the species is naturally reproducing in the Miami River. Similarly, it is commonly believed that the brown trout and lake trout are also fish originally stocked into Indian Lake. In summer, run-of-the-mill brown trout go anywhere from 1 to 4 pounds and are often taken on stickbaits and streamers. Fish in the 5- to 8-pound range, however, are caught on large minnows through the ice. Lake trout average 3 pounds, but fish of better than 10 pounds are available. They are mostly taken through the ice on minnows and by jigging. Northern pike in the 3- to 8-pound

Lewey Lake · Indian Lake · Lake Abanakee · Indian River

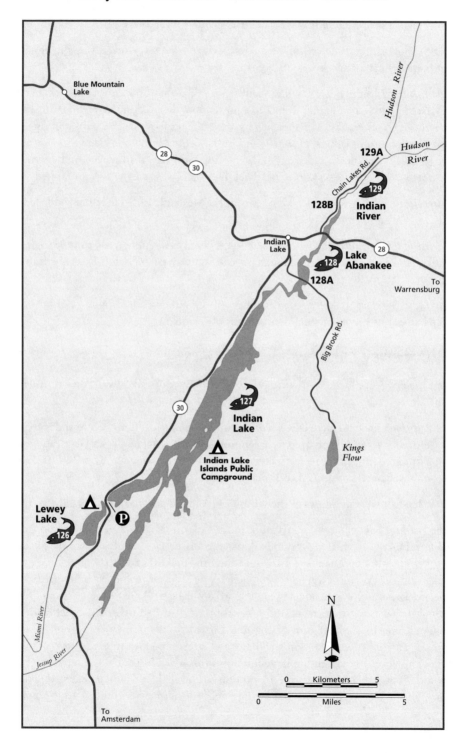

range are plentiful in the grass and weed beds surrounding the lake. They bite best on minnows but are more exciting to catch on buzzbaits.

Directions: From NY Thruway exit 27 (Amsterdam), head north on NY 30 for about 65 miles.

Additional information: Lewey Lake Public Campground is a fee area offering 209 campsites, a hard-surface boat launch, parking for fifteen rigs, hot showers, a sand beach, and a trailer dumping station. A day-use fee is charged when the campgrounds are open, from mid-May through mid-November. Day use is free off-season.

Contact: New York State Department of Environmental Conservation Region 5, and Hamilton County Tourism.

127. Indian Lake

Key species: Landlocked Atlantic salmon, brown trout, lake trout, smallmouth bass, northern pike, whitefish, yellow perch, and pumpkinseed.

Description: Developed only on its northwest corner, this largely forested, 4,255-acre impoundment averages 39 feet deep and has a maximum depth of 85 feet.

Tips: Autumn drawdown lowers the lake by up to 10 feet, leaving much of the south end high and dry.

The fishing: A healthy smelt population keeps predators well fed. The state annually stocks about 1,000 landlocked salmon averaging 5 inches into the lake's major tributary, the Jessup River. Survival is fair, and fish ranging from 15 to 18 inches are commonly caught on streamers and Junior ThunderSticks. The state annually releases about 7,500 brown trout averaging 8 inches. Most are caught on worms, flies, and small lures by the time they reach 12 inches. A lot, however, make it to true lunker size—each winter anglers take browns ranging from 5 to 8 pounds through the ice on live smelt. Lake trout fare even better than the browns. About 1,000 fewer are stocked annually, and they're about an inch smaller to boot. Yet they prosper in the lake's deep northern end, typically growing from 1.5 to 4 pounds, with many making it to 10 pounds or better. Fish for them with flutter spoons dragged on Seth Green rigs. Smallmouth bass find the lake's rocky bottom to their liking. Ranging from 12 to 16 inches, they respond well to finesse worms on drop-shot and Carolina rigs. Northern pike aren't very numerous, but when you get one it is generally 8 pounds or better; 20-pounders are taken each year, primarily by ice fishers. Use spinnerbaits in soft water and large minnows through the ice. Lake whitefish ranging from 12 to 20 inches thrive in the deep water at the north end. They are mostly taken through the ice on tiny jigs tipped with fish bellies or grubs. For some reason, pumpkinseeds find this place very agreeable. Indeed, the state record—a 1-pound, 9-ounce monster—was caught here. They average an incredible 8 inches and, along with the plentiful perch supply (which averages 10 inches), provide memorable moments to family groups fishing from shore with worms.

Directions: NY 30 parallels the west bank, south of the village of Indian Lake.

Additional information: The state boat launch on NY 30, at the lake's south end, has a hard-surface launch ramp and parking for fifty rigs. Indian Lake Islands Public Campground has fifty-five campsites scattered around the lake and its islands. Access is by boat only. It's open mid-May through Labor Day.

Contact: New York State Department of Environmental Conservation Region 5, and Hamilton County Tourism.

128. Lake Abanakee *(see map on page 188)*

Key species: Lake trout, brown trout, northern pike, largemouth bass, smallmouth bass, and pumpkinseed.

Description: Formed by a dam on the Indian River (site 129), this 361-acre impoundment is broken into three small lakes separated by bridges too low for boats to pass through. It averages 8 feet deep and has a maximum depth of 21 feet.

Tips: In spring, cast spoons and crankbaits scented with fish oil into the plunge pool, 0.8 mile upstream of Big Brook Road, for large lake trout and brown trout.

The fishing: Considered a warm-water fishery by all standards, this lake offers a unique opportunity for large salmonids. When Indian Lake is drawn down each fall, some large trout invariably go down the tubes. As the water starts warming up in spring, they congregate in the deep water at the mouth of Abanakee and strike anything that resembles a smelt. Since they can't survive in the warm habitat, the state allows taking them year-round. Northern pike range from 18 to 25 inches and provide good sport for anglers casting spinner-rigged 3-inch curly-tailed grubs and tubes. Smallmouth bass go around 12 to 16 inches. These scrappers love crayfish and minnows. Largemouth bass of up to 4 pounds are present and can be coaxed out of cover with jig-'n'-pigs and floating worms. Pumpkinseeds of up to 10 inches can't seem to resist a juicy worm floated in weed openings below a bobber.

There is no closed season or size limit for trout and salmon, but statewide bag limits apply. Yellow perch and pumpkinseeds can be taken in any number.

Directions: About 1 mile east of the village of Indian Lake on NY 28.

Contact: New York State Department of Environmental Conservation Region 5, and Hamilton County Tourism.

128A. Public Access

Description: This site is a picnic area, but anglers use it as an informal cartop launch. There's parking for four cars.

Directions: Head south on NY 30 from the village of Indian Lake for just less than 1 mile, then turn left onto Big Brook Road. Travel about 0.5 mile to the bridge.

128B. Public Access

Description: This informal hard-surface launch is on town property, with parking for about five rigs and additional parking on the shoulder.

Directions: Head east out of Indian Lake village on NY 28. Turn north a little more than 1 mile later, just before the bridge, onto Chain Lakes Road and travel for 0.75 mile.

129. Indian River *(see map on page 188)*

Key species: Brown trout.

Description: The 2-something-mile stretch from the Abanakee Lake Dam to the Indian River's confluence with the Hudson is a jumble of wild and scenic pocket water punctuated with chutes and ledges littered with blowdowns.

Tips: Work Muddler Minnows through the pockets.

The fishing: Each year, the state stocks about 1,900 brown trout averaging 8 inches and an additional 490 two-year-olds that can be as long as 16 inches. The fish normally range from 9 to 14 inches; some holdover trout of up to 20 inches are possible. They hit worms, minnows, and stonefly nymphs by day, and dry flies matching the hatch at dawn and dusk.

Trout and landlocked salmon can be taken year-round, in any size.

Directions: Head east out of Indian Lake village on NY 28. Turn north about 1 mile later, just before the bridge, onto Chain Lakes Road and follow it for a little less than 1 mile.

Additional information: The land beyond the gate on Chain Lakes Road is private, but the club doesn't mind folks fishing the stream. Several campsites marked with disks are found along Chain Lakes Road. Watch for fast-rising water.

Contact: New York State Department of Environmental Conservation, and Hamilton County Tourism.

129A. Forest Preserve Campsites

Description: Numerous roadside campsites, some within view of the Indian River. Camping allowed in designated sites only.

Directions: Head east out of Indian Lake village on NY 28. Turn north just before the bridge onto Chain Lakes Road and follow it for a little more than 1 mile.

130. Upper Hudson River *(see map on page 192)*

Key species: Brown trout, rainbow trout, northern pike, smallmouth bass, and largemouth bass.

Upper Hudson River · Huntley Pond · Boreas River

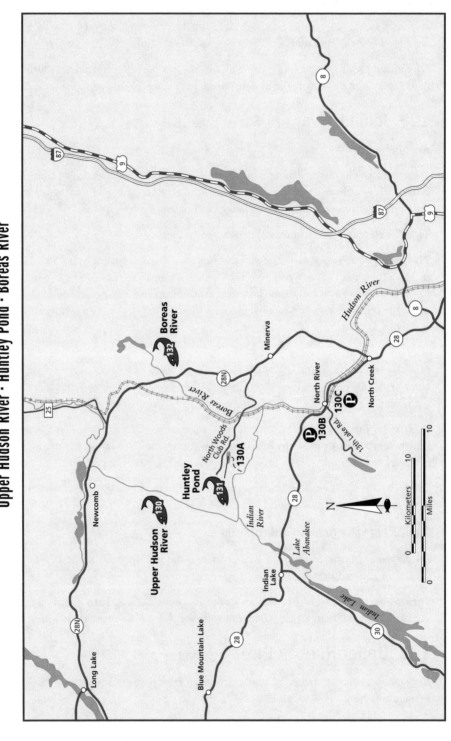

Description: This section of New York's largest river runs from its source for about 110 miles to Hudson Falls. Only about the size of a big creek around Newcomb, it gets nourished by numerous tributaries, becoming a decent-sized river by the time it winds out of the Adirondacks west of Glens Falls. On the way, it slices through a magnificent gorge that, in spring, ranks as one of the country's top ten, adventure-class whitewater venues.

Tips: Use beadhead nymphs just about anytime.

The fishing: The state annually airlifts roughly 4,270 brown trout averaging 7.5 inches and 7,400 rainbow trout averaging 8.5 inches into the remote stretch between Newcomb and North River. Pushed out of the plane without parachutes, those that hit the water, and don't break their fins on the way, find the pickings good, growing anywhere from 10 to 16 inches. In addition, roughly 2,000 two-year-old trout averaging 12 inches are stocked around North River. Some head upstream, but most hang out in the stretch from North River to about 2 miles downstream, offering anglers decent trout fishing at the shoulder of NY 28. They respond well to streamers, large nymphs, worms, and spinners. Downstream of North Creek, the river is wide, shallow, and, according to Rich Preall, a state aquatic biologist, "loaded with black rocks that draw the sun like a magnet, heating the water to levels trout can't tolerate."

Below Warrensburg, the river narrows again and gets deeper. Although some trout are available, the habitat is most suitable for warm-water species. Smallmouth bass ranging from 12 to 15 inches and northern pike from 18 to 24 inches are common and respond well to streamers, spoons, and minnows. From Corinth to Fort Edward, the river and fish get bigger. Smallmouths go 12 to 18 inches, and northern pike can reach 15 pounds. Largemouth bass begin appearing around Glens Falls. They range from 1 to 4 pounds and take spinnerbaits, large minnows, and minnow imitations.

There is no closed season or size limit for trout or bass in the river flowing through Essex and Hamilton Counties. From the Thurman Bridge (NY 418, a couple of miles west of Warrensburg) upstream, black bass can be taken year-round, in any size. From Glens Falls Bridge upstream to Thurman Bridge, the minimum size for black bass is only 10 inches.

Directions: NY 28 parallels the river from North River to a few miles north of Warrensburg. The river forms part of the boundary between Essex and Hamilton Counties and Warren and Saratoga Counties.

Additional information: The vast majority of the Hudson flows through private property; there are no public campgrounds. Primitive camping, however, is allowed in the small patches of state land it runs through. The biggest swath of public property is upstream and downstream of the Indian River's (site 129) mouth. Numerous informal pull-offs punctuate NY 28.

Contact: New York State Department of Environmental Conservation, Hamilton County Tourism, and Warren County Tourism.

130A. Blue Ledges *(see map on page 192)*

Description: Gateway to the Hudson River Gorge, this spectacularly scenic spot is named for its towering limestone cliffs.

The fishing: The largest pool on the Upper Hudson is located here. The pocket water flowing in and out of it is highly oxygenated, making the whole area ideal year-round trout habitat. This spot is favored by purists who enjoy hiking into a wildly remote area for quality fly fishing.

Directions: Take NY 28N north out of North Creek for about 8 miles to Minerva. Continue north for about 1.5 miles beyond the village and turn left (west), at the curve, onto North Woods Club Road. After about 1 mile, the pavement ends. Continue on the hard-surface road for about 4 more miles to the parking area on the east side of Huntley Pond (site 131). Follow the well-worn footpath south for about 2.1 miles to the river.

Additional information: Located deep in the gorge and down a moderately difficult trail, there isn't any level ground far enough from the river for campsites. There are, however, three large campsites at Huntley Pond.

130B. Off-Road Parking *(see map on page 192)*

Description: This site has parking for five cars.

Directions: Across from 13th Lake Road's terminus at NY 28, about 0.25 mile north of the hamlet of North River.

130C. Off-Road Parking *(see map on page 192)*

Description: This site has a beach launch for cartop craft and parking for four cars.

Directions: On NY 28, about 0.5 mile south of the hamlet of North River.

131. Huntley Pond *(see map on page 192)*

Key species: Brook trout.

Description: This 40-acre pond is largely wooded with some wetland on the west end. It averages about 20 feet deep and has a maximum depth of 40 feet.

Tips: Best fished from a rubber raft or canoe.

The fishing: Each year, the state stocks this pond with about 3,800 brook trout averaging 4 inches. They end up ranging from 9 to 11 inches and are popularly targeted by fly fishers casting flashy dry flies such as Royal Coachmen and streamers.

Directions: Head north on NY 28N out of Minerva for about 1.5 miles, turn west onto North Woods Club Road, and continue for about 5 miles.

Blue Ledges, Upper Hudson River (site 130A).

Author holding brook trout caught at Boreas River.

Additional information: The western tip is owned by the North Woods Club. They don't mind folks fishing but frown on trespassers walking the property. Obey posted signs. There are three large clearings near the parking area where camping is permitted.

Contact: New York State Department of Environmental Conservation Region 5.

132. Boreas River *(see map on page 192)*

Key species: Brook trout and brown trout.

Description: Spawned by Boreas Ponds, this river winds south for about 18 miles to feed the Hudson River on the east end of the Hudson Gorge.

Tips: Use Woolly Worms in late summer.

The fishing: The headwaters are native brook trout habitat. The fish range from 4 to 8 inches and take worms and flies. Near the river's mouth, the state annually stocks about 1,350 brown trout averaging 8 inches. They find the highly oxygenated pocket water to their liking and thrive, growing to average 10 inches. They like worms and nymphs.

Directions: Flowing mostly through wild forest, the Boreas's only easily accessible stretches are at two bridges: the North Woods Club Road bridge (take NY 28N north out of Minerva for 1.5 miles, turn west onto North Woods Club Road, and continue for about 3 miles) and the NY 28N bridge, about 8 miles north of Minerva.

Contact: New York State Department of Environmental Conservation Region 5.

133. Piseco Lake *(see map on page 200)*

Key species: Lake trout, landlocked Atlantic salmon, lake whitefish, and small-mouth bass.

Description: Surrounded by wild forest and wilderness areas, this 2,842-acre lake averages 58 feet deep and has a maximum depth of 125 feet. Its cottages and lakeshore businesses offer the only civilization for miles around.

Tips: Using a very light line, ice fish with minnows suspended about 2 feet below the ice on tip-ups.

The fishing: Lake trout are the dominant predators. The state annually stocks close to 5,000 of them—averaging 7.5 inches. They end up ranging from 18 to 26 inches and are mainly targeted by ice fishers jigging with minnows. About 3,400 land-locked Atlantic salmon are also stocked annually. They do very well, typically reaching between 18 and 20 inches. While some are caught in summer by trolling streamers and crankbaits, most are targeted by ice anglers suspending live smelt a couple of feet below the ice. Lake whitefish run from 14 to 22 inches and respond well to strips of smelt bellies jigged through the ice. The locally favored technique involves chumming an area with ground-up fish parts and oatmeal, then returning in a day or so and working bottom with a tiny jig tipped with a small strip of fish belly, piece of worm, or perch eye. Smallmouth bass of up to 16 inches rule the rocky drops and have an appetite for minnows and crayfish.

Lake trout and salmon can be taken year-round. The minimum length for lak-ers is 18 inches, and the daily limit is three; the minimum for salmon is also 18 inches, and the daily limit is two. Use or possession of alewives or blueback herring as bait is prohibited.

Directions: Head east out of Utica on NY 8 for about 57 miles. NY 8 parallels the lake's east side.

Contact: New York State Department of Environmental Conservation Region 5.

133A. Point Comfort Public Campground

Description: This fee area offers seventy-six campsites, a paved boat launch with parking for six rigs, picnic areas, a sandy swimming beach, a bathhouse, and toilets. It's open mid-May through Labor Day. Free day use is permitted off-season.

Directions: On Old Piseco Road, about 0.5 mile from its western terminus at NY 8.

Ice fishing yields a large catch.

133B. Little Sand Point Public Campground *(see map on page 200)*

Description: This fee area offers seventy-eight campsites (more than half of them on the lake shore), a paved boat launch with parking for six rigs, a picnic area, a swimming beach, a bathhouse, toilets, and a trailer dumping station. It's open mid-May through Labor Day. Off-season day use is permitted.

Directions: On Old Piseco Road, 3 miles east of its western terminus at NY 8.

133C. Poplar Point Public Campground *(see map on page 200)*

Description: This fee area offers twenty-one campsites, all on shore, along with a paved boat launch with parking for fifteen rigs, a sandy beach, a bathhouse, and toilets. It's open mid-May through Labor Day. Free day use is allowed off-season.

Directions: On Old Piseco Road, 4 miles east of its western terminus at NY 8.

134. Sacandaga Lake *(see map on page 200)*

Key species: Brown trout, rainbow trout, walleye, chain pickerel, and smallmouth bass.

Description: This 1,600-acre lake's entire northern half is in the Jessup River Wild Forest. It averages roughly 25 feet deep and has a maximum depth of 60 feet. It is connected to Lake Pleasant (site 135) by a navigable channel.

Tips: Don't confuse this lake with its mighty offspring, Great Sacandaga Lake (site 139).

The fishing: Managed as a two-story fishery, the state stocks this lake each year with 3,330 brown trout averaging 9 inches and kicks in an additional 490 averaging 14 inches. Survival is good, and the general population averages 12 inches, with a lot of fish taken each year that measure more than 20 inches and weigh up to 5 pounds. Minnows and worms work best, but trolling minnow-imitating crankbaits scented with fish oil also produces well. Roughly 3,500 rainbow trout averaging 9 inches are stocked yearly. They end up averaging about 12 inches, but a lot reach 18 inches. They respond well to trolled spoons and crankbaits.

Walleyes run from 15 to 24 inches, with 27-inchers possible. They have a taste for minnows, worms drifted on plain and spinner-rigged harnesses, and diving crankbaits such as the MirrOlure 92LSR and C. C. Shads. Smallmouth thrive on this lake's rocky, irregular floor. Ranging from 1 to 3 pounds, they respond well to scented tubes and curly-tailed grubs bounced and dragged along bottom. Chain pickerel averaging 18 inches cruise shallow, weedy areas and strike fast-moving Krocodiles, ThunderSticks, and Rooster Tails. Recently the lake has been experiencing a developing largemouth bass fishery, and bucketmouths of up to 5 pounds are being reported with increasing regularity. They like spinnerbaits and jerkbaits.

Trout season is open year-round. Fishing is prohibited in all tributaries and the outlet from March 16 until the first Saturday in May to protect spawning walleyes. Use or possession of alewives or blueback herring as bait is prohibited.

Piseco Lake · Sacandaga Lake · Lake Pleasant · Sacandaga River

To Hague

East Branch
Sacandaga River

137

P

8

Main Stem
Sacandaga River

138

30

8

Sacandaga River

30

Wells

Lake
Algonquin

Sacandaga Public Campground

P

To Amsterdam

Lake
Pleasant

135

South Shore Rd.

Lake Pleasant

Speculator

P

30

Moffitt Beach
Public Campground

navigable channel

Sacandaga
Lake

Lake Pleasant

8

Sacandaga
Lake

134

West Branch
Sacandaga River

136

West Branch Sacandaga River

Old Piseco Rd.

Piseco
Lake

133

Piseco Outlet

Piseco Lake

Poplar Point
Public Campground
133C

Little Sand Point
Public Campground 133B

Point Comfort
Public
Campground
133A

10

8

To Utica

N

0   Kilometers   4

0   Miles   4

Directions: From NY Thruway exit 27 (Amsterdam), head north on NY 30 for about 24 miles to Speculator, then continue west on NY 8 for about 3 miles.

Additional information: Moffitt Beach Public Campground is a fee area offering 261 campsites, a beach launch with parking for thirty rigs, hot showers, and picnic areas. A day-use fee is charged to noncampers when the campground is open, mid-May through mid-October. Free day use is permitted off-season, and the road is plowed in winter.

Contact: Hamilton County Tourism, and New York State Department of Environmental Conservation Region 5.

135. Lake Pleasant

Key species: Walleye, smallmouth bass, brown trout, and rainbow trout.

Description: This 1,504-acre lake has an average depth of 29 feet and a maximum depth of 65 feet. Although surrounded by roads, it is far enough off the beaten path to discourage crowding. It is connected to Sacandaga Lake by a navigable channel.

Tips: The largest walleyes are females, which are most active at night.

The fishing: This lake's inlet allows its fish to intermingle with Sacandaga Lake (site 134) fish, making them almost identical fisheries. Walleyes, however, fare better here. Indeed, they were stocked into the lake in the 1920s and took like tadpoles to pond water. Stocking was discontinued a few years later because the fish started reproducing naturally. They range from 14 to 24 inches, but some reach 27 inches. Minnows, worms, and crankbaits all work well. The bottom here is much more regular than its sister lake, so the smallmouth bass aren't as plentiful. Still, there are enough 1- to 3-pounders around to make talking about them in bars a local pastime. They are mostly taken by drifting minnows and crayfish, especially off the longest point and island. Each year, the state stocks roughly 3,230 brown trout averaging 9 inches and an additional 490 averaging 14 inches. They generally average 12 inches, with a lot of fish taken each year weighing up to 5 pounds. Minnows and worms work best, but trolling minnow-imitating crankbaits scented with fish oil also produces well. About 3,400 rainbow trout averaging 9 inches are also stocked annually. They end up averaging about 12 inches, but many reach 18 inches. They respond well to flatlined spoons and crankbaits, particularly in spring and fall.

Trout season is open year-round. Fishing is prohibited in all tributaries from March 16 until the first Saturday in May to protect spawning walleyes. Use or possession of alewives or blueback herring as bait is prohibited. Like its sister lake, Lake Pleasant is experiencing a developing largemouth bass fishery.

Directions: From NY Thruway exit 27 (Amsterdam), head north on NY 30 for about 24 miles to Speculator.

Additional information: A beach launch with parking for ten cars is located near the NY 30/NY 8 bridge crossing the outlet. Camping is available at Moffitt Beach Public Campground on adjoining Sacandaga Lake (site 134).

Contact: Hamilton County Tourism, and New York State Department of Environmental Conservation Region 5.

136. West Branch Sacandaga River *(see map on page 200)*

Key species: Brook trout and brown trout.

Description: Springing from the Silver Lake Wilderness, this branch runs north, then northeast, for about 20 miles to join the main stem at the Sacandaga Public Campground.

Tips: The only public access is at the Sacandaga Public Campground.

The fishing: The state used to stock thousands of trout into the stream, but in 2001 the 5 miles of river that used to be open to the public was posted and developed. Still, Rich Preall, the senior aquatic biologist through whose beat the river runs, says, "I plan on stocking good numbers of two-year-old browns at the public campground, where there is good road access." Recently released two-year-old browns will hit anything from worms to cork flies imitating food pellets.

Directions: Head south out of Wells on NY 30 for 2 miles.

Additional information: Sacandaga Public Campground is a fee area offering 143 campsites, hot showers, and a trailer dump station. A day-use fee is charged to non-campers when the campground is open, mid-May through Labor Day. Free day use is permitted off-season.

Contact: New York State Department of Environmental Conservation Region 5.

137. East Branch Sacandaga River *(see map on page 200)*

Key species: Brook trout and brown trout.

Description: This river pours out of the west side of Gore Mountain, snakes around a bit in the Siamese Ponds Wilderness, then comes to NY 8 and follows it south for a good 10 miles before feeding the main stem at the NY 8/NY 30 junction, 8 miles east of Speculator.

Tips: Wear a Bug-Out Outdoorswear head net in spring to keep blackflies from bugging you.

The fishing: The lower portion of this stream gets stocked with some of the browns designated for the main stem. They end up ranging from 8 to 12 inches. Native brook trout ranging from 4 to 8 inches are plentiful in the wilderness headwaters. Both take worms early in the year, brown and tan nymphs in summer.

Directions: Head east out of Speculator on NY 30/NY 8 for about 8 miles, then continue on NY 8, which parallels the East Branch for about 10 miles.

Contact: New York State Department of Environmental Conservation Region 5.

138. Main Stem Sacandaga River *(see map on page 200)*

Key species: Brown trout, smallmouth bass, chain pickerel, northern pike, and walleye.

Description: This beautiful trout stream is deceiving. Although it is loaded with dynamite-looking trout habitat, the vast majority of it gets too warm in summer to support salmonids.

Tips: The best trout fishing stretches from the fast water downstream of Speculator to the head of Lake Algonquin.

The fishing: Close proximity to NY 8/NY 30 qualifies this warm stream for some heavy annual stocking—about 4,550 brown trout averaging 8 inches. Most only make it to about 9 inches before being driven by rising temperatures into tributaries or downstream into Great Sacandaga Lake. Still, they provide a lot of exciting action for fly fishers casting mayfly, caddis, and terrestrial patterns into July. Smallmouth bass ranging from 12 to 14 inches and chain pickerel of up to 20 inches inhabit the entire river. Their populations are especially great in Lake Algonquin, an impoundment about 15 miles south of Speculator, on NY 30. Both hit Mepps Aglias, Junior ThunderSticks, Berkley Jerk Shads, and, in quiet stretches, 1/16- and 1/24-ounce Hula Poppers. Northern pike of up to 36 inches and walleyes ranging from 18 to 23 inches are available in the lower reaches; the closer you fish to Great Sacandaga Lake (site 139), the better your chances of catching one. Both species take minnows, bucktail jigs, C. C. Rattlin' Shads, and Rattlin' Red Fins. In addition, walleyes will hit a worm slowly pulled upstream on bottom or trolled on a spinner-rigged harness.

There is no minimum size for chain pickerel. Fishing is prohibited from March 16 through the first Saturday in May, from the mouth to the NY 30 bridge in Hamilton County, to protect spawning walleyes.

Directions: NY 30 parallels the entire river north of the hamlet of Northville.

Additional information: The main stem flows into Great Sacandaga Lake (site 139) and flows out again, to flow an additional 4 miles before feeding the Hudson River in Hadley. Sacandaga Public Campground, located on NY 30 a couple of miles south of Wells, is a fee area offering 143 campsites, picnic sites, hot showers, and a trailer dump station. A user fee is charged to noncampers when the campground is open, mid-May through Labor Day. Free day use is permitted off-season.

Contact: New York State Department of Environmental Conservation Region 5.

139. Great Sacandaga Lake

Key species: Northern pike, walleye, smallmouth bass, brown trout, and rainbow trout.

Description: Formed in 1930 when a dam was built on the Sacandaga River, this 26,860-acre lake averages 32 feet deep and has a maximum depth of 70 feet. Subject to wildly fluctuating water levels, it's a dangerous place for boats—especially during low water, when its numerous shoals reach propeller level. Totally contained within the Adirondack Park, ancient peaks loom over the reservoir's northern horizon.

Tips: Use large suckers and shiners suspended below bobbers in tributary mouths.

The fishing: This lake has broken several northern pike state records and surrendered the current contender, a 46-pound, 2-ounce monster. Trophy northerns didn't get that way by being stupid, and catching one is a real challenge. Ron Kolodziej, the lake's only guide who specializes exclusively in northern pike, says that trophy seekers must use minnows "one-third the size of the fish you're after. In other words, a 10-inch minnow for a 30-inch pike and so on." Still, many large pike are taken serendipitously on smaller minnows targeting walleyes and bass. Walleyes are generally small, ranging from 15 to 20 inches. But there are a lot of them. They respond well to ThunderSticks and bucktail jigs tipped with minnows or worms. Smallmouth bass stretching the tape from 12 to 20 inches are plentiful and hang out along the old river bottom on the lake's long eastern arm, where they are popularly targeted with minnows, crayfish, curly-tailed grubs, and tubes. Perch ranging from 7 to 11 inches are taken on small minnows and Beetle Spins. Local clubs stock rainbow and brown trout. Rich Preall, a senior aquatic biologist with the state, says the impoundment has "a thin zone where some trout can survive. Most of the stockies are stressed for their entire time here and eventually end up in the mouth of a northern pike." Still, trout ranging from 8 to 14 inches are available and respond to worms fished in tributary mouths early and late in the season.

From March 16 until opening day of walleye season, fishing is prohibited in all tributaries up to the first highway bridge. Trout can be taken year-round.

Directions: Take exit 27 (Amsterdam) off the NY Thruway and get onto NY 30 north. Stay on NY 30 north for the west shore, or take CR 110 for the east shore.

Additional information: Northampton Beach Public Campground, off NY 30 about 3 miles south of Northville, is a fee area offering 223 no-frills campsites, public showers, handicapped access, a hard-surface boat launch, parking for a hundred rigs, hot showers, a playground, picnic facilities, and a picnic pavilion. A day-use fee is charged to noncampers when the campground is open, early May through mid-October. Free day use is allowed off-season.

Contact: New York State Department of Environmental Conservation Region 5, and Fulton County Chamber of Commerce.

Great Sacandaga Lake · East and West Caroga Lakes

139A. Boat Launch *(see map on page 205)*

Description: This site has a hard-surface ramp and parking for sixty rigs.

Directions: On NY 30 in the village of Northville.

139B. Boat Launch *(see map on page 205)*

Description: This site has a hard-surface launch and parking for seventy rigs.

Directions: On CR 110, 3 miles north of the village of Broadalbin.

139C. Boat Launch *(see map on page 205)*

Description: This site has a hard-surface ramp and parking for forty-four rigs.

Directions: Off CR 4, 5 miles north of Edinburg.

140. East Caroga Lake *(see map on page 205)*

Key species: Splake, chain pickerel, smallmouth bass, yellow perch, black crappie, and panfish.

Description: This 246-acre lake averages 13 feet deep and has a maximum depth of 48 feet. A little more than half its shoreline is developed with private residences. It is connected to West Caroga Lake (site 141) by a navigable channel.

Tips: Work Mepps Spin Flies over submerged weed beds.

The fishing: Some splake come in through the channel from West Caroga Lake (site 141). They range from 8 to 12 inches and are usually taken incidentally by anglers casting spoons or spinners for smallmouth bass. Chain pickerel are the dominant warm-water predator. They typically go from 15 to 20 inches and strike spoons and surface baits. Bronzebacks are small, averaging 12 inches. But they're scrappy and eagerly take Mister Twister BigySmal Meatloaf Shad and Zara Pooches. Yellow perch average 8 inches, black crappies range from 9 to 11 inches, pumpkinseeds typically go 7.5 inches, and bullheads reach 12 inches. The crappies and perch like small Beetle Spins and Exude 2-inch curly-tailed grubs. Pumpkinseeds hit wet flies and ½-ounce Hula Poppers. The bullheads, perch, and sunfish all love worms. Trout can be taken year-round.

Directions: From NY Thruway exit 29 (Canajoharie), head north on NY 10 for about 17 miles.

Additional information: Caroga Lake Public Campground (at the southeastern corner of the lake, off NY 29A) is a fee area offering 161 campsites, a boat launch with a paved ramp and parking for ten rigs, a swimming beach, picnic tables, hot showers, and a trailer dump station. A day-use fee is charged to noncampers when the campground is open, mid-May through Labor Day. Free day use is allowed off-season.

Contact: New York State Department of Environmental Conservation Region 5.

141. West Caroga Lake *(see map on page 205)*

Key species: Splake, landlocked Atlantic salmon, whitefish, smallmouth bass, chain pickerel, and yellow perch.

Description: Oval-shaped with symmetrical contours steadily sliding into its deep center, this 227-acre lake averages 34 feet deep and has a maximum depth of 74 feet. It is connected to East Caroga Lake (site 140) by a navigable channel, and much of its shoreline is developed with private residences.

Tips: Ice fish with minnows.

The fishing: This lake is one of the state's top splake hot spots. More than 5,000 are stocked each year averaging 9.5 inches. Most grow to between 12 and 18 inches, but there are some longer than 25 inches down there. Locals ice fish for them by jigging minnows or Swedish Pimples. Three hundred landlocked salmon averaging 7 inches are stocked annually. They end up ranging from 15 to 18 inches and are primarily targeted in winter by suspending a minnow a couple of feet below the ice. Whitefish averaging 15 inches are plentiful and are fished for through the ice by working a teardrop jig tipped with a piece of fish belly or grubs. Smallmouth bass range from 12 to 15 inches and hit jigheads tipped with scented curly-tailed grubs or tubes and dragged on bottom in 10 to 20 feet of water. Chain pickerel up to 20 inches are guaranteed to provide explosive action on worms retrieved rapidly over weed beds on spinner-rigged worm harnesses. Yellow perch averaging 9 inches hit worms, minnows, and 2-inch Exude curly-tailed grubs. Trout can be taken year-round.

Directions: From NY Thruway exit 29 (Canajoharie), head north on NY 10 for about 17 miles.

Additional information: Camping and a boat launch are available at Caroga Lake Public Campground on neighboring East Caroga Lake (site 140).

Contact: New York State Department of Environmental Conservation Region 5.

142. Horseshoe Lake *(see map on page 208)*

Key species: Tiger muskie, largemouth bass, smallmouth bass, and yellow perch.

Description: This 384-acre lake averages 9 feet deep and has a maximum depth of 16 feet. Its shoreline is completely forested.

Tips: Flatline a Mepps Timber Doodle tipped with a minnow.

The fishing: This lake is the best norlunge spot in Region 6. Most range from 7 to 12 pounds, but 18-pounders are caught regularly. They respond well to trolled Bomber Long "A"s and Z-Ray spoons, and to large minnows suspended below tip-ups in winter. Largemouth bass between 1 and 4 pounds are plentiful and hit surface lures and jig-'n'-pigs. Smallmouths generally go from 0.75 to 2 pounds and are taken mostly on crayfish and minnows. Yellow perch average 10 inches and are often

Horseshoe and Lows Lakes · Hitchins and Grassy Ponds · Bog River

caught on crayfish and minnows targeting smallmouths. Many are also taken by drifting worms and 2-inch jig-rigged, scented curly-tailed grubs. The minimum size for black bass is 10 inches.

Directions: From Long Lake village, take NY 30 north for about 14 miles, turn west onto NY 421, and travel for about 5 miles.

Additional information: Cartop launches, with parking for about five cars each, are located on NY 421, on the southeast and southwest banks. Fifteen beach campsites are available. Camp only in sites designated by a CAMP HERE disk.

Contact: New York State Department of Environmental Conservation Region 6, and St. Lawrence County Chamber of Commerce.

143. Hitchins Pond

Key species: Largemouth bass and yellow perch.

Description: This 147-acre pond averages 12 feet deep and has a maximum depth of 33 feet.

Tips: The north basin is the deepest part of the lake.

The fishing: A decent largemouth bass fishery has developed over the past decade or so. Bucketmouths typically range from 1.5 to 3.5 pounds and react with extreme prejudice to just about any rattling crankbait. Yellow perch from 6 to 10 inches are abundant and hit worms and spinner-rigged soft plastics such as Berkley Power Grubs. Use or possession of minnows as baitfish is prohibited. No motors are allowed.

Directions: Paddle down the Horseshoe Lake outlet (site 142) for about a mile to its confluence with the Bog River (site 146), then head upstream (west) on the Bog for about a mile.

Additional information: There are three beach campsites, and one with a pit toilet.

Contact: New York State Department of Environmental Conservation Region 6.

144. Lows Lake

Key species: Largemouth bass and brook trout.

Description: Its western half set in the deep woods of the Five Ponds Wilderness, fringed in spots with vast bogs and marshes, this 2,844-acre lake averages 5 feet deep and has a maximum depth of 55 feet.

Tips: Store food away from the campsite to prevent visitations from bears.

The fishing: Trophy largemouth bass in a wilderness setting are the lake's major draw. Bucketmouths typically range from 2 to 4 pounds, but some monsters tipping the scales at more than 6 pounds have been taken. Spinnerbaits, rattling crankbaits, and plastic worms, fished on Texas rigs or skipped over the surface around vegetation and windfalls, all produce. Brook trout from 6 to 14 inches occupy pockets of deep water. These wild fish will take a worm, wet fly, or streamer trolled behind a wobbler or small dodger.

Possession or use of baitfish is prohibited. No motors are allowed.

Directions: Head southwest on NY 30 for about 8 miles out of Tupper Lake village and turn west onto NY 421. Travel for about 4 miles, skirting the south shore of Horseshoe Lake, and at the end take the gravel road heading south to the lower dam. Launch on the Bog River (site 146) and head upstream. If a barrier prevents access to the gravel road, continue on NY 421 to Horseshoe Lake's outlet (site 142), launch there and paddle downstream to the confluence with the Bog River, then head upstream. You will have one short portage around the upper dam.

Additional information: The state has twenty-six primitive campsites spread around the lake and on the large island, some with pit privies. Beach camping is permitted only in sites designated by a disk. Several islands and points are off limits to the general public from June through August.

Contact: New York State Department of Environmental Conservation Region 6.

145. Grassy Pond (Grasse and Grass) *(see map on page 208)*

Key species: Brook trout and largemouth bass.

Description: This 125-acre pond averages 20 feet deep and has a maximum depth of 30 feet.

Tips: Dead-drift nymphs at the mouths of tributaries.

The fishing: Native brook trout ranging from 6 to 16 inches are available in the mouths of tributaries, in the deep hole off the northwestern tributary, and in the deep center. They hit worms and Muddler Minnows trolled about 8 inches behind an attractor. Largemouth bass of up to 4 pounds roam the shallow shoreline and the outlet channel. They hit Carolina-rigged, scented crayfish imitations, and wacky-style-rigged Exude Poc'it Fry worms.

Use or possession of baitfish is prohibited.

Directions: This pond is the north arm on Lows Lake's (site 144) west end.

Additional information: The pond has five beach campsites (two primitive, three with pit toilets).

Contact: New York State Department of Environmental Conservation Region 6.

146. Bog River *(see map on page 208)*

Key species: Brook trout and largemouth bass.

Description: Gathering the flows from Lows and Horseshoe Lakes and Hitchins and Grassy Ponds, this river tumbles over a dam and flows east for about 7 miles to feed Tupper Lake's south end.

Tips: Scout all rapids.

The fishing: Downstream of the Bog River Flow's lower dam, the state stocks 2,500 fingerling brook trout annually. They grow to between 8 and 12 inches and respond to worms, Mepps Spin Flies, and Phoebes. Some largemouth bass are also available near the mouth. Ranging from 1 to 2.5 pounds, they can be taken in holes on Rebel Crawfish, by fly fishing with bass streamers and ¼-ounce Hula Poppers tight to vegetation and structure, and by walking topwater lures such as Zara Spooks over open water.

Directions: Head southwest on NY 30 for about 8 miles out of Tupper Lake village and turn west onto NY 421. Travel for about 4 miles, skirt the south shore of Horseshoe Lake, take the gravel road heading south, and continue for 1 mile to the dam.

Additional information: The best way to fish here is to float in a rubber raft or whitewater canoe. Always scout rapids. Even during low water, there are stretches of technical Class III rapids, as well as a Class V and a killer Class VI waterfall. Primitive camping is allowed in the state forest lining most of both banks.

Contact: New York State Department of Environmental Conservation Region 6.

147. Lower Brown Tract Pond *(see map on page 212)*

Key species: Brook trout, smallmouth bass, largemouth bass, and panfish.

Description: Located on the seam of the Pigeon Lake Wilderness and the Moose River Plains Wild Forest, this 150-acre pond averages 14 feet deep and has a maximum depth of 33 feet.

Tips: Walk Zara Pooches on calm days.

The fishing: A few brook trout find their way here via tributaries. Ranging from 6 to 14 inches, they are often caught serendipitously by surprised campers targeting bullheads and pumpkinseeds with worms. Smallmouth bass in the 12- to 14-inch range are plentiful, and a few largemouths up to 18 inches are also available. Both take surface lures and spinnerbaits. Brown bullheads averaging 9 inches and pumpkinseeds of up to 8 inches can be taken by fishing worms on bottom.

No motorboats are allowed.

Directions: Head west out of the hamlet of Raquette Lake village on Uncas Road, a well-maintained dirt road.

Lower and Upper Brown Tract Ponds · Shallow, Blue Mountain, and Raquette Lakes

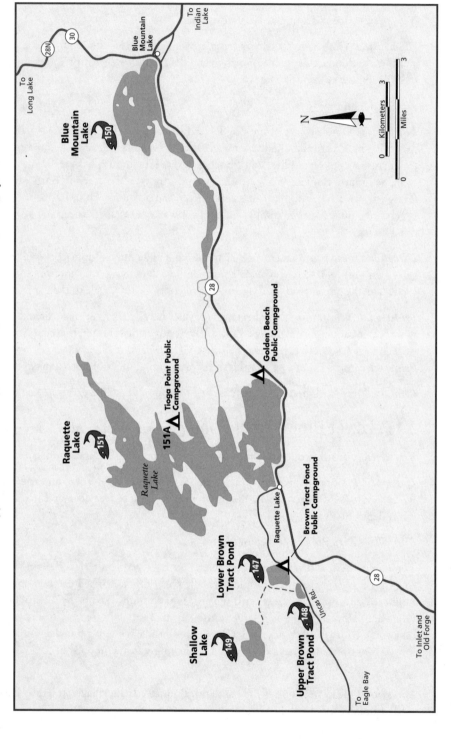

Additional information: Brown Tract Pond Public Campground is a fee area offering ninety campsites, picnic areas, vault toilets, and a hard-surface boat launch. A day-use fee is charged to noncampers when the campground is open, mid-May through Labor Day. Free day use is permitted off-season.

Contact: New York State Department of Environmental Conservation Region 5.

148. Upper Brown Tract Pond

Key species: Largemouth bass and brown bullheads.

Description: This 51-acre pond is totally surrounded by woods, averages 14 feet deep, and has a maximum depth of 33 feet.

Tips: Walk gently and wear camouflage.

The fishing: Largemouth bass range from undersized to 16 inches. They take in-line spinners and crankbaits ranging from Excalibur Fat Free Shallows to Rat-L-Traps. Brown bullheads average 9 inches and take worms fished on bottom.

Directions: A little less than 1 mile west of Lower Brown Tract Pond (site 147) on Uncas Road.

Contact: New York State Department of Environmental Conservation Region 5.

149. Shallow Lake

Key species: Brook trout and smallmouth bass.

Description: Located deep in the Pigeon Lake Wilderness, this 268-acre lake averages 11 feet deep and has a maximum depth of 30 feet.

Tips: It is best to fish this wooded pond from a canoe.

The fishing: The state annually air-drops about 6,400 brook trout averaging 4 inches. They grow to commonly range from 8 to 15 inches, but Rich Preall, a senior aquatic biologist with the state, says he has seen brookies here that will go 3 pounds. They take nymphs and streamers trolled 100 feet behind the canoe in a figure-8 pattern. Smallmouth bass ranging from 12 to 14 inches are common and also hit streamers—but they are just as likely to hit Beetle Spins, worms, or crayfish.

Possession or use of minnows as bait is prohibited. No motors allowed.

Directions: Head northwest for 1.5 miles on the footpath at the north end of Lower Brown Tract Pond (site 147).

Contact: New York State Department of Environmental Conservation Region 5.

150. Blue Mountain Lake

Key species: Lake trout, landlocked Atlantic salmon, and smallmouth bass.

Floating in the morning mist on Blue Mountain Lake.

Description: Less than 20 feet from the road in spots, punctuated by several forested islands, shaded by its 3,759-foot-tall namesake looming over the east bank, this 1,220-acre lake averages 46 feet deep and has a maximum depth of 102 feet.

Tips: Fishing is best in June.

The fishing: Lake trout are the bread-and-butter species here. Annually, the state stocks 2,600 averaging 7 inches. They grow to range from 3 to 9 pounds on the lake's smelt and can be taken by jigging spoons or minnows on bottom in deep water. The state releases about 1,300 landlocked Atlantic salmon averaging 6.5 inches yearly, as well. These easily reach their 15-inch size limit on the smelt, too, and are mostly targeted with silver Rapalas or Black Nose Dace. Smallmouths range from 12 to 15 inches—monsters of more than 4 pounds are reported every year. Most are taken by drifting golden shiners along breaklines and drop-offs. Trout can be taken year-round.

Directions: Head south out of the hamlet of Long Lake on NY 30 for about 9 miles.

Additional information: There is no free public access on the lake, but the village of Blue Mountain Lake has a couple of commercial launches. Primitive camping is allowed in the Blue Ridge Wilderness, on the south side of NY 28, about 2 miles west of the village of Blue Mountain Lake. The divide separating the Hudson and St. Lawrence River drainages is about 1 mile east of the hamlet.

Contact: New York State Department of Environmental Conservation Region 5, and Hamilton County Tourism.

151. Raquette Lake *(see map on page 212)*

Key species: Largemouth bass, lake trout, brook trout, smallmouth bass, yellow perch, and brown bullhead.

Description: Covering 4,927 acres, this lake averages 44 feet deep and has a maximum depth of 96 feet. Its shoreline has many cottages and boasts several Great Camps—fabulous log palaces constructed by industrialists and robber barons between 1870 and 1930.

Tips: The best time to troll for lakers in summer is around high noon.

The fishing: The state's regional fish biologist, Rich Preall, says that an exciting largemouth bass fishery has been developing here over the past few years. While this deep lake isn't exactly swimming in bucketmouth habitat, the little it has—primarily in its shallow, weedy back bays—is loaded with largemouths ranging from 1 to 5 pounds. Indeed, a local fish-and-game club that holds annual potluck fishing tournaments has seen lake trout pushed out of the top spot the past few years by largemouths. Search for them with slugs and topwater lures in and around fallen timber, along bulrush colonies and lily pads. Lake trout are the most common game fish. Most range from 1 to 3 pounds, and fish of more than 10 pounds are possible. May is the best month to fish for them because the water is cold enough for them to swim near shore, within range of anglers casting spoons and minnow-imitating crankbaits, especially around Beech Island on the lake's north end. In summer, they go deep and respond to minnows and spoons. The state stocks thousands of brook trout averaging 4 inches annually. Those lucky enough to escape being dinner for the lakers grow to range from 8 to 14 inches and respond well to worms, Mepps Aglia Long Spin Flies, and Panther Martins. Smallmouth bass range from 12 to 15 inches and will hit diving crankbaits such as the Poe's Super Cedar series. Yellow perch in the 6- to 12-inch range and brown bullheads of up to 13 inches are plentiful and are commonly targeted in spring with worms fished on bottom.

The limit for lake trout is two per day. Trout can be taken year-round.

Directions: Take NY 28 north out of Inlet for about 7 miles.

Additional information: Big Island, east of the village of Raquette Lake, has three primitive lean-tos. Several other lean-tos are found on the lake's west and north shores. These structures are available to the public on a first-come, first-served basis, for one night. The state brochure "Adirondack Canoe Routes: Adirondack Forest Preserve Map and Guide" shows their locations. Golden Beach Public Campground, a fee area on NY 28 about 3 miles east of the hamlet of Raquette Lake, offers 205 no-frills sites, many on the beach, along with a paved launch suitable for small trailered craft, parking for fifteen rigs, shore fishing, hot showers, picnic areas with fireplaces, and a swimming beach. A day-use fee is charged to non-campers during the camping season, mid-May through Labor Day. Free day use is allowed off-season.

Contact: New York State Department of Environmental Conservation Region 5.

151A. Tioga Point Public Campground *(see map on page 212)*

Description: This fee area has fifteen lean-tos, ten no-frills sites, picnic tables, and fireplaces. There's no potable water. It's open from mid-May through Labor Day.

Directions: Accessible only by water, this facility is on the third point on the east bank as you head north up the lake.

152. Upper Raquette River

Key species: Brown trout, walleye, northern pike, largemouth bass, and smallmouth bass.

Description: Spawned as the outlet of Raquette Lake, this stretch of the river feeds and drains Forked and Long Lakes, Simon and Raquette Ponds, and Piercefield Flow, and comes to rest in Carry Falls Reservoir.

Tips: Douse yourself in insect repellent and wear a Bug-Out head net in spring.

The fishing: From the river's headwaters to a couple of miles below Raquette Falls is considered a cold-water habitat. The state annually stocks about 400 brown trout

Upper Raquette River · Piercefield Flow and Nearby Lakes and Ponds

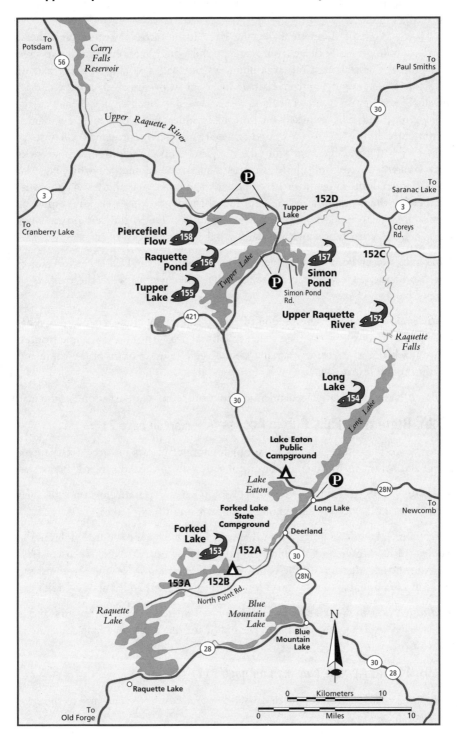

averaging 14 inches here to supplement naturally occurring populations of brook trout. Both species take worms during high water, nymphs and in-line spinners the rest of the time.

Downstream of Raquette Falls, the river turns into a warm-water fishery. Northern pike normally range from 3 to 5 pounds, but larger ones can be expected at any time. They hit best on large minnows but will also take a spinnerbait or crankbait. Walleyes ranging from 18 to 23 inches grow progressively more common the closer you get to Tupper Lake and respond well to bucktail jigs, 3-inch curly-tailed grubs, and tubes worked on bottom in holes and along undercut banks. Smallmouths in the 0.5- to 1.5-pound range are also well represented. They share habitat with the walleyes and will take the same baits. In addition, bronzebacks react violently to anything flashy such as a spoon or spinnerbait whipping past them. Largemouths range from 1 to 4 pounds and seem well on their way to out-numbering the smallmouths. Search for them with topwater lures such as MirrOlure's Prop Baits, Humpback Mules, and Top Dogs, and soft plastic slugs worked around vegetation and windfalls in oxbows and backwaters.

Directions: North Point Road, which strikes southwest from Deerland, runs alongside the Raquette's headwaters. NY 3 parallels the river between the hamlets of Tupper Lake and Sevey.

Additional information: This section of river is a popular canoe route and is spotted with numerous lean-tos. The state's free brochure "Adirondack Canoe Routes: Adirondack Forest Preserve Map and Guide" gives a description of the route and locations of all lean-tos.

Contact: New York State Department of Environmental Conservation Region 5.

152A. Buttermilk Falls Public Access *(see map on page 217)*

Description: This site has shoulder parking for about five cars and access to the river above and below one of the most beautiful waterfalls in the Adirondack Park.

The fishing: This stretch has brown and brook trout above and below the falls. Bass and northern pike occupy some holes just upstream of Long Lake.

Directions: Take NY 28 north out of Raquette Lake village for about 13 miles to the hamlet of Blue Mountain Lake and head north on NY 30/NY 28N. When you pass the Adirondack Museum on the edge of town, continue for 6.4 miles to the sharp curve in Deerland, take a left onto North Point Road, and go for about 1 mile.

Additional information: There are three public lean-tos near the falls—one above and two below. They are available to the public for one night on a first-come, first-served basis.

152B. Public Access *(see map on page 217)*

Description: Parking for about ten cars and river access at the entrance to the state campgrounds.

Buttermilk Falls (site 152A).

The fishing: This stretch of river has native brook trout ranging from 5 to 12 inches and brown trout averaging 14 inches. They take worms and nymphs.

Directions: Continue heading down North Point Road from the above site for about 2 miles and turn into the Forked Lake State Campground.

152C. Axton Landing *(see map on page 217)*

Description: Parking for ten cars and a beach launch for cartop craft.

The fishing: Walleyes, northern pike, and smallmouth bass occupy this relatively quiet section of river, which runs through a massive marsh whose habitats include steep shorelines, undercut banks, blowdowns, cattail mats, bulrush colonies, lily pads, and tributary mouths. Minnows and spinnerbaits are effective for bass and northerns; worms and minnow-imitating crankbaits are popularly used for the bronzebacks and walleyes.

Directions: From Tupper Lake, head east on NY 3 for about 7 miles, then turn south onto Coreys Road and follow it for about 1.5 miles.

Additional information: Raquette Falls is about 3 miles upstream.

152D. Raquette River Public Access *(see map on page 217)*

Description: This state site is downstream of Raquette Falls and has a double-wide ramp, two lots with parking for more than fifty rigs, and toilets.

The fishing: The river is aimless here. Flowing slowly, quietly through one of the largest wetlands in the Adirondacks, it looks like a watery web whose strands of creeks, backwaters, and oxbows shoot out in all directions. This navigable network of channels is home to good populations of northern pike, smallmouth bass, bucketmouths, and walleyes.

Directions: Head north out of the village of Tupper Lake on NY 30/NY 3 for about 3 miles.

Additional information: Much of this section, in both directions, runs through or along the High Peaks Wilderness Area, where primitive camping is allowed.

153. Forked Lake *(see map on page 217)*

Key species: Largemouth bass, smallmouth bass, yellow perch, pumpkinseed, and brown bullhead.

Description: Set in deep woods, this crooked, 1,248-acre lake averages 10 feet and has one deep spot dropping to 40 feet.

Tips: Work soft plastic slugs around tree stumps and submerged logs.

The fishing: This warm-water fishery is loaded with bass. Largemouths are the predominant species, outnumbering the smallmouths four to one. They range from 12 to 20 inches and respond to tubes, slugs, Texas-rigged soft plastic worms, and jig-'n'-pigs. Smallmouths range from 12 to 15 inches and will take the same lures, as well as fat-bodied crankbaits. Yellow perch thrive here, reaching up to 12 inches. They take minnows and small lures. Pumpkinseeds ranging from 4 to 7 inches and bullheads averaging a whopping 13 inches are also abundant and are fond of worms. This lake's deepest areas are acidic and have low oxygen levels.

Directions: Take NY 28 north out of Raquette Lake village for about 13 miles. In the hamlet of Blue Mountain Lake, take NY 30/NY 28N for about 8 miles to Deerland. Turn west onto North Point Road, travel for 3 miles, turn right at the FORKED LAKE STATE CAMPGROUND sign, and travel for about 1 mile.

Additional information: Forked Lake State Campground has eighty no-frills campsites, a boat launch, picnic facilities, canoe and boat rentals, hiking trails, and pit toilets. It's open from mid-May through Labor Day; a day-use fee is charged to noncampers during the season. Free day use is permitted off-season.

Contact: New York State Department of Environmental Conservation Region 5.

153A. Canoe Carry Access

Description: This hard-surface beach launch is suitable for small trailered craft. There's parking for about ten rigs.

Directions: Head southeast for about 5 miles on North Point Road from its intersection with the campground entrance road, then turn right.

154. Long Lake *(see map on page 217)*

Key species: Smallmouth bass, largemouth bass, and northern pike.

Description: Really just a long, wide hole in the Raquette River, this 4,077-acre widewater stretches for 16 miles, averages 13 feet deep, and has a maximum depth of 50 feet.

Tips: Find habitat and you'll find fish.

The fishing: This lake is poor in habitat. While the shoreline may look fishy, the lake floor just a few feet off the beach is generally barren. Still, there's a good population of smallmouth bass in the 0.75- to 2.5-pound range. They are especially numerous around the north end's two sets of islands—the deepest part of the lake—where they respond well to scented, 3-inch curly-tailed grubs and 4-inch finesse worms worked on drop-shot rigs.

An exciting largemouth fishery is developing on the lake. Rare just five years ago, fish ranging from 2 to 4 pounds are being caught with increasing regularity. Most are taken on Rat-L-Traps, floating baits such as Mann's Chug-N-Spits, and jerkbaits worked around everything from docks and fallen timber to lily pads. The northern pike fishery, the lake's former main attraction, seems to have deteriorated lately. They used to range from 3 to 8 pounds but now go only from 2 to 4 pounds. They hang out anywhere there is cover and respond to Lazy Ikes, C.C. Rattlin' Shads, and live minnows.

Directions: Head north out of Blue Mountain Lake on NY 30/NY 28N for about 7 miles.

Additional information: The Long Lake fishing access site, located right in the heart of Long Lake village (turn east at the flashing light onto NY 30), has a boat launch with a triple-wide paved ramp, parking for forty rigs, and toilets.

Contact: New York State Department of Environmental Conservation Region 5.

155. Tupper Lake *(see map on page 217)*

Key species: Northern pike, walleye, largemouth bass, smallmouth bass, lake trout, landlocked Atlantic salmon, cisco, and yellow perch.

Description: Covering roughly 4,000 acres, averaging 39 feet deep, and having a maximum depth of 100 feet, half of this two-story fishery's shoreline is heavily developed and includes the village of Tupper Lake, one of the largest in the Adirondacks, on its northeastern corner.

Tips: Be creative with presentations so your bait stands out.

The fishing: This lake's incredible rainbow smelt population supports large populations of a variety of game species. Northern pike are the most famous. Although they range from 3 to 15 pounds, specimens pushing the 20-pound mark are caught annually, mostly through the ice on large minnows. Walleyes are the lake's best-kept secret. They range from 4 to 10 pounds, and larger ones are caught frequently. In fact, Richard Preall, a state biologist, says he wouldn't be surprised if a new state record is swimming in the lake. They respond well to worms and minnows drifted or trolled on harnesses. Smallmouth bass range from 0.75 to 3 pounds. They congregate around island drop-offs and rocky points and respond well to salted tubes and spinnerbaits. Preall notes that this lake, like many of the lakes on the Raquette River, is experiencing an explosion of largemouth bass. Relatively rare just five years ago, fish ranging from 2 to 4 pounds, with a smattering of 5-pounders, are being caught with increasing regularity. They hang out in the lake's bays and stream mouths and are mostly taken on spinnerbaits, buzzbaits, and Texas-rigged worms meant for smallmouths. Yellow perch range from 6 to 14 inches and hit worms, minnows, and scented, 2-inch curly-tailed grubs.

Roughly 10,000 lake trout averaging 6.5 inches are stocked annually. Still, surveys show that 20 percent of the lakers taken are naturally reproducing. They range from 20 to 30 inches and are generally taken through the ice on minnows fished throughout the water column. Landlocked salmon range from 15 to 22 inches and hit crankbaits such as Junior ThunderSticks and Bomber Long "A"s. Ciscoes ranging from 9 to 15 inches thrive in the lake. With all the glamorous species around, few anglers pay any attention to these freshwater herring until winter, when they are often caught by ice anglers targeting perch with tiny Swedish Pimples or jigs tipped with grubs.

Trout and salmon can be taken year-round.

It is often said big fish didn't get that way by being stupid. Tupper Lake is an exception to that rule. Here the fish get big because of the unusually abundant forage base. In fact, the population of rainbow smelt is so vast, the biggest problem anglers face is getting the fish to see their bait.

Directions: Take NY 3 south out of Saranac Lake for about 20 miles to the village of Tupper Lake. NY 30 parallels the east bank.

Additional information: The Tupper Lake Boat Launching Site is located on NY 30, about 2 miles south of the village. It has a paved four-lane ramp, parking for about seventy-five rigs, shore-fishing access, handicapped access, and toilets. The village of Tupper Lake publishes a free fishing guide containing maps and tips. Numerous inns and motels can be found in the area.

Contact: New York State Department of Environmental Conservation Region 5, and Tupper Lake Chamber of Commerce.

156. Raquette Pond *(see map on page 217)*

Key species: Northern pike, walleye, and yellow perch.

Description: Although this pond is impossible to differentiate from the main lake, it was created by a dam built on the Raquette River, a couple of miles downstream of Tupper Lake's outlet, and is known formally as Raquette Pond. Covering 1,180 acres, it averages 5 feet deep and has a maximum depth of 12 feet.

Tips: Troll the channel running down the center.

The fishing: Northern pike range from 3 to 15 pounds. They hang out along the weed edges, where they hit large minnows, YUM Walleye Grubs (the yellow is especially effective), and spinnerbaits. Walleyes ranging from 3 to 10 pounds are available in spring and fall and respond to above-mentioned grubs, trolled crankbaits, and worms on spinner harnesses. Yellow perch range from 6 to 12 inches and take worms, minnows, and jigs fished plain or tipped with 2-inch Exude grubs.

Directions: NY 3 parallels the lake's north side in the hamlet of Tupper Lake.

Additional information: The municipal park on NY 3 has a beach launch suitable for small trailered craft.

Contact: New York State Department of Environmental Conservation Region 5, and Tupper Lake Chamber of Commerce.

157. Simon Pond *(see map on page 217)*

Key species: Northern pike, walleye, and perch.

Description: This 689-acre pond averages 10 feet deep and has a maximum depth of 36 feet. It is connected to Tupper Lake (site 155) by a canal-like, navigable channel.

Tips: Ice fish with minnows in the weedy areas on the northwestern corner.

The fishing: This pond is the hottest ice-fishing spot around Tupper Lake. Northern pike of up to 18 pounds are taken here each winter. While they will hit spoons tipped with minnows and jigged on bottom, the technique favored by locals is to fish minnows, off tip-ups, in weed clearings. Walleyes ranging from 3 to 8 pounds are also taken through the ice on minnows, primarily in the deep eastern corner. Perch of up to 13 inches occupy the entire pond and hit minnows or grubs.

Directions: On the east side of the NY 30 bridge, in the village of Tupper Lake.

Additional information: The access site most favored by ice fishers is the local rod-and-gun club's gravel boat launch on Simon Pond Road. There's parking for ten cars.

Contact: New York State Department of Environmental Conservation Region 5, and Tupper Lake Chamber of Commerce.

158. Piercefield Flow *(see map on page 217)*

Key species: Northern pike, smallmouth bass, and walleye.

Description: This 365-acre impoundment averages 7 feet deep and has a maximum depth of 50 feet. Surrounded by forest, it is littered with numerous, barely submerged stumps.

Tips: Fish below Setting Pole Dam for early- and late-season walleye.

The fishing: This water body is loaded with northern pike habitat. They range from 18 to 30 inches and eagerly take minnows and spinnerbaits. Smallmouth bass ranging from 12 to 14 inches are abundant and respond to drop-shotting with 3-inch Berkley Drop-shot Pulse Worms and 4-inch Power Worms. Walleyes range from 15 to 22 inches and respond well to bucktail and marabou jigs and minnow-imitating crankbaits.

Directions: Head west on NY 3 out of the village of Tupper Lake for about 4 miles.

Additional information: Primitive camping is allowed at Setting Pole Dam. A beach launch for cartop craft is on NY 3. The state publishes a free brochure titled "The Raquette River in St. Lawrence County: Official Maps and Guide."

Piercefield Flow (site 158).

Contact: New York State Department of Environmental Conservation Region 6, and St. Lawrence County Chamber of Commerce.

159. Carry Falls Reservoir *(see map on page 226)*

Key species: Tiger muskie, northern pike, walleye, smallmouth bass, and brown bullhead.

Description: This 3,170-acre impoundment averages 18 feet deep and has a maximum depth of 50 feet; its shoreline is almost entirely forested.

Tips: Fish for walleyes on moonless nights.

The fishing: Lately the state has annually been stocking 1,500 muskies averaging 9 inches. In a 2001 survey, they were not doing too well, and the state was reconsidering the program. Norlunge ranging from 7 to 12 pounds should be available until the end of the decade. They like minnows and have a reputation for aggressively hitting bucktail spinners and Red Fins. Northern pike ranging from 2 to 6 pounds are also present. They respond to the same baits as their larger half-breed kin. Walleyes can go anywhere from 15 to 26 inches. They take Wally Divers and C. C. Shads, as well as worms trolled on spinner harnesses. Smallmouth bass from 12 to 14 inches are typical and take crayfish, minnows, scented curly-tailed grubs, tubes, and finesse worms. Brown bullheads ranging from 8 to 12 inches are widespread and hit worms fished on bottom, especially on cloudy days and at night.

Directions: Head south out of Potsdam on NY 56 for about 18 miles, turn east onto Stark Road, travel for about 2 miles, turn south onto Carry Falls Road, and continue for about 1.5 miles.

Additional information: A hard-surface launch ramp with parking for about five cars is found next to the dam. Parmenter Campsites, a fee area on the south end of the lake off NY 56, offers sixteen primitive sites and a boat launch. It's open Memorial Day through Labor Day.

Contact: New York State Department of Environmental Conservation Region 6, and St. Lawrence County Chamber of Commerce.

160. Stark Falls Reservoir *(see map on page 226)*

Key species: Tiger muskie, northern pike, walleye, smallmouth bass, brown bullhead, and yellow perch.

Description: This 704-acre impoundment averages 24 feet deep and has a maximum depth of 52 feet.

Tips: Pitch wacky-rigged Exude 5-inch Poc'it Fry.

The fishing: Recently the state has been stocking 1,000 norlunge annually. They aren't doing so hot, and the state is reconsidering the program. Still, tiger muskies

Reservoirs between Upper and Lower Raquette River · Colton Flow · Hannawa Falls Flow · Potsdam Flow · Norwood Lake

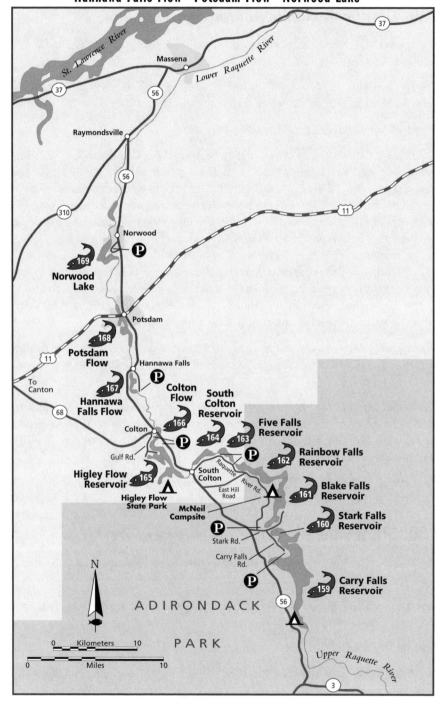

from 7 to 12 pounds should be available until the end of this decade. They respond well to large minnows drifted just off bottom, or suspended under bobbers and fished over weed edges. Northerns run 2 to 6 pounds and are quick to strike at 3- to 4-inch scented curly-tailed grubs worked at a steady retrieve, punctuated by a twitch of the rod every now and then. Walleyes ranging from 15 to 22 inches hit bucktail jigs tipped with minnows and worms and bounced slowly on bottom, in 15 to 20 feet of water. The breaklines at the mouths of bays hold good numbers of smallmouths up to 14 inches. They respond well to drop-shotting with 3- and 4-inch, scented, soft plastic baits. Brown bullheads and yellow perch range from 7 to 11 inches and are the local remedy for cabin fever right after ice-out. The bullheads take worms fished on bottom at night or on rainy days, and the perch go for small minnows suspended below tiny bobbers on sunny days.

Directions: Head south out of Potsdam on NY 56 for about 19 miles, then turn east onto Stark Road and travel for about 1.5 miles.

Additional information: A hard-surface ramp, with parking for about five rigs, is found at the dam. While reversing out of the launch area, watch out for boulders on the left.

Contact: New York State Department of Environmental Conservation Region 6, and St. Lawrence County Chamber of Commerce.

161. Blake Falls Reservoir

Key species: Walleyes, smallmouth bass, northern pike, yellow perch, and brown bullheads.

Description: This 710-acre impoundment averages 7 feet deep and has a maximum depth of 45 feet. The large bays are relatively shallow; the deepest part is a narrow, 0.5-mile-long trench right in the middle.

Tips: Cast diving crankbaits such as C. C. Shads at the dam.

The fishing: Walleyes range from 2 to 5 pounds and respond well to minnows fished deep on Lindy Rigs. In the evening, they rise to the bays and can be taken on diving and shallow-running, hard minnowbaits. Smallmouth bass from 12 to 14 inches are abundant, responding to crayfish crankbaits. Northerns range from 18 to 26 inches and are partial to spinnerbaits. Bullheads and perch reach 13 inches and take worms.

Directions: Head south out of Potsdam on NY 56 for about 19 miles; go east on Stark Road for about 1.5 miles, then north on Raquette River Road for about 1.5 miles more.

Additional information: McNeil Campsite, a fee area on Raquette River Road, offers fifty-eight sites, a hard-surface launch ramp, and toilets.

Contact: New York State Department of Environmental Conservation Region 6, and St. Lawrence County Chamber of Commerce.

162. Rainbow Falls Reservoir *(see map on page 226)*

Key species: Walleye, smallmouth bass, and northern pike.

Description: This 717-acre impoundment's south shore is heavily developed in cottages, but the north shore is heavily wooded. It averages 7 feet deep, drops to a maximum depth of 45 feet, and has a huge island.

Tips: Work buzzbaits over the tops of weeds.

The fishing: Walleye ranging from 15 to 22 inches are plentiful. Most are taken on bucktail jigs tipped with minnows or scented 3-inch curly-tailed grubs. Smallmouths can go as large as 3 pounds, but 1-pounders are the norm. They also hit baited jigs but will take stubby crankbaits like Wiggle "O"s just as quickly. Northerns rule the lake's copious weed beds. They respond well to a jig-rigged tube baited with a minnow and worked in weed openings and along the edges.

Directions: Head south out of Potsdam on NY 56 for about 15 miles. Head south out of Potsdam on NY 56 to South Colton, about 15 miles. A little south of the village, turn east on East Hill Road and travel about 2 miles to Raquette River Road, which parallels the reservoir.

Additional information: A public boat launch with a hard-surface ramp and parking for ten rigs is located on Raquette River Road.

Contact: New York State Department of Environmental Conservation Region 6, and St. Lawrence County Chamber of Commerce.

163. Five Falls Reservoir *(see map on page 226)*

Key species: Walleye, northern pike, and smallmouth bass.

Description: The smallest of the Raquette River impoundments, this place is shallow, features vast weed beds, and has little shoreline development—characteristics that make it look more like a beaver pond than a hydroelectric reservoir.

Tips: Fish the pools in the upper reaches for scrappy smallmouths.

The fishing: Walleyes can range anywhere from too little to just big enough. They hang out in the channels and take worms drifted on bottom. Smallmouths generally hang out in the same places and are often taken on worms drifted for walleyes—but things even out, because the walleyes often hit crankbaits targeting bronzebacks. This whole lake is northern pike territory. They reach up to 26 inches, though they're typically a few inches smaller. Go for them with minnows and soft slugs worked in and around the weeds.

Directions: Follow directions to Raquette River Road as described in site 162. Turn left on Raquette River Road and head north about 1 mile.

Additional information: A public launch site with a hard-surface ramp and parking for five cars is found on Raquette River Road.

Contact: New York State Department of Environmental Conservation Region 6, and St. Lawrence County Chamber of Commerce.

164. South Colton Reservoir *(see map on page 226)*

Key species: Walleye, northern pike, and smallmouth bass.

Description: Almost entirely in private hands, this 230-acre reservoir is ringed by cottages. It averages 14 feet deep and has a maximum depth of 47 feet.

Tips: Avoid crowding by fishing early in the morning.

The fishing: Walleyes average 18 inches and respond well to Rat-L-Traps and bucktail jigs, fished plain or tipped with scented curly-tailed grubs or minnows. Northern pike range from 20 to 28 inches and will take rattling crankbaits and buzzbaits. Smallmouth bass reach 14 inches and are partial to jigged tubes, Exude finesse worms dragged on Carolina rigs, live crayfish, and minnows.

Directions: Three Falls Lane (Raquette River Road), just east of the village of South Colton, parallels the reservoir.

A typical northern pike found in the Raquette River Reservoirs.

Additional information: Undeveloped access, with a beach launch for cartop craft, is found on Raquette River Road.

Contact: New York State Department of Environmental Conservation Region 6, and St. Lawrence County Chamber of Commerce.

165. Higley Flow Reservoir (Higley Falls Reservoir)
(see map on page 226)

Key species: Northern pike, smallmouth bass, largemouth bass, walleye, black crappie, yellow perch, and brown bullhead.

Description: This 1,135-acre impoundment averages 11 feet deep and has a maximum depth of 32 feet. Its shoreline is heavily developed with private residences.

Tips: Walleyes hang out below the dam in May and June.

The fishing: Northern pike ranging from 18 to 36 inches rule this pond, especially the shallow southern half near the mouth of the Raquette River. They respond well to buzzbaits and Zara Spooks but will take just about any lure, prompting cost-conscious anglers to use about 18 inches of TyGer stainless-steel leader material. Smallmouth bass ranging from 12 to 16 inches, and walleyes averaging 17 inches, reign in the northern half. They share the drop-offs. The walleyes like it a little deeper during the day, between 20 and 30 feet in summer. Both species respond well to minnows and worms. At night they move into shallow water, within reach of minnow crankbaits cast from shore. Panfish are a big draw, particularly around the south shore. This is about the only Raquette River reservoir where crappies ranging from 9 to 12 inches are plentiful enough to warrant targeting. They respond to scented, spinner-rigged, 2-inch curly-tailed grubs fished along weed edges. Yellow perch ranging from 6 to 10 inches, and brown bullheads in the 8- to 12-inch range are also plentiful. Perch take the same small lures as crappies and, just like bullheads, are fond of worms fished on bottom.

Directions: Head south out of Potsdam on NY 56 for about 10 miles.

Additional information: A paved boat launch with parking for about five rigs is found on Pine Road (off Gulf Road). Higley Flow State Park, a 1,250-acre fee area, occupies much of the south shore. It offers a single-lane paved launch, 135 campsites (43 with electrical hook-ups), playing fields, a swimming beach, and hiking trails. It's open from Memorial Day through Labor Day. Although free day use is permitted off-season, a barrier prevents vehicles from entering.

Contact: New York State Department of Environmental Conservation Region 6, and St. Lawrence County Chamber of Commerce.

166. Colton Flow (see map on page 226)

Key species: Northern pike, largemouth bass, yellow perch, and panfish.

Description: Slow moving and narrow, this weedy, 154-acre impoundment averages 4 feet deep and has a maximum depth of about 10 feet.

Tips: Drift a worm below a tiny bobber down the channels between the weeds.

The fishing: Northern pike range from 18 to 22 inches and respond well to jerkbaits. Largemouth bass run 1 to 3 pounds and love Texas-rigged worms and spinner-rigged soft plastic minnows flipped into weed openings. Bluegills and pumpkin-seeds averaging 5 inches, yellow perch of up to 10 inches, and bullheads averaging 10 inches are plentiful and respond enthusiastically to worms.

Directions: Head south out of Potsdam on NY 56 for about 8 miles to the south end of the village of Colton.

Additional information: A cartop launch and parking for five cars is located on Gulf Road, on the west side of the reservoir (off NY 68, about 0.5 mile west of the NY 56/NY 68 intersection). An informal shore-fishing access site with parking for about twenty cars is located on NY 56 just after you cross the bridge while heading south out of Colton.

Contact: New York State Department of Environmental Conservation Region 6, and St. Lawrence County Chamber of Commerce.

167. Hannawa Falls Flow (see map on page 226)

Key species: Smallmouth bass, walleye, and panfish.

Description: Its shoreline heavily developed with homes, this 200-acre impound-ment averages about 6 feet deep and has a maximum depth of 15 feet.

Tips: Cast perch-colored spoons.

The fishing: Smallmouth bass ranging from 12 to 14 inches respond well to 3-inch, scented curly-tailed grubs and salted tubes worked slowly on bottom. Walleyes are few but can be taken by dragging a worm, or by bouncing a scented curly-tailed grub on bottom. Brown bullheads of up to 12 inches and rock bass averaging 6 inches hit worms still-fished on bottom. In addition, rock bass respond to wet flies and small surface poppers.

Directions: Head south out of Potsdam on NY 56 for about 3 miles to Hannawa Falls.

Additional information: Postwood Park (from Main Street, turn south onto Church Street, then right onto Postwood Road) has beach access where launching cartop craft is permitted, bathrooms, playgrounds, picnic tables, and parking for about a hundred cars. You have to walk about 200 yards to get to the beach.

Contact: New York State Department of Environmental Conservation Region 6, and St. Lawrence County Chamber of Commerce.

168. Potsdam Flow *(see map on page 226)*

Key species: Northern pike, smallmouth bass, yellow perch, and rock bass.

Description: This shallow, 540-acre "pocket wilderness" runs right through the middle of the village of Potsdam.

Tips: Work twitch baits through the channels between the marshy islands.

The fishing: Northern pike ranging from 18 to 22 inches are fairly common and respond to minnow baits. Smallmouth bass in the 12- to 14-inch range are available, though you'll have to go through perhaps ten undersized fish to catch a keeper. They hit well on in-line spinners and spoons. Yellow perch between 5 and 9 inches and rock bass of up to 8 inches are common and are popularly sought by family groups fishing on bottom with worms while picnicking in Ives (Water Street) and Fall Island Parks.

Additional information: There is no launch suitable for trailered craft, but several village parks offer shore fishing and beach launching of canoes.

Contact: New York State Department of Environmental Conservation Region 6, and St. Lawrence County Chamber of Commerce.

169. Norwood Lake *(see map on page 226)*

Key species: Northern pike, smallmouth bass, and walleye.

Description: Located on the village of Norwood's southwest shore, this 352-acre reservoir averages about 10 feet deep. The east shore is moderately developed with private residences, while the west bank is a mixture of forest and farmland.

Tips: Drift crayfish on bottom.

The fishing: Northern pike range from 18 to 26 inches and have a taste for spinnerbaits. Smallmouth bass of up to 15 inches and walleyes of up to 20 inches are possible. They are often taken on lipless crankbaits and by drifting with worms on harnesses.

Directions: Head north out of Potsdam on NY 56 for 4 miles, then go west on CR 35.

Additional information: The village of Norwood has a hard-surface launch ramp and parking for about five cars off Lake Shore Drive.

Contact: New York State Department of Environmental Conservation Region 6, and St. Lawrence County Chamber of Commerce.

170. Lower Raquette River

Key species: Walleye, northern pike, smallmouth bass, and muskellunge.

Lower Raquette River

Description: This stream's final 15 miles, from Raymondsville to the St. Lawrence River, is free of barriers. Its long stretches of flatwater are punctuated by rapids that can be run by skilled canoeists during low water. The surrounding shoreline is mostly farmland and mixed bottomland forest.

Tips: Obtain permission from the Indians before fishing their water.

The fishing: Walleyes range from 15 inches to 8 pounds and are normally targeted by trolling floating-diving, minnow-imitating crankbaits. Northern pike as long as 36 inches are common and respond well to spinnerbaits and minnows fished below bobbers. Although smallmouth bass can reach up to 4 pounds, they average about 2 pounds. They bite best on minnows and crayfish but are also taken on scented, finesse worms on Carolina rigs. Though rare, muskellunge are here as well. They typically range from 8 to 12 pounds but have been known to go better than 20 pounds. They respond best to large minnows and minnow crankbaits. The size limit for muskellunge is only 40 inches.

Directions: North Raquette River Road (CR 40) breaks off from NY 56 about 3 miles north of Raymondsville and parallels the river to Rooseveltown.

Additional information: The last 5.6 miles of the river are on the St. Regis Indian Reservation, and you need permission from the sovereign nation to fish there. From Massena downstream, the river is polluted and grows progressively dirtier the closer you get to the mouth. Indeed, by the time it reaches the St. Lawrence, it is so contaminated with industrial wastes that the state has issued a health advisory warning against eating any fish.

Contact: New York State Department of Environmental Conservation Region 6, St. Lawrence County Chamber of Commerce, and Mohawk Council of Akwesasne Conservation Department.

170A. Springs Park *(see map on page 233)*

Description: This village park has a paved single-lane ramp, parking for ten rigs, shore-fishing access, picnic facilities, playgrounds, and toilets.

The fishing: The slow stretches upstream and downstream are ideal habitat for walleyes, northerns, smallmouths, and muskies.

Directions: Off Hatfield Street, below the NY 420 bridge, in the village of Massena.

171. Lake Eaton

Key species: Landlocked Atlantic salmon, lake trout, brown trout, smallmouth bass, yellow perch, pumpkinseed, and brown bullheads.

Description: Set in the north tip of the Sargent Ponds Wild Forest, this 556-acre lake's wooded shoreline is spotted with campsites. It averages 26 feet deep and has a maximum depth of 56 feet.

Lakes Eaton, Harris, and Lila - Little Tupper Lake

Tips: Use cork flies imitating food pellets.

The fishing: The state annually stocks almost 1,000 landlocked salmon averaging 6.5 inches. They typically grow to range from 15 to 18 inches and are usually taken by flatlining streamers and Junior ThunderSticks. Some years, usually in autumn, the local hatchery releases twenty-five to fifty brood stock landlocked salmon up to 38 inches long. Those that aren't caught almost immediately on flies imitating food pellets—or, later on, through the ice on minnows—are usually taken in spring or summer on big crankbaits such as Red Fins and Krocodile spoons. Roughly 6,500 lake trout averaging 6.5 inches are stocked annually. Growth is good, and anglers take quite a few keepers (21 inches) by casting spoons and crankbaits from shore in spring and fall, and by ice fishing with minnows. Lately the state has been stocking about 500 brown trout each year averaging 14 inches. The savviest of the species, they grow to average 3 pounds, with a lot of 6-pounders present. They respond well to minnows, worms, and crankbaits scented with herring oil. Finally, 3,100 rainbow trout averaging 9 inches are stocked yearly. They will take kernel corn, Berkley Trout Bait, and flies that imitate food pellets. A few naturally spawned brook trout are also available, and respond to dry flies and spinners. Smallmouth bass range from 12 to 14 inches and take crayfish, worms, jigs, and crankbaits. Bullheads and perch reach up to 14 inches; pumpkinseeds run as big as 8 inches. These are favored by family groups bottom fishing from shore with worms.

Trout and landlocked salmon can be taken year-round. The daily limit for lake trout is two. Yellow perch and sunfish can be taken in any number.

Directions: Take NY 30 for 1.5 miles north of Long Lake village.

Additional information: Lake Eaton Public Campground is a fee area offering 135 no-frills campsites (roughly half are along the shore), a hard-surface beach launch with parking for twelve rigs, boat and canoe rentals, hot showers, a swimming beach, and a trailer dumping station. When the campground is open, mid-May through Labor Day, a day-use fee is charged to noncampers. Free day use is permitted off-season.

Contact: New York State Department of Environmental Conservation Region 5.

172. Lake Harris *(see map on page 235)*

Key species: Northern pike, smallmouth bass, largemouth bass, brown bullhead, and yellow perch.

Description: Bordered on its entire north side by state land, this 287-acre lake averages 11.5 feet deep and has a maximum depth of 40 feet.

Tips: Wash lures with scent-free soap after handling.

The fishing: This warm-water fishery is completely natural. Northern pike range from 18 to 24 inches and are mostly caught on 4-inch shiners. Smallmouth bass range from 12 to 15 inches and take minnows, crayfish, and diving crankbaits.

Largemouth bass go from 12 to 20 inches and strike spinnerbaits, buzzbaits, and plastic worms. Perch average 9 inches; bullheads go from 8 to 12 inches. Both will take worms fished on bottom.

Use or possession of alewives or blueback herring as bait is prohibited.

Directions: From the village of Long Lake, head east on NY 28N for about 14 miles to Newcomb, then go north on Campsite Road for about 1 mile.

Additional information: Lake Harris Public Campground is a fee area offering eighty-nine no-frills campsites (fifty-seven of them on shore), a boat launch, canoe and rowboat rentals, hot showers, picnic areas, and a trailer dump station. A day-use fee is charged to noncampers when the campground is open, mid-May through Labor Day. Free day use is allowed off-season.

Contact: New York State Department of Environmental Conservation Region 5.

173. Little Tupper Lake (see map on page 235)

Key species: Brook trout.

Description: Nestled in the William C. Whitney Wilderness, this 2,305-acre pond is surrounded by forest, averages 10 feet deep, and has a maximum depth of 25 feet.

Tips: Use single-hooked lures such as Mepps Bantam Syclops and Aglia Long Spin Flies.

The fishing: This lake is famous for its Little Tupper Lake "heritage" strain of brook trout, classified by Cornell University scientists as genetically unique. Fishing is restricted to catch-and-release with artificial lures only. Like brook trout everywhere, these fish have an awesome appetite and will take properly presented flies, streamers, and lures. The tributaries have low densities of trout. Fishing is prohibited on the Charley Pond Outlet, the tributary on the west end, from July 1 through September 15. Other tributaries may be closed to fishing as well—check the *Fishing Regulations Guide*. Land a fish by wetting your hand first then gently grasping it. Do not insert your fingers under its gill cover or remove the fish from the water. Instead, keep it submerged as you unhook it, then release it immediately.

The use or possession of baitfish is prohibited. No motors are allowed.

Directions: From Long Lake village, take NY 30 north for 7 miles to Sebattis Road (CR 10). Turn west and travel for 4 miles.

Additional information: A cartop launch with parking for about ten cars is found on Sebattis Road. There are numerous primitive beach campsites around the lake and on some islands. Beach camping is only allowed in sites designated with CAMP HERE disks. The state's free brochure "William C. Whitney Wilderness: Adirondack Forest Preserve Map and Guide" shows the locations of all campsites.

Contact: New York State Department of Environmental Conservation Region 5.

174. Lake Lila *(see map on page 235)*

Key species: Lake trout and smallmouth bass.

Description: Set in the William C. Whitney Wilderness, this 1,414-acre lake averages 25 feet deep and has a maximum depth of 75 feet. The largest body of water in the forest preserve totally bound by state land, it is named for railroad magnate William Seward Webb's wife—the adjoining township is named for the man himself.

Tips: Beetle Spins work great for smallmouths.

The fishing: This lake has a remarkable number of lake trout ranging from 15 to 30 inches—so many, in fact, that the state has lowered the minimum length to 15 inches in the hope of thinning the population a bit. They are easiest to catch in spring and fall when they cruise shallow water, within reach of anglers casting and flatlining spoons, streamers, and silver crankbaits. The lake's smallmouth fishery is just short of legendary. Rich Preall, a state aquatic biologist, says they range from 12 to 15 inches, and fifty-fish days are possible. They respond best to spinnerbaits, diving crankbaits such as Wiggle "O"s and crayfish.

Use or possession of baitfish is prohibited. No motors are allowed.

Directions: From Long Lake village, take NY 30 north for 7 miles to Sebattis Road (CR 10). Turn west, travel for about 8 miles, turn left onto Lake Lila Road, and continue for about 5.75 miles. The trail to the canoe launch is found about 100 yards before the barrier.

Additional information: This lake has a lean-to and numerous primitive campsites along the shore and on its islands. Beach camping only allowed in sites designated by CAMP HERE disks. The state's free brochure "William C. Whitney Wilderness: Adirondack Forest Preserve Map and Guide" shows the locations of beach campsites.

Contact: New York State Department of Environmental Conservation Region 5.

175. Stillwater Reservoir

Key species: Smallmouth bass, splake, yellow perch, and bullhead.

Description: This 6,195-acre impoundment averages 6 feet deep and has a maximum depth of 32 feet. Almost totally surrounded by public woods, rich in points and islands, this is one of the most popular destinations for earth travelers in these mountains.

Tips: Keep your eyes peeled for shoals, sandbars, and barely submerged stumps.

The fishing: Smallmouth bass ranging from 2 to 4 pounds are plentiful, and larger ones are available. Indeed, the reservoir was partially drained in the summer of 2001 for repairs on the dam and numerous bronzebacks of better than 5 pounds were caught in the pools. Minnows and crayfish work best but crankbaits and soft plastics are also productive. Annually, the state stocks 1,500 splake averaging 9.5 inches

Stillwater Reservoir · Beaver River Canoe Route: Moshier Reservoir to Effley Falls Reservoir

Beaver River

Stillwater Reservoir

175

Stillwater Reservoir

Adirondack Scenic Railroad

Big Moose

1

To Eagle Bay

Stillwater Reservoir

Stillwater Big Moose Rd.

Moshier Reservoir

176

Moshier Rd.

Stillwater Rd.

Beaver Lake

177

White Water Release Section

Eagle Falls Dam

177A

Adsit Trail

Buck Point Road

Soft Maple Reservoir

178

Soft Maple Recreation Area

Effley Falls Reservoir

179

Soft Maple Rd.

Number Four Rd.

To Croghan

To Lowville

N

Kilometers
0   5   5

Miles
0   5

into the Burnt Lake and Trout Pond (natural lakes that were "drowned" by the reservoir) sections in the northeastern corner. Holdover is fair, and the fish range from 10 to 16 inches. They respond to worms, minnows, and streamers deep-trolled behind wobblers. Yellow perch range from 6 to 9 inches, and bullheads average 10 inches. Both take worms.

Directions: Take NY 28 north out of Old Forge for about 9 miles to Eagle Bay. Turn north onto Big Moose Road (CR 1) and travel for about 8 miles to the hamlet of Big Moose, where the pavement ends. Continue on the hard-surface, gravel road for about 10 miles and turn right, at the sign, into the state boat launch and parking area.

Additional information: The launch area has a double-wide paved ramp, a loading dock, parking for about fifty rigs, picnic tables, toilets, a convenience store, and a restaurant. The shoreline and islands have numerous hardened campsites. Campers must register at the state forest ranger headquarters at the boat launch. The state offers the free brochure "Stillwater Reservoir: Adirondack Forest Preserve Map and Guide."

Contact: New York State Department of Environmental Conservation Region 6.

176. Moshier Reservoir (see map on page 239)

Key species: Tiger muskie.

Description: This long, narrow 281-acre impoundment starts below Stillwater Reservoir Dam, averages 19 feet deep, and has a maximum depth of 75 feet. The shoreline is largely forested.

Tips: Suspend large shiners 3 to 5 feet below bobbers. Keep the floats as small as possible.

The fishing: This reservoir gets stocked annually with 900 norlunge averaging 9.5 inches. Although they have a lot of forage, primarily perch and white suckers, the vast majority end up growing to weigh only between 5 and 8 pounds. Still, they attract a following of anglers who enjoy fishing for them in the pristine setting with large crankbaits and minnows.

Directions: From the launch at Stillwater Reservoir (site 175), continue west on Stillwater Road for about 3 miles, then turn north onto Moshier Road and follow it for about 2.5 miles to the whitewater release parking lot above the dam.

Additional information: A beach launch with parking for about five cars is found at the dam.

Contact: New York State Department of Environmental Conservation Region 6, and Reliant Energy.

177. Beaver Lake (see map on page 239)

Key species: Chain pickerel, smallmouth bass, brown bullhead, and yellow perch.

Description: This 234-acre impoundment averages 8 feet deep and has a maximum depth of 30 feet. It has several back bays and a long narrow stretch.

Tips: If you are fishing for perch and catch a small one, leave. Continue moving until you locate one of at least 8 inches, then work the area thoroughly.

The fishing: Pickerel are the main predator. They range from 15 to 25 inches and respond well to worms on spinner harnesses retrieved at a moderate speed. Smallmouth bass range from 10 to 13 inches and like crayfish and scented curly-tailed grubs. Perch average 6 inches, but schools of fish ranging from 8 to 10 inches are present. They can be anywhere; a good technique is to work a scented, 2-inch curly-tailed grub through the entire water column until you locate one—generally there will be more. Brown bullheads range from 6 to 12 inches and love worms still-fished on muddy bottoms.

The minimum length for black bass is 10 inches.

Directions: Follow the above directions to Moshier Reservoir (site 176), but when you turn onto Moshier Road, only continue about 0.5 mile to the powerhouse.

Additional information: There is parking for about five cars at the powerhouse. If you want to launch a canoe, you'll have to portage about 0.25 mile, crossing Sunday Creek on a footbridge, to the beach launch.

Contact: New York State Department of Environmental Conservation Region 6, and Reliant Energy.

177A. Public Access

Description: This site has parking for about three cars above the Eagle Falls Dam.

Directions: Head west on Stillwater Road to its end. Turn right (north) onto Buck Point Road, then left (west) 0.5 mile later onto Adsit Trail, an unpaved road. Travel for 2.6 miles, turn right, go downhill for 0.2 mile, and bear right to the launch site.

Additional information: This site is above the dam, on Eagle Reservoir, an arm of Beaver Lake separated from the main body by a long strait swollen in spots by bays.

178. Soft Maple Reservoir *(see map on page 239)*

Key species: Norlunge, smallmouth bass, and brown bullhead.

Description: This 326-acre impoundment averages 23 feet deep and has a maximum depth of 63 feet. A channel on the southwest side leads into its smaller kin, lower Maple Reservoir. The islands offer just enough extra habitat to make this pond one of the most productive in the chain.

Tips: Cast MirrOlure Lipped 52M minnows.

The fishing: Tiger muskies range from 30 to 36 inches and respond well to large minnows, crankbaits, and Mepps Muskie Killers. Smallmouth bass range from 10 to

14 inches and like crayfish and minnows. Brown bullheads average 10 inches and take worms fished on bottom.

Minimum size for black bass is 10 inches.

Directions: From site 177A, continue on the Adsit Trail for about 0.7 mile to the canoe launch.

Additional information: The canoe launch at the foot of the powerhouse has parking for about five cars. The Soft Maple Recreation Area, about a mile farther west on Adsit Trail, is a fee area offering campsites, picnic facilities, a canoe launch, and toilets. There are several free, no-frills campsites on the islands and on the long point on the northeastern end.

Contact: New York State Department of Environmental Conservation Region 6, and Reliant Energy.

179. Effley Falls Reservoir *(see map on page 239)*

Key species: Chain pickerel, smallmouth bass, brown bullhead, and rock bass.

Description: This 339-acre impoundment is the first formed by the Beaver River after it leaves the Adirondack Park. Averaging 17 feet deep, its maximum depth is 31 feet.

Tips: Fly fish with ¼-ounce poppers.

The fishing: Chain pickerel are plentiful. They range from 15 inches to 25 inches and respond well to Hula Poppers and worms on spinner-rigged harnesses retrieved at a moderate to rapid clip. Smallmouth bass average 12 inches and will take surface lures, crayfish, and minnows. Brown bullheads ranging from 8 to 11 inches, and rock bass averaging 6 inches, both readily take worms.

The minimum size for black bass is 10 inches.

Directions: From site 178, continue down Adsit Trail for about 2.5 miles.

Additional information: The cartop launch below the Soft Maple powerhouse has parking for five cars. There are no public roads along the south side.

Contact: New York State Department of Environmental Conservation Region 6, and Reliant Energy.

180. Taylorville Reservoir

Key species: Chain pickerel, smallmouth bass, and brown bullhead.

Description: This 95-acre impoundment averages 9 feet deep and has a maximum depth of 25 feet.

Tips: Still-fish with worms on bottom in spring and bring lots of insect repellent.

Beaver River Canoe Route: Taylorville Reservoir to High Falls Reservoir · Lower Beaver River

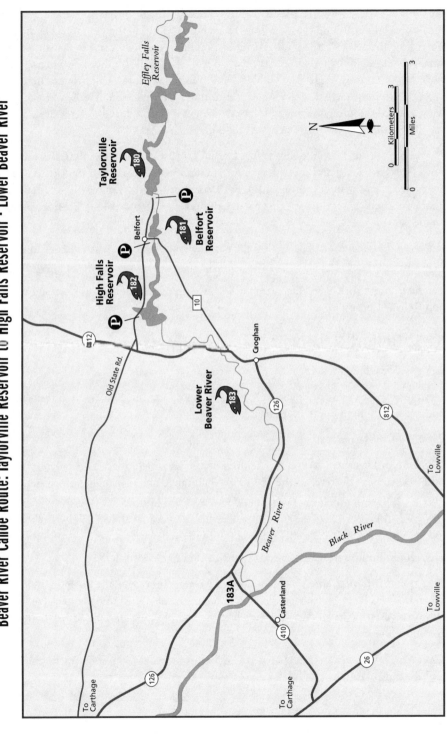

The fishing: Chain pickerel ranging from 15 to 21 inches are plentiful. They respond well to a variety of soft plastics, but especially slugs and curly-tailed grubs. Smallmouth bass are the typical 10- to 13-inch fish found in the system. They hang out a little deeper than the pickerel and respond best to worms but will also take a small, diving crankbait such as a Poe's Super Cedar 1100. Bullheads averaging 10 inches are plentiful. While they will hit a worm fished on bottom almost any time of year, they are especially hungry—and plentiful near shore—from late April through May, and are popularly targeted by family groups at the Taylorville picnic area.

The minimum size for black bass is 10 inches.

Directions: From Lowville, head north on NY 812 for about 13 miles. Turn east onto Old State Road and travel for about 3 miles into the hamlet of Belfort. About 0.1 mile east of the intersection with CR 10, turn south onto Taylorville Road, then bear left 0.3 mile later onto the dirt road. Continue for 0.6 mile, along the huge pipe, to the dam.

Additional information: The Taylorville parking and picnic area has a canoe launch, shore-fishing access, picnic facilities, and toilets.

Contact: New York State Department of Environmental Conservation Region 6, and Reliant Energy.

181. Belfort Reservoir *(see map on page 243)*

Key species: Chain pickerel and yellow perch.

Description: Covering only about 40 acres, this impoundment averages 5 feet deep and has a maximum depth of 14 feet.

Tips: Fly fish with streamers.

The fishing: This small reservoir is seldom fished because it doesn't have many fish. Still, some chain pickerel in the 15- to 18-inch range are available and respond to Storm's SubWarts, Rooster Tails, and just about anything bite sized that whips past them. The perch are small, 5- to 7-inchers, and are a lot of fun to catch on worms and wet flies fished below tiny bobbers with ultralight tackle.

Directions: Follow the directions to Belfort listed under site 180.

Additional information: A new bridge was being built over the river in Belfort when this was being written, and a boat launch was scheduled to be constructed on its northwestern corner. A canoe launch at the end of Taylorville Road has parking for about five cars.

Contact: New York State Department of Environmental Conservation Region 6, and Reliant Energy.

182. High Falls Reservoir *(see map on page 243)*

Key species: Smallmouth bass, rock bass, and brown bullhead.

Description: The last of the Beaver River impoundments, this 185-acre reservoir averages 5 feet deep and has a maximum depth of 18 feet.

Tips: The area around the dam holds most of the bass.

The fishing: Smallmouths range from 10 to 14 inches. They respond well to 3-inch Exude curly-tailed grubs fished on drop-shot rigs. Rock bass go anywhere from 5 to 8 inches. The larger ones will sometimes hit drop-shot-rigged soft plastics—but they always hit minnows and worms. Bullheads up to 12 inches take worms fished on bottom. The formal and shoulder access sites at the culverts on Old State Road are local hot spots in spring.

The minimum size for black bass is 10 inches.

Directions: Head west for 2 miles out of Belfort on Old State Road.

Additional information: A canoe launch on the west side of the Old State Road culverts has parking for about ten cars, picnic facilities, and shore access. Primitive camping is allowed on the two largest islands.

Contact: New York State Department of Environmental Conservation Region 6, and Reliant Energy.

183. Lower Beaver River *(see map on page 243)*

Key species: Walleye, smallmouth bass, and northern pike.

Description: Tamed by the reservoirs, the Beaver River slowly snakes west for about 10 miles to feed the Black River, 1 mile east of Castorland. Dark, deep, steep sided, and loaded with windfalls, this stretch runs through relatively flat farm country and bottomland forests.

Tips: Work Lindy No-Snagg Timb'r Rock Jigs tipped with minnows, worms, or scented curly-tailed grubs through the holes below log piles.

The fishing: Walleyes ranging from 15 to 22 inches are plentiful in these dark waters. Although they respond well to Rapalas and Bomber Long "A"s worked through the channels, daytime anglers have better luck casting live bait under structure and along steep banks. Smallmouths typically run from 10 to 16 inches, but 20-inchers are possible. They will take 3-inch scented curly tails, tubes, and Texas-rigged worms. Northerns prowl shallow areas. Fish in the 30-inch range are common and respond well to Rat-L-Traps bounced off emergent branches then worked tight to the submerged timber.

The minimum length for black bass is 10 inches.

Directions: NY 126 and 812 parallel most of the river.

Contact: New York State Department of Environmental Conservation Region 6, and Lewis County Chamber of Commerce.

183A. Public Access *(see map on page 243)*

Description: This site offers a paved single-lane ramp, a hard-surface double-lane ramp, shore-fishing access, parking for fifty rigs, and toilets.

Directions: Head north out of Lowville on NY 26 for 6 miles. Turn east onto NY 410, travel for 3.2 miles, cross the bridge, and turn left.

184. Lake Durant

Key species: Tiger muskie, largemouth bass, pumpkinseed, and yellow perch.

Description: Named for William West Durant, a nineteenth-century developer famed as the father of the Adirondack Great Camp, this 293-acre impoundment averages about 8 feet deep and has a maximum depth of 20 feet.

Tips: Fly fish the back bays with large bass bugs.

The fishing: This lake's claim to fame is norlunge. The state annually stocks about 1,300 averaging 9 inches. Although few, if any, reach true trophy proportions, there are a lot of 5- to 7-pound fish, making this one of your best bets in the "Dacks" for catching a tiger. They hit large bucktail spinners and crankbaits such as Ripplin' Red Fins. Largemouth bass range from 3 to 5 pounds and also respond to crankbaits and spinners. Yellow perch go from 5 to 9 inches and can be counted on to hit worms and 2-inch scented, curly-tailed grubs. Pumpkinseeds average 5 inches and like worms, wet flies, and tiny poppers.

Directions: Take NY 28/NY 30 for about 1 mile east of the village of Blue Mountain Lake.

Additional information: Lake Durant Public Campground, a fee area, offers sixty-one no-frills sites, hot showers, a paved launch ramp with parking for ten rigs, a handicapped-accessible fishing platform, hiking trails, and a sand beach. A day-use fee is charged to noncampers when the campground is open, mid-May through Columbus Day. Free day use is permitted off-season.

Contact: New York State Department of Environmental Conservation Region 5.

185. Limekiln Lake

Key species: Splake, yellow perch, and panfish.

Description: Set in the northwestern corner of the Moose River Plains Wild Forest, under the shadow of Fawn Lake Mountain, this 460-acre lake is mostly ringed by forest, averages 20 feet deep, and has a maximum depth of 71 feet.

Lake Durant · Limekiln Lake

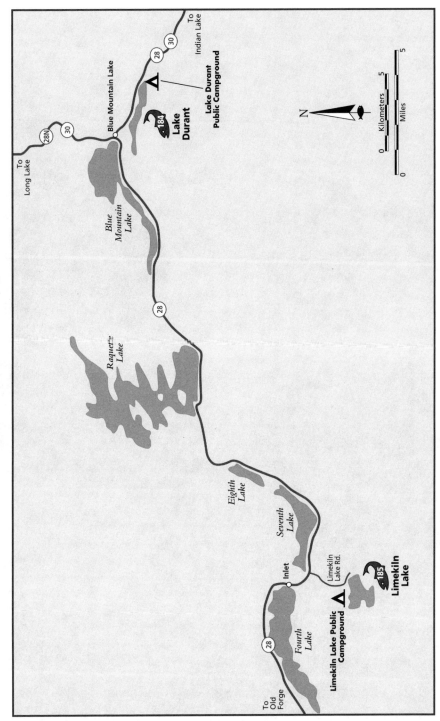

Enjoying the relaxing view at Lake Durant.

Tips: Slowly troll a Gray Ghost streamer 12 to 24 inches behind a gold wobbler.

The fishing: This lake is one of only a handful in the state that are stocked with splake. These fish range from 0.5 to 1.5 pounds—and there are a lot of them—but specimens up to 9 pounds have been taken. Most are caught on streamers or worms trolled deep, behind attractors. Trout can be taken year-round. Yellow perch ranging from 6 to 10 inches are plentiful and hit small jigs and worms. Bullheads of up to 12 inches and pumpkinseeds averaging 5 inches are also numerous, and both love worms.

Trout can be taken year-round. No motors are allowed on the lake.

Directions: Head north out of Utica on NY 12 for 24 miles to Alder Creek. Get on NY 28 north and travel for about 35 miles, going through the village of Inlet and turning right, about a mile later, onto Limekiln Lake Road. Travel for 1.5 miles, turn right onto Campsite Road, and continue for 0.5 mile.

Additional information: Limekiln Lake Public Campground is a fee area offering 271 no-frills sites, a gravel launch ramp, parking for twenty cars, swimming area, canoe rentals, nature trails, and hot showers. A day-use fee is charged to noncampers when the campground is open, mid-May through Labor Day. Free day use is allowed off-season.

Contact: New York State Department of Environmental Conservation Region 6.

186. Old Forge Pond *(see map on page 250)*

Key species: Largemouth bass, northern pike, and tiger muskie.

Description: Covering about 30 acres, this pond averages 5 feet deep and has a maximum depth of 9 feet. A 0.5-mile-long channel averaging 3 feet deep connects it to First Lake.

Tips: Spinnerbaits work well on all three species.

The fishing: Compared to its siblings in the Fulton Chain, this pond looks like the runt. Yet, gallon for gallon, it holds more than its fair share of hawg bucketmouths and northern pike of truly pikasaurus dimensions. Rumors of the pond containing 20-pound northerns have been circulating through the watering holes of Old Forge since the turn of the century, and Frank Flack, senior aquatic biologist, confirms their presence. This is a developing fishery and while you don't catch many, the ones you get are usually worth writing home to Mom about. They love large minnows. Flashy and noisy crankbaits and spinners ignite their conservative instincts, however, driving these pillars of the aquatic community to strike with extreme prejudice. Largemouth bass in the 1- to 3-pound range are common. They hang out under docks and in vegetation, responding well to Texas-rigged worms dragged over mud, and to fly-rod-sized Hula Poppers ($\frac{1}{32}$ to $\frac{1}{16}$-ounce) tossed onto lily pads and "bounced on the roof" to the water's edge. Tiger muskies in the 30- to 40-inch range are available and Mepps Muskie Killers trigger their suicidal tendencies.

Fulton Chain · Nicks Lake

To Blue Mountain Lake

Eighth Lake Public Campground

194 Eighth Lake

193 Seventh Lake

192 Sixth Lake

191 Fifth Lake

Inlet

190 Fourth Lake

South Shore Rd.

Petrie Rd.

190B

190A

Alger Island Public Campground

189 Third Lake

188 Second Lake

187 First Lake

186 Old Forge Pond

Old Forge

Bisby Rd.

Nicks Lake Public Campground

195 Nicks Lake

Middle Branch Moose River

To Alder Creek

N

Kilometers 0   5
Miles   0   5

Directions: Head north out of Utica on NY 12 to Alder Creek (about 22 miles). Get on NY 28 and travel north for about 25 miles to Old Forge.

Contact: New York State Department of Environmental Conservation Region 6, and Town of Webb Tourist Information Center.

187. First Lake

Key species: Smallmouth bass, largemouth bass, northern pike, and tiger muskie.

Description: This 736-acre lake averages 13 feet deep and has a maximum depth of 52 feet.

Tips: Drift large minnows.

The fishing: Smallmouth bass ranging from 1 to 3 pounds are common and are targeted with deep diving crankbaits such as C. C. Rattlin' Shads and MirrOlure 92LSRs. Bucketmouths range from 1 to 4 pounds and are targeted with jerkbaits and slugs worked in and around vegetation. A northern pike fishery has been developing lately and, as in all lakes when they first appear, they reach pikasaurus proportions. Frank Flack, a senior aquatic biologist with the state, says a 34-pounder was caught here in September 2001, and several 20-pounders have also been reported. They hit large minnows, crankbaits, and spinnerbaits. Over the past few years, the state has annually been stocking about 1,800 tiger muskies averaging 9 inches. They have grown to range a respectable 30 to 40 inches and relish the same baits northerns do.

A few rainbow trout drift in from Fourth Lake (site 190), and some brook trout migrate from tributaries. Their size ranges from tiny to trophy; most are caught incidentally by anglers targeting smallmouths with small crankbaits, spinners, and worms. They can be taken year-round, and their minimum size is 9 inches.

Directions: At the end of the channel running east out of Old Forge Pond (site 186).

Contact: New York State Department of Environmental Conservation Region 6, and Town of Webb Tourist Information Center.

188. Second Lake

Key species: Smallmouth bass, largemouth bass, northern pike, and tiger muskie.

Description: This 262-acre lake averages 51 feet deep and has a maximum depth of 85 feet.

Tips: Work salted tubes off points.

The fishing: Smallmouth bass range from 12 to 15 inches. They take crayfish, minnows, and diving crankbaits such as Fat Raps and Poe's Super Cedar series 1100. Largemouth bass go from 1 to 4 pounds and slam slugs jerked around docks and timber. Northern pike got into this system when someone dumped a couple illegally and, as in all places when they first appear, reached truly gargantuan proportions. In September 2001, a 34-pound pikasaurus was caught in adjoining First Lake, and several 20-pounders have been taken in Second Lake. They hit large minnows, spinnerbaits, and crankbaits. First Lake's tiger muskies know no boundaries and can be caught here. Ranging from 30 to 40 inches, they respond well to the same baits northerns do, as well as large Mepps Muskie Killers.

Landlocked salmon, as well as rainbow, lake, and brook trout, periodically wander in from adjoining lakes and tributaries and are caught incidentally by anglers targeting bass or pike and panfish. Salmonids can be taken year-round. The minimum size for brook and rainbow trout is 9 inches.

Directions: Just beyond the island on First Lake's (site 187) west end.

Contact: New York State Department of Environmental Conservation Region 6, and Town of Webb Tourist Information Center.

189. Third Lake *(see map on page 250)*

Key species: Lake trout, rainbow trout, smallmouth bass, largemouth bass, northern pike, and tiger muskie.

Description: This 179-acre lake averages 31 feet deep and has a maximum depth of 59 feet.

Tips: Cast propbaits and buzzbaits onto the shallow shelves on the north and west banks at dusk and dawn.

The fishing: Lake trout range from 21 to 25 inches and are usually taken in spring and fall by flatlining spoons and crankbaits, and through the ice with smelt. The state stocks about 1,200 8-inch rainbow trout annually. They typically grow to between 8 and 14 inches and hit worms, Mepps Black Fury spinners, and Mister Twister BigySmall Meatloaf Shad. Smallmouth bass ranging from 12 to 17 inches are common and respond well to crayfish and Carolina-rigged finesse worms. Bucketmouths in the 1- to 5-pound range thrive in the shallows and gentle drop-offs skirting the north and east banks and respond to Rat-L-Traps, Red Fins, and spinnerbaits. Someone illegally released a pair of northern pike here, and the species found the habitat good. They can go 30 to 45 inches and respond best to large minnows. Tiger muskies range from 30 to 40 inches and can be taken on large minnows, crankbaits, and Mepps bucktail spinners.

Some landlocked salmon, rainbow trout, and brook trout are also available and respond to worms, spinners, and crankbaits. Salmonids can be taken year-round. The minimum size for rainbow and brook trout is 9 inches.

Directions: Connected to the northwest corner of Second Lake (site 188) by a channel.

Contact: New York State Department of Environmental Conservation Region 6, and Town of Webb Tourist Information Center.

190. Fourth Lake *(see map on page 250)*

Key species: Landlocked Atlantic salmon, lake trout, rainbow trout, smallmouth bass, largemouth bass, northern pike, and tiger muskie.

Description: The largest and most popular lake in the chain, it covers 2,137 acres, averages 33 feet deep, and has a maximum depth of 85 feet.

Tips: Ice fish with live smelt for lunker lake trout.

The fishing: This lake is a traditional ice-fishing hot spot for lake trout. Each year, the state stocks about 5,800 averaging 7 inches. They grow to range from 2 to 10 pounds, with some reaching more than 20 pounds. Most are taken by ice fishers who first catch smelt by jigging, then use them for the lakers. Come warm weather, lakers are targeted with spoons trolled on Christmas tree or Seth Green rigs. Rainbow trout have fallen on hard times recently. Locals blame their disappearing act on tiger muskies and northern pike that prey heavily on the stockies. Still, the state annually releases more than 9,000 averaging 9 inches, and lucky anglers catch quite a few in spring on worms, minnows, spinners, and spoons—cast from shore, no less. Each year, about 4,300 landlocked Atlantic salmon averaging 6 inches are stocked. Enough manage to reach the 15-inch minimum length to make targeting them with streamers and crankbaits popular. In addition, the hatchery's surplus landlocked salmon brood stock is released here in some years, usually in autumn, creating pleasant surprises for anglers targeting lakers that winter.

Smallmouth bass can reach 17 inches and take minnows and crayfish and salted tubes fished deep, especially around the islands. Largemouths of up to 20 inches can be found in the back bays, where they respond to jig-'n'-pigs and Carolina-rigged Exude Super Craws. Northerns of up to 20 pounds are being reported with increasing regularity, along with tiger muskies in the 30- to 40-inch range. Both love large minnows, crankbaits, and bucktail spinners. In addition, the northerns just can't seem to keep their mouths shut around a red-and-white spinnerbait.

Salmonids can be taken year-round. The minimum size for brook and rainbow trout is 9 inches. The state has issued a health advisory against eating any lake trout from this water, because their flesh contains high levels of DDT, residues from the 1950s.

Directions: Head north from Old Forge on NY 28 for about 12 miles to Inlet.

Additional information: The state launch on NY 28 in the village of Inlet has a paved double-wide ramp, a loading dock, parking for thirty rigs, and toilets. Shore fishing is prohibited in the boat launch area. However, bank fishing is allowed in the village park, located in the heart of town, at the curve on NY 28. The park also offers a boat dock, picnic facilities, and toilets.

Contact: New York State Department of Environmental Conservation Region 6, and Town of Webb Tourist Information Center.

190A. Fourth Lake Picnic Area *(see map on page 250)*

Description: This site has a cartop boat launch and shore-fishing access. It's the reservation center for camping on Alger Island.

Directions: Traveling north on NY 28 in Old Forge, turn right onto Gilbert Street (at the post office), then left onto Park Avenue. Follow Park Avenue to its end, turn right onto South Shore Road, and continue for almost 5 miles to Petrie Road. Then turn left and travel for 0.75 mile.

190B. Alger Island Public Campground and Day Use Area
(see map on page 250)

Description: This operation, located on a wooded, 40-acre island, is a fee area offering fifteen lean-tos, two tent sites, outhouses, well water, picnic areas, a boat dock, and hiking trails. The campground is open mid-May through Labor Day. Free day use is permitted off-season.

Directions: Located on the west side of Fourth Lake.

191. Fifth Lake *(see map on page 250)*

Key species: Smallmouth bass, largemouth bass and rainbow trout.

Description: Covering only 14 acres, the smallest lake in the Fulton Chain averages 10 feet deep and has a maximum depth of 20 feet.

Tips: Drift with minnows or crayfish.

The fishing: Although any of the species found in its sister lakes can show up, this pond is mostly known for its smallmouths. They run from 12 to 18 inches and respond to drifted live bait, and curly-tailed grubs and salted tubes dragged on bottom. Largemouth bass range from 12 to 18 inches and mostly hang out in the weedy areas on the west shore, where they can be taken with soft and hard jerkbaits and Texas-rigged worms. The state used to annually stock about 400 rainbow trout averaging 9 inches, but stopped in 2002. Still, some between 9 and 18 inches should be available for years to come, because they migrate here from the other lakes in the chain. They take worms fished on bottom around the inlet in spring and fly patterns that match the hatch on summer evenings.

Possession or use of blueback herring or alewives as bait is prohibited.

Directions: Off NY 28 in downtown Inlet.

Additional information: The short portage between Fifth and Sixth Lakes starts at Fifth Lake's inlet, on its southeast side. Climb the hill and turn east along NY 28. Then cross NY 28 and take Sixth Lake Road to the dam.

Contact: New York State Department of Environmental Conservation Region 5.

192. Sixth Lake *(see map on page 250)*

Key species: Lake trout, landlocked Atlantic salmon, rainbow trout, and small-mouth bass.

Description: This 108-acre lake averages 12 feet deep and has a maximum depth of 38 feet. Though it's separated from Seventh Lake (site 193) by a navigable bottle-neck created by an island and a point, "these lakes are the same, from a management standpoint," says Rich Preall, the state aquatic biologist on whose beat they lie.

Tips: Flatline spoons parallel to shore, in 5 to 15 feet of water, in spring and fall.

The fishing: This lake is loaded with frying-pan-sized lake trout ranging from 18 to 20 inches—so many, in fact, that the state has reduced the minimum length to 18 inches in the hope of reducing populations a bit. At last word, the authorities were considering reducing the minimum length even further. Most are taken early and late in the season by casting or trolling spoons and crankbaits in shallow water. The state annually stocks 1,300 rainbow trout averaging 9 inches. They quickly grow to at least 10 inches, and many reach 16 inches. Most accessible in spring and fall, when they cruise the shallows near shore, they respond well to small spoons. Landlocked Atlantic salmon averaging 16 inches swim over from Seventh Lake all the time and are mostly taken by flatlining streamers. Smallmouth from 12 to 15 inches can be taken almost anywhere by fishing crayfish on bottom, in 10 to 20 feet of water.

There is no closed season for trout and salmon.

Directions: Take NY 28 about a 0.5 mile east of Inlet and turn left onto Sixth Lake Road.

Contact: New York State Department of Environmental Conservation Region 5.

193. Seventh Lake *(see map on page 250)*

Key species: Lake trout, landlocked salmon, rainbow trout, brown trout, and small-mouth bass.

Description: This 851-acre lake averages 70 feet deep and has a maximum depth of 120 feet. Its shoreline is mostly ringed by forest.

Tips: Cork-bodied flies that imitate food pellets work well.

The fishing: Like Sixth Lake (site 192), Seventh Lake is also loaded with lake trout in the 18- to 25-inch range. The state has been annually stocking more than 1,000 averaging 7 inches for years, and there are so many—and natural reproduction is so good—that the authorities are seriously thinking about discontinuing stocking. Indeed, the minimum length for lakers has already been reduced to 18 inches and, at last word, the authorities were thinking of reducing the size further still. Most are taken by flatlining spoons near shore in spring and fall. Ice fishers take quite a few on smelt. In summer, they are sought by anglers jigging spoons, or deep-trolling spoons on Seth Green and Christmas tree rigs. Roughly 800 landlocked salmon averaging 6.5 inches are also stocked each year. They manage to reach an average of 16 inches and like worms fished on bottom around tributary mouths in spring, in fall, and after a summer rain. Surplus landlocked salmon brood stock is released here occasionally, always in fall. Ranging from 5 to 15 pounds, these monsters are enthusiastically sought by ice anglers suspending smelt or shiners a couple feet below the hard water. About 3,800 rainbow trout averaging 9 inches are stocked annually. They end up ranging from 10 to 20 inches and are targeted, late spring through fall, with dry flies, streamers, and worms. Two hundred brown trout averaging 14 inches are also stocked each year. They can be caught in warm weather on worms, especially after a rain, and in winter by ice fishing with smelt. Smallmouth bass ranging from 12 to 15 inches are popularly sought by anglers drifting minnows and crayfish or jigging and drop-shotting scented 3-inch curly-tailed grubs and 4-inch finesse worms along drop-offs.

Trout and salmon can be taken year-round. The minimum size for lake trout is 18 inches.

Directions: Take NY 28 north for about 1 mile out of Inlet.

Additional information: A fishing access site on NY 28 has a double-wide paved ramp and parking for thirty rigs.

Contact: New York State Department of Environmental Conservation Region 5.

194. Eighth Lake *(see map on page 250)*

Key species: Lake trout, landlocked Atlantic salmon, rainbow trout, and smallmouth bass.

Description: The last lake in the Fulton Chain, it covers 303 acres, averages 39 feet deep, and has a maximum depth of 81 feet. The shoreline is almost completely forested and undeveloped.

Tips: Anchor at night and suspend a light over the side. Chum with kernel corn to attract trout and fish for them with a worm.

The fishing: This lake is notorious for large lake trout. The state stocks about 1,600 averaging 7 inches each year, and many grow to range from 6 to 10 pounds. Some make it all the way to 20 pounds. They respond well to live smelt fished on bottom, and to spoons trolled behind Christmas tree and Seth Green rigs. About 500 landlocked salmon yearlings averaging 6.5 inches are released annually. They do very well on the smelt and grow to average a respectable 20 inches. They will hit worms, smelt, and streamers. Rainbows averaging 9 inches are stocked to the tune of 2,800 annually. Most end up measuring 10 to 16 inches and are taken on worms, spoons, and spinners. Smallmouth bass go 12 to 16 inches and mostly hang out on the drop-offs along the rocky west bank. Often found in water exceeding 20 feet deep, the best way to catch them is by fishing a crayfish or minnow on bottom, or with Carolina-rigged Exude finesse worms.

Directions: Six miles east of Inlet on NY 28.

Additional information: Eighth Lake Public Campground, a fee area on NY 28 on the southern tip of the lake, offers 126 tent and trailer sites, a hard-surface launch ramp suitable only for small trailered craft, picnic areas, hiking trails, and showers. A day-use fee is charged to noncampers in-season, mid-April through mid-November. Free day use is allowed during the off-season.

Contact: New York State Department of Environmental Conservation Region 5.

195. Nicks Lake *(see map on page 250)*

Key species: Brown trout, rainbow trout, brown bullhead, and rock bass.

Description: This 205-acre reservoir averages 8 feet deep, has a maximum depth of 17 feet, and is completely surrounded by forest.

Tips: Cast mayfly and caddis patterns at dawn and dusk.

The fishing: This pond is managed as a trout fishery. Recently the state has been annually stocking about 15,000 browns averaging 6 inches. Winter survival is average, and browns range from 6 to 18 inches. The smaller ones take dry flies, but fish of more than 10 inches generally hang low and respond to streamers, minnow crankbaits scented with herring oil, and worms. A couple of thousand rainbows

Brown trout are plentiful in stocked Adirondack lakes such as Nicks Lake (site 195).

averaging 8 inches are also stocked each year. They generally reach up to 12 inches and respond to Krocodiles flatlined more than 5 to 10 feet of water in spring and fall, and to worms, natural kernel corn, or Exude Corn Niblets fished on bottom or below bobbers all season long. Rock bass range from 4 to 8 inches; bullheads average 10 inches. Both take worms.

In 2002 the state stocked black bass into the lake, hoping to develop a natural population. The fish management plan calls for catch-and-release bass fishing only — until they take, anyway — and this has been passed into law. Check the Herkimer County Special Regulations section in the state *Fishing Regulations Guide.*

No motors are allowed. Use or possession of minnows as baitfish is prohibited.

Directions: Take Bisby Road south out of Old Forge for about 1 mile.

Additional information: Nicks Lake Public Campground offers a cartop boat launch, parking for about ten cars, 112 campsites, hot showers, picnic facilities, ball fields, and hiking trails. A day-use fee is charged to noncampers in-season, mid-May through late October. Free day use is permitted off-season.

Contact: New York State Department of Environmental Conservation Region 6, and Town of Webb Tourist Information Center.

196. Cranberry Lake

Key species: Brook trout, smallmouth bass, northern pike, and rock bass.

Description: This 6,975-acre lake averages 6 feet deep, has a maximum depth of 38 feet, and has so many nooks and crannies that if you straightened out its shoreline it would stretch for 55 miles. The north bay has a little development, but the rest of the lake is ringed by wilderness.

Tips: The hot spot for big brookies is the bay at Dead Creek Flow.

The fishing: Though this was traditionally a brook trout lake, the species was all but wiped out by acid rain. Frank Flack, a senior aquatic biologist with the state, says his office started stocking the Temiscamie hybrid strain of brook trout late in the last century. A native of Canada known for its ability to tolerate acidic waters, the strain took, and currently fish ranging from 12 to 16 inches are common; some up to 4 pounds are caught every year. They respond well to worms and Muddler Minnows trolled slowly behind wobblers. Smallmouth bass are plentiful, but their numbers have been decreasing as the brookies have been increasing. Still, bronze-backs ranging from 10 to 18 inches are abundant and respond well to scented slugs, tubes, and curly-tailed grubs. Someone dumped northern pike into the lake and the illegal aliens found the place to their liking, with some growing to 15 pounds on the lake's abundant forage. They have a taste for red-and-white Dardevles.

The rock bass fishery sounds like a tall tale. Fish of 0.5 pound are common and 0.75-pounders are reported regularly. They hit worms, 2-inch scented curly-tailed grubs, minnows, small spinners, and spoons.

Cranberry Lake - Oswegatchie River (to Gouverneur)

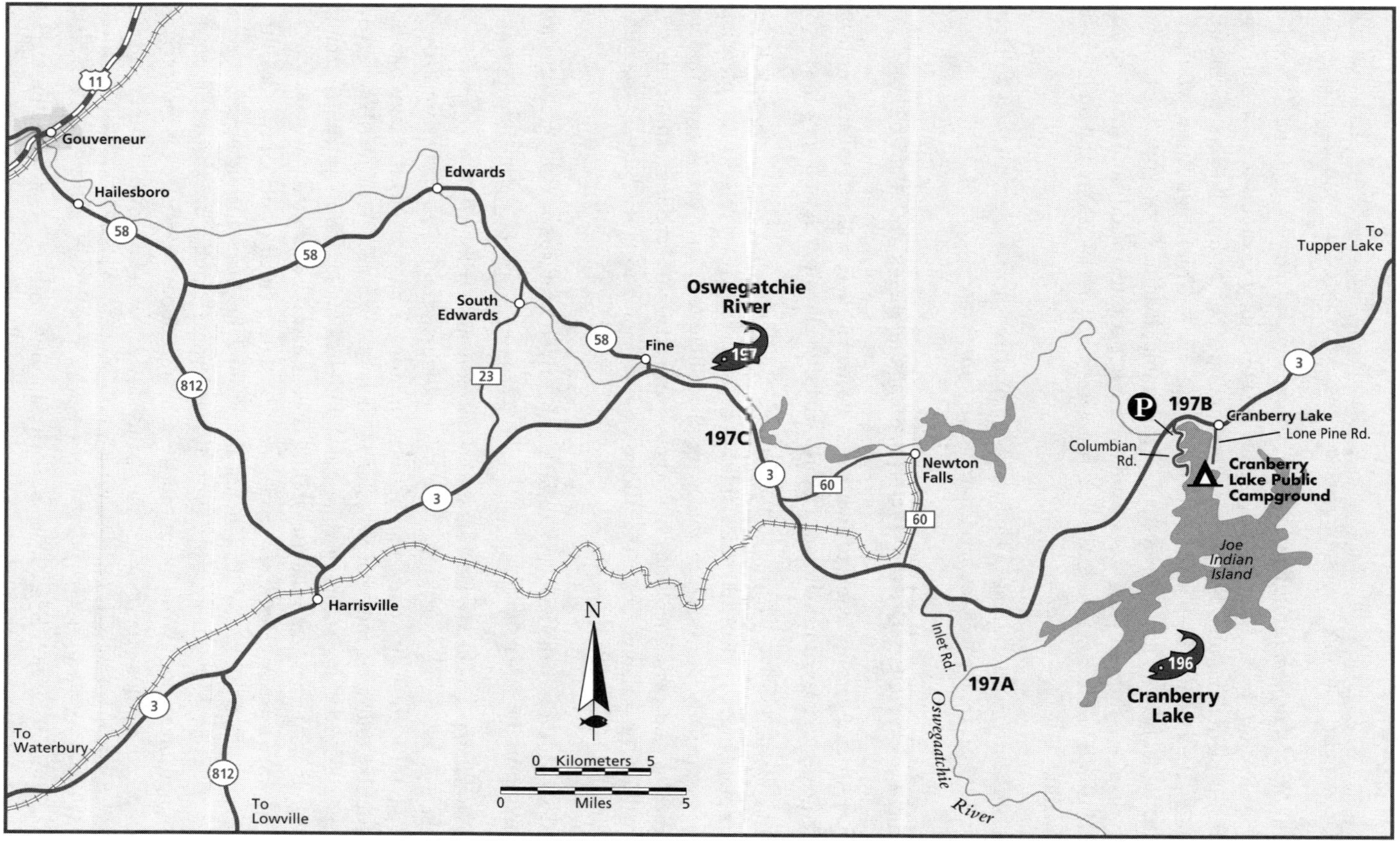

To Tupper Lake

3

Granberry Lake
Lone Pine Rd.

Cranberry Lake
Public
Campground

197B

Columbian Rd.

196

Cranberry Lake

Joe Indian Island

197A

Inlet Rd.

Oswegaatchie River

Newton Falls

60

60

Oswegatchie River

197

3

197C

Fine

58

Edwards

South Edwards

23

3

Harrisville

N

0 Kilometers 5

0 Miles 5

58

812

Gouverneur

Hailesboro

58

111

To Lowville

812

3

To Waterbury

The minimum size for black bass is 10 inches. There is no size limit on northern pike.

Directions: Take NY 3 west out of Tupper Lake village for about 21 miles.

Additional information: The Cranberry Lake Public Campground, located on Lone Pine Road, 1 mile south of NY 3, is a fee area offering 173 campsites, a handicapped-accessible fishing pier, hiking trails, a swimming beach, hot showers, picnic areas, and a trailer dump station. The state boat launch on Columbian Road (west side of the outlet bridge) has a paved double-wide ramp, loading docks, parking for seventy-five rigs, shore-fishing access, and overnight parking. In addition, there are forty-six primitive clearings designated as campsites along the lakeshore and on Joe Indian Island.

Contact: New York State Department of Environmental Conservation Region 6, and the St. Lawrence County Chamber of Commerce.

197. Oswegatchie River *(see maps on pages 259 and 261)*

Key species: Brook trout, brown trout, northern pike, walleye, smallmouth bass, largemouth bass, muskellunge, channel catfish, yellow perch, and rock bass.

Description: Snaking from the Five Ponds Wilderness to the St. Lawrence River, a distance of more than 100 miles, this boulder-strewn stream offers a complete menu of angling adventures, from wilderness fly fishing for native brook trout under the gaze of bald eagles demonstrating their own version of catching fish on the fly, to trolling for walleyes under the bridge in cosmopolitan Ogdensburg. It has numerous small impoundments.

Tips: A canoe is the best way to tackle this river because the fishing always looks better on the other side.

The fishing: The headwaters are native brook trout territory. The state supplements their population by stocking about 350 brookies averaging 9.5 inches annually. You won't find the 5-pounders that used to lure robber barons into this fabulous backcountry following the Civil War, but 14-inchers—or better—are possible on worms dead-drifted along submerged logs and undercut banks. This stretch is in the Five Ponds Wilderness, and the use of minnows as bait is prohibited.

Downstream from Cranberry Lake, the state annually stocks a couple of thousand brook trout averaging 9 inches and about 2,400 brown trout averaging 8 inches. Another 350 two-year-old browns averaging 14 inches are thrown in to make things interesting. While trout can show up just about anywhere on the river, their population thins progressively the farther downstream you go. The best trout water is from South Edwards upstream to Cranberry Lake. Salted minnows, worms, and in-line spinners work well.

Warm-water species thrive downstream of Cranberry Lake. Smallmouth bass ranging from 10 to 18 inches respond well to minnows, tubes, and spinner-rigged

Oswegatchie River: Gouverneur to Ogdensburg

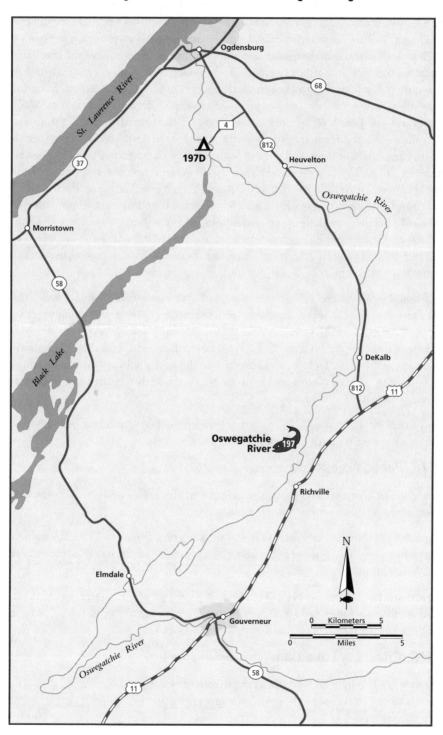

3-inch Exude Curly Tail Grubs. Come summer, the bigger ones migrate to impoundments above dams, where they will take spinnerbaits worked deep, along the edge of the old riverbed. Largemouth bass range from 1 to 4 pounds and are targeted mostly with topwater lures and spinnerbaits. Northern pike ranging from 3 to 20 pounds claim quiet stretches and impoundments, where they will take large minnows, minnow-imitating crankbaits, and spinnerbaits. Walleyes range from 2 to 6 pounds and will hit jigs worked through pockets in fast water, minnow-imitating and lipless crankbaits cast in slow-moving areas, and diving baits such as Wally Divers and MirrOlure 92LSRs in impoundments. Channel catfish ranging from 3 to 10 pounds—20-pounders are possible—hug the floor in deep holes and respond to cut bait, minnows, shrimp, and gobs of worms fished on bottom. Purebred muskellunge in the 5- to 25-pound class rule the lower reaches and respond to large crankbaits and surface baits, cast and trolled. Yellow perch ranging from 6 to 12 inches and rock bass ranging from 4 to 8 inches are found in most impoundments and slow stretches, and love worms, minnows, and small lures.

From Cranberry Lake downstream, trout season runs from April 1 to November 30. The minimum length for black bass is 10 inches. Above the dam in Ogdensburg, the minimum length for muskies is 40 inches.

Additional information: This stream is riddled with canoe-eating rapids, waterfalls, and dams. Head for shore to scout your course whenever you hear rushing water up ahead. Most communities on the river have informal public access with shoulder parking. They include Newton Falls, Fine, South Edwards, Edwards, Hailesboro, Gouverneur, Elmdale, Dekalb, and Heuvelton. The state publishes the free brochure "Fishing/Canoeing the Oswegatchie River: Newton Falls to Ogdensburg," containing maps and other information.

Contact: New York State Department of Environmental Conservation Region 6, and St. Lawrence County Chamber of Commerce.

197A. Public Access *(see map on page 259)*

Description: This site, known as the Inlet, is in the Five Ponds Wilderness, and offers a beach launch and parking for fifty cars.

The fishing: The native brook trout in this section range from 4 to 14 inches and will take worms, in-line spinners, streamers, and caddis variations. No baitfish or motors are allowed.

Directions: Head west on NY 3 for about 9 miles out of Cranberry Lake village. Turn south onto Sunny Lake Road, then immediately turn left onto Inlet Road and continue for 3.5 miles on the hard-surface unpaved road.

197B. Cranberry Lake Dam *(see map on page 259)*

The fishing: The state heavily stocks the stretch of water downstream of NY 3 with trout, and one of the river's hottest trout spots is below this dam.

View of the Oswegatchie River (site 197).

Directions: On the west side of the village of Cranberry Lake.

Additional information: There is no developed access. Anglers either park along the shoulder of Columbian Road or in the state boat launch parking lot.

197C. Reliant Power's Flat Rock Public Access *(see map on page 259)*

Description: This site has a canoe launch, parking for five cars, shore-fishing access, and picnic facilities.

The fishing: This tiny reservoir's waters hold ideal habitat for smallmouth bass, northern pike, catfish, yellow perch, and rock bass.

Directions: On NY 3, about 16 miles west of Cranberry Lake.

197D. Eel Weir State Park *(see map on page 261)*

Description: This fee area offers thirty-eight campsites, bathrooms, a picnic area, a paved launch ramp, and 600 feet of shore-fishing access. It's open Memorial Day through Columbus Day.

The fishing: This site sits between the river's mouth and the hamlet of Heuvelton, a stretch known for walleyes, bucketmouths, monster catfish, and a few muskies.

Grass River

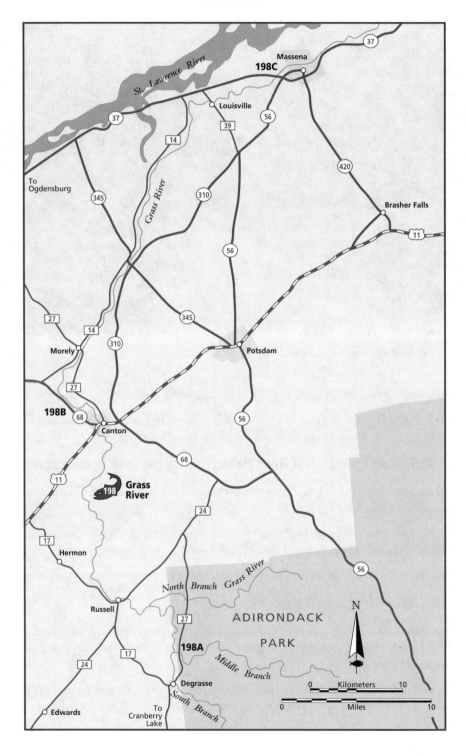

Directions: Head south out of Ogdensburg on NY 812 for about 3 miles, turn right (west) onto CR 4, and travel for about 2 miles.

198. Grass River

Key species: Brown trout, brook trout, walleye, northern pike, smallmouth bass, and muskellunge.

Description: Springing from the foothills of the Adirondacks, this river has three branches in its upper reaches, mostly on private property. It gathers them together about 1 mile east of Russell to form the main stem. From this point, the river slices north for about 50 miles—mostly canoeable—to feed the St. Lawrence River at Massena.

Tips: The best water for large muskies is the 21-mile stretch from Morley to Louisville.

The fishing: The state annually stocks this river's upper reaches around Russell with about 1,680 brown trout averaging 8 inches. They join native brook trout to offer decent angling for fish ranging from 8 to 14 inches. Trout habitat extends as far north as the village of Pyrites; the fish will take worms, flies, and spinners.

From here downstream, the habitat is strictly warm water. Smallmouth bass range from too short to about 13 inches—but there is a lot of them. Local guide and author Mike Seymour says eighty- to a hundred-fish days are common for folks using crayfish, worms, minnows, or casting spinners and small crankbaits. Northerns running from 18 to 30 inches are plentiful all the way to Massena. They hit minnows and their imitations. Walleyes from 18 to 22 inches are typical, but specimens of up to 30 inches are caught occasionally. They hang out in deep holes, where they'll hit a jig, drifted worm, or nightcrawler trolled on a spinner harness. Purebred muskies are available, but there aren't too many. Still, Mike Seymour leads clients to dream-sized muskies every year. The vast majority is taken in the most exciting and personal way: by casting large crankbaits and Mepps Muskie Killers.

Although the dam in Massena gave out late in the last century, state aquatic biologist Frank Flack says his office still considers it the first barrier impassable by fish. The minimum length for muskies above it is 40 inches. The minimum length for black bass is 10 inches.

Additional information: The state's free brochure "Fishing and Canoeing the Grass River: Degrasse to Massena" contains maps and pertinent information on the canoeable water. Informal canoe access is available at most bridge crossings.

Contact: New York State Department of Environmental Conservation Region 6.

198A. Informal Canoe Access

Description: This bridge crossing is on the Middle Branch, about 0.75 mile upstream of its confluence with the South Branch.

Canoeing on the Grass River (site 198).

The fishing: Brown trout, wild brook trout, and bronzebacks are available.

Directions: Head north out of Cranberry Lake on Tooley Pond Road for about 16 miles to Degrasse. Then take CR 27 north for 2 miles.

198B. Fishing Access *(see map on page 264)*

Description: This site, located on the eastern edge of the Upper and Lower Lakes State Wildlife Management Area, offers a hard-surface launch ramp and parking for twenty-five rigs.

The fishing: For 2 miles downstream of the boat launch, the river is flatwater averaging 4.5 feet deep, providing good northern pike, smallmouth bass, and walleye habitat.

Directions: Head north out of Canton on NY 68 for about 3 miles.

198C. Massena Municipal Boat Launch *(see map on page 264)*

Description: Although this site has a paved ramp, the dam downstream gave out several years ago and the water is well below it, making it unsuitable for trailered craft most of the time. There's parking for about twenty-five rigs. Picnic tables and toilets are found in the adjacent park.

The fishing: This stretch's shallow areas are good northern pike habitat, and the deep holes and channels contain walleyes and smallmouth bass. Some muskies are also available.

Directions: Behind the firehouse on Andrews Street.

199. North Lake *(see map on page 268)*

Key species: Tiger muskie, yellow perch, and brown bullhead.

Description: This 307-acre lake is the major source of the Black River. Averaging about 18 feet deep, having a maximum depth of roughly 50 feet, its shoreline is mostly forested. The bottom is strewn with rocks and huge boulders. The lake has suffered acidification problems in the past, wiping out all the fish for a while, including those in the Black River just downstream. Dan Buehler, the local forest ranger, says that strict air pollution laws have resulted in the condition remedying itself.

Tips: Use Mepps bucktail spinners for tiger muskies.

The fishing: The state began stocking norlunge in the late 1990s to the tune of 5,000 7-inchers annually. Currently they range from 32 to 38 inches and hit minnows, bucktail spinners, and crankbaits. Yellow perch get big, reaching 14 inches. They bite best on minnows and 2-inch, scented curly-tailed grubs. Bullheads average only 8 inches, but there are enough of them to make going after a bullhead dinner worthwhile. Fish for them on bottom with worms. A couple of thousand splake averaging 10 inches were stocked in 1999, and a few hardy individuals should be around

Black River from Its Source to Lowville

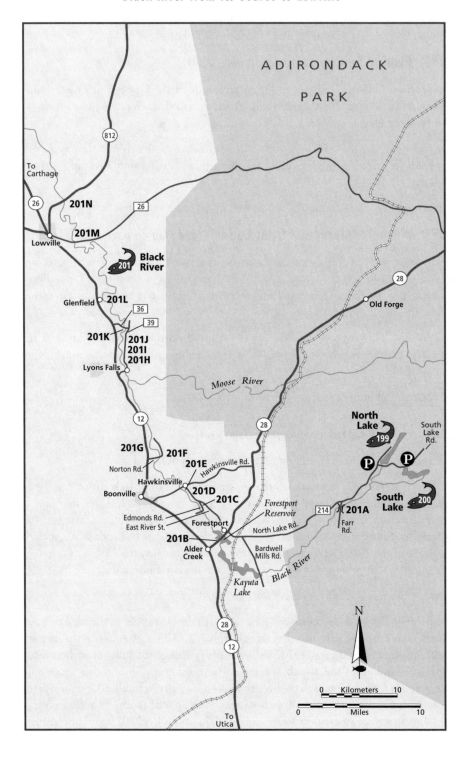

for part of this decade. They like streamers and worms trolled a few inches behind wobblers, in deep water, near bottom. Some brook trout, migrants from tributaries, are also available. Their numbers are few, and they hit the same lures as splake.

Directions: Head north out of Utica on NY 12 for about 22 miles to Alder Creek. Get on NY 28 north and go 2 miles to Forestport. Cross the bridge and take the first right onto Woodhull Road. Cross the railroad tracks 1.2 miles later, and continue straight on North Lake Road for 15 miles.

Additional information: There are several campsites on the north and south shores. The ones on the north shore can be reached via an improved unpaved road, while the south-shore sites can only be reached by hiking or by boat.

Contact: New York State Department of Environmental Conservation Region 6.

200. South Lake

Key species: Brook trout and lake trout.

Description: This 486-acre lake is the second source of the Black River. It averages about 25 feet deep and has a maximum depth of 60 feet. Its shoreline is moderately developed with private camps.

Tips: Early in the season, work weighted streamers slowly at right angles to shore.

The fishing: This lake has suffered major damage from acidification in the past. Currently, according to local forest ranger Dan Buehler, the situation is correcting itself and fish can once again survive. The state restocked the lake in the early 1990s, and the bread-and-butter species is brook trout. They average 12 inches and can be taken on flies and worms. Some, though not many, lakers up to 21 inches are also available. They hit streamers near shore in spring, minnows and spoons fished deep the rest of the season. In 1999, 2,000 landlocked salmon averaging 7 inches were stocked. Follow-up surveys hadn't been conducted by press time. If they took, they should be available for most of this decade and are known to hit small crankbaits and streamers.

Directions: After reaching its namesake, North Lake Road (see the directions in site 199 above) turns into South Lake Road. Follow it for 2.3 miles.

Additional information: A beach launch suitable for small trailered craft is located on South Lake Road. In addition, there are three beach campsites just off the road.

Contact: New York State Department of Environmental Conservation Region 6.

201. Black River (see maps on pages 268 and 274)

Key species: Brook trout, brown trout, rainbow trout, smallmouth bass, northern pike, walleye, chain pickerel, rock bass, sunfish, and bullhead.

Description: Running for more than 100 miles, this river contains three distinct fisheries. The upper section pours out of the western Adirondack Mountains and supports cold-water species. The middle section, from the base of Lyons Falls to Watertown, is warm water. The lower section, from the Mill Street Dam in Watertown to the mouth, is warm water but supports seasonal runs of salmonids.

Tips: Wild brook trout and brown trout are available in all tributary mouths in the spring.

The fishing: This river is one of the state's wildest. Dammed at least twenty-five times, it nonetheless manages a stiff current and several sets of awesome rapids for much of its course. Brook trout ranging from 6 to 10 inches, with a smattering of brown and rainbow trout a few inches longer, occupy the headwaters stretching from North and South Lakes all the way to Kayuta Lake. Rainbow and brown trout ranging from 8 to 14 inches, and brook trout averaging 8 inches, are available from Forestport to Lyons Falls. These fish hit worms and salted minnows from opening day through mid-June and after a summer rain; they take spinners and flies during the dog days of summer.

While a few smallmouth bass are caught in the upper reaches, the greatest numbers are found in the quiet stretches downstream of Forestport. Generally ranging from 10 to 13 inches, they are fond of worms, crayfish, and just about every lure imaginable. Pickerel share the river from Forestport to Lyons Falls with the smallmouths. They can reach 25 inches and are usually caught incidentally on bass lures. Still, a faithful following targets them with spoons such as Daredevles and Rooster Tail spinners.

Below Lyons Falls, smallmouths range from 10 to 15 inches. Northern pike of up to 36 inches become available and are most likely to hit large minnows or their imitations. Although some walleyes have been caught as far upstream as the Denley Dam, they reach fishable populations downstream of Lyons Falls. Ranging from 15 to 23 inches, "eyes" generally hang out in deep holes, where they hit worms trolled on spinner harnesses, 3-inch Mister Twister Exude Grubs, hard minnowbaits, and worms fished eel fashion (worked slowly upstream, on bottom, along current edges). Rock bass grow to range between 0.5 and a respectable 0.75 pound. They hit worms, small minnows, and Mister Twister's 2-inch Exude Grubs. Sunfish ranging from 0.3 to 0.75 pound and brown bullheads ranging from 6 to 14 inches occupy all impoundments. Both take worms, and the sunfish hit surface poppers and flies.

Additional information: From the Oneida and Herkimer County line downstream to the Mill Street Falls in Watertown, the minimum length for black bass is 10 inches.

Contact: New York State Department of Environmental Conservation Region 6.

201A. Farr Road Bridge Access *(see map on page 268)*

Description: Shoulder parking for about five cars.

Fishing the Black River (site 201) below Forestport Reservoir Dam (site 203).

Directions: Heading north on NY 28 in Forestport, cross the bridge and take a right onto Woodhull Road. A mile later, in Forestport Station, the road turns to North Lake Road; continue on it for about 9 miles and turn right onto Farr Road.

201B. Forestport Public Access *(see map on page 268)*

Description: There are two lots here: a formal access site above the dam with parking for about thirty cars, and an adjacent, informal lot below the dam with parking for twenty cars.

Directions: From NY 28 north in Forestport, take a left onto River Street (just before the bridge) and travel for 0.1 mile.

201C. Edmonds Road Bridge Access *(see map on page 268)*

Description: This informal access is at the foot of an abandoned bridge. There's shoulder parking for about five cars.

Directions: Get on River Street in Forestport (see site 201B). Continue straight when the road turns to East River Street. Bear left at the fork with the DEAD END sign. For the next couple of miles, the road changes from paved to gravel a couple of times before ending at Edmonds Road. Turn left at the stop sign.

201D. Edmonds Road Public Access *(see map on page 268)*

Description: This formal site has parking for about five cars.

Directions: Head downstream from site 201C, above, for about 0.7 mile.

201E. Hawkinsville Public Access *(see map on page 268)*

Description: This formal site has parking for about ten cars and access above and below the dam.

Directions: Follow Edmonds Road from site 201D for 2.5 miles.

201F. Norton Road Public Access *(see map on page 268)*

Description: This formal site has parking for three cars.

Directions: Head north on NY 12 out of Boonville for 3.7 miles. Turn east onto Norton Road and travel for 1 mile.

201G. Denley Power Project Dam Public Access *(see map on page 268)*

Description: This site offers shore-fishing access above and below the dam.

Directions: Head north out of Booneville on NY 12 for about 5 miles, then turn right onto the gravel road about 100 yards after the road narrows to two lanes.

201H. Upper Lyons Falls Public Access *(see map on page 268)*

Description: This site is designed as a canoe launch and portage. The Moose River joins the Black River here. There's shore-fishing access on both rivers and parking for about twenty cars.

Tips: During summer's low water levels, the current is slow here. Work a bait tight to the old bridge abutments in the mouth of the Moose River for smallmouth bass.

Directions: Head east on South Street in the village of Lyons Falls, cross the bridge, and turn left onto Lyons Falls Road (CR 39).

201I. Lower Lyons Falls Public Access *(see map on page 268)*

Description: This site was specifically designed as a canoe launch. There is a long stretch of shore-fishing access, including access to the massive pool below the 100-foot-high falls. Parking for about ten cars is available.

The fishing: The pool below the falls is a good spot for walleyes and bullheads in May.

Directions: Head downstream on Lyons Falls Road (CR 39) for about 0.3 mile from site 201H.

201J. High Towers State Forest *(see map on page 268)*

Description: Primitive camping is permitted in these large woods.

Directions: On CR 39, a little more than 1 mile north of Lyons Falls.

201K. Burdicks Crossing Public Access *(see map on page 268)*

Description: This parklike site has picnic facilities, a canoe launch, and shore access.

Directions: Head north on NY 12 from Lyons Falls for about 4 miles, then turn east onto Burdick Crossing Road (CR 36) and travel about 0.8 mile.

201L. Public Fishing Access Site *(see map on page 268)*

Description: This site has a paved ramp, picnic facilities, and parking for about twenty rigs.

Directions: Head south on NY 12 from Lowville for about 3 miles to Glenfield. Get on Main Street, then turn east onto River Street. The ramp is across the bridge.

201M. Public Fishing Access *(see map on page 268)*

Description: This site has a paved launch, parking for ten rigs, and toilets.

Directions: Head east on River Street out of Lowville. When it turns to Number Four Road (CR 26) outside of town, continue for 1.6 miles.

201N. Handicapped Platform *(see map on page 268)*

Description: This wooden platform is about 10 feet above a slow-moving section of the river. The railings have holes for resting your rod. There's parking for five vans.

Directions: Head north on NY 812 for 0.8 mile out of Lowville. Turn east onto Waters Road, then turn left a couple of hundred feet later and travel for about 200 feet to the ramp at the end of the road.

201O. Castorland Public Fishing Access Site *(see map on page 274)*

Description: This site has a paved single-lane ramp and a hard-surface, unpaved double-wide ramp right next to it. There's parking for fifty rigs, as well as toilets.

Directions: Take NY 26 north out of Lowville for 6 miles. Turn east onto NY 410 and travel for 3.2 miles, cross the bridge, and turn left.

201P. NY 3 Fishing Access Site *(see map on page 274)*

Description: This site offers fishing access above a dam. You'll find a beach launch for cartop craft, parking for twenty cars, and a handicapped-accessible fishing platform.

Black River: Lowville to Watertown

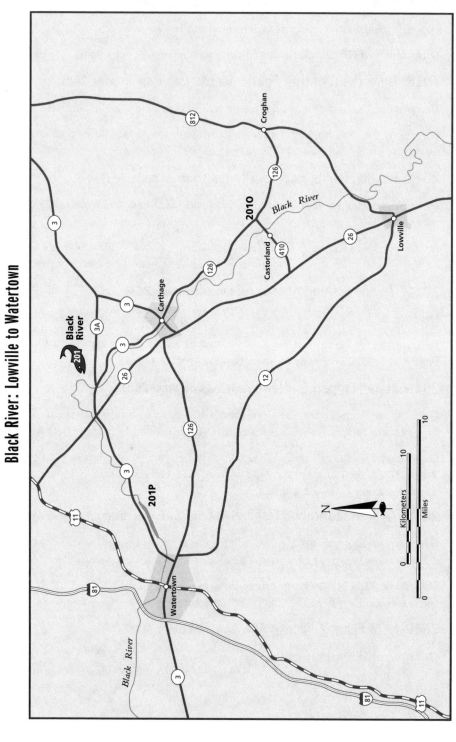

Directions: On the east side of the NY 3 bridge, just over Watertown's eastern boundary.

202. Kayuta Lake *(see map on page 276)*

Key species: Brook trout, smallmouth bass, norlunge, pickerel, yellow perch, and brown bullhead.

Description: This 422-acre Black River impoundment averages 10 feet deep and has a maximum depth of 22 feet.

Tips: The area around the mouth of the Black River always holds fish.

The fishing: Brook trout enter this lake from the Black River and several smaller tributaries. They range from 8 inches to 12 inches and hit worms, spinners, and spoons. The Adirondacks' short growing season keeps the smallmouth bass small. Ranging only from 8 to 14 inches, they are nevertheless fat and feisty and battle their little hearts out when caught on jigs and spinners with ultralight tackle. The state stocked 2,000 7-inch tiger muskies in 2000. If things go as expected, they will range from 30 to 40 inches for most of this decade. Pickerel do pretty well here, reaching up to 25 inches. They'll hit soft plastic slugs ripped over the surface, Rooster Tail spinners, and worms worked on spinner-rigged harnesses. Yellow perch range 6 to 12 inches and take worms, minnows, and small streamers. Bullheads from 6 to 10 inches are plentiful and are partial to worms still-fished on bottom.

Directions: Head north out of Utica on NY 12 for about 22 miles to Alder Creek. Get on NY 28 north and go 2 miles to Forestport. Cross the bridge and turn right onto Woodhull Road. About 1 mile later, bear right (south) onto Bardwell Mills Road (CR 72) and travel 2.8 miles.

Additional information: There is a shoulder parking area big enough for about two cars before you cross the bridge.

Contact: New York Department of Environmental Conservation Region 6.

202A. Kayuta Hydro Recreation–Boat Launch Area

Description: This site has a concrete ramp, parking for ten rigs, and shore-fishing access above and below the dam.

Directions: Take NY 12 north out of Utica for about 24 miles, bearing right onto NY 28 at Alder Creek. While still in the curve of the transition, turn right onto Old State Dam Road and travel for 0.8 mile.

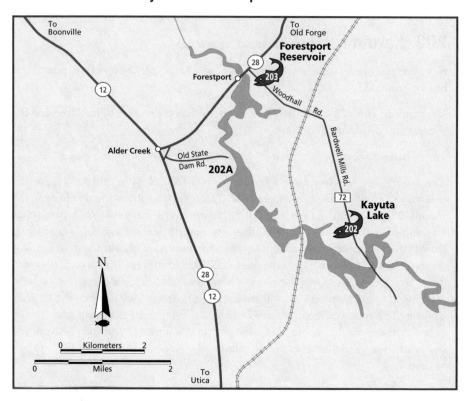

203. Forestport Reservoir

Key species: Brook trout, largemouth bass, smallmouth bass, chain pickerel, yellow perch, and brown bullhead.

Description: This 101-acre Black River impoundment averages a little more than 6 feet deep and has a maximum depth of 25 feet. Its north end is flanked by the hamlet of Forestport.

Tips: Work loud surface baits such as Hula Poppers and MirrOlure's Top Dogs on calm summer days.

The fishing: This impoundment is primarily warm-water habitat, but some brook trout migrate from tributaries. They range from 6 to 12 inches and take worms and spinners. Largemouth bass ranging from 10 to 14 inches are common and hang out in weed beds and emergent vegetation, where they eagerly take noisy surface baits. Chain pickerel also occupy this range and take the same lures. Smallmouths range from 8 to 12 inches and like hanging out on the bottom in channels where there is moving water—at the discharge pipe below Kayuta Lake's (site 202) dam, for instance. They take crayfish, minnows, and jigs. Yellow perch running as big as 12 inches can turn up just about anywhere and will respond to worms, minnows, small crayfish—you name it. Bullheads ranging from 6 to 10 inches scour the bottom, looking for crayfish and juicy worms.

Directions: Head north out of Utica on NY 12 for 22 miles, then bear north onto NY 28 for about 2 miles.

Additional information: A fishing access site on River Road, on the south side of the NY 28 bridge, has two parking lots next to each other with combined parking for about fifty cars. Woodhull Road, the right turn at the other end of the bridge, has an informal lot with parking for about fifteen cars.

Contact: New York State Department of Environmental Conservation Region 6.

204. Fish Creek (Lewis County) *(see map on page 278)*

Key species: Brook trout and brown trout.

Description: This rift-pool stream flows for about 11 miles and feeds the Black River. In its upper reaches, the bottom is sand, gravel, and boulders; the lower portion is loaded with windfalls and tangles of woody debris.

Tips: The biggest trout are in the lower section.

The fishing: This stream's brown and brook trout are wild. Brookies range from 6 to 12 inches, and the browns go from 6 to 16 inches. These fish will take worms early in the season and a gently presented dry fly in late spring. Worms still work well after a summer rain, while Muddler Minnows and Black Nose Dace, stripped rapidly across the surface around dawn and dusk, produce during the dog days of summer. The state owns 5.5 miles of public fishing rights downstream of North South Road.

Directions: Head north out of Lyons Falls for about 3 miles on Lyons Falls Road (CR 39) to Fish Creek Road, which parallels most of the public fishing rights section.

Contact: New York State Department of Environmental Conservation Region 6.

204A. Public Access

Description: Parking for about five cars.

Directions: Head north on Lyons Falls Road (CR 39) out of Lyons Falls for a little less than 2 miles and bear left onto River Road.

204B. Public Access

Description: Parking for about five cars.

Directions: About 100 feet east on Fish Creek Road from its intersection with CR 39.

Fish Creek · Crystal Creek

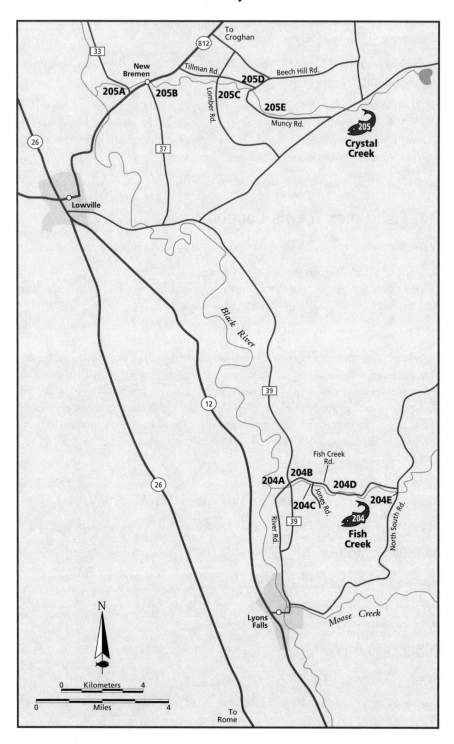

204C. Public Access

Description: Parking for about five cars.

Directions: From site 204B, head east on Fish Creek Road for about 1 mile to Jones Road and turn right.

204D. Public Access

Description: This scenic county park has picnic facilities, two footbridges crossing the creek, and parking for ten cars.

Directions: From site 204C, take Fish Creek Road east for about 0.5 mile.

204E. Public Access

Description: Parking for about five cars.

Directions: From site 204D, travel east about 1.5 miles on Fish Creek Road to North South Road and turn right to the bridge.

205. Crystal Creek

Key species: Brook trout and brown trout.

Description: This rift-pool stream flows for about 12 miles and feeds the Black River.

Tips: Cast spinners into the backwashes and pools below the fallen willows and woody debris downstream of New Bremen.

The fishing: Frank Flack, the local state fisheries biologist, considers this the best trout stream in Lewis County. Like all the Black River tributaries, it has native brook trout in its upper reaches. Flack claims that there are a lot of browns up there, too—they're just a lot savvier and harder to catch. From New Bremen downstream, the state annually stocks about 800 browns averaging 9 inches, and 200 averaging 14 inches. Flack says this section has a nice combination of wild and stocked fish, many better than 2 pounds—and he has a five-pound brown hanging on his wall to prove it.

The state owns public fishing rights on 10.6 miles of the stream.

Directions: Head north on NY 812 from Lowville for about 3 miles to New Bremen.

Contact: New York Department of Environmental Conservation Region 6, and Lewis County Chamber of Commerce.

205A. Public Access

Description: This informal site has parking for about four cars.

Directions: From Lowville, head north on NY 812 for 3 miles to Van Amber Road (CR 33), turn north, and travel to the bridge.

205B. Public Access *(see map on page 278)*

Description: This site is at a small town park above a dam and has parking for five cars.

Directions: From Lowville, head north on NY 812 for about 3.5 miles to New Bremen. The park is on CR 37.

205C. Public Access *(see map on page 278)*

Description: This site offers access at a bridge and parking for five cars.

Directions: Take NY 812 east out of New Bremen. About 1 mile later, turn right onto Tillman Road, then right again, 1 mile later, onto Lomber Road.

205D. Public Access *(see map on page 278)*

Description: This site offers access at a bridge and parking for five cars.

Directions: Continue east on Tillman Road (see site 205C) for about 1.5 miles to the access at the old bridge just before Beech Hill Road.

205E. Public Access *(see map on page 278)*

Description: This site offers bridge access and parking for five cars.

Directions: From site 205D, continue east on Tillman Road to Beech Hill Road. Turn right, then left 0.3 mile later, onto Muncy Road.

206. West Canada Creek

Key species: Brown trout, brook trout, and smallmouth bass.

Description: This stream springs from the western Adirondacks, runs for about 75 miles, and pours into the New Erie Canal at Herkimer. Along the way, it fills and drains Hinckley and Prospect Reservoirs.

Tips: Use Green Drakes in the first two weeks of June.

The fishing: This is one of the most popular trout streams in the state. Curiously, the stretch feeding Hinckley Reservoir is pretty much a washout. The state annually stocks this section with 1,620 brown trout averaging 8 inches and 2,500 brook trout averaging 9 inches. The stream is austere and acidic, however; survival isn't easy for the browns, and they don't grow much. Brookies do a little better, and 12-inchers are possible. Both take worms, salted minnows, and nymphs.

Downstream of the Hinckley Reservoir is a different story. The fishery improves immediately (see Prospect Reservoir, site 208) and remains top-notch all the way to the mouth. Special arrangements between the state and power companies

West Canada Creek · Hinckley Reservoir · Prospect Reservoir

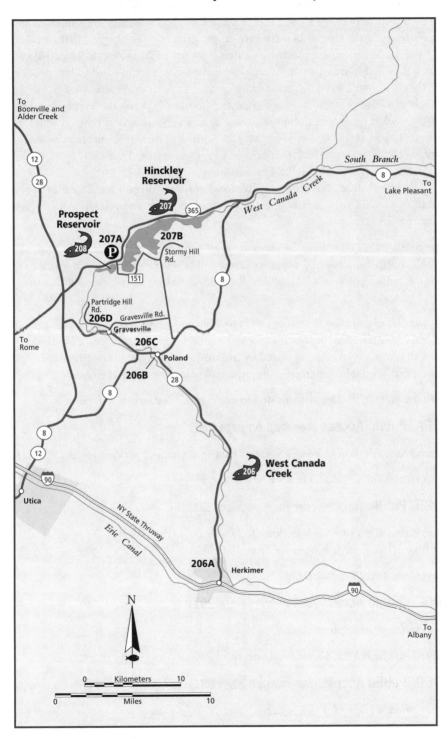

ensure a cool flow year-round. The state annually stocks roughly 17,000 brown trout averaging 8 inches, 2,300 14.5-inchers, and 300 17-inchers. Survival is good, and trout typically range from 10 to 18 inches; 19- to 23-inchers are common, and some stretching the tape to 28 inches are caught each year. The biggest fish are taken on worms and minnows. Fly fishers catch a lot up to 20 inches on Gold Ribbed Hare's Ears and March Brown nymphs. Variations on mayflies and caddis provide dry-fly purists with exciting action from spirited little trout. Brook trout from 8 to 14 inches are also available, primarily near the mouths of the tributaries they outgrew. Most are taken on worms, minnows, and spinners. Smallmouth bass typically go between 12 and 14 inches, but 16-inchers are possible. Their numbers are sufficient to warrant locals targeting them specifically with crayfish, Dardevle spoons, and crankbaits such as Excalibur Fat Free Shallows.

The stretch from the bridge at Trenton Falls downstream for 2.5 miles to the mouth of Cincinnati Creek is open year-round to catch-and-release trout fishing with artificial lures only.

Directions: NY 28 parallels the creek from the village of Herkimer (NY Thruway exit 30) north for about 20 miles to Gravesville. NY 365 parallels the stream for about 8 miles upstream of Hinckley Reservoir. Parking areas are plentiful along both highways.

Additional information: Easement rights, public land, and agreements with private property owners open most of the creek to public fishing. Downstream of Hinckley Dam, the river's level is manipulated by utilities, so watch out for fast-rising waters. Motels and several commercial campgrounds are located along the river.

Contact: New York Department of Environmental Conservation Region 6.

206A. Public Access *(see map on page 281)*

Description: Algonquin Power Systems fishing access and parking for twenty cars.

Directions: On NY 28, 1.3 miles north of Herkimer.

206B. Public Access *(see map on page 281)*

Description: This site offers parking for about twenty cars and is the favored take-out for anglers float-fishing from Trenton Falls.

Directions: NY 28 in Poland.

206C. Public Access *(see map on page 281)*

Description: Parking for ten cars.

Direction: On NY 28, about 1 mile north of Poland.

206D. Public Access *(see map on page 281)*

Description: Parking for twenty cars.

Directions: Head north on NY 28 from Poland for about 7 miles. Turn right onto Gravesville Road, then immediately turn left onto Partridge Hill Road.

207. Hinckley Reservoir (Kuyahoora Lake)
(see map on page 281)

Key species: Brook trout, brown trout, yellow perch, and rock bass.

Description: This 2,800-acre body of water averages about 7 feet deep and has a maximum depth of 20 feet. Its main tributary and outlet is West Canada Creek (site 206). Its waters are acidic and infertile, making it one of the most austere reservoirs in the state. What few nutrients it gets are washed away during winter drawdown.

Tips: Fish the mouths of tributaries.

The fishing: Some brook trout and brown trout flee the slim pickings and acidic water of upper West Canada Creek by migrating to the reservoir. Unfortunately, the vast majority find survival even tougher here. People fishing with worms report catching skinny brown trout every now and then ranging from 8 to 16 inches, famished brookies averaging 6 inches, 4- to 7-inch perch, and rock bass from 3 to 6 inches. Indeed, the state Department of Environmental Conservation classifies this fishery as poor, and finding someone willing to say something positive about the fishing is about as difficult as finding hair on a catfish.

Directions: Head north out of Utica on NY 12 for 14 miles. Turn east onto NY 365 and travel for about 5 miles.

Additional information: Close proximity to NY 365 makes this scenic reservoir a very popular recreational spot. Primitive camping is allowed on Prices Point and the lake's island.

Contact: New York State Department of Environmental Conservation Region 6.

207A. Public Boat Launch

Description: This informal site is on state land, just beyond the commercial marina. It has a soft-surface beach launch suitable for small trailered craft and parking for about forty rigs.

Directions: On NY 365, about 2 miles east of the dam (0.7 mile east of the commercial launch).

207B. Hinckley Day-Use Area

Description: This fee area is for day use during summer. Beach launching of cartop craft is permitted, and there's ample shore-fishing access, a swimming beach, playing fields, hiking trails, picnic tables, a bathhouse, toilets, and parking for a hundred cars. It's open from Memorial Day through Labor Day.

Directions: From the NY 12/NY 365 intersection in Barnveld, head east for 4.4 miles and turn right, just before the Hinckley Reservoir Dam, onto South Side Road (CR 151). Travel 4 miles to the stop sign and turn left onto Grant Road/Stormy Hill Road. Travel for 0.6 mile and turn left.

208. Prospect Reservoir *(see map on page 281)*

Key species: Brown trout and rainbow trout.

Description: This reservoir starts directly below the Hinckley Reservoir Dam and stretches for about 1 mile to the Power Dam.

Tips: Drift the fast water below Hinckley Dam with live bait.

The fishing: The state annually stocks 1,200 rainbow trout and 1,550 brown trout averaging 8.5 inches. The rainbows are usually caught before they reach 12 inches. The brown trout, however, end up ranging from 14 to 24 inches. The rainbows are taken on flies and spinners, while the browns respond best to minnows, worms, and crayfish.

Directions: Head north on NY 12 from Utica for 14 miles, then turn east onto NY 365 and travel 3.9 miles.

Additional information: Reliant Energy Company's West Canada Creek Recreation Area access site on NY 365 has a hard-surface launch ramp and parking for about fifteen rigs. It's open Memorial Day through Labor Day.

Contact: New York State Department of Environmental Conservation Region 6.

MOHAWK VALLEY

ts roots stretching deep into the Tug Hill Plateau, the Mohawk River is spawned by the union of its East and West Branches just downstream of the hamlet of West Branch. Flowing southeast for nearly 150 miles, the river carves a fabulous valley all the way to Troy, where it spills into the Hudson River. Downstream of Rome, the river is incorporated into the New Erie Canal, weaving in and out of the human-made waterway in a braid of backwaters.

209. Lansing Kill (see map on page 286)

Key species: Brown trout and brook trout.

Description: This small stream pours out of the hills a couple of miles south of Booneville and feeds the Mohawk River about 8 miles later.

Tips: Cast white caddis imitations early in the evening.

The fishing: The state annually stocks more than 3,000 brown trout averaging 8 inches. Growth is good, and many reach 12 inches—with a few making it to 16 inches and then some. They take worms, flies, and in-line spinners. Natural brook trout, scions of tiny tributaries, migrate into the stream when they outgrow their natal turf. Ranging from 4 to 10 inches, they take worms and flies.

Directions: NY 46 parallels the stream.

Additional information: The state owns public fishing rights on 2.5 miles of the stream, and informal access at bridges and off the shoulder of the road is plentiful.

Contact: New York State Department of Environmental Conservation Region 6.

209A. Public Access

Description: This site has parking for about five cars.

Directions: Head north out of Rome on NY 46 for 13 miles.

209B. Pixley Falls State Park

Description: The Lansing Kill and Old Black River Canal run through this 375-acre fee area. It offers twenty-two campsites, showers, a trailer dumping station, playing fields, and hiking trails. The campground is open mid-May through Labor Day, and a day-use fee is charged to noncampers. Free day use off-season.

Directions: Take NY 46 north out of Rome for about 14 miles.

Lansing Kill · Upper Mohawk River · Delta Lake

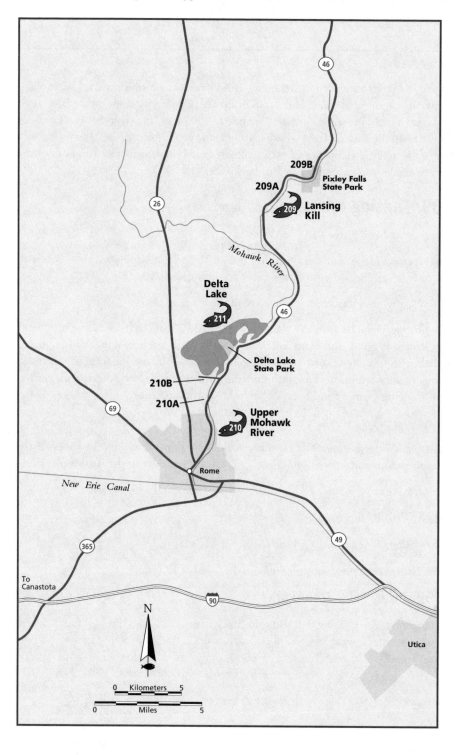

210. Upper Mohawk River

Key species: Brown trout, brook trout, northern pike, and walleye.

Description: This section covers the cold-water portion of the Mohawk River, stretching from its headwaters to its mouth on the New Erie Canal in Rome.

Tips: Fish the pool below the Delta Lake Dam.

The fishing: The state annually stocks almost 5,000 brown trout averaging 8 inches into the river above Delta Lake. Habitat is good, and the trout easily reach 12 inches. Indeed, Frank Flack, regional fisheries biologist, says there are enough big browns here to warrant raising the minimum length to 12 inches. About 1,000 rainbow trout averaging 8.5 inches are also stocked here each year. They are much easier to catch and seldom make it beyond 10 inches. A relatively wide, open stream, this is good water to fly fish; many big trout are taken on nymphs and streamers.

The state annually stocks almost 10,000 brown trout averaging 8 inches, and about 1,500 averaging 14 inches, in the 6-mile stretch below Delta Lake. In some years, a couple of hundred stretching the tape to 17 inches are thrown in to make things interesting. Huge brook trout also like this spot. Close to a hundred 15-inchers are stocked annually, and 4-pounders were caught here in 2000 and 2001. Both trout species take worms, minnows, Mepps Aglias, Rapalas, and diving plugs such as MirrOlure 91LSRs and C. C. Shads.

Northern pike range from 26 to 40 inches and are partial to minnows and their imitations. Walleyes run from 1 to 5 pounds and are taken on worms, jigs, and minnow-imitating crankbaits.

Directions: NY 46 parallels much of the river.

Additional information: Special trout seasons stretching from April 1 to November 30 are in effect in the Mohawk River from the bridge in Westernville upstream to its confluence with the Lansing Kill, and from Delta Dam downstream to the New Erie Canal. The state owns several miles of public fishing rights, designated by yellow steel signs nailed to trees, and informal access is plentiful at bridges and the shoulder of the road.

Contact: New York State Department of Environmental Conservation Region 6.

210A. Public Access

Description: Located across the street from the state fish hatchery, this site boasts handicapped access and parking for a hundred cars.

Directions: Head north out of Rome on NY 46 for 1.2 miles.

210B. Delta Lake Dam Access

Description: This informal site has parking for about ten cars.

The Lansing Kill running through locks on the Old Black River Canal, north of Pixley Falls State Park.

Directions: Head north out of Rome on NY 46 (Black River Boulevard) for about 2.5 miles, then turn left (west) onto Golf Course Road, just below the dam.

211. Delta Lake *(see map on page 286)*

Key species: Northern pike, walleye, black bass, yellow perch, and black crappie.

Description: This 2,500-acre reservoir averages 22 feet deep and has a maximum depth of 60 feet.

Tips: From opening day through June, drift the shoreline and swim-and-jig (aka *yo-yo*) spinnerbaits for monster northern pike.

The fishing: This reservoir has a reputation for huge northern pike more than 40 inches long. Most are taken on large minnows suspended below bobbers. Flatlining with Red Fins and Rapalas also works, however, especially in May and again in October. Walleyes range from 2 to 6 pounds and are taken with jigs, YUM Walleye Grubs, and crankbaits such as Rat-L-Traps and MirrOlure's Shad Rattlers. Smallmouth bass in the 1- to 3-pound range are common and take worms, minnows, and crayfish. Largemouths from 1 to 4 pounds can be taken on topwater lures and spinnerbaits in the eastern bay. Perch ranging from 6 to 12 inches and black crappies from 9 to 12 inches are plentiful, taking small minnows and 2-inch scented curly-tailed grubs.

Directions: Head north out of Rome for 2.5 miles on NY 46.

Additional information: Delta Lake State Park, a fee area, offers a paved double-lane ramp, parking for about twenty-five rigs, 101 campsites, hot showers, playgrounds and playing fields, picnic facilities, and hiking trails. The campground is open mid-May through Columbus Day. Free day use is permitted off-season.

Contact: New York State Department of Environmental Conservation Region 6, and Oneida County Convention and Visitors Bureau.

212. New Erie Canal East: Waterford to Rome
(see maps on pages 291, 294, and 296)

Key species: Black bass, northern pike, walleye, tiger muskie, channel catfish, and panfish.

Description: Originally named the Barge Canal, this waterway replaced the Old Erie Canal in 1918. Stretching from Waterford to Tonawanda, a distance of 338 miles, the canal incorporates the Seneca, Oneida, and Mohawk Rivers, bypassing their largest oxbows with cuts. All told, there are thirty-three locks and fifteen lift bridges. In this section (from Rome to its mouth), the minimum depth in the channel is 14 feet. The word's highest canal lift in the shortest distance is where the Mohawk River pours into the Hudson River at Waterford. Called the Waterford Flight, a series of five locks here raises canal traffic 169 feet in 1.25 miles.

Tips: Use a Lindy No-Snagg Slip Sinker to drag worms on bottom in the rapids below dams for walleyes.

The fishing: Largemouth bass up to 6 pounds, smallmouth bass up to 4 pounds, and northern pike up to 15 pounds thrive in the canal and the backwaters of the Mohawk River. All three like minnows, spinnerbaits, and jerkbaits. In addition, the bass have a taste for crayfish. Walleyes ranging from 15 to 28 inches are present throughout the canal—but the greatest number by far is found between Troy and Utica. They hang out on the channel floor by day and move into rapids below dams in the evening. In fast water, they hit nightcrawlers dragged slowly on bottom, against the current, and minnow-imitating crankbaits. In the canal, they like crankbaits, bucktail jigs fished plain or tipped with a scented 3-inch curly-tailed grub, and nightcrawlers drifted plain or trolled on spinner harnesses. Catfish in the 15- to 20-inch range are most common, but monsters the size of miniature Minotaurs are caught regularly. They like meat: worms, minnows, cut bait, raw chicken liver, and shrimp fished on bottom. Tiger muskies have been stocked heavily recently. The water from Frankfort to Little Falls is notorious for these beasts. Fish for them with large minnows, their imitations, and Mepps bucktail spinners. The canal is loaded with keeper crappies, yellow perch ranging from 6 to 12 inches, white perch and white bass up to 14 inches, and 0.25- to 0.5-pound sunfish and rock bass. The white perch and white bass hang out everywhere—stillwater and fast—while the crappies, perch, and rock bass seem to prefer the shallow shelves lining both sides of the canal, especially around weed edges, riprap, and the edges of drop-offs. They all take minnows and small lures. Sunfish like the same shallow habitat but also like the mouths of swamps and weedy mudflats, and are partial to worms, wet flies, and 1-inch Exude Curly Tail Grubs. Bonus brown and rainbow trout, many more than 20 inches, can be found around tributary mouths. They are usually caught incidentally in spring by folks targeting panfish.

Additional information: A two-day or seasonal pass is required to go through locks. The Erie Canal Heritage Trail, a recreation path, opens much of the waterway to shore fishing. There are no public campgrounds on the canal, but numerous private campgrounds are nearby.

Travelling east to west, the Mohawk River and the Erie Canal are one until the last couple of miles, where the canal is diverted by a crescent dam to flow north of the river and is paralleled by the Waterford Flight A Road. East of Utica, the Mohawk River is separated from the Erie Canal for about 8 miles and rejoins it in Frankfort.

Contact: New York State Canal Corporation, Mohawk Valley Heritage Corridor, and New York State Department of Environmental Conservation Regions 4, 5, and 6.

212A. Waterford State Boat Launch Ramp *(see map on page 291)*

Description: This single-lane paved ramp is located right where the Erie Canal pours into the Hudson River (Champlain Canal). There's parking for about five rigs.

New Erie Canal East: Waterford to Fonda

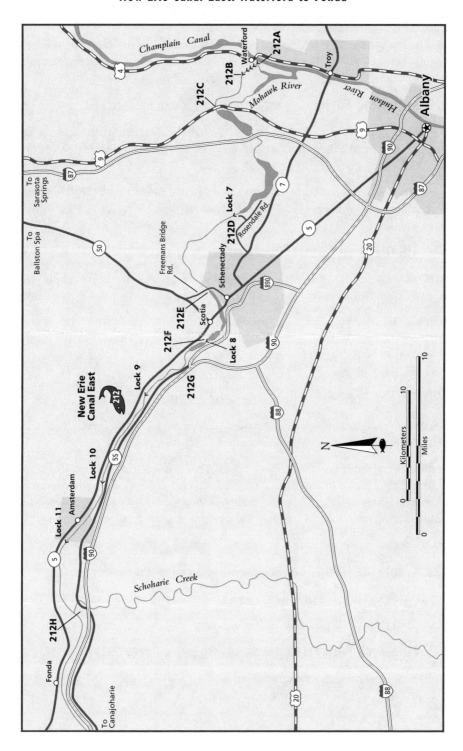

The fishing: Catch-and-release fishing only downstream of the NY 32 bridge.

Directions: At the end of First Street in Waterford.

Additional information: First Street is narrow, with cars often parked on both sides, especially between 4:00 and 7:00 P.M. Wide craft should use Troy's 123rd Street ramp (off US 4, behind Riverside Plaza) directly across the Hudson River.

212B. Waterford Flight Recreation Area *(see map on page 291)*

Description: This linear park offers a paved single-lane launch in the widewater above the Waterford Flight, parking for about three rigs, shore-fishing access on both sides of the canal, picnic tables, and bathrooms.

Directions: Take Washington Street (which turns into Fonda Road, CR 97) north out of Waterford, bear west (left) onto Waterford Flight A Road, and travel for about 1.5 miles.

212C. US 9 Bridge Access Sites *(see map on page 291)*

Description: Shore-fishing access on both sides of the bridge, parking for about ten cars, a handicapped-accessible ramp, and picnic tables.

Directions: Head north out of Albany on US 9 for about 9 miles, then turn right just before the bridge crossing the canal for the south shore access. For the north side, cross the bridge, turn left onto Vischer Ferry Road, and immediately turn left again onto Towpath Road.

212D. Lock 7 Park *(see map on page 291)*

Description: This park offers a gravel launch, parking for twenty-five rigs, hundreds of yards of shore-fishing access, picnic tables, and bathrooms.

The fishing: The stretch of the Mohawk River between Locks 7 and 8 is loaded with islands, making it one of the canal's most productive areas for hawg largemouth bass, pikasauruses of more than 10 pounds, walleyes of up to 10 pounds, small-mouths ranging from 1.5 to 4 pounds, and tiger muskies of 20-something pounds.

Directions: In Schenectady, at the end of Lock 7 Road (off Rosendale Road, CR 158).

212E. Freemans Bridge Launch *(see map on page 291)*

Description: This state boat launch has a paved ramp and parking for about fifteen rigs.

Directions: Freemans Bridge Road in Schenectady.

212F. Maalwyck Park Fishing Access *(see map on page 291)*

Description: This park offers shore fishing near Lock 8.

Directions: Off NY 5, just west of Scotia.

212G. Kiwanis Boat Launch Ramp *(see map on page 291)*

Description: This site has a paved ramp and parking for about twenty-five rigs.

Directions: Take I–890 west out of Schenectady for about 3 miles to its end and head west on NY 5S for about 0.5 mile.

212H. Schoharie Crossing Fishing Access *(see map on page 291)*

Description: Located at the mouth of Schoharie Creek, this site offers a double-wide paved ramp, parking for thirty rigs, 2.5 miles of shore-fishing access on the creek and the New Erie Canal, portable toilets, picnic tables, and a shelter.

Directions: Head west out of Amsterdam on NY 5S for about 4 miles. Cross the Schoharie Creek Bridge and make a right onto North Dufel Road.

Additional information: This is the only remaining site in the state where all three stages of the Erie Canal—the original, expanded, and new—exist side by side. The ruins of an aqueduct built of cut limestone during the expansion in 1841 cross the creek.

212I. Canajoharie State Boat Launch *(see map on page 294)*

Description: This site has a paved ramp, parking for thirty rigs, portable toilets, picnic facilities, and a shelter.

Directions: In the village, on the southeastern corner of the NY 10 bridge.

212J. Nelliston Fishing Access *(see map on page 294)*

Description: This site has a hard-surface ramp, parking for fifteen rigs, and shore-fishing access.

Directions: Railroad Street (the service road on the northeast end of the NY 80 bridge).

212K. St. Johnsville Marina and Campsite *(see map on page 294)*

Description: This fee area has a paved ramp, parking for fifty rigs, and five transient campsites.

Directions: On the northeast side of the Bridge Street Bridge.

212L. Lock 17 Park *(see map on page 294)*

Description: This site offers handicapped-accessible fishing off the canal wall, parking for twenty-five cars, and access to Moss Island's primitive shoreline on the Mohawk River.

Directions: Head east on NY 5 in Little Falls, turn right onto NY 169, cross the canal, and turn right.

New Erie Canal East: Fonda to Utica

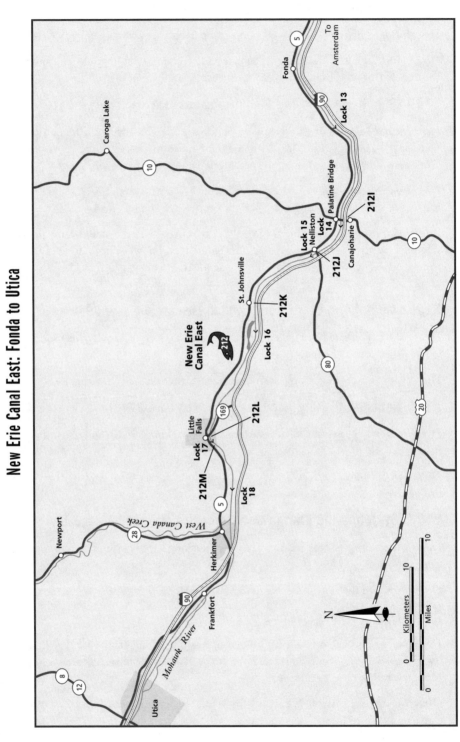

Additional information: Ruins of Old Erie Canal locks run parallel to new ones. Moss Island's sheer cliffs tower more than 40 feet, making it the area's most popular rock climbing venue. A permit is required to rock climb. The island's web of trails lead to spectacular potholes, one more than 20 feet high.

212M. Little Falls Launch Ramp *(see map on page 294)*

Description: This site has a double-wide paved ramp, parking for about twenty-five rigs, loading docks, and picnic tables.

Directions: Located at the end of Industrial Drive: Take Main Street (NY 5) to Lock Street, cross the railroad tracks, and bear right onto Industrial Drive.

212N. Utica Marsh Fishing Access *(see map on page 296)*

Description: This site offers a beach launch for cartop craft and parking for ten cars.

Directions: In Utica, head north on Barnes Avenue off Oriskany Boulevard (NY 5A).

Dam on Mohawk River at Little Falls as seen from Moss Island in Lock 17 Park (site 212L).

New Erie Canal East: Utica to Rome

Bellamy Harbor Park, where the upper Mohawk feeds the New Erie Canal, in Rome.

2120. Bellamy Harbor Park

Description: This linear park offers shore-fishing access at the dam where the Mohawk River enters the New Erie Canal, two parking lots (twenty-five cars total), and a pedestrian bridge across the Mohawk River.

The fishing: Walleyes of up to 5 pounds mill around the dam for the first couple of weeks of the season. Catfish and carp are available all the time.

Directions: On Harbor Way (take Mills Street off East Dominick Street), Rome.

212P. Muck Road Boat Launch

Description: This site has a hard-surface ramp, parking for about thirty rigs, and a handicapped-accessible fishing ramp.

Directions: On Muck Road (off South James Street), Rome.

213. Chenango Canal *(see map on page 299)*

Key species: Brown trout.

Description: Built in the 1830s to connect the Erie Canal with Binghamton, this waterway went out of service in 1877. Much of it has been filled in, but numerous short stretches, fed by springs and brooks, slice through central New York's southern tier. The most popular section runs through Bouckville and feeds Oriskany

Creek (site 214) about 1.5 miles north of the village. Wide, shallow, lined by brush, and carpeted with waving fields of weeds, it is ideal habitat for brown trout.

Tips: Free-float nymphs in narrow channels slicing through weeds.

The fishing: The state annually stocks about 1,200 brown trout averaging 8 inches. They grow well, ranging from 10 to 14 inches by late summer, with many stretching the tape even more. Wet flies work best during the heat of day, and tiny caddis and mayfly imitations are great at dusk and dawn.

Directions: Head east out of Morrisville for about 3 miles to the village of Bouckville. The canal runs through the heart of town.

Additional information: Trout season is open year-round in the 3-mile stretch from the NY 46 bridge downstream to the canal's mouth. This section is restricted to artificial lures only, the minimum length for trout is 12 inches, and the daily limit is two.

Contact: New York State Department of Environmental Conservation Region 7, and Madison County Tourism.

214. Oriskany Creek

Key species: Brown trout.

Description: This creek flows for about 25 miles through Madison and Oneida Counties and feeds the Mohawk River between Utica and Rome.

Tips: In late summer, cast dry flies in the wide, slow-moving channels on the stretch between Clinton and Kirkland.

The fishing: Frank Flack, regional senior fisheries biologist for the state, says that this creek is "one of the most productive streams in upstate New York, [with] all wild fish above Deansboro." Still, the state annually stocks more than 13,000 brown trout averaging 7 inches, plus 750 two-year-olds averaging 14 inches. The stream is lined in many areas with heavy brush crawling with insects, and the trout grow big on all these terrestrials. Many survive the winter—the creek is notorious for trout ranging from 14 to 18 inches. Worms and salted minnows are the baits of choice among most locals who, quite naturally, consider trout food fish.

Additional information: The state owns 9.2 miles of public fishing rights. From October 16 through March 31, catch-and-release fishing, with artificial lures only, is allowed in the 13-mile stretch from the bridge in Deansboro to the mouth.

Contact: New York State Department of Environmental Conservation Region 6.

214A. Mouth of Chenango Canal Access Site

Description: A dirt trail about 50 feet long ends at the falls where the Chenango Canal tumbles into the headwaters of Oriskany Creek. There's informal shoulder parking for three cars.

Chenango Canal · Oriskany Creek

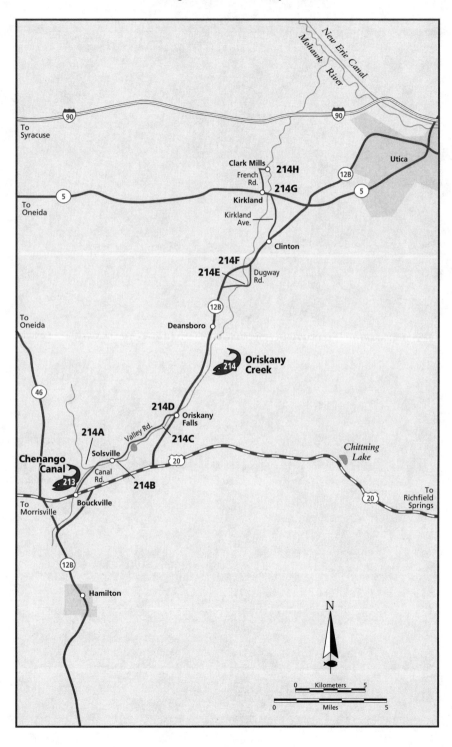

What a great catch at Oriskany Creek.

Directions: Head east out of Morrisville for about 4 miles to Bouckville. Turn north onto Canal Road and travel about 2 miles to the CHENANGO CANAL SPECIAL REGULATION AREA sign. Park in the slot at the shoulder 50 feet up the road.

214B. Fishing Access *(see map on page 299)*

Description: The stream undermined the floor of an old mill dam here. There's shoulder parking.

Directions: Head north out of Bouckville on Canal Road for about 2.3 miles and turn right.

214C. Fishing Access *(see map on page 299)*

Description: This official access site has parking for about seven cars and a trail to the creek.

Directions: From site 214B, continue north on Canal Road for a few hundred yards into Solsville, then take Valley Road east for 2.4 miles.

214D. Fishing Access *(see map on page 299)*

Description: This site has parking for five cars and a handicapped fishing platform.

Directions: Located in Oriskany Falls, at the NY 12B bridge.

214E. Fishing Access *(see map on page 299)*

Description: This site has parking for fifteen cars.

Directions: Head north on NY 12B out of Oriskany Falls for about 6 miles, turn east onto Dugway Road, and travel about 1 mile.

214F. Fishing Access *(see map on page 299)*

Description: This site has parking for about ten cars.

Directions: Head south out of Clinton on NY 12B for about 1.5 miles.

214G. Kirkland Fishing Access Site *(see map on page 299)*

Description: This site has parking for about five cars.

Directions: Head north out of Clinton on Kirkland Avenue for about 1.5 miles to NY 5 in the village of Kirkland. Turn right and go to the bridge.

214H. Clarks Mills Fishing Access Site *(see map on page 299)*

Description: This informal access site has parking for about five cars on the east side of the bridge.

Directions: Head north on French Road for 0.8 mile out of Kirkland. Turn right at the stop sign in Clarks Mills and travel 0.3 mile to the bridge.

SUSQUEHANNA DRAINAGE: EAST

One of the country's major rivers, the Susquehanna winds for about 450 miles, draining an area of roughly 27,550 square miles before pouring into the north end of the Chesapeake Bay. Only tributaries feeding the river east of Binghamton are covered in this volume.

215. Tully Lake

Key species: Largemouth bass, pickerel, walleye, black crappie, yellow perch, and sunfish.

Description: This weedy, shallow, 230-acre glacial lake is punctuated with kettle holes ranging from 2 to 10 acres, one of which is 34 feet deep. A massive weed bed that some call "the island" is located a couple of hundred feet off the west shore, midway down the lake. The shoreline is heavily developed with private residences.

Tips: Ice fish with grubs baited on dot jigs.

The fishing: This is marvelous largemouth bass habitat. Most are between 2 to 4 pounds, but larger ones are available. They hit floating worms worked over weeds. Pickerel, ranging from 15 to 25 inches, are popular because of their propensity for heart-jolting assaults on topwater offerings such as Slug-Gos and Jitterbugs. Walleye up to 2 feet long like worms drifted through deep holes in summer and minnows fished on bottom in winter. Yellow perch up to 12 inches and sunfish ranging from palm sized up to 0.75 pound take worms. The perch and black crappies—averaging 10 inches—hit Beetle Spins and minnows.

The minimum length for walleye is 18 inches, and the daily limit is three. Motors above 7.5 horsepower are prohibited.

Directions: From the village of Tully, take I–81 south for 2 miles to Preble, exit 13. Head north on NY 281 for 1.4 miles and hook a left onto Song Lake Crossing. Take a right 0.6 mile later onto Saulsbury Road, then turn right 0.4 mile later onto Friendly Shore Drive.

Additional information: The fishing access site at the end of Friendly Shore Drive offers a beach launch for cartop craft and parking for about thirty cars. There are no other services on the lake.

Contact: New York State Department of Environmental Conservation Region 7.

216. Upper Little York Lake

Key species: Largemouth bass, brown trout, rainbow trout, and pickerel.

Tully Lake · Upper Little York Lake · Casterline Pond

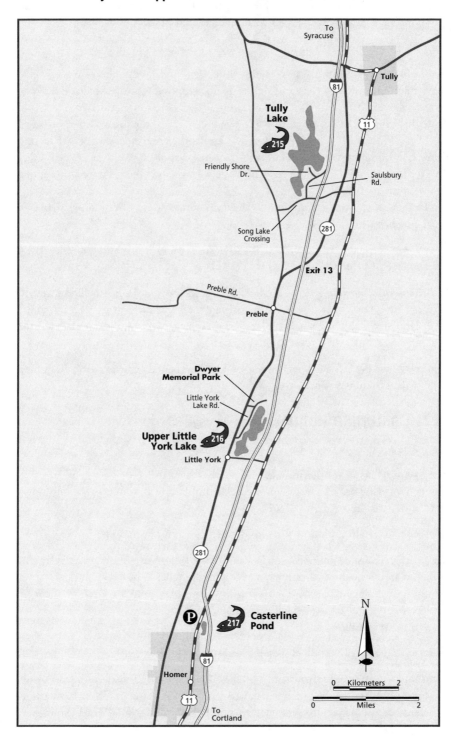

Description: A link on the chain of small lakes along I–81 between Homer and Tully, this 150-acre lake averages 15 feet deep and has a maximum depth of 75 feet. The shoreline is heavily developed with cottages and homes.

Tips: The best time to fish in summer is early in the morning or at dusk.

The fishing: Largemouth bass averaging about 2 pounds and pickerel averaging 20 inches hang out in the weeds and under docks, responding to jerkbaits and prop-baits. Each year, the state stocks thousands of 8-inch brown and rainbow trout. While the ratio favors rainbows five to one, almost 200 of the browns are two-year-olds of better than 14 inches. Both species like Panther Martin spinners cast around tributary mouths in spring and fall, and mayflies cast close to shore, at dusk, May through June. In winter, trout cruise near the surface and take minnows suspended a few feet below the ice.

Trout season is open year-round. The daily limit is five with no more than two over 12 inches.

Directions: The lake is in the village of Little York, on NY 281, about 4 miles north of the village of Homer (I–81 exit 12).

Additional information: Dwyer Memorial Park, located on the north end of the village off Little York Lake Road, offers fishing access, parking for fifty cars, and a beach launch suitable for small trailered craft. There is no public camping on the lake, but several private campgrounds are nearby.

Contact: New York State Department of Environmental Conservation Region 7, and Cortland County Tourism.

217. Casterline Pond *(see map on page 303)*

Key species: Rainbow trout, brown trout, and panfish.

Description: This is another one of the ponds that brush I–81 between Tully and Homer. Covering only 11 acres, it nonetheless holds a lot of water, averaging 13 feet deep, with a maximum depth of 25 feet.

Tips: From May through mid-June, fly fish with mayfly imitations.

The fishing: The state annually stocks hundreds of two-year-old browns averaging 14 inches and almost 1,000 rainbows averaging 8 inches. They respond to worms, streamers, in-line spinners, and marshmallows. Sunfish up to 8 inches are plentiful and like worms and Exude 1-inch curly-tailed grubs.

No boats are allowed.

Directions: On US 11, at the north end of Homer (I–81 exit 12).

Additional information: Trout can be taken from the pond year-round, but only two over 12 inches can be taken per day. A public access site on US 11 has parking for twenty cars, plus picnic tables. There is no public campground nearby, but there are several private ones.

Contact: New York State Department of Environmental Conservation Region 7, and Cortland County Tourism.

218. West Branch Tioughnioga River *(see map on page 306)*

Key species: Brown trout

Description: This branch is the outlet of Tully Lake. It flows south for about 10 miles, filling and draining several small ponds and lakes before joining the East Branch in Cortland to form the main stem of the Tioughnioga River.

Tips: Terrestrials are most productive in summer.

The fishing: This branch is creek sized. The state annually stocks more than 3,000 brown trout averaging 8 inches and an additional 600-something of better than 14 inches. Many survive winter, and 16-inch fish are common. They respond to worms, salted minnows, flies, and in-line spinners. Daily limit for trout is five, with no more than two over 12 inches, plus five brookies under 8 inches.

Directions: NY 281 and the stretch of US 11/NY 41 just north of Cortland parallel the river.

Additional information: The state owns about a mile of public fishing rights just north of Cortland. Unfortunately, there isn't any formal public access. Most anglers find a productive-looking stretch from the road, ask the landowner's permission to cross his or her property, then just park on the shoulder. Most of the section running through Cortland isn't posted.

Contact: Cortland County Visitors Bureau, and New York State Department of Environmental Conservation Region 7.

219. Fabius Brook *(see map on page 306)*

Key species: Brook trout.

Description: This tiny stream starts out in the hills above Apulia and flows at a gentle pace for about 5 miles before feeding the West Branch of Tioughnioga Creek. Averaging only about 8 feet wide and a couple of feet deep, it is loaded with cover—from root systems and logjams to undercut banks—and gets so overgrown in summer that it's nearly impossible to fish.

Tips: This stream is best fished in the beginning weeks of the season.

The fishing: The state stocks this stream annually with 500 brook trout averaging 9.5 inches; Onondaga County kicks in an additional 900. Most are taken on worms or salted minnows. In addition to stocking, this brook is visited by some monster brown trout that run up from the Tioughnioga River each fall to spawn. Finding the environs suitable, they spend the winter and are taken during the opening week of trout season. These fish can range from 2 to 5 pounds. Daily limit for trout is five,

Tioughnioga River: East and West Branches · Fabius Brook · Labrador Pond

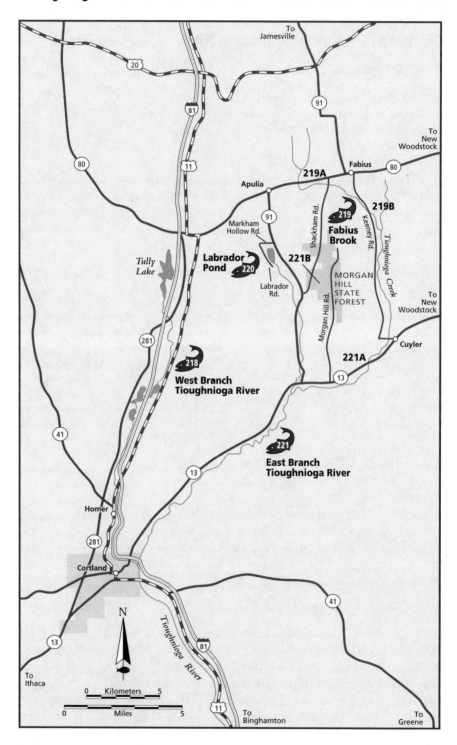

with no more than two longer than 12 inches, plus five brook trout under 8 inches.

Additional information: The state owns public fishing rights to most of the stream.

Contact: New York State Department of Environmental Conservation Region 7.

219A. Fabius Public Fishing Access

Description: This site has parking for about fifty cars.

Directions: On NY 80/NY 91, on the western edge of the village of Fabius.

219B. Keeney Road Bridge Access

Description: Informal shoulder access to the brook and one of its largest pools. There's parking for four cars.

Directions: Head south out of Fabius on Keeney Road for about 1.5 miles.

220. Labrador Pond

Key species: Largemouth bass and carp.

Description: Nestled in an extremely narrow valley, this 120-acre pond averages only 4 feet deep. Hills tower 800 feet above it on the east and west sides, shrouding it in shade most of the day.

Tips: Drift along with a Slug-Go, lizard, or snake, jerking it every few feet.

The fishing: Largemouth bass in the 1.5- to 3-pound range are most common, but some real hawgs are available. Almost any shallow-water baits and techniques, from casting Johnson silver spoons into lily pads to working jig-'n'-pigs around downed timber, will work. Carp reach 25 pounds and respond to small garden worms.

Bank fishing is prohibited to protect the unique habitat. No motors are allowed on the pond.

Directions: Head west out of Fabius on NY 80/NY 91 for about 2.5 miles to Apulia. When NY 91 separates, follow it south for about 2.25 miles and turn right onto Markham Hollow Road.

Additional information: A fishing access site on Labrador Road has a beach launch and parking for five cars. Primitive camping is allowed in Morgan Hill State Forest, across NY 91. This pond is in the Labrador Hollow Unique Area, containing plants normally found in alpine meadows. The clearing atop the eastern hill is the most popular hang-gliding launch in central New York.

Contact: New York State Department of Environmental Conservation Region 7.

221. East Branch Tioughnioga River

Key species: Brown trout, smallmouth bass, and northern pike.

Description: Spawned by the West Branch and Middle Branch Tioughnioga Creeks merging just north of Cuyler, this stream winds for about 15 miles through a fertile valley. Slicing through soft soil, it's constantly changing, moving, and rearranging riverwide logjams, digging new holes and filling in old ones. Its banks are often steep.

Tips: Use brown or tan nymphs, in sizes 6 to 12.

The fishing: Numerous tributaries keep the first 10 miles of this arm of the river at temperatures brown trout can tolerate. Annually, the state stocks 3,200 of them averaging 8 inches and almost 1,000 averaging 14.5 inches. Survival is decent, and many trout reach a respectable 18 inches. Smallmouth bass in the 8- to 12-inch range are available, and their numbers increase the closer you get to Cortland. Work diving crayfish-imitation crankbaits through deep pools. Northern pike from 18 to 24 inches are abundant and can be caught on minnows and their imitations.

Daily limit for trout is five, with no more than two longer than 12 inches, plus five brookies under 8 inches. The minimum length for black bass is 10 inches.

Directions: NY 13 parallels this stream.

Additional information: Most anglers access this stream from the shoulder and bridge crossings.

Contact: Cortland County Visitors Bureau, and New York State Department of Environmental Conservation Region 7.

221A. Tioughnioga River Public Access *(see map on page 306)*

Description: Parking for fifteen cars.

Directions: Take NY 13 for 1.2 miles south of Cuyler.

221B. Morgan Hill State Forest *(see map on page 306)*

Description: Primitive camping is allowed in this 5,560-acre forest.

Directions: Head south on NY 13 out of Cuyler for 2 miles, turn right onto Morgan Hill Road, and continue for 2 miles more.

222. Tioughnioga River

Key species: Brown trout, smallmouth bass, northern pike, walleye, tiger muskie, rock bass, and brown bullheads.

Description: Formed by the confluence of the East and West Branches in Cortland, this stream flows south for about 30 miles to feed the Chenango River. Wide and open, its long runs and deep pools are linked together by stretches of ripples.

Tips: Drift or troll worms on spinner rigs tight to logjams.

Tioughnioga River

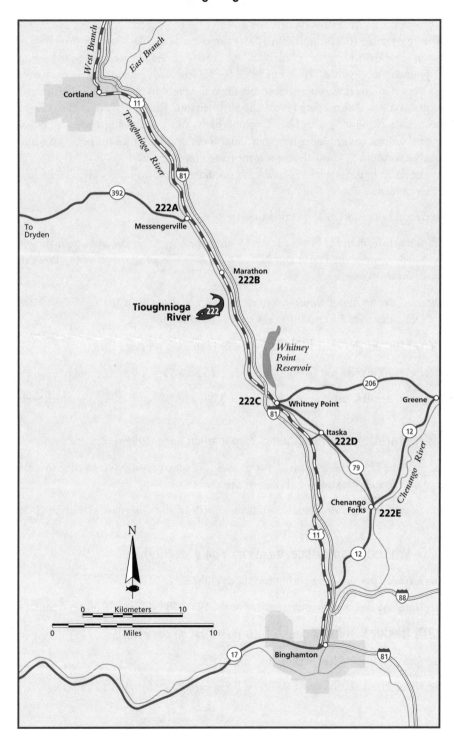

The fishing: Brown trout averaging 12 inches can be caught in spring pools and around stream mouths with worms and small spoons. Smallmouth bass in the 10- to 16-inch range can be taken virtually anywhere on spinners. Northern pike typically range from 3 to 5 pounds, but 10-pounders are available. They respond best to big minnows fished in quiet pools. Walleyes thrive in the murky waters; fish of up to 7 pounds are possible. Work minnows on jigheads along drop-offs and the bottoms of pools. The state-record tiger muskie was caught in this river. Biologists suspect it was a fish that migrated from the Susquehanna River. Most tigers are caught near the mouth on large crankbaits, spinnerbaits, and minnows intended for other game fish. Rock bass ranging between 5 and 8 inches and bullheads between 6 and 12 inches respond to crayfish and worms fished on bottom.

The daily limit for trout is five, with no more than two longer than 12 inches, plus five brookies under 8 inches.

Directions: I–81 and US 11 parallel the stream.

Additional information: From March 16 until the first Saturday in May, fishing is prohibited between the US 11 and NY 26 bridges in the village of Whitney Point to protect spawning walleyes.

Contact: Greater Binghamton Convention and Visitors Bureau, and New York State Department of Environmental Conservation Region 7.

222A. Messengerville Fishing Access *(see map on page 309)*

Description: This site has parking for five cars and a 50-yard trail to the river.

Directions: Head south out of Cortland on US 11 for about 8 miles, then turn west onto NY 392.

222B. Marathon Public Access *(see map on page 309)*

Description: This site is located on a wide shoulder; you have to step over a guardrail. There's parking for about ten cars.

Directions: On the shoulder of US 11, just north of the village of Marathon (I–81 exit 9).

222C. Whitney Point Access *(see map on page 309)*

Description: This site has parking for about eight cars.

Directions: At the southwestern corner of the NY 206 bridge in Whitney Point.

222D. Itaska Fishing Access Site *(see map on page 309)*

Description: This site has parking for eight cars.

Directions: Head south out of Whitney Point on NY 79 for about 5 miles.

Additional information: Follow the arrows on the north end of the parking lot to the wide, gently sloping, 50-yard trail to the river. This spot is a popular put-in for canoe anglers, who float 4 miles and take out at the Chenango Forks (site 222E).

222E. Chenango Forks Fishing Access Site *(see map on page 309)*

Description: This site is about 20 yards from the river, up a gentle slope, and offers parking for ten cars. The mouth of the Tioughnioga River is only a few hundred feet downstream. This is a popular takeout for canoeists launching at site 222D.

Directions: About 9 miles north of Binghamton on NY 12.

223. Otselic River *(see map on page 312)*

Key species: Brown trout, walleyes, and smallmouth bass.

Description: Springing out of the hills north of the Madison County village of Georgetown, this stream winds its way south for more than 40 miles, forms Whitney Point Reservoir (site 224), and feeds the Tioughnioga River about 1 mile below the dam.

Tips: Work Junior ThunderSticks in deep holes and along undercut banks.

The fishing: Annually, the state stocks roughly 10,000 8-inch brown trout and an additional 2,000 averaging 14 inches. Locals fish for them with salted minnows and worms. Fly-fishing purists do well with nymphs and streamers in the upper reaches, while spin casters do well on Vibrax spinners and Dardevles in the wide and slow sections just above and below the reservoir. Walleyes ranging from 18 inches to 23 inches and smallmouths from 12 inches to 16 inches are abundant a couple of miles above Whitney Point Reservoir and in the river's lower reaches. They like crayfish, worms, minnows tipped on jigheads, and Cotton Cordell's Spot Minnows.

The daily limit for trout is five, with no more than two longer than 12 inches, plus five brookies under 8 inches. The minimum length for black bass in the Cortland County length of river is 10 inches. The minimum length for walleyes from the reservoir up to the CR 169 bridge is 18 inches, and the daily limit is three. Fishing is prohibited from the mouth upstream to the Whitney Point Reservoir Dam from March 16 until the first Saturday in May to protect spawning walleyes.

Directions: NY 26 parallels the river.

Contact: New York State Department of Environmental Conservation Region 7.

223A. Willet Public Access Site

Description: This site offers access at the bridge and parking for eight cars.

Directions: NY 26 in the village of Willet.

Otselic River · Whitney Point Reservoir

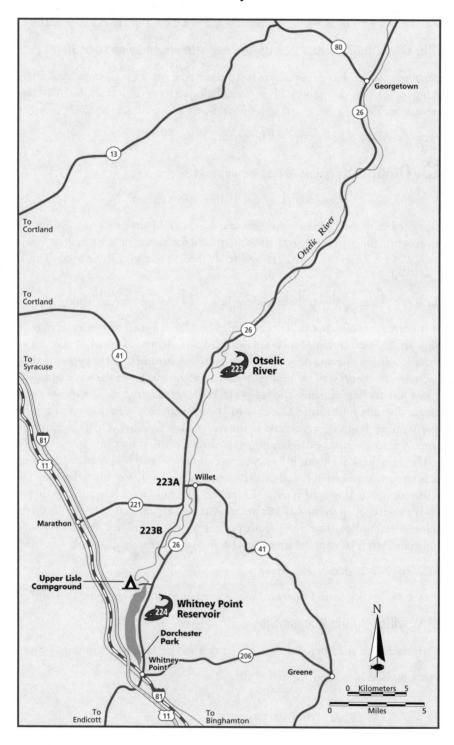

223B. Landers Corners Road Fishing Access Site

Description: This site has a beach launch for cartop craft and parking for seven cars.

Directions: Head south on NY 26 from Willet for about 4 miles, turn west onto Landers Corners Road, and travel about 0.5 mile.

224. Whitney Point Reservoir

Key species: Walleye, black bass, tiger muskie, yellow perch, black and white crappie.

Description: This 3,168-acre impoundment is set in gently rolling countryside, averages 10 feet deep, and has a maximum depth of 25 feet. It is fed and drained by the Otselic River (site 223).

Tips: Smallmouths and walleyes hang out in the old river channel all summer long.

The fishing: Walleyes usually go 18 to 23 inches, but many of more than 25 inches are caught annually. Jig for them with shiners, scented curly-tailed grubs, and blade-baits such as Heddon's Sonar Flash. Smallmouth bass between 12 and 18 inches share the range with walleyes and respond to crayfish and minnows drifted on bottom. Largemouth bass from 1 to 5 pounds and some northern pike hang out in the shallows and can be taken on spinnerbaits, jerkbaits, and crankbaits worked around vegetation and timber. The state stocked thousands of tiger muskies in the waning years of the last century, but the fishery didn't develop as expected and the program was discontinued. Survivors top 20 pounds now, and some should be around until the end of this decade. Most are taken on lures targeting other game fish. This place contains the state's greatest population of white crappies. Ranging from 9 to 14 inches, they are popularly targeted with minnows and spinner-rigged curly-tailed grubs and tubes from spring through autumn, and with minnows and grubs through the ice. Yellow perch go 6 to 9 inches and can be caught just about anywhere with tiny minnows, worms, and 2-inch curly-tailed grubs.

The minimum length for walleyes is 18 inches, and the daily limit is three. The speed limit is 10 miles per hour; motors exceeding 25 horsepower are prohibited.

Directions: From Binghamton, take I–81 north for 15 miles to Whitney Point (exit 8). Turn right onto NY 26 north and travel for 1.7 miles.

Additional information: Dorchester Park on NY 26 is open year-round and offers a hard-surface ramp, parking for up to seventy rigs, playgrounds, picnic facilities, and toilets. Upper Lisle Campground, a fee area on the north end, is open from the first full weekend in May through Columbus Day, and offers eighty-four no-frills campsites, toilets, potable water, a gravel launch, and parking for ten rigs. The New York State Crappie Derby is held on the reservoir each winter—ice permitting.

Contact: Greater Binghamton Convention and Visitors Bureau, and New York State Department of Environmental Conservation Region 7.

Reservoirs and Ponds from Cazenovia to Hamilton

225. Stoney Pond

Key species: Largemouth bass and sunfish.

Description: This 44-acre pond averages 4 feet deep, has an island, and is loaded with emergent and submerged vegetation. Surrounded by forest, it's circled by a path.

Tips: Fly fish with cork-bodied poppers and hair-bodied bass bugs.

The fishing: Largemouths range from 1.5 to 4 pounds and are partial to spinnerbaits and minnows. Bluegills and pumpkinseeds range from 4 to 7 inches, but some up to 0.75 pound are available. They respond to worms floating over weeds.

Directions: From Cazenovia, take US 20 east for about 3 miles to Nelson. Turn south onto Erieville Road, then left about 1.5 miles later onto Old State Road. About 2 miles later, turn right onto Jones Road and travel for a couple of miles to the dirt road on the left.

Additional information: The pond lies within 1,469-acre Stoney Pond State Forest. This site is so popular, the state has built a campground on the south shore. Camping is allowed in designated sites by permit only. In addition, primitive camping, under regular state rules, is allowed in the forest outside the pond campground. There is a cartop launch and parking for about ten cars at the campgrounds.

Contact: New York State Department of Environmental Conservation Region 7.

226. Eaton Reservoir

Key species: Walleye, rainbow trout, largemouth bass, yellow perch, and black crappie.

Description: One of several Madison County impoundments built early in the nineteenth century to supply water to the Chenango Canal, the reservoir is cradled in gently sloping, forested hills. Covering 268 acres, its shoreline drops quickly to 30-something feet deep. The deepest spot, 52 feet, is at the dam.

Tips: Fish crayfish around the culvert under Eaton Brook Road (CR 52) for early-season rainbow trout and walleyes.

The fishing: This is trophy walleye water, with fish averaging 6 pounds. Most are caught through the ice, but quite a few are also taken from dusk to dawn, spring through fall, on crankbaits such as Ripplin' Red Fins and C. C. Rattlin' Shads. Each year, the DEC stocks about 2,000 yearling rainbow trout. Survival is good, and fish generally range from 1 to 3 pounds. They hit worms fished at tributary mouths, minnows suspended below bobbers, and spoons, wobblers, and minnow-imitating crankbaits flatlined and deep-trolled. Hawg largemouth bass, ranging from 3 to 6 pounds, thrive in the place, especially in the western bay and the pond on the south side, across Eaton Brook Road (CR 52). Fish for them along weed edges and in openings with Texas-rigged scented worms. In late summer, they provide explosive action on hard plastic surface plugs such as MirrOlure's Humpback Mule and Top Dog, as well as Slug-Gos. Panfish, especially crappies and perch, are the species of choice of shore anglers and ice fishers and respond to small minnows, grubs, and worms.

Trout can be taken year-round. The daily limit is five with no more than two longer than 12 inches. Minimum length for walleyes is 18 inches and the daily limit is three.

Directions: At the US 20 light in Morrisville, head south on Eaton Street (CR 105). Bear right onto Eagleville Road (CR 103) a little more than 1 mile later and stay on it for 2 miles to West Eaton. Turn right at the stop sign onto NY 26 south. When the road banks a sharp left a few hundred feet later, continue straight onto Eaton Brook Road (CR 52) and travel for about 4 miles.

Additional information: A fishing access site on Eaton Brook Road (CR 52) has a paved ramp and parking for twenty rigs. Camping is permitted in nearby Stoney Pond State Forest (see site 225).

Contact: New York State Department of Environmental Conservation Region 7, and Madison County Tourism.

227. Hatch Lake *(see map on page 314)*

Key species: Northern pike, smallmouth bass, largemouth bass, chain pickerel, cisco, yellow perch, and black crappie.

Description: Completed in 1836 as a water source for the Chenango Canal, this impoundment covers 134 acres, averages about 20 feet deep, and has a maximum depth of 63 feet.

Tips: Fly fish with wet flies and small streamers in and around weeds for perch and crappies.

The fishing: This is one of the local hot spots for huge northern pike. Fish of better than 15 pounds are caught every year, mostly on big minnows through the ice. Smallmouth bass range from 10 to 14 inches and occupy rocky drop-offs, constantly on the lookout for their favorite food, crayfish. Largemouth bass, ranging from 1 to 4 pounds, can be taken by twitching Bill Lewis' Slapsticks along weed edges. Pickerel also reach trophy size, with many stretching the tape at more than 25 inches. They share the range with bucketmouths and are partial to spinner-rigged worms cast to the edge of vegetation and worked into deep water. This lake is one of the state's most productive cisco fisheries. Ciscoes between 12 and 15 inches can be caught in summer by flatlining small silver spoons such as Luhr Jensen's Kokanee Kings and Needlefish on lead-core line so they reach 15 to 20 feet down. Many are also taken through the ice on teardrop jigs and ice flies tipped with grubs. Perch, ranging from 4 to 7 inches, and crappies of up to 11 inches hang out in shallow cover and are taken on small minnows fished below bobbers, as well as on tiny, spinner-rigged tubes and curly-tailed grubs.

Directions: Head south on NY 26 from West Eaton for about 2 miles.

Additional information: There is no official public access, but folks launch cartop craft or bank fish off the shoulder of NY 26.

Contact: New York State Department of Environmental Conservation Region 7, and Madison County Tourism.

228. Bradley Brook Reservoir *(see map on page 314)*

Key species: Northern pike, chain pickerel, yellow perch and bullhead.

Description: Set 1,430 feet above sea level in wooded, rolling hills, this 140-acre reservoir is ringed by cottages and homes, averages 12 feet deep, and has a maximum depth of 28 feet.

Tips: Troll large minnow crankbaits such as Red Fins for monster northern pike.

The fishing: This is another local favorite for huge northern pike tipping the scale at more than 15 pounds. Most are taken through the ice on big minnows. Chain pickerel reach 25 inches and are also targeted through the ice with large minnows, and in summer with spoons and in-line spinners. Yellow perch average only about 8 inches, but they are fat and juicy. Work weed edges, in 3 to 10 feet of water, with tiny spinners. In winter, jig for them with an ice dot tipped with a grub or perch eye. Shore fishing for spring bullheads from the dam is a local tradition here. The fish reach a whopping 14 inches and are taken at night with worms still-fished on bottom.

Directions: Take NY 26 south for about 2 miles out of West Eaton to Hatch Lake. At the lake's southwest corner, take a left onto Westcott Road and follow it for about 2 miles to the dam.

Additional information: There is no formal public access, but nonresidents have been fishing and launching canoes from the dam for years without being challenged.

Contact: New York State Department of Environmental Conservation Region 7, and Madison County Tourism.

229. Lebanon Reservoir *(see map on page 314)*

Key species: Rainbow trout, largemouth bass, black crappie, and yellow perch.

Description: Heavily developed with cottages, this 92-acre lake averages 10 feet deep and has a maximum depth of 48 feet.

Tips: Night fish for rainbow trout from a boat by hanging a Coleman lantern over the side and fishing below the light with corn.

The fishing: The state stocks around 2,000 yearling rainbow trout annually. Most are caught fairly quickly, but enough survive to offer decent summer fishing for trout ranging from 1 to 2 pounds. They respond to flatlined spoons and streamers. Largemouth bass were stocked late in the last century and average 2 pounds. A good technique for catching them is to hook a worm in the head and tail to form a circle, suspend it 1 to 3 feet below a tiny bobber, and paddle-troll slowly along weed edges. Yellow perch and crappies of up to 12 inches share the shallows. Work tiny jigs in weed openings, around submerged timber, and near swimming docks. Trout season is year-round. The daily limit is five, with no more than two longer than 12 inches.

Directions: From the village of Eaton, take River Road (CR 73) south for 3 miles to Reservoir Road (CR 66). Turn right and follow it for a little more than 1 mile.

Additional information: A fishing access site with a paved ramp and parking for fifteen rigs is located on Reservoir Road. There is no public campground on the reservoir, but there is a private one.

Contact: New York State Department of Environmental Conservation Region 7, and Madison County Tourism.

230. Leland Ponds (see map on page 314)

Key species: Largemouth bass, tiger muskie, brown trout, yellow perch, and bullhead.

Description: Actually two ponds connected by a channel that goes under NY 26, the ponds collectively cover almost 100 acres. Heavily developed with summer cottages and year-round homes, the average depth of the upper pond is about 20 feet; the lower pond is about 6 feet deep. Both have a maximum depth of around 50 feet.

Tips: Work surface baits such as Mann's Phat Rat and 4-inch Ghosts.

The fishing: These ponds are loaded with bass habitat. Bucketmouths average 3 pounds and have an appetite for surface critters such as mice, snakes, and frogs, as well as lures that imitate them. The state has stocked tiger muskies into the lower pond recently. They typically reach about 10 pounds and have a knack for startling daydreaming bass anglers drifting minnows and casting spinnerbaits and large minnowbaits. The state stocks brown trout regularly, and the fish usually range from 1 to 2 pounds. They like worms and minnows. Although yellow perch are favorite snacks of resident game fish, these masters of evasion still manage to reach 8 to 10 inches—some even bigger. They have an uncontrollable appetite for small crayfish and minnows. Bullheads are plentiful, reaching up to 14 inches, and take crayfish and worms fished on bottom, especially during a rain or at night.

Trout season is year-round. The daily limit is five with no more than two longer than 12 inches.

Directions: Head east on US 20 from Morrisville for about 2.5 miles and turn south onto NY 46, then west a few hundred yards later onto NY 26 south.

Additional information: Trout can be taken year-round. Both ponds have paved ramps on NY 26 and parking for ten rigs. The North Pond has a handicapped fishing access site. There are no public campgrounds, but there are several private ones nearby.

Contact: New York State Department of Environmental Conservation Region 7, and Madison County Tourism.

231. Lake Moraine (Madison Reservoir) *(see map on page 314)*

Key species: Largemouth bass, tiger muskie, pickerel, bluegill, and black crappie.

Description: Built in 1836 to supply water to the Chenango Canal, this 235-acre lake's shoreline is heavily developed with year-round homes, cottages, and a conference center. Averaging 20 feet deep, its maximum depth is 48 feet.

Tips: Drift large minnows parallel to shore in 7 to 15 feet of water for muskies and bucketmouths.

The fishing: This lake is known for its largemouth bass. They range from 1.5 to 5 pounds, and many grow larger. They respond to Texas-rigged worms pitched under docks; jig-'n'-pigs worked in weed openings, along their edges, and in slop; and buzzbaits and propbaits ripped over cover. Muskies are stocked regularly by the state and are known to reach 20 pounds. Still, fish of around 10 pounds are most common and are mostly taken on large minnows, their imitations, and bucktail spinners. Chain pickerel range from 20 to 25 inches and respond well to Slug-Gos and worms on spinner harnesses retrieved over weed beds. Bluegills of up to 0.5 pound and black crappies averaging 10 inches hang out around cover ranging from windfalls to swimming platforms. Cast ½-ounce poppers for bluegills, and suspend tiny minnows below bobbers for crappies. Both like wet flies, too.

Directions: Head north out of Hamilton on CR 83 for a couple of miles.

Additional information: The causeway has a hard-surface ramp and parking for ten rigs. There is no private campground on the lake, but several private ones are nearby.

Contact: New York State Department of Environmental Conservation Region 7, and Madison County Tourism.

232. Balsam Pond *(see map on page 320)*

Key species: Tiger muskie, largemouth bass, pickerel, black crappie, and brown bullhead.

Description: Located on a high meadow, surrounded by forest and marsh, this 153-acre lake averages 5 feet deep and has a maximum depth of 10 feet. More often than not, a stiff, cold wind sweeps over the place.

Tips: Suspend a small plastic tube on a ½-ounce jighead below a tiny float and work it along weed edges, submerged timber, and brush for crappies.

The fishing: This superb warm-water fishery's primary claim to fame is big largemouth bass ranging from 3 to 6 pounds. They respond to minnows and Texas-rigged plastic worms. The state has stocked tiger muskies in the past, and some should still be around until 2006. They get big—up to 45 inches—and hit suckers suspended below bobbers. This place has a reputation for huge chain pickerel ranging from 25

Balsam Pond · Bowman Lake · Long Pond · Mill Brook Reservoir

to 30 inches. They hit worms on spinner harnesses retrieved over and along submerged weeds. Crappies averaging 0.75 pound take minnows and Bass Pro Shop's Crappie Thunders. Bullheads range from 6 to 14 inches and take worms at night or on cloudy days.

Motors exceeding 5 horsepower are prohibited.

Directions: From Norwich, head west on NY 23 for about 16 miles to CR 10 and turn left. Half a mile later, turn right onto CR 7A to CR 7. Follow CR 7 for 3.4 miles and turn left onto Beckwith Road. Turn left again 0.8 mile later and proceed 1.5 miles.

Additional information: There is a beach launch and parking for ten rigs. Primitive camping is allowed in the state forest covering more than half the shoreline, and there are a couple of hardened campsites near the launch site. The road is plowed up to the dam for ice-fishing access.

Contact: New York State Department of Environmental Conservation Region 7, and Chenango County Tourism.

233. Bowman Lake

Key species: Rainbow and brook trout.

Description: Surrounded by Bowman Lake State Park, which is in turn surrounded by McDonough State Forest, this 35-acre spring-fed lake averages 12 feet deep and has a maximum depth of 17 feet.

Tips: Fly fish with cork-bodied food pellet imitations early in the season.

The fishing: The state stocks the lake annually with 600 rainbow trout and 700 brook trout averaging 8 inches. While the pond gets a lot of fishing pressure, owing to the popular campground on its east shore, some fish manage to survive the season, and 12-inchers of both species are always possible. Daily limit for trout is five, with no more than two over 12 inches, plus five brookies under 8 inches.

Directions: Take NY 220 west from the village of Oxford for 6 miles to the Y in the road at the EAST MCDONOUGH sign. Continue straight on NY 997A for 1.5 miles, then turn left to the park.

Additional information: Bowman Lake State Park offers 198 no-frills sites, hot showers, a sand beach, playgrounds, rowboat rentals, and a hard-surface ramp—a permit, available for a fee at the park office, is needed to use the ramp. The campground is open from May through mid-October, and a day-use fee is charged to noncampers during the season. Motors are prohibited on the pond. Primitive camping is allowed in surrounding state forest.

Contact: Bowman Lake State Park.

234. Long Pond (see map on page 320)

Key species: Largemouth bass, pickerel, tiger muskie, black crappie, pumpkinseed, and bluegill.

Description: Completely surrounded by 3,254-acre Long Pond State Forest, this 117-acre pond averages about 5 feet deep and has a maximum depth of 15 feet.

Tips: The best time to fish here is from autumn through spring, when the weed beds are down.

The fishing: Largemouth bass from 1 to 4 pounds are plentiful, and 6-pounders are possible. In summer, they hide in the weed beds covering 80 percent of the lake and respond to propbaits, poppers, and floating worms worked rapidly over the vegetation. In autumn, most weeds lay down, and bass are taken on Texas-rigged worms and craws and Carolina-rigged lizards worked along edges, in openings, and around timber. Roughly 700 10-inch tiger muskies are stocked annually. They grow quickly—a former state record was caught here in 1983. Most are targeted with large minnows and floating-diving minnow-imitating crankbaits. Chain pickerel ranging from 15 to 20 inches are plentiful and respond to shallow-running crankbaits such as Bomber Shallow "A"s. Pumpkinseeds and bluegills in the 6- to 9-inch range are so common that a lot of anglers target them exclusively, fly fishing for them with wet flies and tiny poppers. Black crappies average 10 inches and are mostly taken through the ice with grubs and minnows.

Directions: Take NY 12 south from Oxford for 2 miles to CR 3. Head west for 10 miles to NY 41. Turn right (north) and continue for 3 miles.

Additional information: Several hardened campsites with fire pits, and a beach launch suitable for small, trailered craft (parking for ten rigs), are located off NY 41.

Contact: New York State Department of Environmental Conservation Region 7, and Chenango County Tourism.

235. Mill Brook Reservoir (see map on page 320)

Key species: Rainbow trout, largemouth bass, yellow perch, and sunfish.

Description: Set in a deep valley, this 100-acre reservoir averages 20 feet deep and has a maximum depth of 60 feet.

Tips: Use buzzbaits and topwater plugs such as Zara Spooks for explosive largemouth bass action, especially at night.

The fishing: The state Department of Environmental Conservation stocks roughly 3,000 8-inch rainbow trout each year. Winter survival is good, and rainbows 2 feet long have been reported. Many anglers fly fish for them at dawn and dusk with terrestrials and fish on bottom with worm-and-corn combinations in broad daylight. Largemouth bass average 2.5 pounds; they take floating lures when the surface is still, crankbaits the rest of the time. Sunfish reach 0.5 pound, and perch grow to 10 inches. They all take worms and wet flies—and the perch respond to minnows and crayfish, too.

Trout season is year-round. The daily limit is five, with no more than two over 12 inches. No motors are allowed on the lake.

Directions: Take CR 29 west out of New Berlin for 1.5 miles and turn left onto Nate Clark Lane.

Additional information: The park at the end of Nate Clark Lane offers a beach launch, parking for fifteen cars, a handicapped-accessible fishing deck, playgrounds, and toilets. Primitive camping is allowed in Skinner Hill State Forest, a couple of miles west on CR 29.

Contact: New York State Department of Environmental Conservation Region 7, and Chenango County Tourism.

236. Chenango River *(see maps on pages 324 and 326)*

Key species: Brown trout, walleye, smallmouth bass, largemouth bass, and northern pike.

Description: Formed by the convergence of several brooks between Morrisville and Hamilton, this stream snakes through pastures, croplands, and woodlots on its 70-something-mile trip to the Susquehanna River. Its combination of long, narrow pools, stretches of bottom-scraping ripples, and short rapids at the bends makes the river perfect canoe habitat.

Tips: Beware of barbed and electrified wire crossing the stream.

The fishing: The state annually stocks roughly 3,500 browns into the river at Eaton. Survival rates are good, and trout in the 10- to 16-inch range are caught on worms, flies, and minnows all the way to Sherburne. Downstream of the village, the river becomes warm-water habitat. Smallmouth bass averaging about 1 pound and walleyes averaging 2 pounds are plentiful. Deeper holes, especially those lined with vegetation, hold pikasaurus in the 3- to 6-pound range. Each of these species has a taste for minnow crankbaits, spinners, and large minnows suspended below bobbers or fished on bottom. From Greene to its mouth, the river widens and supports good populations of northern pike in the 5- to 8-pound range, walleyes up to 6 pounds, and smallmouths running from 1 to 3 pounds. In addition, there's a smattering of muskies up to 20 pounds and largemouth bass from 2 to 4 pounds. Locals drift with minnows for each species. A dedicated following targets walleyes in the evening by working original Rapalas through the heads of pools. Bass enthusiasts catch smallmouths and largemouths on spinnerbaits and crayfish. Northerns and muskies are sought with large Mepps bucktail spinners, Rapala Husky Jerks, and Magnums.

The daily limit for trout is five, with no more than two over 12 inches, plus five brookies under 8 inches. Muskie season runs from the first Saturday in May through March 15. The minimum size is 30 inches.

Chenango River: Hamilton to Brisben

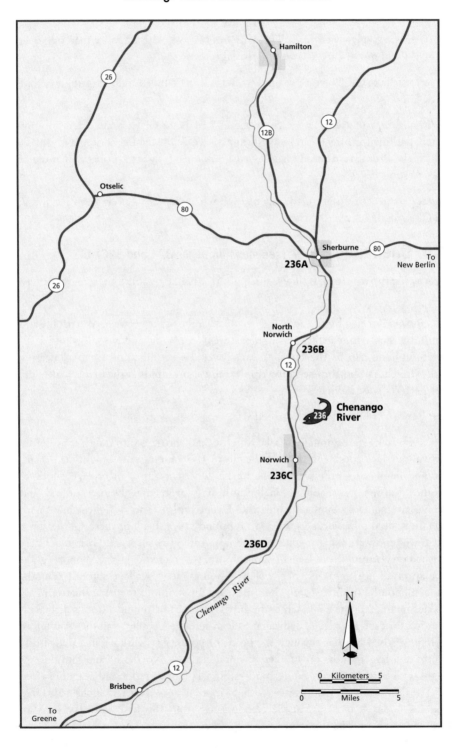

Directions: NY 12 and NY 12B parallel the river for most of its length.

Contact: New York State Department of Environmental Conservation Region 7.

236A. Public Fishing Access

Description: This site has parking for eight cars, shore-fishing access, and a cartop beach launch.

Directions: On the west side of Sherburne, at the NY 80 bridge.

236B. Public Fishing Access

Description: This site has a hard-surface launch ramp and parking for sixteen cars.

Directions: Head north out of Norwich on NY 12 for about 5 miles to North Norwich.

236C. Public Fishing Access

Description: This site offers a hard-surface launch ramp and parking for six rigs.

Directions: In Norwich, take the dirt road heading north on the west side of the Hale Street Bridge.

236D. Public Fishing Access

Description: This site has a beach launch and parking for ten cars.

Directions: Head south out of Norwich on NY 12 for about 3 miles, then turn east onto Halfway House Road to the bridge.

236E. Public Fishing Access *(see map on page 326)*

Description: Beach launch for cartop craft, shore-fishing access, and parking for six cars.

Directions: Head south out of Norwich on NY 12 for about 20 miles to the intersection with NY 41 in the hamlet of Greene.

236F. Chenango Valley State Park *(see map on page 326)*

Description: This 1,075-acre fee area offers 216 campsites (51 of them with electrical hook-ups), twenty-four cabins, playing fields, hiking trails, a swimming beach, an eighteen-hole golf course, and hot showers. A day-use fee is charged to noncampers from 9:00 A.M. to 5:00 P.M. when the campground is open, mid-May through Columbus Day. Noncampers must be out of the park by 10:00 P.M. Free day use off-season.

Directions: Head east out of Binghamton on I–88 for about 4 miles to exit 3, then go north on NY 369 for about 3 miles.

The fishing: This park offers several hundred yards of shore access to the Chenango

Chenango River: Brisben to Binghamton

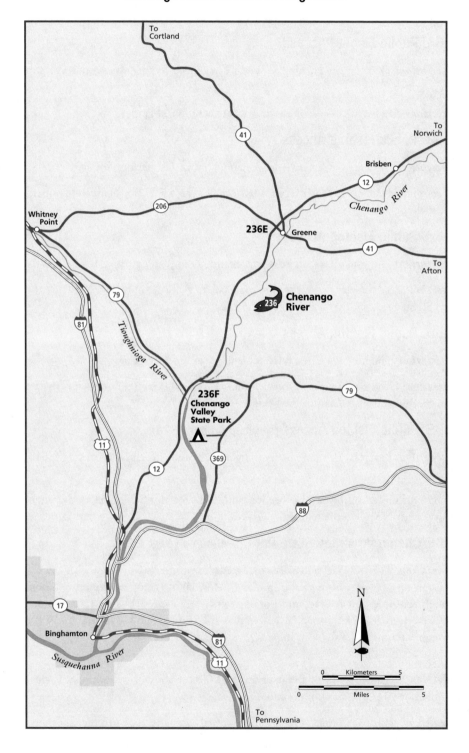

River. In addition, it has two lakes. Chenango Lake is stocked annually with about 7,500 rainbow trout averaging 8.5 inches. They respond to worms, Berkley Trout Bait, and flies. Lily Lake is small and shallow and has sunfish and bullheads that take worms.

Additional information: The park offers rowboat and paddleboat rentals. Private canoes are allowed on the lake during daylight hours—but you need a canoe permit, available from the park office for $5.00 per week or $15.00 per season.

237. Chittning Pond *(see map on page 328)*

Key species: Largemouth bass, chain pickerel, yellow perch, and black crappie.

Description: This 65-acre impoundment averages 7 feet deep and has a maximum depth of 14 feet.

Tips: Jig minnows through the ice.

The fishing: Largemouth bass average 2.5 pounds and respond to surface lures and Texas-rigged worms. Pickerel range from 15 to 25 inches and take scented, 3-inch curly-tailed grubs allowed to drop to bottom then retrieved steadily through the water column. Crappies running from too small to just big enough, and perch of up to 12 inches, are available; all take Road Runners and jigged, 2-inch, scented curly-tailed grubs.

Directions: Take US 20 east for 3.5 miles from the US 20/NY 12 intersection in Sangerfield.

Additional information: The fishing access site offers a paved ramp, parking for twenty cars, and a fishing platform for the handicapped. The pond is located in Tassel Hill State Forest, and primitive camping is allowed 150 feet from water sources, trails, and roads.

Contact: New York State Department of Environmental Conservation Region 6.

238. Unadilla River *(see maps on pages 328 and 330)*

Key species: Brown trout, smallmouth bass, walleye, pickerel, rock bass, white sucker, and carp.

Description: Stretching from southern Herkimer County to its mouth on the Susquehanna River at Sidney, a distance of roughly 75 miles, this mild-mannered river flows along a reasonably level side valley between the Mohawk and Susquehanna Valleys. For most of its distance, it serves as a boundary water between counties, joining the Susquehanna at the corner where Chenango, Otsego, and Delaware Counties touch.

Tips: This river is best fished from a canoe.

The fishing: The state annually stocks about 600 brown trout averaging 8 inches

Chittning Pond · Unadilla River: West Winfield to Rockdale

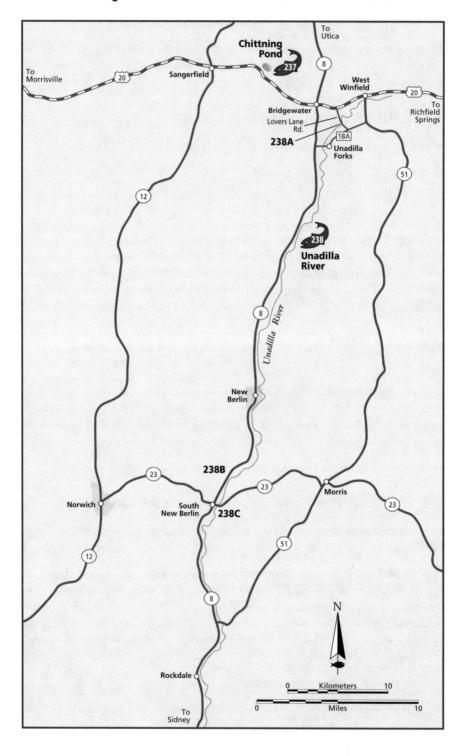

into the upper reaches. The habitat is good, and they survive to average 10 inches, providing decent sport to anglers using worms and salted minnows in spring, flies and spinners in summer. Larger fish are definitely available. Most end up migrating to spring holes in the lower river, where they reach 20-something inches and generate fond memories when caught on lures targeting walleyes and bass. From Leonardsville downstream, the river gradually warms, becoming a respectable warm-water fishery near New Berlin. Smallmouths in the 12- to 16-inch range are plentiful and take crayfish and 3-inch scented curly-tailed grubs slowly jigged or dragged on bottom tight to logjams, undercut banks, and bridge abutments. Rock bass ranging between 4 and 8 inches share the same range and will hit the same baits, plus worms, streamers, and poppers. Walleyes ranging from 2 to 4 pounds can be found in deep pockets, runs, and pools, where they'll take dark-colored bucktail jigs and jigheads tipped with worms and minnows bounced on bottom. Pickerel averaging 15 inches occupy weedy oxbows and bays and react violently to just about any lure worked rapidly along the edges and through the holes of submerged vegetation and lily pads. Suckers grow to 2 feet long and are popular with a dedicated group of anglers who pursue them in spring by fishing worms on bottom. They're said to be very delicious throughout April—"as good as trout," according to some. Carp ranging from 3 to 10 pounds are everywhere. They'll hit a marble-sized dough ball, kernels of corn threaded on a size 6 hook, bouillon-sized cubes of baked potato, and pieces of worm. They're especially thrilling to catch by spot-fishing (locating a school, slowly working the bait into its path with fly-fishing tackle, and watching one swim up, engulf it, then peel out like a locomotive when it feels the hook).

The minimum length for black bass is 10 inches.

Directions: NY 8 parallels most of the river.

Contact: New York State Department of Environmental Conservation Region 4.

238A. Public Access

Description: This informal site has shoulder parking along a lightly traveled road and a beach launch for cartop craft.

Directions: Take US 20 east out of West Winfield for about 1.5 miles, turn south onto Lovers Lane Road, and travel about 1 mile to the bridge.

Additional information: This is the river's uppermost canoe launching site and may require carrying the craft over some shallow spots in summer. The best trout water exists from here to the source. If you head downstream, pull out before the waterfalls at Unadilla Forks.

238B. Public Fishing Access

Description: This site has a beach launch for cartop craft and parking for about eight cars. A short hike along an easy path is required to reach the river.

Directions: Head south out of New Berlin on NY 8 for about 6 miles.

Unadilla River: Rockdale to Sidney

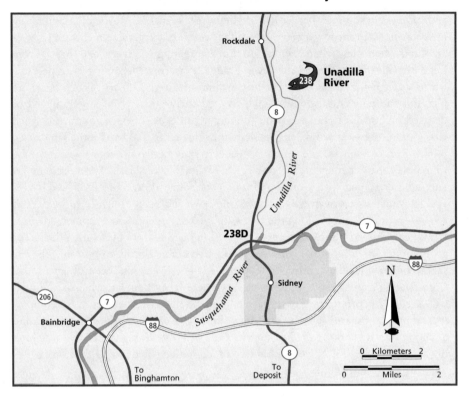

238C. Public Fishing Access *(see map on page 328)*

Description: This site has a beach launch for cartop craft and parking for ten cars.

Directions: Take NY 8 south out of New Berlin for about 8 miles to South New Berlin, then turn east onto NY 23 and travel a few hundred feet to the bridge.

238D. Public Fishing Access *(see map above)*

Description: This site has a beach launch for cartop craft and parking for seven cars.

Directions: At the intersection of NY 8 and NY 7, about 0.5 mile west of Sidney.

239. Canadarago Lake *(see map on page 332)*

Key species: Tiger muskie, black bass, pickerel, walleye, and yellow perch.

Description: This 1,900-acre lake averages 33 feet deep and has a maximum depth of 44 feet. Its east and west sides are heavily developed with cottages.

Tips: Drift worms along the edges of the hump northeast of the launch area.

The fishing: The north and south ends of this lake are shallow and loaded with weed beds and windfalls—the perfect habitat for largemouth bass in the 2- to 4-pound range and pickerel of up to 3 pounds. Both species love ambushing soft stickbaits such as Slug-Gos and Fin-S fish worked over and around cover. Walleyes ranging from 1 to 3 pounds are common. Cast for them with diving crankbaits around "Sunken Island," a shallow hump on the northwestern end. Smallmouth bass of between 1 and 3 pounds can be found along the hump, too. Work crankbaits such as Poe's Super Cedar series 1100s so they bounce bottom, creating puffs of silt. Yellow perch ranging from 6 to 12 inches hang out around weed beds and take worms and small minnows.

The daily limit for perch is twenty-five.

Directions: Take NY 28 south out of the village of Richfield Springs for 1.5 miles.

Additional information: A state fishing access site with a double-lane paved boat launch is found on NY 28, about 4 miles south of Richfield Springs. There's parking for about seventy-five rigs; a fee is charged from mid-May through Labor Day. There are no public campgrounds on the lake, but there are several commercial ones in the area.

Contact: Otsego County Tourism, and New York State Department of Environmental Conservation Region 4.

240. Otsego Lake *(see map on page 332)*

Key species: Lake trout, brown trout, lake whitefish, cisco, landlocked Atlantic salmon, black bass, walleye, and yellow perch.

Description: Cold and clear, this 4,200-acre lake averages 82 feet deep and has a maximum depth of 165 feet. Its shoreline is largely developed and includes Cooperstown on the south end, home of the Baseball Hall of Fame.

Tips: Flatline 0.75-inch to 1-inch shiny spoons off wire line in 50 to 100 feet of water for lake whitefish ranging from 16 to 19 inches.

The fishing: Brown trout typically range from 18 to 25 inches. Fishing for them after ice-out, by casting silver spoons and minnowbaits from the park at Three Mile Point, is a local rite of spring. Lake trout ranging from 21 to 25 inches are commonly caught by trolling spoons off Seth Green rigs through water averaging 50 degrees. Far more warm-water tolerant, landlocked salmon are targeted near the surface by flatlining crankbaits and tandem streamers. Ciscoes ranging from 13 to 15 inches are fished for through the ice by chumming with oatmeal then jigging a grub or tiny piece of worm. Lake whitefish run between 15 and 20 inches and are mostly targeted by trolling tiny spoons. Largemouth bass are plentiful in the weed beds on the north and south basins, in Hyde Bay on the northeastern end, and on the shallow hump on the west side, across from Clark Point. Averaging 2.5 pounds, bucketmouths respond to topwater lures, YUM Walleye Grubs, and scented worms

Canadarago Lake · Otsego Lake · Susquehanna River:
Its Source to Unadilla · Goodyear Lake

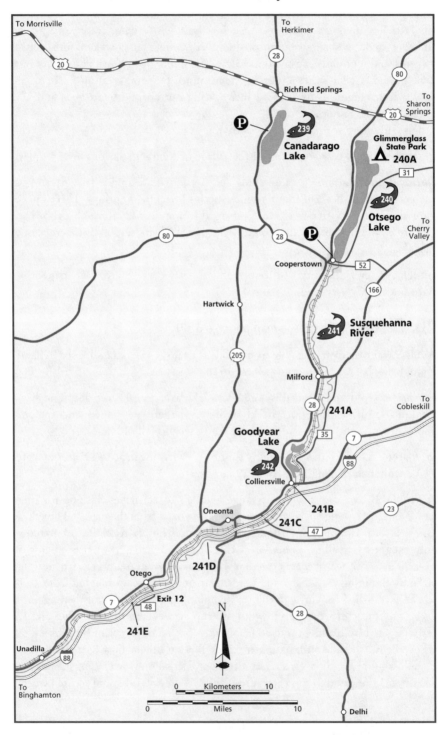

rigged on Slider Heads and swum over deep weeds. Schools of smallmouths ranging between 1 and 2 pounds suspend over steep drop-offs. Fish for them with Bomber Fat "A"s and Texas-rigged YUM CrawBugs. Walleyes are rare, but when one's caught, it's usually better than 8 pounds. The State University of New York at Oneonta is conducting an experimental walleye stocking program designed to increase their numbers. In the evening, from late May through mid-July, lunker "eyes" come in close to feed on alewives, and they'll often take a minnow-imitating crankbait worked parallel to shore. Perch are normally taken through the ice on jigs tipped with perch eyes or grubs and fished a few inches off bottom.

The minimum length for brown trout, rainbow trout, and salmon is 18 inches; the daily limit is two in any combination, including lake trout, which must be 21 inches to keep. In addition, only one lake trout exceeding 27 inches can be taken per day.

Directions: On the north end of Cooperstown. NY 80 clings to the lake's west bank.

Additional information: The year-round trout and salmon season is constantly under attack by locals, who fear that too many are being caught; the rules can change at any time. A public boat launch with a paved ramp and street parking for about fifteen cars is located at the foot of Fair Street in Cooperstown. Additional parking for twenty-five rigs is available in Fairy Springs Park.

Contact: New York State Department of Environmental Conservation Region 4, and Otsego County Tourism.

240A. Glimmerglass State Park

Description: This 593-acre fee area features thirty-nine no-frills campsites, hot showers, a sandy beach, and a covered bridge. A day-use fee is charged to noncampers when the campground is open, mid-May through Labor Day. Free day use off-season.

Directions: On CR 31, 6 miles north of Cooperstown.

241. Susquehanna River *(see maps on pages 332, 336, and 339)*

Key species: Walleye, smallmouth bass, muskellunge, tiger muskie, and channel catfish.

Description: Spawned by Otsego Lake in Cooperstown, this shallow stream wiggles through south-central New York, providing canoe anglers with 150 miles of quiet pools and gentle runs punctuated by low-adventure riffles.

Tips: From October until ice time, work jigs tipped with minnows or worms through the heads of pools, tight to undercut banks, and along drop-offs.

The fishing: Walleyes range between 2 to 5 pounds. They respond to worms drifted through holes on harnesses and crankbaits such as ThunderSticks or Rat-L-Traps cast into pools and runs. Smallmouths between 0.5 and 1.5 pounds are plentiful, sharing the range and tastes with the walleyes. Ohio-strain purebred muskellunge and hybrid norlunge rule this river, especially downstream of Binghamton. They are

"Getaway" on the Susquehanna River.

caught mostly on large crankbaits, jerkbaits, Mepps bucktail spinners, and live minnows. Channel cats of up to 20 pounds hang out at the heads and the eddies of deep holes, where they hit large minnows, cut bait, or shrimp fished on bottom.

Muskie season runs from the first Saturday in May through March 15, and the minimum length is 30 inches. Fishing is prohibited from March 16 until the walleye opener from the Rock Bottom Dam to the Exchange Street Bridge in Binghamton, and from the Erie-Lackawanna Railroad bridge in the towns of Union and Vestal, downstream to Murphy's Island.

Directions: NY 28 parallels the river from Cooperstown to Colliersville; NY 7 picks up from there and follows it to just east of its junction with NY 79. NY 79 follows it to Pennsylvania. It comes back to New York along US 11 and goes through Binghamton, where NY 17C and I–86 follow it until it dips into Pennsylvania for good.

Additional information: Several commercial campgrounds and motels are found in the area. Beware of dams and rapids in Binghamton. The Broome County Department of Parks and Recreation publishes a pamphlet called "Your Guide to Broome County Rivers," showing their locations as well as launch, takeout, and portage sites.

Contact: New York State Department of Environmental Conservation Region 7, Otsego County Tourism, Greater Binghamton Convention and Visitors Bureau, and Tioga County Tourism Office.

241A. Public Access *(see map on page 332)*

Description: This site has a beach launch for cartop craft and parking for twenty-five cars.

Directions: In Milford, cross the river on NY 166 and take CR 35 south for about 2 miles.

241B. Public Access *(see map on page 332)*

Description: This site has a beach launch for cartop craft and parking for about five cars.

Directions: On NY 7 in Colliersville.

241C. Public Access *(see map on page 332)*

Description: This site has a beach launch for cartop craft and parking for ten cars.

Directions: Take NY 7 east out of Oneonta for about 2 miles, then turn right onto CR 47.

241D. Public Access *(see map on page 332)*

Description: This site has a beach launch for cartop craft and parking for twenty cars.

Susquehanna River: Unadilla to Binghamton

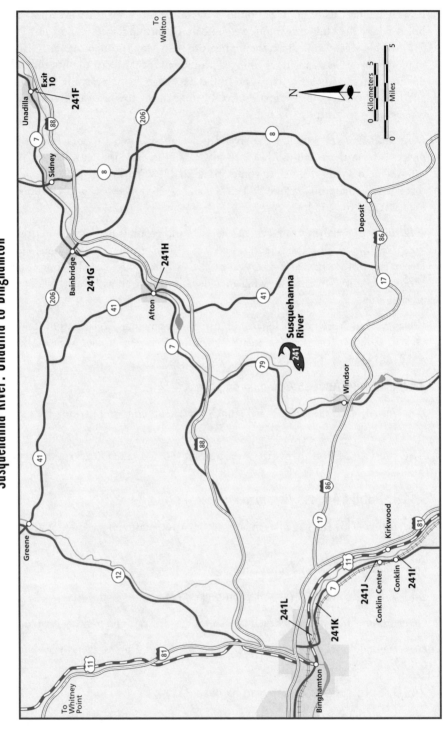

Directions: At the NY 205 terminus, Oneonta.

241E. Public Access *(see map on page 332)*

Description: This site has a beach launch for cartop craft and parking for twenty-five cars.

Directions: From I–88 exit 12 in Otego, take CR 48 south for about 0.3 mile.

241F. Public Access

Description: This site has a beach launch for cartop craft and parking for thirty cars.

Directions: Located on the NY 7 connector to I–88, west side of Unadilla.

241G. Bainbridge Park

Description: This site has a hard-surface ramp, parking for twenty rigs, and picnic facilities.

Directions: Located in Bainbridge, just downstream of the NY 206 bridge.

Additional information: From here to Afton, there's a flat stretch deep enough for small motorboats. Keep an eye open for shallow spots, however.

241H. Foster Park

Description: This site has a beach launch for cartop craft, parking for twenty cars, and picnic tables.

Directions: In the village of Afton, below the NY 41 bridge.

241I. Kirkwood Park

Description: This site has a single-lane concrete ramp and parking for six rigs.

Directions: Below the CR 20 bridge in the hamlet of Kirkwood.

241J. Leo Schnurbush Park

Description: This site has a beach launch for cartop craft and parking for six cars.

Directions: Off NY 7 in Conklin Center.

241K. Sandy Beach Park Public Access

Description: This site has a concrete ramp and parking for eight rigs.

Directions: On NY 7, Binghamton.

241L. Rock Bottom Dam Public Access

Description: This site offers a single-lane concrete ramp and parking for five rigs.

Directions: In Binghamton, off NY 363.

241M. Public Access

Description: This site has a beach launch for cartop craft and parking for ten cars.

Directions: Directly under the NY 201 bridge in Johnson City.

241N. Harold Moore Park

Description: Hard-surface ramp and parking for about ten rigs.

Directions: In the village of Vestal, off Old Vestal Road.

241O. Grippen Park

Description: This site offers a concrete ramp, parking for ten rigs, picnic facilities, and toilets.

Directions: Located in the village of Endicott, on Grippen Avenue (off NY 17C).

241P. Public Access

Description: This site has a hard-surface ramp and parking for ten rigs.

Directions: On Marshland Road, off NY 434, about 2 miles east of Owego.

Additional information: From Appalachia to Owego, the river is big and deep. Still, there are some shallow spots where you can bottom out during dry spells.

241Q. Hickories Park

Description: This site has a paved ramp and parking for six rigs.

Directions: Off NY 17C, about 1 mile east of Owego.

241R. Public Access

Description: This site is a highway rest stop and comes complete with parking for about fifty cars, heated bathrooms, vending machines, picnic tables, and views of a blue heron rookery across the river. Access is through an opening in the fence on the west end, behind the Dumpsters in the tractor trailer lot.

Directions: On NY 17 (I–86), about 1 mile west of the Owego exit.

241S. Nichols East Launch Ramp

Description: This site has a concrete ramp and parking for ten rigs.

Directions: From Nichols, take East River Drive for about 0.5 mile.

241T. Village of Barton Launch

Description: Beach launch for cartop craft with parking for six cars.

Directions: On Barton Road.

Susquehanna River: Binghamton to Barton

Blue heron rookery on the Susquehanna River, across from site 241R.

242. Goodyear Lake *(see map on page 332)*

Key species: Black bass, walleye, chain pickerel, and panfish.

Description: Formed in 1907 by a dam on the Susquehanna River, this 370-acre lake averages 14 feet deep and has a maximum depth of 30 feet.

Tips: Work buzzbaits and poppers over the openings and edges of weed beds.

The fishing: This lake's largemouth bass and pickerel range from 1.5 to 3 pounds. They hang out under all available cover and keep their eyes peeled on the surface for bite-sized critters. They take bass bugs, frogs, buzzbaits, and free-lined minnows. Smallmouths run from 0.5 to 2 pounds and walleyes, up to 5 pounds. They roam the drop-offs and hit jigheads tipped with scented, curly-tailed grubs, tubes, worms, and minnows. Yellow perch, bluegills, and rock bass typically range from 6 to 9 inches and hit worms and wet flies. Black crappies are found around windfalls and docks and take minnows, jig-rigged curly-tailed grubs, and Beetle Spins.

The daily limit for bluegill and yellow perch is twenty-five.

Directions: Take NY 7 east out of Oneonta for 4 miles to Colliersville. Turn north onto NY 28 and continue for 0.5 mile.

Additional information: A cartop launch with parking for ten cars is located on CR 35.

Contact: Otsego County Tourism, or New York State Department of Environmental Conservation Region 4.

Appendix

n most cases, fishing information can be obtained toll-free by contacting county tourism offices, chambers of commerce, or regional councils such as the Mohawk Valley Heritage Corridor. If that doesn't work, or if you require detailed, site-specific information such as stocking reports and future management plans, contact the fisheries office in the Regional Department of Environmental Conservation Office.

Visitor Bureaus, Visitor Associations, and Tourism Offices

Albany County Convention and Visitors Bureau
25 Quackenbush Square
Albany, NY 12207
(800) 258–3582
www.albany.org

Chenango County Tourism
5125 State Highway 12, Suite E
Norwich, NY 13815
(877) 243–6264
www.chenangocounty.org

Columbia County Tourism
401 State Street
Hudson, NY 12534
(800) 724–1846
www.columbiacountyny.com

Cortland County Visitors Bureau
34 Tompkins Street
Cortland, NY 13045
(800) 859–2227
www.cortlandtourism.com

Dutchess County Tourism
3 Neptune Road, Suite M-17
Poughkeepsie, NY 12601
(800) 445–3131
www.dutchestourism.com

Franklin County Tourism
355 West Main Street
Malone, NY 12953
(800) 709–4895
www.adirondacklakes.com

Greater Binghamton Convention and Visitors Bureau
P.O. Box 995
Binghamton, NY 13902-0995
(800) 836–6740
www.binghamtoncvb.com

Greene County Promotion and Tourism Department
P.O. Box 527
Catskill, NY 12414
(800) 355–2287
www.greene-ny.com

Hamilton County Tourism
P.O. Box 771
Indian Lake, NY 12842
(800) 648–5239
www.hamiltoncounty.com

Lake Placid/Essex County Visitors Bureau

Olympic Center
Lake Placid, NY 12946
(800) 447–5224
www.lakeplacid.com

Long Island Convention and Visitors Bureau

330 Motor Parkway, Suite 203
Hauppauge, NY 11788
(800) 441–4601
www.licvb.com

Madison County Tourism, Inc.

P.O. Box 1029
Morrisville, NY 13408
(800) 684–7320
www.madisontourism.com

Oneida County Convention and Visitors Bureau

P.O. Box 551
Utica, NY 13503-0551
(800) 426–3132
www.oneidacountycvb.com

Orange County Tourism

30 Matthews Street, Suite 111
Goshen, NY 10924
(800) 762–8687
www.orangetourism.org

Otsego County Tourism

242 Main Street
Oneonta, NY 13820
(800) 843–3394
www.cooperstown-otsego.com

Rensselaer County Tourism

1600 Seventh Avenue
Troy, NY 12180
(518) 270–2959
www.discoverrensselaer.com

Sullivan County Visitors Association, Inc.

100 North Street
Monticello, NY 12701-5192
(800) 882–2287
www.scva.net

Tioga County Tourism

188 Front Street
Owego, NY 13827
(800) 671–7772
www.visittioga.com

Ulster County Tourism

P.O. Box 1800
Kingston, NY 12402
(800) 342–5826

Town of Webb

Tourist Information Center
Old Forge, NY 13421
(315) 369–6983
www.oldforgeny.com

Warren County Tourism

1340 State Route 9
Lake George, NY 12845-9803
(800) 365–1050
www.visitlakegeorge.com

Chambers of Commerce

Delaware County Chamber of Commerce

114 Main Street
Delhi, NY 13753
(800) 642–4443
www.delawarecounty.org

Fulton County Chamber of Commerce

2 North Main Street
Gloversville, NY 12078
(800) 676–3858
www.fultoncountyny.org

Indian River Lakes Chamber of Commerce
Town Clerk's Office
Commercial & Main Streets
Theresa, NY 13691
(315) 628–5046

Lewis County Chamber of Commerce
7383-C Utica Boulevard
Lowville, NY 13367
(800) 724–0242
www.lewiscountychamber.org

Plattsburgh–North Country Chamber of Commerce
P.O. Box 310
Plattsburgh, NY 12901-0310
(518) 563–1000
www.northcountrychamber.com

St. Lawrence County Chamber of Commerce
Drawer A
Canton, NY 13617
(315) 386–4000
slccoc@northnet.org
www.stlawrencechamber.com

Saranac Lake Area Chamber of Commerce
30 Main Street
Saranac Lake, NY 12983
(800) 347–1992
www.saranaclake.com

Schoharie County Chamber of Commerce
P.O. Box 400
Schoharie, NY 12157
(800) 418–4748

Tupper Lake Chamber of Commerce
60 Park Street
Tupper Lake, NY 12986
(518) 359–3328

Regional Councils

Mohawk Valley Heritage Corridor
60 Montgomery Street
Canajoharie, NY 13317
(518) 673–1045
mvhc@telenet.net

New York City Department of Environmental Protection

1250 Broadway
Eighth Floor
New York, NY 10001
(212) 643–2201
www.nyc.gov/watershedrecreation

New York State Department of Environmental Conservation

Fisheries Office
NYSDEC Region 1
SUNY, Building 40
Stony Brook, NY 11790-2356
(516) 444–0280

Fisheries Office
NYSDEC Region 3
21 South Putt Corners Road
New Paltz, NY 12561-1696
(914) 256–3161

Fisheries Office
NYSDEC Region 4
Route 10, HCR 1
Stamford, NY 12167-9503
(607) 652–7366

Fisheries Office
NYSDEC Region 5
P.O. Box 296
Ray Brook, NY 12977-0296
(518) 897–1200

Fisheries Office
NYSDEC Region 6
State Office Building
317 Washington Street
Watertown, NY 13601-3787
(315) 785–2261

Fisheries Office
NYSDEC Region 7
1285 Fisher Avenue
Cortland, NY 13045-3095
(607) 753–3095

State Parks

State parks generally charge a day-use fee from Memorial Day through Labor Day. To reserve campsites and cabins in state parks, call the New York State Camping Reservation System at (800) 456–2267 or visit www.ReserveAmerica.com.

Caleb Smith State Park Preserve
P.O. Box 963
Smithtown, NY 11787
(631) 265–1054

Chenango Valley State Park
153 State Park Road
Chenango Forks, NY 13746
(607) 648–5251

Connetquot River State Park Preserve
Sunrise Highway
Oakdale, NY 11769
(631) 581–1005

Cumberland Bay State Park
152 Cumberland Head Road
Plattsburgh, NY 12901
(518) 563–5240

Delta Lake State Park
8797 State Route 46
Rome, NY 13440
(315) 337–4670

Eel Weir State Park
R.D. 1
Ogdensburg, NY 13669
(315) 393–1138

Glimmerglass State Park
R.R. 2, Box 580
Cooperstown, NY 13326
(607) 547–8662

Higley Flow State Park
442 Cold Brook Drive
Colton, NY 13625
(315) 769–0127

Hither Hills State Park
R.R. #2, Box 206A
South Fairview Avenue
Montauk, NY 11954
(631) 668–2554

Max V. Shaul State Park
P.O. Box 23, Route 30
Fultonham, NY 12071
(518) 827–4711

Mills-Norrie State Park
U.S. Route 9
Staatsburg, NY 12580
(845) 889–4646

Mine Kill State Park

Box 923
North Blenheim, NY 12131
(518) 827–6111

Moreau Lake State Park

605 Old Saratoga Road
Gansevoort, NY 12831
(518) 793–0511

Pixley Falls State Park

State Route 46
Boonville, NY 13309
(315) 942–4713

Thompson's Lake State Park

Box 99
East Berne, NY 12059
(518) 872–1674

Wildwood State Park

North Wading River Road
Wading River, NY 11792
(631) 929–4314

County Parks

Broome County Parks

P.O. Box 1766
Binghamton, NY 13902
(607) 778–2193

Suffolk County Parks

P.O. Box 144
West Sayville, NY 11796
(631) 854–4949
www.co.suffolk.ny.us/exec/parks

More Contacts

Blenheim-Gilboa Pumped Storage Power Project

c/o Community Relations
P.O. Box 898
North Blenheim, NY 12131
(800) 724–0309

Coast Guard

U.S. Coast Guard Activities NY
212 Coast Guard Drive
Stanton Island, NY 10305
(718) 354–4003

Indian Nations

Mohawk Council of Akwesasne
Conservation Department
P.O. Box 489
Hogansburg, NY 13655-0489
(613) 575–2377

New York State Canal Corporation

P.O. Box 189
Albany, NY 12201–0189
(800) 422–6254

Reliant Energy

225 Greenfield Parkway, Suite 201
Liverpool, NY 13088
(315) 413–2800
www.reliantenergy.com
For information on water releases at power plants on the Salmon, Black, Sacandaga, and Raquette Rivers, as well as West Canada Creek, call the Waterline at (800) 452–1742.

About the Author

Spider Rybaak, son of Ukrainian immigrants who survived years of slave labor under the Nazis, and avoided Stalin's terror by coming to America after the war, learned early in life the spiritual, emotional, and practical benefits of fishing. A professional writer for over eighteen years, his articles and short stories have appeared in magazines such as *In-Fisherman, Great Lakes Angler, Fishing and Hunting News, American Legion,* and *Boating Life.* He resides in central New York with his best friend, Susan, and their ten cats.